THE VIDEO COLLECTION

Approved Certification Courseware
Adobe™

ADOBE
PREMIERE PRO CS5
AFTER EFFECTS CS5
SOUNDBOOTH CS5
ENCORE CS5

REVEALED

THE VIDEO COLLECTION

Adobe Approved Certification Courseware ™

COLLECTION

ADOBE
PREMIERE PRO CS5
AFTER EFFECTS CS5
SOUNDBOOTH CS5
ENCORE CS5

REVEALED

DEBBIE KELLER

DELMAR
CENGAGE Learning™

Australia • Brazil • Japan • Korea • Mexico • Singapore • Spain • United Kingdom • United States

DELMAR
CENGAGE Learning™

The Video Collection CS5 Revealed
Debbie Keller

Vice President, Career and Professional Editorial:
Dave Garza

Director of Learning Solutions: Sandy Clark

Senior Acquisitions Editor: Jim Gish

Managing Editor: Larry Main

Product Managers: Jane Hosie-Bounar, Meaghan O'Brien

Editorial Assistant: Sarah Timm

Vice President Marketing, Career and Professional:
Jennifer Baker

Executive Marketing Manager: Deborah S. Yarnell

Marketing Manager: Erin Brennan

Marketing Coordinator: Erin Deangelo

Production Director: Wendy Troeger

Senior Content Project Manager: Kathryn B. Kucharek

Developmental Editor: Ann Fisher

Technical Editor: Sebastian Guerra

Senior Art Director: Joy Kocsis

Cover Design: Joe Villanova

Cover Art: Spitting Images

Cover Photos:
Lion: © istockphoto.com/Kristian Sekulic;
Theatre: © istockphoto.com/Anja Hild

Text Designer: Liz Kingslein

Copy editor: Harold Johnson

Production House: Integra Software Services Pvt. Ltd.

Proofreader: Kim Kosmatka

Indexer: Alexandra Nickerson

Technology Project Manager: Christopher Catalina

For product information and technology assistance, contact us at **Cengage Learning Customer & Sales Support, 1-800-354-9706**
For permission to use material from this text or product, submit all requests online at **www.cengage.com/permissions**
Further permissions questions can be emailed to **permissionrequest@cengage.com**

Adobe® Premiere Pro®, Adobe® After Effects®, Adobe® Soundbooth®, Adobe® Encore, Adobe® Photoshop®, Adobe® InDesign®, Adobe® Illustrator®, Adobe® Flash®, Adobe® Dreamweaver®, Adobe® Fireworks®, and Adobe® Creative Suite® are trademarks or registered trademarks of Adobe Systems, Inc. in the United States and/or other countries. Third party products, services, company names, logos, design, titles, words, or phrases within these materials may be trademarks of their respective owners.

Adobe product screenshot(s) reprinted with permission from Adobe Systems Incorporated.

The Adobe Approved Certification Courseware logo is a proprietary trademark of Adobe. All rights reserved. Cengage Learning and The Video Collection CS5—Revealed are independent from ProCert Labs, LLC and Adobe Systems Incorporated, and are not affiliated with ProCert Labs and Adobe in any manner. This publication may assist students to prepare for an Adobe Certified Expert exam in Premiere Pro, however, neither ProCert Labs nor Adobe warrant that use of this material will ensure success in connection with any exam.

Library of Congress Control Number: 2010921377

Hardcover edition:
ISBN-13: 978-1-4390-5756-8
ISBN-10: 1-4390-5756-7

Soft cover edition:
ISBN-13: 978-1-4390-5758-2
ISBN-10: 1-4390-5758-3

Delmar
5 Maxwell Drive
Clifton Park, NY 12065-2919
USA

Cengage Learning is a leading provider of customized learning solutions with office locations around the globe, including Singapore, the United Kingdom, Australia, Mexico, Brazil, and Japan. Locate your local office at: **international.cengage.com/region**

Cengage Learning products are represented in Canada by Nelson Education, Ltd.

To learn more about Delmar, visit **www.cengage.com/delmar**

Purchase any of our products at your local college store or at our preferred online store **www.cengagebrain.com**

Notice to the Reader
Publisher does not warrant or guarantee any of the products described herein or perform any independent analysis in connection with any of the product information contained herein. Publisher does not assume, and expressly disclaims, any obligation to obtain and include information other than that provided to it by the manufacturer. The reader is expressly warned to consider and adopt all safety precautions that might be indicated by the activities described herein and to avoid all potential hazards. By following the instructions contained herein, the reader willingly assumes all risks in connection with such instructions. The publisher makes no representations or warranties of any kind, including but not limited to, the warranties of fitness for particular purpose or merchantability, nor are any such representations implied with respect to the material set forth herein, and the publisher takes no responsibility with respect to such material. The publisher shall not be liable for any special, consequential, or exemplary damages resulting, in whole or part, from the readers' use of, or reliance upon, this material.

Printed in the United States of America
1 2 3 4 5 6 7 14 13 12 11 10

Revealed Series Vision

The Revealed Series is your guide to today's hottest multimedia applications. These comprehensive books teach the skills behind the application, showing you how to apply smart design principles to multimedia products such as dynamic graphics, animation, Web sites, software authoring tools, and digital video.

A team of design professionals including multimedia instructors, students, authors, and editors worked together to create this series. We recognized the unique learning environment of the multimedia classroom and created a series that:

- Gives you comprehensive step-by-step instructions
- Offers in-depth explanation of the "Why" behind a skill
- Includes creative projects for additional practice
- Explains concepts clearly using full-color visuals
- Keeps you up to date with the latest software upgrades so you can always work with cutting edge technology

It was our goal to create a book that speaks directly to the multimedia and design community—one of the most rapidly growing computer fields today. We think we've done just that, with a sophisticated and instructive book design.

—The Revealed Series

Author's Vision

The idea of writing a book has always been in the back of my mind. Also in the back of my mind was the question "How many people ever really get this chance?" Well, I got mine. I met a Cengage Sales Rep named Debbie Henson about a year ago and it started with "You look familiar, where might I have seen you?" When I provided my answer, she told me I should be working with Cengage. Amazingly, in the next few days my world would change. Debbie contacted me and asked that I forward my "credentials"; she had a Senior Acquisitions Editor named Jim Gish who was interested in learning more about me. Being in education most of my adult life, I asked if a resume would be okay (it was).

Just a few short days later, Jim Gish contacted me and said he was interested in having me write a book for the Revealed series, and asked if I was familiar with it. At that time, I had just heard of it and was waiting for my evaluation copies. He asked me which title I would like to write, Premiere Pro or After Effects. I wanted to write a Video Collection that would include Premiere Pro, After Effects, Soundbooth, and Encore. I thought it made more sense than just one title. Boy was I being ambitious. I would not realize that until many months later. Jim agreed and the process began, and what a quick process it was.

I was introduced to the team and assigned a Project Manager, Jane Hosie-Bounar, and a Development Editor named Ann Fisher. I received my contract over Thanksgiving break; it was official, I was going to write a book! Over a period of six quick months, the book was written. Jane was wonderful to work with. She was always patient with my questions and extremely helpful through the entire process. Ann's questions in her edits helped make this book better. As a first time author, I was very fortunate to work with both of these women.

My goal was to write a project-based book that integrated the software applications. I hope that is what the reader experiences and I hope the reader is able to embrace the way I approached this book. It was a challenge to write, and so very rewarding.

Thank you Jim Gish for taking a chance on me, I hope I have made you proud.

Thank you to Barry Britt of Soundzabound, and Joel Holland of Footage Firm, for making many of the audio and video clips available. Thank you to Eric Franke, an art teacher at the school where I work, for making his photography available.

Thank you to my friends at Adobe, who connected me with the right people when they were not able to answer my questions: Michelle Galina, Claire Erwin, Anuja Dharkar, Daniela Birch and Tom Dent. Also, thank you to Johann Zimmern and Megan Stewart who brought me into the Adobe Education Leaders program back when it was Macromedia.

Thank you to my mother, Catherine Harrington, for understanding the time constraints that were put on me for the last six months and for cleaning my house every Wednesday so I had one less thing to worry about.

Thank you to my husband Glenn for being supportive of me in everything I do. Last summer, he drove me around the Hill Country of Texas to film video and take pictures to be used as resources for this text. Thanks to him, we had some shaky footage to work with when working with Mocha. Then, when the process of actually writing began, while I was teaching high school fulltime, he started doing the grocery shopping. Thank you for your continued encouragement and reminding me that I could in fact do this. You will see our dogs, Lucky and Potus, in the pages of this book as well as in video clips used in the projects. (Lucky learns to sing in one of the later chapters!) Thank you to Potus for making me take a break once in a while, and reminding me when it was time to go to bed.

— Debbie Keller

Introduction to The Video Collection Revealed

Welcome to *The Video Collection—Revealed*. This book offers creative projects, concise instructions, and complete coverage of basic to advanced video skills, helping you to create polished, professional-looking video. Use this book both in the classroom and as your own reference guide.

The text is written in an integrated approach to utilize the benefits from each of four applications: Adobe Premiere Pro, After Effects, Soundbooth, and Encore. A chapter is dedicated to each application to help you gain familiarity with the program. The last three chapters incorporate what you have learned and have you work with more than one application, or work dynamically with more than one application with Adobe Dynamic Link. (Note that this feature is only available if your software was installed as part of a suite and not as individual point products.)

What You'll Do

A What You'll Do figure begins every lesson. This figure gives you an at-a-glance look at what you'll do in the chapter, either by showing you a page or pages from the current project or a tool you'll be using.

Comprehensive Conceptual Lessons

Before jumping into instructions, in-depth conceptual information tells you "why" skills are applied. This book provides the "how" and "why" through the use of professional examples. Also included in the text are tips and sidebars to help you work more efficiently and creatively, or to teach you a bit about the history or design philosophy behind the skill you are using.

Step-by-Step Instructions

This book combines in-depth conceptual information with concise steps to help you learn about working with video in CS5. Each set of steps guides you through a lesson where you will create, modify, or enhance a file. Step references to large colorful images and quick step summaries round out the lessons. The Data Files for the steps are provided on the DVDs at the back of this book.

The zoo in your area has contracted you to create a PSA they would like to air on local television and on their Web site bringing public awareness to a campaign about endangered animals. They are providing you with 12 video clips featuring animals they would like included in the commercial. A sample workspace is shown in Figure 106.

Using your skills in Premiere Pro and After Effects, create a 30-second commercial with appropriate text and a voice over from your own research concerning these endangered animals. You will need to export your movie in the MPEG-2 and FLV file formats.

1. Import the video clips into Premiere Pro.
2. Trim clips and combine them on a sequence (needs to be 30 seconds).
3. Use Adobe Dynamic Link to create an After Effects composition from the Premiere Pro sequence.
4. Add special effects of your choosing in After Effects.
5. Add appropriate text either in Premiere Pro or in After Effects.
6. Return to Premiere Pro and add a voice over.
7. Export as an MPEG-2 and FLV.

PORTFOLIO PROJECT

Figure 106 *Sample Portfolio Project*

Develop a PSA & Commercial Using Premiere Pro & After Effects CS5

THE VIDEO COLLECTION CS5/PREMIERE PRO & AFTER EFFECTS 5-75

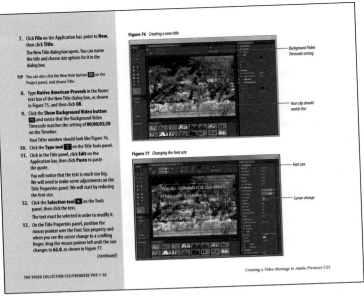

7. Click **File** on the Application bar, point to **New**, then click **Title**.
   The New Title dialog box opens. You can name the title and choose size options for it in the dialog box.

   TIP You can also click the New Item button on the Project panel, and choose Title.

8. Type **Native American Proverb** in the Name text box of the New Title dialog box, as shown in Figure 75, and then click **OK**.

9. Click the **Show Background Video button** and notice that the Background Video Timecode matches the setting of **00;00;03;20** on the Timeline.
   Your Titler window should look like Figure 76.

10. Click the **Type tool** on the Title Tools panel.

11. Click in the Title panel, click **Edit** on the Application bar, then click **Paste** to paste the quote.
    You will notice that the text is much too big. We will need to make some adjustments on the Title Properties panel. We will start by reducing the font size.

12. Click the **Selection tool** on the Tools panel, then click the text.
    The text must be selected in order to modify it.

13. On the Title Properties panel, position the mouse pointer over the Font Size property and when you see the cursor change to a scrolling finger, drag the mouse pointer left until the size changes to **62.0**, as shown in Figure 77.

(continued)

THE VIDEO COLLECTION CS5/PREMIERE PRO 5-58

Figure 76 *Creating a new title*

Background Video Timecode setting

Your clip should match this

Figure 77 *Changing the font size*

Font size

Cursor change

Creating a Video Montage in Adobe Premiere CS5

Projects

This book contains a variety of end-of-chapter materials for additional practice and reinforcement. The Skills Review contains hands-on practice exercises that mirror the progressive nature of the lesson material. The chapter concludes with three projects: two Project Builders, and one Portfolio Project. The Project Builders require you to apply the skills you've learned in the chapter. Portfolio Projects encourage you to address and solve challenges based on the content explored in the chapter, and to develop your own portfolio of work.

What Instructor Resources Are Available with this Book?

The Instructor Resources CD-ROM is Delmar's way of putting the resources and information needed to teach and learn effectively into your hands. All the resources are available for both Macintosh and Windows operating systems.

Instructor's Manual

Available as an electronic file, the Instructor's Manual includes chapter overviews and detailed lecture topics for each chapter, with teaching tips. The Instructor's Manual is available on the Instructor Resources CD-ROM.

Sample Syllabus

Available as an electronic file, the Sample Syllabus includes a suggested syllabus for any course that uses this book. The syllabus is available on the Instructor Resources CD-ROM.

PowerPoint Presentations

Each chapter has a corresponding PowerPoint presentation that you can use in lectures, distribute to your students, or customize to suit your course.

Data Files for Students

To complete most of the chapters in this book, your students will need Data Files. The Data Files are available on the DVDs at the back of this text book. Instruct students to use the Data Files List at the end of this book. This list gives instructions on organizing files.

Solutions to Exercises

Solution Files are Data Files completed with comprehensive sample answers. Use these files to evaluate your students' work. Or distribute them electronically so students can verify their work. Sample solutions to all lessons and end-of-chapter material are provided with the exception of some portfolio projects.

Test Bank and Test Engine

ExamView is a powerful testing software package that allows instructors to create and administer printed and computer (LAN-based) exams. ExamView includes hundreds of questions that correspond to the topics covered in this text, enabling students to generate detailed study guides that include page references for further review. The computer-based and LAN-based/online testing component allows students to take exams using the EV Player, and also saves the instructor time by grading each exam automatically.

Certification

This book covers the objectives necessary for Adobe Premiere Pro certification. Use the Certification Grid at the back of the book to find out where an objective is covered.

BRIEF CONTENTS

CONTENTS

 CHAPTER 1: CREATING A VIDEO MONTAGE IN ADOBE PREMIERE CS5

Supported Features

The Adobe Dynamic Link feature is only available if your software was installed as part of a suite and not as individual point products. In addition, please note that if you installed a trial version of the Suite, Encore and other features will be disabled.

Intended Audience

This book is designed for the beginner or intermediate user who wants to learn applications from the Video Production Suite. The book is written in a project-based format to provide basic and in-depth material that not only educates, but also encourages you to explore the nuances of each of the applications discussed in this book.

Approach

The text is designed to work at your own pace through step-by-step tutorials. A concept is presented and the process explained, followed by the actual steps. To take advantage of what this text has to offer, you should work as follows:

- Read the introduction for each chapter to understand the overall concept that is being used to teach the tools and techniques the applications have to offer.

- The introduction for each lesson provides greater explanation than the actual steps. Refer back to this area of the text while working on the steps.
- As you work on the steps, pay attention to what you are doing and why; do not just go through the motions of following directions.
- After completing a set of steps, ask yourself if you could use these skills without referring to the steps. If you feel you cannot, review the steps.

Icons, Buttons, and Pointers

Symbols for icons, buttons, and pointers are shown each time they are used in the steps. Try to become familiar with their names and their location.

Data Files

To complete the lessons in this book, you need the Data Files located on the DVDs provided in the back of this book. Your instructor will tell you where to store the files as you work, such as to your hard drive or network server. The instructions will refer to the drive and folder where these data files are stored.

The software in this text creates reference files to assets or footage being used in the individual applications. As a result, there may be instances when your files are missing. The application may alert you to this when it is opening a project, or it may show a missing link in the Project panel. In either case, it will be necessary to locate the missing files in order for the project to work properly. Once the files have been re-linked and the project file saved, it will not be necessary to locate these files again. Therefore, it is extremely important not to move or delete any files that are being used.

Building an Electronic Portfolio

The final chapter in this book addresses Encore, which will be used to create an electronic portfolio of the portfolio projects from each chapter in this book. It is suggested you work on the chapters in the book in consecutive order so that as your skills are developed you are able to utilize them in later chapters.

Windows and Macintosh

The Video Production Suite works virtually the same on both the Windows and Macintosh operating systems. In those cases where there is a difference, the abbreviations (Win) and (Mac) are used.

System Requirements for Adobe Creative Suite 5 Production Premium

Windows

- 64-bit support required: Intel® Pentium® 4 or AMD Athlon® 64 processor (Intel Core™2 Duo or AMD Phenom® II recommended); Intel Core 2 Duo or AMD Phenom II required for Adobe Premiere® Pro
- 64-bit operating system required: Microsoft® Windows Vista® Home Premium, Business, Ultimate, or Enterprise with Service Pack 1 (Service Pack 2 recommended) or Windows 7
- 2 GB of RAM (4GB or more recommended)
- 16.3 GB of available hard-disk space for installation; additional free space required during installation (cannot install on removable flash-based storage devices)
- 1280x900 display (1280x1024 recommended) with qualified hardware-accelerated OpenGL graphics card, 16-bit color, and 256 MB of VRAM
- Adobe-certified GPU card for GPU-accelerated performance in Adobe Premiere Pro
- Some features in Adobe Bridge rely on a DirectX 9–capable graphics card with at least 64 MB of VRAM
- 7200 RPM hard drive for editing compressed video formats; RAID 0 for uncompressed
- Adobe-certified card for capture and export to tape for SD/HD workflows
- OHCI-compatible IEEE 1394 port for DV and HDV capture, export to tape, and transmit to DV device
- Sound card compatible with ASIO protocol or Microsoft Windows Driver Model
- DVD-ROM drive compatible with dual-layer DVDs (DVD+-R burner for burning DVDs; Blu-ray burner for creating Blu-ray Disc media)
- Java™ Runtime Environment 1.5 (32 bit) or 1.6
- QuickTime 7.6.2 software required for QuickTime features
- Adobe Flash® Player 10 software required to play back DVD projects exported as SWF files
- Broadband Internet connection required for online services

Macintosh System Requirements

- Multicore Intel processor with 64-bit support
- Mac OS X v10.5.7 or v10.6.3; Mac OS X v10.6.3 required for GPU-accelerated performance in Adobe Premiere Pro
- 2 GB of RAM (4 GB or more recommended)
- 20.6 GB of available hard-disk space for installation; additional free space required during installation (cannot install on a volume that uses a case-sensitive file system or on removable flash-based storage devices)
- 1280x900 display (1280x1024 recommended) with qualified hardware-accelerated OpenGL graphics card, 16-bit color, and 256 MB of VRAM
- Adobe-certified GPU card for GPU-accelerated performance in Adobe Premiere Pro
- 7200 RPM hard drive for editing compressed video formats; RAID 0 for uncompressed
- Core Audio–compatible sound card
- DVD-ROM drive compatible with dual-layer DVDs (SuperDrive for burning DVDs; external Blu-ray burner for creating Blu-ray Disc media)
- Java Runtime Environment 1.5 or 1.6
- QuickTime 7.6.2 software required for QuickTime features
- Adobe Flash Player 10 software required to play back DVD projects exported as SWF files
- Broadband Internet connection required for online services

Certification

This book covers the objectives necessary for Adobe Premiere Pro ACE certification. Use the Certification Grid at the back of the book to find out where an objective is covered.

1

CHAPTER

CREATING A VIDEO MONTAGE
IN ADOBE PREMIERE CS5

1. Create a new project and explore the workspace
2. Import assets
3. Work with the Timeline panel and sequences
4. Apply video transitions
5. Work with motion effects
6. Design and insert titles
7. Export a movie

CHAPTER 1

CREATING A VIDEO MONTAGE
IN ADOBE PREMIERE CS5

Adobe Premiere Pro CS5 is a professional digital video editing application that allows you to capture, edit, and publish video. It can be purchased as a stand-alone application or as part of either the Creative Suite 5 Production Premium or the Creative Suite 5 Master Collection.

You have probably heard of Adobe Systems and have already used some of their applications such as Photoshop or Illustrator. Premiere Pro should therefore have some familiarity to you as you begin to work with it because of the similarity in workspace design with other Adobe products.

When working with Premiere Pro you bring together video clips, digital images, audio, and vector graphics to create a **project file**. A project file is the name used for the movie you are creating and is saved with the .prproj file extension.

In this project, we will create a video montage. A **video montage** is a video created with digital images, words, transitions, and music.

Create a New Project
AND EXPLORE THE WORKSPACE

What You'll Do

In this lesson, you will start Premiere Pro, create a new project, and explore the workspace.

Exploring the Premiere Pro Workspace

When you start Premiere Pro, you will be prompted to create a new project or open an existing project. Once you have done that, you will see the **application window**, which is the main window comprised of various panels. The arrangement of panels in the application window is known as the **workspace**. Premiere Pro offers several preformatted workspaces which are designed for specific tasks. Figure 1 shows the default workspace which is called **Editing**.

Figure 1 *Editing workspace*

Creating a Video Montage in Adobe Premiere CS5

The Editing workspace, as its name implies, is designed to facilitate video editing. The panels that are necessary to perform editing functions are the active panels.

The workspace can be changed by selecting a default workspace or by rearranging the panels to your individual preference. Preformatted workspaces can be changed using the Workspace command on the Window menu or by making a selection from the drop-down menu on the Tools panel.

Panels can be moved by clicking and dragging the **panel tabs**. As you drag the panel, an area becomes highlighted; this is called the **drop zone**, as shown in Figure 2, and provides a visual reference to where the panel can be placed.

If you wish to save a custom workspace, you may do so by selecting the New Workspace command on the Workspace menu or from the drop-down menu on the Tools panel. A **custom workspace** is one that has been created by the user and saved with a unique name.

The panels used most often in Premiere Pro are:

Project panel: The Project panel organizes all the assets for your project. **Assets** can include video clips, digital images, and audio clips.

Timeline panel: The Timeline panel is where you assemble assets and edit them. It is here that you can also add special effects, transitions, and titles. The Timeline plays the items from left to right creating a movie.

Figure 2 *Moving panels in the workspace*

Drop zone

Preformatted workspaces

Source and Program Monitor panels:

The Source Monitor is used to preview assets from the Project panel or the Media Browser before you place them in a sequence, and the Program Monitor displays the contents of the Timeline—your project in progress.

Capturing Video from an External Device

Adobe Premiere Pro supports the control of devices such as camcorders and VCRs for capturing video via the Control Settings dialog box. DV and HDV devices are controlled with the IEEE 1394 (FireWire, i.Link) connections. On the Windows platform Adobe Premiere Pro can also control serial devices by way of RS-232 or RS-422 controllers if they are installed on the computer.

The Control Settings dialog box can be activated via the Device Control panel in the Preferences dialog box or from the Settings pane of the of the Capture panel. This controls how Premiere Pro transfers video and audio from a VCR or a camera. The options may differ depending on installed software or capture cards. In the Capture panel, if you are connecting a DV or HDV Device, select the device you want to control from the Device pop-up menu. You will then have the option to select the model, or one from the same family. If these are not available options, choose Standard. If you are connecting a serial device, make your selections from the Protocol, Port, Time Source, and Time Base menus. Check either or both check box selections available for the protocol you choose.

The Capture panel, activated from the File menu, provides controls similar to those in the Source and Program Monitor panels to operate the device during playback and capture. These are called transport controls and include a Record button. The Record button is used for a manual capture.

In the Logging pane, you can create metadata for your imported footage and set up the capture to import the entire footage as one clip or based on scene detection. Extra frames, or handles, can also be set to be added to the clip to provide additional frames at each end to assist in editing. Additionally, you can log clips and identify In/Out points without capturing so that you can utilize batch capturing. Batch capturing allows you to capture logged clips automatically and then leave them unattended, allowing you to minimize Premiere Pro and switch to another application without stopping capture. (*Note*: This option is selected from the File menu.)

Premiere Pro supports editing footage from a multi-camera shoot, of up to four cameras. Make sure each camera has a sync point, such as a clapper slate, to easily synchronize the footage. Capture your footage as you normally would, and stack the synchronized footage on separate video tracks and create a nested sequence. You can then open the Multi-Camera Monitor panel and target the nested sequence. You will then be able to see the footage from each of the cameras and edit from this panel. You will have the ability to switch between camera footage and assemble an edited sequence from the footage from each of the cameras while viewing all of them at one time. The Capture panel is shown in Figure 3 and the DV/HDV Device Control Settings dialog box is shown in Figure 4.

Figure 3 *Using the Capture panel*

Capture
panel

Status area

Preview

Transport controls

Figure 4 *DV/HDV Device Control Settings*

Understanding the New Project Dialog Box

When you create a new project, the New Project dialog box opens. The New Project dialog box is where you specify the settings for your Premiere Pro project. It has two tabs: General and Scratch Disks. The General tab is where you adjust settings regarding safe margins and video/audio formats. It is recommended that these settings be left to their defaults. We will be using the DV Capture setting. If you capture or have access to your own high definition footage, you will need to change this setting to HDV. The General tab is also where you name and set the location where you will be saving your project file.

The Scratch Disks tab, as shown in Figure 5, provides settings for a variety of files associated with the video editing process including where they are stored. Premiere Pro sets the default for each of these files as the Same as Project. Using the Same as Project setting is an excellent way to keep your project organized and to be able to clean up project files as they become

Figure 5 *Scratch Disks tab in the New Project dialog box*

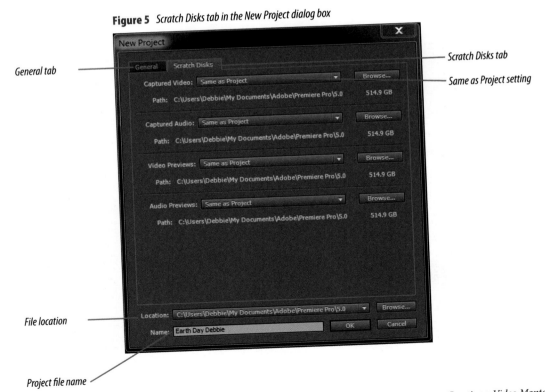

General tab

File location

Project file name

Scratch Disks tab

Same as Project setting

Creating a Video Montage in Adobe Premiere CS5

memory intensive. We will be using the default settings as we work through the projects in this book.

Understanding the New Sequence Dialog Box

The New Sequence dialog box appears after you click OK in the New Project dialog box. A **sequence** is where the digital assets are placed and edited. At least one sequence is required in a Premiere Pro project, which is why you are prompted to create one when beginning a project. The New Sequence

dialog box has three tabs: Sequence Presets, General, and Tracks. We will be working with the default settings, as shown in Figure 6, unless otherwise noted.

The Sequence Presets tab has a number of categories of sequence settings for commonly used capture devices. It is recommended that you choose the preset that matches the settings for your device if it is available.

The General tab is available to customize settings if there is not a preset available for

your device. It is recommended that you use the preset that is the closest match to your device and continue with any necessary customizations on the General tab. You can then save this custom preset.

The Tracks tab allows you to indicate how many video and audio tracks will be added when the sequence is created; by default, three video tracks and three stereo audio tracks are created. Tracks can be added or deleted later.

Figure 6 *New Sequence dialog box*

Create a new project and explore the workspace

1. Click **Start** 🪟 on the Application bar, point to **All Programs**, then click **Adobe Premiere Pro CS5**. (Win) or open the **Finder** from the dock and click **Applications** from the sidebar, select the **Adobe applications folder** then click **Adobe Premiere Pro CS5** (Mac).

   You may need to look in a subfolder if you have installed the Creative Suite.

   TIP Pressing and holding [Ctrl][Alt][Shift] (Win) or ⌘ [Shift][option] (Mac) while starting Premiere Pro restores default preference settings.

2. Click **New Project** in the Welcome to Adobe Premiere Pro window as shown in Figure 7.

   The New Project dialog box opens.

3. Click the **Browse button** and navigate to the drive and folder where your Data Files are located.

4. Click **OK** to close the Browse for Folder window but keep the New Project dialog box open.

   The Browse button allows you to choose a destination to save the project in. As shown in Figure 8, the path where the project will be saved appears in the Location field.

   (continued)

Figure 7 *Welcome to Adobe Premiere Pro window*

New Project

Figure 8 *New Project dialog box*

File path

Browse button

Project / file name

Creating a Video Montage in Adobe Premiere CS5

Figure 9 *Effects workspace*

5. Type **Earth Day** followed by your name in the Name text box of the New Project dialog box.

6. Click **OK** to close the New Project dialog box.

   The New Sequence dialog box appears.

7. Accept the default settings, then click **OK**.

   The Premiere Pro CS5 workspace appears.

8. Locate the Project panel, Source Monitor, Program Monitor, and Timeline.

9. Click **Window** on the Application bar, point to **Workspace**, then click **Effects**.

   The Effects workspace is used for working with Video and Audio Effects. As shown in Figure 9, the Effects panel moved into the original location of the Project panel and the Effect Controls panel moved to the forefront in place of the Source Monitor panel.

10. Click **Window** on the Application bar, point to **Workspace**, then click **Editing** to return to the default workspace.

You started Adobe Premiere Pro CS5, created a new project named Earth Day, and explored the workspace.

Import ASSETS

What You'll Do

In this lesson, you will continue to work with the project you began in Lesson 1 and familiarize yourself with the Project panel and the Media Browser.

Importing Assets

The Premiere Pro CS5 project is a single file that stores all references to **digital assets** used in the project. Digital assets may include: video, audio, still images, and Photoshop and Illustrator files. The project file also contains **sequences** (or timelines); these are where the digital assets are placed and edited. Only one project may be opened at a time. When you save a project, the name will appear in the title bar along with the path to where it is being saved.

The assets you use for your project are imported into the Project panel. You will have the option when importing to select single or multiple clips, folders and their content, and numbered stills. Video projects characteristically take up a lot of memory so to help keep the file size down, Premiere Pro creates **reference files** that point to the original file being imported. Keep this in mind as you work with your project file. If you move any of the reference files, the Project panel will no longer be able to find them.

Organizing the Project Panel

The Project panel is your "file cabinet" of assets. You can create **bins** to help organize your file cabinet, as shown in Figure 10. Bins work the same way as folders in Windows Explorer or the Mac OS Finder. Bins may contain assets, sequences, or other bins.

Figure 10 *Project panel with bins and assets*

Creating a Video Montage in Adobe Premiere CS5

You may want to use them to organize your source files by category, such as text or images, or if you are creating multiple sequences, to organize sequences with their own source files.

Working with the Media Browser

The Media Browser provides a convenient way to locate, sort, preview, and import assets that you plan to use in your Premiere Pro project, as shown in Figure 11. It also provides access to the assets that you are using while you edit. Since the Media Browser is a panel it can be treated like any other panel—docked, left open, or floating.

If you double-click or right-click an asset in the Media Browser it will open in the Source Monitor for preview; it will not import the file into the Project panel.

Organizing a Storyboard

In addition, the Project panel can be used for storyboarding when changed to Icon view.

Storyboarding is a way to plan your video by placing **clips** or digital assets in the order you plan to have them play. **Icon view** shows **thumbnails**, smaller versions of the digital assets you imported, as shown in Figure 12. To arrange the thumbnails, click and drag any square. As you drag, a vertical bar indicates where the item is going; when you release the mouse button the thumbnail will drop into place.

Figure 11 *Media Browser*

Media Browser
Computer directory
Folders and files

Figure 12 *Organizing a storyboard in Icon view*

Preview
Return to Parent bin
List View button
Icon View button

Import assets using the Media Browser

1. Open your Earth Day your name.prproj file, if necessary.

2. Click the **Media Browser panel tab**, if it is not already active.

   The Media Browser displays the hard drive(s) on your computer.

3. On the Media Browser, navigate to the drive and folder where the Chapter 1 Data Files are located as shown in Figure 13.

4. Select **70s Soft Rock - 60.mp3**. in the Chapter 1 Data Files folder.

5. Click **File** on the Application bar, then click **Import from Media Browser**.

   TIP You can also right-click a file on the Media Browser and select Import or drag the file from the Media Browser into the Project panel.

   The Project panel now contains the reference to the 70s Soft Rock - 60.mp3 file from the Chapter 1 Data Files folder.

6. Save your project file and leave it open for the next exercise.

You used the Media Browser to import an audio file for your Earth Day project.

Figure 13 *The Media Browser panel*

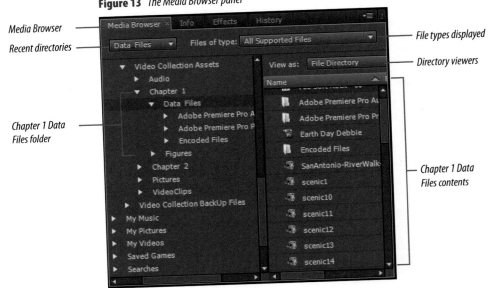

Media Browser

Recent directories

Chapter 1 Data Files folder

File types displayed

Directory viewers

Chapter 1 Data Files contents

Viewing Files in the Media Browser

To view only files of certain types in the Media Browser, click the Files of type list arrow in the Import dialog box, and select a file type. To select an additional type, open the menu again and make another selection. Repeat until all desired types have been selected. Select one or more files from the list of files. To select more than one noncontiguous file, [Ctrl]-click (Win) or ⌘-click (Mac) the filenames. To select more than one contiguous file, [Shift]-click the filenames.

Figure 14 *Creating a new bin*

Type Scenic Pictures here

Figure 15 *Scenic Pictures bin opened as a dockable panel*

Bin name

Work with bins

1. Open your Earth Day your name.prproj file, if it is not already open.

2. Click the **New Bin button** on the Project panel to create a new bin.

3. Click **Bin01**, as shown in Figure 14, then type **Scenic Pictures** to rename the bin.

4. Double-click the **Scenic Pictures bin** to open the bin as a dockable panel.

   Opening a bin as a dockable panel allows you to resize the window to get a better view, as shown in Figure 15.

TIP To open a bin on the Project panel, [Ctrl]-double-click (Win) or ⌘-double-click (Mac) the bin. Click the Parent bin button to close the bin if you opened the bin on the Project panel.

5. Click the **Close box** to close the Scenic Pictures dockable panel.

6. Save your project file and leave it open for the next exercise.

You created a new bin titled Scenic Pictures, opened it as a dockable panel, and then closed it.

Import assets with the Import command

1. Open your Earth Day your name.prproj file, if necessary.

2. [Ctrl]-double-click (Win) or ⌘-double-click (Mac) the **Scenic Pictures bin** to open it within the Project panel.

3. Click **File** on the Application bar, click **Import**, as shown in Figure 16, then navigate to the drive and folder where your Data Files are located.

   TIP Alternatively, you can right-click a bin, then click Import.

4. Select the range of files **scenic1.jpg** through **scenic32.jpg** located in the Data Files folder, then click **Open**.

   TIP To select more than one contiguous file, press and hold [Shift] as you click the filenames.

   (continued)

Figure 16 *Import command on the File menu*

Import command

Figure 17 *Scenic Pictures bin with imported images*

Imported assets

The Scenic Pictures bin now contains the references to the files from the Data Files folder, as shown in Figure 17.

5. Click the **Parent bin button** 📁 to close the Scenic Pictures bin.

6. Save your project file and leave it open for the next exercise.

You imported images into the Scenic Pictures bin using the Import command.

Create a storyboard

1. Open your Earth Day your name.prproj file, if necessary.

2. Double-click the **Scenic Pictures bin** to open it as a dockable panel.

3. Click the **Icon View button** 🖥 on the Scenic Pictures bin.

   Clips in the Project panel can be viewed in List view (default view) or in Icon view. To change from one view to another, click the List View button 🗒 or the Icon View button 🖥 on the Project panel.

(continued)

Configure Premiere Pro Preferences for a Project

Premiere Pro can be customized using the Preferences panel. Options range from setting the brightness of the interface under the Appearance category, to changing the default length of transitions under the General category. Some preferences will remain for all projects, while others such as setting a location for scratch disks, under the Media category, will be specific to a project file.

Lesson 2   Import Assets

4. Click the **Scenic Pictures bin options button** ▼≡ , point to **Thumbnails**, then click **Medium**.

5. Click the **scenic3.jpg image**, drag the image after **scenic1.jpg**, then release the mouse button.

As you drag, a vertical line appears to show you where the item will be placed, as shown in Figure 18.

(continued)

Figure 18 *Dragging an image in the Scenic Pictures bin*

Vertical line

Preparing Still Images for Import

To reduce rendering time and improve quality, images should be prepared prior to importing into your Adobe Premiere Pro project. The pixel dimensions should be set to the resolution you will use in Adobe Premiere Pro. If you plan to scale the image, set the image dimensions to the largest size the image will be in the project. Scaling an image larger than its original size can cause loss of sharpness. Crop the parts of the image that you don't want to be visible in Adobe Premiere Pro.

Figure 19 *Images rearranged in the Scenic Pictures bin*

Odd numbered images

Even numbered images

Icon View button

6. Reorder all of the images so that the odd numbered images are first (scenic1.jpg, scenic3.jpg, scenic5.jpg, and so on).

TIP You may need to resize the Scenic Pictures bin to drag all of the images.

Your bin should resemble Figure 19.

7. Close the Scenic Pictures bin.

8. Save your project file and leave it open for the next exercise.

You created a storyboard by rearranging the images in the Scenic Pictures bin.

Work with the Timeline Panel
AND SEQUENCES

What You'll Do

 In this lesson, you will work with a sequence in the Timeline panel by placing clips on the sequence.

Understanding the Timeline Panel

The Timeline panel, as shown in Figure 20, is where most editing takes place in a **sequence**. Adobe Premiere Pro can have multiple sequences and you can place sequences inside other sequences to break your project up into manageable pieces. Sequences are comprised of video and audio tracks. **Tracks** are where the clips are assembled, edited, and enhanced with effects and transitions. A sequence can consist of multiple audio and video tracks, but must contain at least one of each. Multiple tracks are used to blend clips together.

Exploring the Timeline Panel Controls

The Timeline panel includes the following features:

Time ruler: The Time ruler measures the time in the sequence horizontally. Icons for markers and In and Out points are also displayed here.

Current time display: The Current time display shows the timecode for the current frame. The **timecode** marks specific frames with unique addresses and is recorded onto videotape during the recording process.

To change the timecode, click the timecode display and enter a new timecode, or place the pointer over the display and drag left or right. Changing the Current time display is a way to adjust the location of the Current-time Indicator.

Play head and Current-time Indicator (CTI): The Current-time Indicator (CTI) indicates the current frame displayed in the Program Monitor. The CTI is a light blue triangle in the Time ruler with a vertical red line extending through the video and audio tracks. The CTI can be moved by clicking and dragging on the blue triangle. This can also be used as a preview method, referred to as **scrubbing**.

Work area bar: The work area bar is the area of the sequence that you want to preview or export. The brackets on either end, located just below the Time ruler, are adjustable so you can export portions of a large project for preview.

Viewing area bar: The viewing area bar is the area which corresponds with the visible portion of the Timeline panel and allows you to quickly move to different parts of the sequence. It is located just above the Time ruler.

Creating a Video Montage in Adobe Premiere CS5

Zoom slider: The Zoom slider increases or decreases the number of visible frames within the current viewing area.

Adding Clips to a Sequence

There are many options for adding clips to a sequence on the Timeline panel. The most obvious is to simply drag the clip from the Project panel to the sequence. If it is an audio clip it needs to be placed on an audio track; all other clips are placed on video tracks.

Any edits or effects that are done to the clip do not alter the clip on the Project panel, so you are able to use clips multiple times in the same project and apply different effects to the same clip.

You are also able to add clips to a sequence while previewing them on the Source Monitor. You can either drag an image from the Source Monitor to a track, or use the Insert button or the Overlay button on the Source Monitor to place the clip on the sequence.

Using the Insert button places the clip at the location of the CTI and shifts any clips at that location to the right to make room for the clip. If you are placing items on a video track and have already placed audio on an audio track you will need to lock the audio track to keep it from shifting. To lock a track, you click the Toggle Track Lock box to the left of a track name. A padlock icon appears, indicating that the track is locked. The Overlay button replaces the clip, as shown in Figure 21.

Figure 20 *Timeline panel*

Current time display

Time ruler

Video tracks

Audio tracks

Viewing area bar

Zoom slider

Playhead and Current-time Indicator

Work area bar

Using the Automate to Sequence Command

In a previous lesson, we learned how to organize digital images in a storyboard. Premiere Pro has a command that will let you place the images from a storyboard on a sequence in the order that they were organized. This feature is called Automate to Sequence.

The clips you would like to be included in the Automate to Sequence process must be selected. The Automate to Sequence command is located on the Project panel menu by clicking the Project panel options button. You can also use the Automate to Sequence button on the Project panel.

If you do not want to organize your clips using a storyboard, you may select the clips in the order that you would like them placed in the sequence while pressing and holding [Ctrl] (Win) or ⌘ (Mac) and then choosing Selection Order from the Ordering list in the Automate To Sequence dialog box, as shown in Figure 22.

Deleting Clips from a Sequence

During the editing process you may decide you want to remove a clip from a sequence. When you remove a clip from a sequence, it is not removed from the Project panel. If you remove a clip from the Project panel, and it

Figure 21 *Example of Insert and Overlay insertions*

Original sequence

scenic14.jpg

scenic2.jpg

scenic29.jpg placed with Insert button

scenic14.jpg

scenic29.jpg placed with Overlay button

scenic2.jpg

Figure 22 *Automate To Sequence dialog box*

Ordering

Creating a Video Montage in Adobe Premiere CS5

is still in a sequence, it will be removed from the sequence. Premiere Pro will give you a warning before it will delete the clip from the Project panel.

The Selection tool is the main tool used in Premiere Pro. It is used to select menu items and objects in the Premiere Pro workspace, and it is used for selecting clips in a sequence and in the Project panel.

The Track Select tool selects everything to the right of where you click in the sequence. See Figure 23. To select the clip and everything to the right on all tracks, [Shift]-click the clip.

The **Ripple Delete** command removes a clip from the sequence without leaving any gaps if the clip being removed is located between two other clips. Be cautious when working with this command if you have assets on other tracks; it will shift the clips on those tracks as well. In order to keep clips from shifting on other tracks they need to be locked before using the Ripple Delete command.

Previewing Your Project in the Program Monitor

The Program Monitor plays back the clips you are assembling in the active sequence on the Timeline panel for you to preview. The Play-Stop Toggle button plays and stops the sequence from the location of the CTI. The Shuttle button moves either forward or backward, fast or slow, depending on how you adjust the slider. The more you move the slider to the right the faster the video will play forward, the more you move the slider to the left the faster the video will rewind.

The Safe Margins guides are available to reference the title-safe and action-safe zones. The inner rectangle is the title-safe zone and the outer rectangle is the action-safe zone. We will discuss this in detail in Chapter 2.

Figure 23 *Selecting clips with the Track Select tool*

All tracks including scenic15.jpg are selected to the right

Track Select tool

Add clips to a sequence by dragging

1. Open your Earth Day your name.prproj file, if necessary.

2. Verify that the Current-time Indicator (CTI) is at the beginning of the sequence, as shown in Figure 24, by clicking the CTI (blue triangle) and dragging it to the left until the Current time display shows all zeroes.

TIP Another method for placing the CTI at the beginning of the sequence is to click the Timeline panel tab and then press [Home]. The [Home] key equivalent is [FN]+left arrow (Mac).

3. Click the **Project panel tab** to activate the Project panel.

4. Double-click the **Scenic Pictures bin**.

5. Click **scenic5.jpg**, then drag the clip to the beginning of the Video 1 track on the Timeline panel.

   When you drag a clip to add it to a sequence, you target the track by dropping the clip into the track.

TIP To make clip edges align when you drag them, make sure that the Snap button is active on the Timeline panel.

(continued)

Figure 24 *CTI with timecode displaying all zeroes*

Current time display showing all zeroes

Current-time Indicator (CTI)

A Note About Rendering

Rendering is part of the exporting process and it is what determines the quality of the playback of the final product. You may have noticed a red or green line below the Work area bar in the Timeline panel. This line indicates whether your project has been **rendered**. A rendered project will play the video more smoothly and much closer to real time. A red line indicates that Premiere Pro is not able to play back your project in real time in the Project Monitor. A green line indicates the project has been rendered. Adjusting the length of the Viewing area bar will allow you to control portions of the video you wish to preview in rendered mode. **Note:** Each time you render your project, a unique preview file is created and can become memory intensive.

Figure 25 *The scenic5.jpg clip on the Video 1 track*

Snap button

Video track 1   Zoom In slider   scenic5.jpg

Figure 26 *The Video 1 track with five clips*

6. Click the **Zoom In slider** on the Timeline panel to enlarge the thumbnail of the image on the Video 1 track until you can view the image better, as shown in Figure 25.

7. Continue dragging clips **scenic6.jpg**, **scenic7.jpg**, and **scenic8.jpg** to the sequence one after the other.

8. Drag clip **scenic9.jpg** directly on top of **scenic6.jpg**.

   The scenic9.jpg file replaces scenic6.jpg in the sequence.

9. Press and hold **[Ctrl]** (Win) or ⌘ (Mac), then drag **scenic6.jpg** directly on top of **scenic9.jpg**.

   The scenic6.jpg is added to the sequence and scenic9.jpg is shifted to the right.

10. Compare your sequence to Figure 26, save your project file, and leave it open for the next exercise.

You added five clips to the sequence by dragging them from the Project panel.

Use the Automate to Sequence command

1. Open your Earth Day your name.prproj file, if necessary.

2. Be sure the Current-time Indicator (CTI) is at the end of the sequence by dragging it to the right until the Current time display shows **00;00;25;00**.

   TIP Another method for placing the CTI at the end of the sequence is to click the Timeline panel tab and press [End]. The [End] key equivalent is [FN]+right arrow (Mac).

3. Click the **Project panel tab** to activate the Project panel.

4. Open the Scenic Pictures bin, as a dockable panel, if necessary.

   The bin should still be in Icon view and sorted by odd numbers first.

5. Select all of the images in the bin.

   TIP You can select all images by pressing [Ctrl][A] (Win) or ⌘[A] (Mac).

6. Click the **Scenic Pictures panel options button** ▾≡, then click **Automate to Sequence**, as shown in Figure 27.

   The Automate To Sequence dialog box opens.

   TIP You can also use the Automate to Sequence button ▦ on the Project panel to access the Automate To Sequence dialog box.

   (continued)

Figure 27 *Using the Automate to Sequence command*

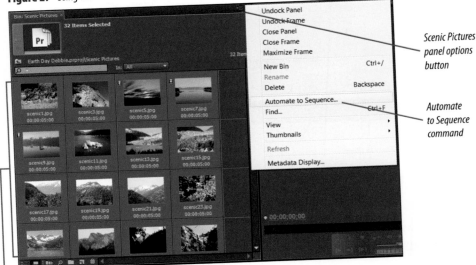

Scenic Pictures panel options button

Automate to Sequence command

All images selected

Figure 28 *Automate To Sequence dialog box*

Sort Order

Figure 29 *Source Monitor*

Play-Stop Toggle button

Insert button

Overlay button

7. In the Automate To Sequence dialog box, click the **Ordering list arrow**, click **Sort Order**, as shown in Figure 28, then click **OK**.

   The clips are added to the sequence in sort order beginning at timecode 00;00;25;00, after the previous five clips that were already on the sequence.

8. Close the Scenic Pictures bin.

9. Save your project file and leave it open for the next exercise.

You added clips to the sequence using the Automate To Sequence dialog box.

Place clips in a sequence using the Source Monitor

1. Open your Earth Day your name.prproj file, if necessary.

2. Be sure the CTI is at the beginning of the sequence.

3. Double-click the **70s Soft Rock-60.mp3** audio file on the Project panel to preview the clip in the Source Monitor.

   The Source Monitor, as shown in Figure 29, allows you to preview any asset from either the Project panel or the Media Browser.

4. Click the **Play-Stop Toggle button** on the Source Monitor to preview the audio file.

(continued)

5. Click in the **header area** of the Video 1 track, as shown in Figure 30, to turn off the target on the Video 1 track.

   The highlight needs to be removed so that when the audio file is placed from the Source Monitor, it knows to affect only the Audio 1 track.

6. Target the **Audio 1 track** by clicking in the header area and then clicking the **source track indicator**, as shown in Figure 31.

   Each area highlights independently; both areas need to be highlighted for the next steps to work properly. The **source track indicator** represents that an audio clip is open on the Source Monitor.

7. Click the **Insert button** 🔲 on the Source Monitor to place the audio file on the sequence in the Audio 1 track.

   To accommodate inserting the audio track, all of the digital images shifted to the right, as shown in Figure 32. We want the music to play with the images, so we need to undo our last action.

8. Click **Edit** on the Application bar, then click **Undo**.

   TIP You can also undo your last step by pressing [Ctrl] [Z] (Win) or ⌘ [Z] (Mac).

   (continued)

Figure 30 *Selecting header area of the Video 1 track*

Selecting header area

Figure 31 *Highlighted tracks*

Source track indicator

Header area

Figure 32 *Using the Insert button to place the audio file*

Notice that the Audio 1 track is selected

Images shifted right

Creating a Video Montage in Adobe Premiere CS5

Figure 33 *The audio file placed with the Overlay button*

Figure 34 *Closing the file on the Source Monitor*

Drop-down menu

9. Click the **Overlay button** [⬇] on the Source Monitor to place the audio file on the sequence.

   Notice this time the audio track is lined up directly below the images on the video track, as shown in Figure 33.

10. Click the **drop-down menu** next to **70s Soft Rock-60.mp3** on the Source Monitor, as shown in Figure 34, then click **Close** to close the audio clip.

11. Save your project file and leave it open for the next exercise.

You added an audio clip to the Audio 1 track using the Insert and Overlay buttons on the Source Monitor.

Delete clips from a sequence

1. Open your Earth Day your name.prproj file, if necessary.

2. Verify that the Editing workspace is chosen.

3. Select the first five clips in the sequence: **scenic5.jpg**, **scenic6.jpg**, **scenic9.jpg**, **scenic7.jpg**, and **scenic8.jpg**.

4. Zoom in on the sequence if necessary.

TIP To select more than one clip, [Shift]-click the clips or drag a selection marquee over them.

(continued)

Lesson 3   Work with the Timeline Panel and Sequences

5. Press **Delete** on the keyboard.

   Notice that the clips are removed, but a gap is left as shown in Figure 35.

6. Click **Edit** on the Application bar, then click **Undo**.

   We will use the Ripple Delete command to remove the clips without leaving a gap in the sequence.

7. Click **Edit** on the Application bar, then click **Ripple Delete**.

   The Ripple Delete command closes the gap and removes the clips from the sequence.

TIP Alternatively, you can right-click (Win) or [Ctrl]-click (Mac) the clips you wish to delete and then choose Ripple Delete.

8. Click the **Track Select tool** ▦ on the Tools panel, then click **scenic2.jpg**.

   The Track Select tool is used to quickly select a range of items. The range of images beginning with scenic2.jpg to the end of the sequence is selected.

9. Press **Delete**.

   Since these images are at the end of the sequence, we do not need to use the Ripple Delete command.

10. Click the **Selection tool** ▸ on the Tools panel before continuing.

11. Save your project file and leave it open for the next exercise.

You deleted clips from a sequence using the Ripple Delete command.

Figure 35 *Removing clips with the Delete key*

Gap left after
clips deleted

Archive your Premiere Pro Project with the Project Manager

The Project Manager can be used to archive a project by consolidating all of the project's source media files, or to create a variation of the project called a trimmed project. There are options to consider in the Project Manager dialog box to conserve disk space. If the Include Preview Files and Include Audio Conform Files options are selected, the rendered effects will remain rendered and the conformed audio will remain conformed in the project, thus taking up more disk space. Remove the check marks to conserve disk space. (Note: These options are only available if the Collect Files And Copy to New Location option is selected.) Once the project is opened again, the audio will be conformed and the file can be rendered.

The Rename Media File To Match Clip Names option provides the opportunity to organize footage files based on the names given to the footage in the Project panel.

The Include Handles option specifies the number of frames that will be preserved before and after the In and Out points of each trimmed clip, the default value is 30 frames. This provides extra frames in the new project if minor adjustments need to be made.

Creating a Video Montage in Adobe Premiere CS5

Figure 36 *Edited Timeline panel*

Preview contents of the Timeline on the Program Monitor

1. Open your Earth Day your name.prproj file, if necessary.

2. Be sure the CTI is at the beginning of the sequence.

3. Press the **Play-Stop Toggle button** ▶ on the Program Monitor to view the contents of the Timeline.

   Each image clip transitions from one to the other as the CTI moves from left to right in the sequence. Premiere Pro applies the default transition called Cross Dissolve to all clips.

   TIP Pressing [Spacebar] will also preview the sequence. Pressing [Enter] (Win) or [return] (Mac) will preview the sequence and begin the rendering process.

4. Drag the **CTI** on the Timeline panel left and right to preview the sequence on the Program Monitor.

   TIP Viewing the clip in this manner is referred to as **scrubbing** (so named because of the back-and-forth motion).

5. Compare your Timeline panel to Figure 36.

6. Save your project file and leave it open for the next exercise.

You previewed the sequence in the Program Monitor.

Apply Video
TRANSITIONS

What You'll Do

In this lesson, you will apply video transition to images.

Applying Video Transitions

A **transition** is used to move from one clip to the next in your sequence. Transitions can add additional interest to your video and can be as simple as phasing out one image and phasing in another. Adobe Premiere Pro CS5 has a large library of video transitions to choose from with categories that include: Dissolve, Page Peel, Slide, and Zoom. Video transitions are stored on the Effects panel. Cross Dissolve is set as the default transition and has already been placed between each of our clips in the Timeline panel.

Applying a Transition Between Clips

After you find the transition you want to apply on the Effects panel, simply drag the transition to the **cut line** (vertical line) between two clips and release the mouse button when you see the cut icon you want to apply. As shown in Figure 37, you can place or align the transition in one of three ways: Center at Cut, Start at Cut, or End at Cut. By default, the transition is placed centered on the **cut**, the space between two clips. The other options either start or end the transition at the cut. These options can

Figure 37 *Three alignment options for placing a transition*

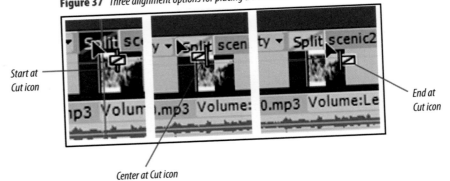

Start at
Cut icon

End at
Cut icon

Center at Cut icon

be chosen on the Effect Controls panel using the Alignment drop-down menu.

Customizing Transitions on the Effect Controls Panel

When working with transitions, it is a good idea to change to the Effects workspace. In the Effects workspace, you can customize transitions on the Effect Controls panel, as shown in Figure 38. Each transition has different options available on the Effect Controls panel.

Some transitions have **edge selectors**, arrows that change the orientation or direction of

the transition. To change the orientation or direction of a transition, you click an edge selector arrow on the transition's thumbnail. For example, the Slide transition can be oriented vertically, horizontally, or diagonally.

Start and **End sliders** can be changed with the three alignment settings as previously mentioned, or as a custom setting by pressing and holding [Shift] to move the start and end sliders together or by dragging one slider to change the position of one end.

The **Show Actual Sources** setting displays the starting and ending frames of the clips.

The **Border Width** setting adjusts the width of the optional border on the transition. The default border width setting is set to 0.0. Some transitions do not have borders.

The **Border Color** setting specifies the color of the transition's border. For the border color to show, the border width setting must be set to a value higher than 0.0.

Figure 38 *Additional transition options on the Effect Controls panel*

Edge selectors would be located here if available

Show Actual Sources

Border Color

Anti-aliasing Quality

Show/Hide Timeline View button

Slider

Border Width

Reverse

Custom

The **Reverse** setting plays the transition backward.

The **Anti-aliasing Quality** setting adjusts the smoothness of the transition's edges.

The **Custom** setting changes settings specific to the transition. Most transitions do not have custom settings.

QUICK TIP

If you have created a custom transition and you would like to use it again in the same Premiere Pro project, you can copy and paste it to any other track as long as you are copying and pasting a video transition to a video track and an audio transition to an audio track.

QUICK TIP

Video transitions on the Mac are very limited compared to the Windows version of Premiere Pro. In this text, transitions have been selected using the Windows platform to demonstrate and take advantage of the customizing options that are available. If you are on a Mac, you will need to make a substitution, when a transition is not available.

Figure 39 *Effects panel for Windows and Mac*

Windows

Mac

Contains box

Effects bins

New Custom
Bin button

Searching for Video Transitions

In the Effects panel, filed in several folders and subfolders, there is an extensive library of transitions, as shown in Figure 39. Therefore, if you know the name of the transition you are looking for, or even if you have an idea of what it might be called, you can search for it by typing its name in the Contains box to find it more quickly.

Creating a Video Montage in Adobe Premiere CS5

Figure 40 *Viewing the default transition between clips*

Cross Dissolve
transition

Figure 41 *Center at Cut placement of Pinwheel transition*

Center at
Cut icon

Apply a transition between two clips

1. Open your Earth Day your name.prproj file, if necessary.

2. Click **Window** on the Application bar, point to **Workspace**, then click **Effects** to change the workspace to the Effects workspace.

   We will be working with the Effects panel and the Effect Controls panel during this lesson.

3. Be sure the CTI is at the beginning of the sequence, then zoom in on the Timeline panel, if necessary, so you can easily see the transitions between the clips, as shown in Figure 40.

   The Cross Dissolve transition has already been applied between the clips placed on the Timeline.

4. Target the **Video 1 track** by clicking in the **Video 1 header**.

5. Click the **triangle** to the left of the Video Transitions bin on the Effects panel to expand it.

6. Inside the Video Transitions bin, expand the Wipe bin.

7. Click and drag the **Pinwheel transition** to the Cross Dissolve transition between **scenic1.jpg** and **scenic3.jpg**, then release the mouse button when you see the **Center At Cut icon** as shown in Figure 41.

8. Click the **Pinwheel transition** on the sequence between **scenic1.jpg** and **scenic3.jpg** to select it.

   The Effect Controls panel displays the settings for the Pinwheel transition because it is selected on the Timeline. The settings can be changed to customize the transition.

(continued)

9. Click the **Show/Hide Timeline View button** on the Effect Controls panel to show the timeline section of the Effect Controls panel, if necessary.

   The timeline section on the Effect Controls panel represents the same time of the sequence on the Timeline panel.

10. Click and drag the **CTI** over the transition to preview it on the Program Monitor.

11. Save your project file and leave it open for the next exercise.

You applied a video transition between two clips in a sequence.

Customize a transition

1. Open your Earth Day your name.prproj file, if necessary.

2. Verify that the Effects workspace is chosen.

3. Click the **Pinwheel transition** between the **scenic1.jpg** and the **scenic3.jpg** clips to preview the transition on the Effect Controls panel.

4. Click the **Show Actual Sources check box** to select it, as shown in Figure 42.

   The scenic1.jpg and scenic3.jpg images replace the A-roll/B-roll format. A preview window appears above the two thumbnails and is useful for previewing the transition as it will look applied to the clips.

5. Click the **Alignment list arrow**, then click **Start at Cut**.

   The transition moves to the right in the timeline section on the Effect Controls panel so that it is placed at the beginning of the second clip.

   (continued)

Figure 42 *Effect Controls panel*

Play the transition button

Scenic1.jpg

Scenic3.jpg

Show Actual Sources check box

Figure 43 *Customizing the pinwheel transition*

12 wedges

Start at Cut

2.0 Border width

Light blue border color

Transition moved to the right of the cut line

Figure 44 *Play the transition button on the Effect Controls panel*

Play the transition button

Figure 45 *Custom Pinwheel transition*

6. Click the **Custom button** on the Effect Controls panel to open the Pinwheel Settings dialog box.

7. Type **12** in the Number of Wedges text box to add extra wedges to the wheel, then click **OK**.

TIP You may need to scroll down in the Effect Controls panel to see additional options if they are available.

8. Click the **Border Width value**, then type **2.0** to change the width of the border.

9. Click the **color box** next to Border Color to open the Color Picker dialog box, pick a **light blue color**, then click **OK**.

   Your Effect Controls panel should resemble Figure 43.

10. Click the **Play the transition button** on the Effect Controls panel, as shown in Figure 44, to preview any changes you make.

11. Click the **Play-Stop Toggle button** ▶ on the Program Monitor to preview the changes made to the transition, as shown in Figure 45.

TIP If the transition is not smooth on the Program Monitor you will need to render the sequence. Press [Enter] (Win) or [return] (Mac) to do so.

12. Save your project file and leave it open for the next exercise.

You customized the Pinwheel transition using settings on the Effect Controls panel.

Search for video transitions

1. Open your Earth Day your name.prproj file, if necessary.

2. On the Effects panel, type **SW** in the Contains box 🔍 , as shown in Figure 46.

   As you type, the Effects panel filters out any effects not containing the characters you have typed.

   TIP Click the Close button to the right of the Contains box to clear what has been typed.

3. Drag the **Swirl transition** between **scenic3.jpg** and **scenic5.jpg** on the Timeline panel and place it as a Center at Cut transition.

4. Save your project file and leave it open for the next exercise.

You searched for a video transition on the Effects panel.

Copy video transitions

1. Open your Earth Day your name.prproj file, if necessary.

2. Click the **Pinwheel transition** between the **scenic1.jpg** and **scenic3.jpg**.

3. Click **Edit** on the Application bar, then click **Copy**.

4. On the Timeline panel drag the **CTI** to the cut line between scenic3.jpg and scenic5.jpg.

5. Click **Edit** on the Application bar, then click **Paste**, as shown in Figure 47.

   TIP Press Page Down to jump quickly to the next cut line.

(continued)

Figure 46 *Searching for a transition*

Contains box

Swirl transition

Figure 47 *Pasting transitions*

Paste command

Video 1 track targeted

CTI at cut line

Creating a Video Montage in Adobe Premiere CS5

Figure 48 *Sequence after pasting Pinwheel transition*

Pinwheel transition
between all clips

6. Repeat Steps 4 and 5 to continue pasting the copied transition over the remaining cut lines in the sequence, then compare your Timeline panel to Figure 48.

7. Preview the changes in the Program Monitor.

8. Save your project file and leave it open for the next exercise.

You copied and pasted video transitions between the remaining clips in the sequence.

Specifying a Default Transition

If you prefer to use another video transition instead of Cross Dissolve you can change the default. Changing the default transition does not affect transitions already applied to a sequence; it only affects future projects.

Expand the Video Transitions bin on the Effects panel. Select the transition that you want to set as the default. Click the Effects panel options button, then click Set Selected As Default Transition.

Work with MOTION EFFECTS

What You'll Do

In this lesson, you will add motion effects and video transition images.

Working with Motion Effects

Motion effects have been used on still images in documentaries to make the footage more visually interesting when video was not available. This effect of panning and zooming has been commonly termed the "Ken Burns Effect." He popularized the use of the effect in his widely seen Civil War documentary on PBS in the fall of 1990. This can be done by scaling or changing the position or the rotation of the image. Motion effects are created using keyframes. A **keyframe** is a "snapshot" of how you want a clip to look at a specified time, and is defined on the Effect Controls timeline, as shown in Figure 49. Premiere Pro recognizes the "snapshots" you have created and fills in the gaps to create a smooth movement between keyframes. For motion effects to work properly, at least two keyframes need to be created.

Understanding Keyframes in More Detail

When working with keyframes you always need to define at least two keyframes, a start point and an end point. It is a good idea to create two keyframes before making any changes. In Figure 50, start and end keyframes have been created for the Position, Scale, and Rotation properties.

By clicking the Toggle animation button, the first keyframe is inserted for you at the location of the CTI. To insert or remove additional keyframes, the Add-Remove Keyframe button needs to be clicked. Remember to move the CTI to the location where you would like the keyframe to be placed. Keyframes can always be adjusted later if you didn't get the location quite right the first time.

Let's work with the Position property in greater detail first. The CTI needs to be positioned on a keyframe before you can change the property values to it. To return to the start keyframe click the Go to Previous Keyframe button.

When creating the Pan effect (scrolling across the image) you need to look at the image and decide what you want the final view of the image to be. In this example, using scenic1.jpg, if the goal is to have the

Creating a Video Montage in Adobe Premiere CS5

image in its original state in the final frame, the start keyframe needs to be adjusted.

The Position coordinates 360.0, 240.0 represent the center of the screen—the upper-left corner is 0.0, the lower-right corner is 720.0, 480.0 (720 × 480 is the standard NTSCDV screen size and is our sequence preset). These coordinates can get quite confusing; therefore, one of the simpler ways to adjust the coordinates is by using the mouse pointer. Hover the mouse pointer over one of the coordinates and it becomes a pointing finger cursor with a double-sided arrow.

Adjusting the coordinates is a matter of dragging left or right. As you drag the left coordinate (360.0) to the left, the image moves left, move it to the right and the image moves right; whereas moving the right coordinate (240.0) to the left moves the image up, and moving it to the right

Figure 49 *Working with keyframes on the Effect Controls panel*

Timeline

Show/Hide Timeline View button

Toggle animation button

Add/Remove Keyframe button

Toggle animation button

Zoom slider

Keyframe navigators

Figure 50 *Working with keyframes in greater detail*

Reset button

Start keyframe

End keyframe

CTI

Add/Remove Keyframe button

moves the image down. As you adjust the coordinates on the Effect Controls panel, you will see the image change location on the Program Monitor, as shown in Figure 51.

Zoom is the second part of the Pan and Zoom effect, and Scale is the Motion Effects property that is used to create this effect. We are completing the Pan and Zoom effect on the scenic1.jpg image and we again want the final frame of the image to appear in its original state.

Adjusting the Scale property works in much the same way as adjusting the Position property. It can be done by either typing the percentage or with the pointing finger cursor. If you deselect the Uniform Scale check box, you will have the option to scale the image's height and width. On the Program Monitor, you will see the image scale change to assist you visually, as shown in Figure 52.

The Pan and Zoom effect can be as creative as you want to make it. This was a very basic version to demonstrate the concept of keyframes. We will work with motion effects throughout this lesson. The Reset button is available on the Effect Controls panel to reset the motion effects back to their default settings without removing the keyframes. If you want to delete keyframes and start over, just click the Toggle animation button. A Warning dialog box appears asking you if you want to remove all of your keyframes from that effect. Click OK, and all the keyframes are removed.

Fading an Image

A basic effect that provides a lot of impact is to fade an image in and out. **Fading** is created by applying the Opacity effect. **Opacity** adjusts the level of transparency on a scale of 0% to

Figure 51 *Adjusting the Position property*

Modified coordinates

Pointing finger cursor

scenic1.jpg position change

Figure 52 *Adjusting the Scale property*

Uniform Scale

Modified coordinates

Reset button

scenic1.jpg scale change

Creating a Video Montage in Adobe Premiere CS5

100%. If you set the Opacity at 0% your clip will be completely transparent; at 100% it will have no transparency. Figure 53 shows two clips set at 100% Opacity and another clip with the same images overlapping with the top clip set with a 50% Opacity. Notice how the two images become blended together.

When creating a fade in/fade out effect you need to create four keyframes. The start and end keyframes are set to 0% Opacity, and the second and third keyframes remain at 100% Opacity. Click the expansion arrow in front of the Opacity property to display a graphical representation of the keyframes actions, as shown in Figure 54. Preview the effect on the Program Monitor. If the fade in is too fast, click and drag the second keyframe to the right to slow the effect down. To reset the Opacity settings, select the start keyframe, click the Reset button, select the end keyframe, and click the Reset button.

Using the Program Monitor to Apply Motion Effects

The Program Monitor provides another option to work with applying motion effects. The Motion properties—Position, Scale, and Rotate—are spatial in nature and therefore easier to manipulate on the Program Monitor where you will have the ability to adjust the clip with handles. The handles allow you to move, size, and rotate the clip visually.

Figure 53 *Examples of Opacity*

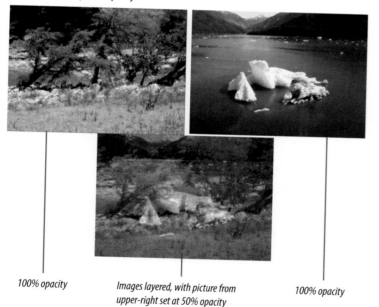

100% opacity

Images layered, with picture from upper-right set at 50% opacity

100% opacity

Figure 54 *Adjusting the Opacity property*

Opacity

Uniform Scale

Reset button

To activate the Motion Effects' controls, click the Transform button, found to the left of Motion on the Effect Controls panel. You may need to adjust the Zoom Level on the Program Monitor to see the transform handles, as shown in Figure 55.

As before, keyframes need to be created before any changes are applied. Using the mouse pointer, click the handles to resize, scale and rotate the image, then notice the property values change on the Effect

Controls panel as you adjust the image on the Program Monitor, as shown in Figure 56.

QUICK TIP

The Rotation effect is applied in the same manner as the Position and Scale effects. It can either be manipulated on the Effect Controls panel, or on the Program Monitor.

As you select other video effects from the library on the Effects panel, you may come across some that will allow you to manipulate

their properties on the Program Monitor. Look for the Transform button to the left of the name of the effect. Some of the effects that provide this feature include: Lightning, Twirl, Transform, Lens Flare, and Checkerboard.

QUICK TIP

The Transform button to the left of a video effect name indicates that the effect's properties can be manipulated on the Program Monitor. Lightning, Twirl, Transform, Lens Flare, and Checkerboard are examples.

Figure 55 *Applying motion effects on the Program Monitor*

Transform button   Handles   Rotate cursor   Select Zoom Level

Figure 56 *Adjusting motion effects on the Program Monitor*

Properties values adjusted based on location on Program Monitor

Resize cursor

Figure 57 *Viewing scenic1.jpg in the Timeline section of the Effect Controls panel*

Timeline section

scenic1.jpg

CTI

Fade an image in and out

1. Open your Earth Day your name.prproj file, if necessary.

2. Reset the workspace to the Effects workspace, if necessary.

3. Be sure the CTI is at the beginning of the sequence, then click **scenic1.jpg**.

4. Click the **Show/Hide Timeline View button** on the Effect Controls panel to show the Timeline section, as shown in Figure 57.

5. Click the **triangle** to the left of **Opacity** on the Effect Controls panel to expand the Opacity properties.

6. Click the **Toggle animation button** to the left of Opacity on the Effect Controls panel.

   A keyframe is added where the CTI is located on the Effect Controls panel. Keyframes do not become available until you activate them with the Toggle animation button, and the first keyframe is added automatically when the Toggle animation button is clicked.

7. Press the → key 10 times to move the CTI 1/10 of a second to the right.

8. Click the **Add/Remove Keyframe button** to add another keyframe.

9. Press **Page Down** to move the CTI to the end of the clip, then add a third keyframe.

10. Press the ← key 10 times to move the CTI 1/10 of a second to the left, then add the fourth keyframe.

(continued)

You should now have four keyframes on the Timeline section of the Effect Controls panel, as shown in Figure 58.

11. Click the **Go to Previous Keyframe button** repeatedly until you return to the first keyframe.

12. Click the **Opacity value**, **100.0%**, then type **0**.

The first keyframe now has 0% opacity. This means the image is invisible and will fade into the next keyframe, as shown in Figure 59.

(continued)

Figure 58 *Four keyframes on the Effect Controls panel*

Keyframes

Figure 59 *First keyframe set to 0% Opacity*

First keyframe

Image on Preview Monitor

0% Opacity

Creating a Video Montage in Adobe Premiere CS5

Figure 60 *Opacity effect shown as a graph*

100% Opacity

100% Opacity

0% Opacity

0% Opacity

13. Click the **Go to Next Keyframe button** repeatedly until you return to the last keyframe, then change its Opacity to **0%**, as shown in Figure 60.

Clicking the expand arrow in front of the Opacity Toggle animation button reveals a line graph in the Timeline section of the Effect Controls panel, which provides a visual representation of opacity.

14. Return the CTI to the beginning of the Timeline and preview the transition on the Program Monitor.

TIP Keyframes can be adjusted by clicking and dragging them to adjust the speed at which the effect takes place.

15. Drag the **second keyframe** to the right to fade the image in more slowly.

16. Preview the clip again to see how the effect has changed.

17. Save your project file and leave it open for the next exercise.

You faded an image in and out using the Opacity property.

Add a Pan and Zoom effect

1. Open your Earth Day your name.prproj file, if necessary.

2. Be sure the CTI is at the beginning of the sequence.

   Remember, the Opacity for this clip has been set to 0% so you will not be able to preview the image in the Program Monitor.

3. Click the **triangle** to the left of Motion on the Effect Controls panel to expand the Motion properties.

4. Click the **Toggle Animation button** to the left of Position and Scale to activate keyframes, as shown in Figure 61.

   This adds a keyframe at the beginning of the clip for both Position and Scale.

5. Move to the end of the clip and add another keyframe for both Position and Scale.

   TIP Another way to move to the end of the clip is to click the Go to Next Keyframe button in the Opacity effect.

6. Go back to the first keyframe, change the Scale setting to **250%**, then change the Position settings to: **346.0**, **436.0**, as shown in Figure 62.

7. Return the CTI to the beginning of the Timeline and preview on the Program Monitor.

8. Save your project file and leave it open for the next exercise.

Figure 61 *Adding a keyframe to the Position and Scale effect*

Motion Properties

0% Opacity   Keyframes

Figure 62 *Changes made to the Position and Scale settings*

Keyframes

Setting changes on first keyframe

Figure 63 *Changing the Rotation setting*

Keyframes

Rotation setting

Add a rotation effect to a clip

1. Open your Earth Day your name.prproj file, if necessary.

2. Be sure the CTI is at the beginning of the sequence.

3. Click the **triangle** to the left of Motion on the Effect Controls panel to display the Motion properties.

4. Click the **Toggle Animation button** 🕹 to the left of Rotation to activate keyframes to add the first keyframe at the beginning of the clip.

5. Move to the end of the clip, then add another keyframe to Rotation.

6. Go to the first keyframe, then change the Rotation setting to **20.0°**, as shown in Figure 63.

7. Return the CTI to the beginning of the Timeline and preview on the Program Monitor.

8. Save your project file and leave it open for the next exercise.

You applied a rotation effect to a clip.

Pan, zoom, and rotate in the Program Monitor

1. Open your Earth Day your name.prproj file, if necessary.

2. Move the CTI to the beginning of the second clip.

3. Click the **triangle** to the left of Motion on the Effect Controls panel to display the Motion properties, if necessary.

4. Activate keyframes for Position, Scale, and Rotation.

5. Add keyframes at the end of the clip for Position, Scale, and Rotation, and return the CTI to the first keyframe on the clip.

6. Click the **Transform button** 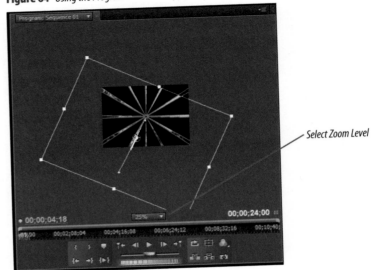 to the left of Motion on the Effect Controls panel.

   A transform box appears around the clip on the Program Monitor.

7. Click the **Select Zoom Level arrow** on the Program Monitor, then click **50%**.

   Using your cursor, you can now position, scale, and rotate the clip, as shown in Figure 64.

8. Position your cursor over the upper-right handle on the transform box, click then drag until you see **26.0 °** in the Rotation setting, as shown in Figure 65.

   (continued)

Figure 64 *Using the Program Monitor to apply effects*

Select Zoom Level

Figure 65 *Using the Program Monitor to rotate the image*

Rotation setting

Rotate cursor

Figure 66 *Using the Program Monitor to resize the image*

Scale setting

Resize cursor

9. Position your cursor over the top-middle handle, then drag down until the Scale setting becomes **76.5%,** as shown in Figure 66.

10. Position your cursor over the center of the image and drag your image to the bottom-left corner until your Position settings become **185.0** and **308.0,** as shown in Figure 67.

11. Return the CTI to the beginning of the Timeline and preview on the Program Monitor.

12. Save your project file and leave it open for the next exercise.

You rotated, resized, and moved the image in the Program Monitor.

Figure 67 *Using the Program Monitor to move the image*

Position setting

Position cursor

Design and
INSERT TITLES

What You'll Do

In this lesson, you will add text to your project using the Titler.

Adding Text to a Video Montage

Titling is an important way to enhance your message and to provide credit by adding text to the video montage. In the video montage we have been working on, we have been using photographs of images from various regions of the United States, but that only conveys a portion of our message. Titling will allow us to bring a stronger message or meaning to our video montage, through the addition of quotes.

As you continue to work in Premiere Pro, you will find other uses for titling. For example, you can superimpose a person's name on the screen while they are speaking as a way to introduce them, or later in an interview to re-introduce them to the viewer. Using titles, you can establish your video with an opening title sequence and provide closing credits at the end for the digital assets that you may have borrowed.

Working with the Titler

In Premiere Pro, you will be creating titles in a mini application called the Titler. The **Titler** is a free-floating window that is made up of a group of panels that are all related to creating titles. The panels in the Titler can be rearranged and docked to your liking. The following panels are included in the Titler, and shown in Figure 68.

The Titler includes the following panels:

- **Title panel** – The Title panel is where you design and preview your text and graphics. It is the central panel in the Titler window.
- **Title Properties panel** – The Title Properties panel is where you choose a font, change the font size, kerning, leading, or font characteristics, such as bold or italics.
- **Title Tools panel** – The Title Tools panel is where the tools are located to draw basic shapes, create text paths, and create vertical or horizontal text.
- **Title Actions panel** – The Title Actions panel is where you align, center, or distribute objects and text vertically and horizontally.
- **Title Styles panel** – The Title Styles panel is where you can apply preset styles to titles. You can also create and save your own titles to maintain consistency throughout a project.

Creating a Video Montage in Adobe Premiere CS5

Creating a New Title

Premiere Pro offers the option to create a title from either the File menu or the Title menu. If you choose to create a title from the Title menu you can choose among three types of titles: Default Still, Default Roll, or Default Crawl. You can base a new title on a template or the current title. Creating a title from the File menu creates a Default Still title.

A title that has fixed text is called **still** (Default Still). Titles in which text moves vertically over the footage are called **rolls** (Default Roll). If the text moves horizontally, it is referred to as a **crawl** (Default Crawl).

Creating a title based on the current title does just what it sounds like. It duplicates the current title allowing you to replace the text while maintaining the current formatting. The Based on a Template option opens up a library of templates in a preview window for you to select a template, as shown in Figure 69. Once you select a template,

Figure 68 *Titler window*

Title Tools panel

Title panel

Title Actions panel

Title Properties panel

Title Styles panel

Figure 69 *Templates dialog box*

Template library

Template preview

THE VIDEO COLLECTION REVEALED

it opens and you are able to replace the placeholder text with your own.

After titles are created, they can be changed into one of the three available types: still, roll, or crawl. To modify a title, click the Roll/Crawl Options button on the Title panel; the Roll/Crawl Options dialog box appears, as shown in Figure 70. You can also choose to apply a template after you have created a title as well, by clicking the Templates button on the Title panel.

Once created, titles are saved on the Project panel and can be edited by simply double-clicking the title clip from either the bin or the sequence. While designing your title, you have the ability to view the footage from the sequence to help with the placement and design of the title. This is done by putting the CTI in the sequence where you plan to place the title, and activating the Show Background Video button on the Title panel. The CTI can be moved while in the Titler by moving the Background Video Timecode on the Title panel, as shown in Figure 71.

QUICK TIP

The length of a title clip in a sequence determines the speed of the text moving in the title. The longer you make the length of the title clip in the sequence, the slower the text will roll or crawl.

Figure 71 *Previewing a clip behind a title*

Show Background Video button

Background Video Timecode

Figure 70 *Roll/Crawl Options dialog box*

Title Type

Creating a Video Montage in Adobe Premiere CS5

The Title panel is where you can make basic formatting decisions such as Font family, Font style, Font size, and Alignment options, as shown in Figure 72. You can also find many of these same options on the Title menu on the Application bar. More advanced options can be found on the Title Properties panel, as shown in Figure 73.

The Title Properties panel provides the opportunity to get very creative with your titles and their appearance using fills, strokes, and shadows.

Working with Title Styles

While working with the Title Properties panel, if you create a format you really like

Figure 73 *Title Properties panel*

Figure 72 *Title panel*

Title tab

New Title Based on Current Title

Roll/Crawl options

Templates Font family Font styles Kerning Font size Leading Tabs stops Alignment options Background Video Timecode

Show Background Video button

Strokes

Shadow

you can save it as a style and add it to the Title Styles panel. The style you create will then become part of the Style library in Premiere Pro and will be available to you in all projects that you create.

Styles are a great way to keep a consistent look and feel when working in a project without having to remember all the settings you chose to make the style.

Premiere Pro also has many preset styles available for you to use, as shown in Figure 74. Styles can be used as they are or as a great springboard for designing your own text and creating your own original style.

Figure 74 *Title Styles panel*

Styles

New Style command

Creating a Video Montage in Adobe Premiere CS5

Figure 75 *New Title dialog box*

*These are the same
dimensions as the
sequence*

Name the title here

Create a new title

1. Open your Earth Day your name.prproj file,
   if necessary.

2. Create a new bin on the Project panel and name
   it **Titles**.

3. [Alt]-double-click (Win) or [option]-double-click
   (Mac) the **Titles bin** to open it in place.

TIP Opening the Titles bin will cause the titles we create to
be automatically saved into the bin as we create them.

4. Click **File** on the Application bar, click **Import**,
   navigate to the location where your Data Files are
   stored, click **Earth Day Text**, and then click **Open**.

   This is a Notepad file we will be using to copy text
   from and paste into the Title panel.

TIP Mac users will need to import the text with the Media
Browser; remember to choose All Files from the Files of
type drop-down menu.

5. Double-click the **Earth Day Text file**, copy the
   first quote (**Native American Proverb**), then
   close the Earth Day Text file.

6. Drag the **CTI** to **00;00;03;20**.

   The new title will start at the 3:20 mark on
   the sequence.

TIP Another way to move the CTI to a specific location is to
click the Current time display on the Timeline, type the
new timecode, and then press [Enter] (Win) or [return]
(Mac). You do not have to type the semicolons (;).

(continued)

7. Click **File** on the Application bar, point to **New**, then click **Title**.

   The New Title dialog box opens. You can name the title and choose size options for it in the dialog box.

TIP You can also click the New Item button 🔲 on the Project panel, and choose Title.

8. Type **Native American Proverb** in the Name text box of the New Title dialog box, as shown in Figure 75, and then click **OK**.

9. Click the **Show Background Video button** 🔲 and notice that the Background Video Timecode matches the setting of **00;00;03;20** on the Timeline.

   Your Titler window should look like Figure 76.

10. Click the **Type tool** 🔳 on the Title Tools panel.

11. Click in the Title panel, click **Edit** on the Application bar, then click **Paste** to paste the quote.

    You will notice that the text is much too big. We will need to make some adjustments on the Title Properties panel. We will start by reducing the font size.

12. Click the **Selection tool** 🔳 on the Tools panel, then click the text.

    The text must be selected in order to modify it.

13. On the Title Properties panel, position the mouse pointer over the Font Size property and when you see the cursor change to a scrolling finger, drag the mouse pointer left until the size changes to **62.0**, as shown in Figure 77.

    (continued)

Figure 76 *Creating a new title*

Background Video Timecode setting

Your clip should match this

Figure 77 *Changing the font size*

Font size

Cursor change

Creating a Video Montage in Adobe Premiere CS5

Figure 78 *Making adjustments on the Title Properties panel*

Quote aligned horizontally and vertically

14. With the text still selected, click **Title** on the Application bar, point to **Position**, then click **Vertical Center**, to adjust the placement of the text vertically.

15. Click **Title** on the Application bar, point to **Position**, then click **Horizontal Center** to adjust the placement of the text horizontally, so that your title is in the approximate location shown in Figure 78.

16. Close the Native American Proverb title.

    Titles save automatically when you close them.

17. Save your project file and leave it open for the next exercise.

In this lesson, you created a new title.

Work with the Title Styles panel

1. Open your Earth Day your name.prproj file, if it is not already open.

2. [Alt]- (Win) or [option]- (Mac) double-click the **Titles bin** to open it in place.

3. Double-click the **Native American Proverb title**.

4. Verify that the Show Background Video button is selected and set the Background Video Timecode to **00;00;03;20**, if necessary.

5. Resize the Title Styles panel, as your screen permits, so you can see the available styles.

   TIP You can also scroll in the Title Styles panel to see all of the available styles.

6. Click the **Selection tool** ▶ on the Tools panel, select the **quote**, and choose the style **TektonPro Narrow Yellow 100** as shown in Figure 79.

   When hovering over a style, the name of the style appears as a tooltip.

   TIP If you click the Title Styles panel options button you can change the view to Text Only and find the style more quickly.

   (continued)

Figure 79 *Applying a title style*

Style name

Creating a Video Montage in Adobe Premiere CS5

Figure 80 *Making changes to the style*

Preview of new style

Height

Font Size

Fill Type

Color picker

Figure 81 *Placing the title in the sequence*

Timecode at 00;00;03;20

Snap button

Video 2 track

Overlay icon   Color picker   Fill type

7. With the quote still selected, make the following changes on the Title Properties panel: Height: **300.0**, Fill Type: **Solid**, Color: **White (FFFFFF)**, Aspect: **79.5%**, and then compare your title to Figure 80.

8. With the quote still selected, click the **Title Styles panel options button** , then click **New Style**.

   We will save this style so that we can use it again on other quotes.

9. Type **Quote Style** in the Name text box of the New Style dialog box, then click **OK**.

   The new style appears at the bottom of the Title Styles panel.

10. Close the American Indian Proverb title.

11. Drag the **American Indian Proverb clip** to the Video 2 Sequence so it snaps to the right of the CTI (which should still be at the **00;00;03;20 Timecode**), as shown in Figure 81.

12. Preview the project on the Program Monitor.

TIP If the text looks blurry, you will need to render the sequence and preview again.

13. Save your project file and leave it open for the next exercise.

In this lesson, you created a new style and saved it on the Title Styles panel.

THE VIDEO COLLE

Create a rolling title

1. Open your Earth Day your name.prproj file, if necessary.

2. **[Alt]**- (Win) or **[option]**- (Mac) double-click the **Titles bin** to open it in place.

3. Double-click the **Earth Day Text file** to open it in Notepad.

4. Copy the **credit information** for the song Subtle Storm, and for the photography, then close the file.

5. Place the CTI at **00;00;56;15**.

6. Click **Title** on the Application bar, point to **New Title**, then click **Default Roll**.

7. Name the new title **Credits** in the Name text box.

8. Click the **Type tool** 🅣 on the Title Tools panel and paste the credits into the Title panel.

9. Apply the **Quote Style** from the Title Styles panel.

10. Change the Font Size to **37.0**.

11. On the Title Properties panel adjust the Leading to **52.0** to create more spacing between the lines of text, then compare your Title panel to Figure 82.

12. Click the **Roll/Crawl Options button** 📰 on the Title panel.

(continued)

Figure 82 *Rolling title preview*

Timecode at 00;00;56;15

Font Size

Leading

Quote Style

Figure 83 *Settings for Roll/Crawl Options*

Preroll

Ease-In   Ease-Out   Postroll

13. Specify the following options in the Roll/
    Crawl Options dialog box: Preroll: **5**, Ease-In: **5**,
    Ease-Out: **5**, Postroll: **5**, as shown in Figure 83,
    then click **OK**.

    The Preroll/Postroll values specify the number
    of frames to play before and after the roll
    begins. The Ease-In/Ease-Out values specify the
    number of frames the roll will ease in or out
    before playing at regular speed.

14. Close the Credits title.

15. Drag the **Credits clip** to the Video 2 Sequence
    so it snaps to the right of the CTI (which should
    still be at the 00;00;56;15 timecode), as shown
    in Figure 84.

16. Render and preview the project on the Program
    Monitor panel.

17. Save your project file and leave it open for the
    next exercise.

In this lesson, you created a rolling title.

Figure 84 *Credits clip placed on sequence*

Credits clip

Create a title from a template

1. Open your Earth Day your name.prproj file, if necessary.

2. **[Alt]**- (Win) or **[option]**- (Mac) double-click the **Titles bin** to open it in place.

3. Place the CTI at **00;00;00;00**.

4. Click **Title** on the Application bar, point to **New Title**, and then click **Based on Template**.

5. Click the **expand triangle** next to Title Designer Presets, if necessary, to open the Template library.

6. Scroll down in the Templates dialog box, expand the General category, then expand Inspire.

7. Select **Inspire_low3**, as shown in Figure 85, name the title **Earth Day**, then click **OK**.

   The Titler window appears ready for you to edit the placeholder text. This title will be used to introduce the project.

8. Click the **Type tool** 🅣 on the Title panel, highlight all of the NAME GOES HERE text and replace it with EVERY DAY IS EARTH DAY ~ ANONYMOUS.

9. Replace TITLE GOES HERE with **your name**, reconfigure both lines of text using fonts and sizes of your choice, then compare your title to Figure 86.

   TIP You may need to reduce the font size of the first line of text before you can select the TITLE GOES HERE text.

   (continued)

Figure 85 *Templates dialog box*

Inspire_low3

Preview of template

Name of title

Figure 86 *Earth Day title clip*

Sample layout of text

Creating a Video Montage in Adobe Premiere CS5

Figure 87 *Locking the tracks*

Locked track

Click here to
lock the track

10. Close the Earth Day title clip, then close the Titles bin.

11. Lock the Video 1 and Audio 1 tracks by clicking the **Toggle Lock Track box** on both tracks, as shown in Figure 87.

12. Target the **Video 2 track**.

13. Click the **Earth Day title clip** in the Titles bin on the Project panel, click **Clip** on the Application bar, then click **Insert**.

    The clip is placed on the Video 2 track while shifting the Native American Proverb to the right, as shown in Figure 88.

14. Preview the project on the Program Monitor.

    TIP If the text looks blurry, you will need to render the sequence and preview again.

15. Save your project file and leave it open for the next exercise.

In this lesson, you created a title based on a template, locked two tracks, and inserted the new title on the Video 2 track.

Figure 88 *Using the Insert command to place a clip*

Shifted clip

Inserted clip

Export a
MOVIE

What You'll Do

In this lesson, you will export your project.

Exporting the Movie

Now it is time to export, or **encode**, your movie so that other people with be able to view it. Premiere Pro has a variety of options from which to choose. You can export to videotape, create a file for viewing on a computer or the Internet, or put your project on a DVD or Blu-ray disc with or without menus and other features. We will be exploring the DVD option in detail in Chapter 7 when we create an Electronic Portfolio using Adobe Encore CS5. Throughout the projects in this book, we will mainly focus on creating files for viewing projects on computers and the Internet.

You need to consider a few options when you are exporting a movie for others to view on another computer or the Internet. File size is important for reducing the size of a movie for storage, transmission, and effective playback. Adobe Premiere Pro Help has an extensive chapter on exporting and options to consider when compressing video for playback on the Web and mobile devices. Adobe Premiere Pro Help is a Web-based feature and is updated frequently to support new mobile devices as they become available.

Exporting for the Web

When exporting video for the Web, your target audience becomes much larger and their software, hardware, and Internet access methods are too numerous to determine. Fortunately, there are a number of **codecs** (compressor/decompressors, also known as encoder/decoders) considered for this purpose to make video Web-friendly. According to Adobe, 98 percent of the world's computers that are connected to the Internet have a Flash Player installed, and of those Flash Players at least 90 percent are capable of playing the latest H.264 codec. Therefore, we will export using the H.264 encoded video for Flash when saving video for the Web.

Many of these codecs use two types of technologies that should be considered when viewing videos on the Web: streaming video and progressive downloadable video. A **streaming video** is also referred to as **live streaming video**. Streaming video occurs when a video is played much like a traditional broadcast, and is affected by the bandwidth that is available. **Buffering** (delay before the video begins to play) may occur when the bandwidth does not meet the required need of the video that is playing; that is, the video will pause until the bandwidth becomes sufficient again. **Progressive video** looks like streaming video because it plays the movie without interruption. The movie player software determines how long it will take to download an entire movie for viewing and begins playing

the movie when enough of the movie has been downloaded so it will playback uninterrupted. The H.264 codec with Flash takes advantage of the Progressive video technology.

The settings we will be using include the following: Format: FLV|F4V; Preset:

FLV- Match Source Attribute (Medium Quality), as shown in Figure 89. When setting the Output Name, the Save As dialog box opens, prompting you to name the file and choose a location to save your project in its exported state.

Figure 89 *Export Settings dialog box*

Format

Preset

Output name

Estimated file size

Queue button

Export button

You have two options to export a file from the Export Settings dialog box: you can choose either the Queue button or the Export button.

The Queue button launches the Adobe Media Encoder application and uses the export settings that have been designated and will then render and save the file. This is an excellent option when exporting to multiple file formats. The Adobe Media Encoder creates a rendering queue and processes the files in the order in which they were received, as shown in Figure 90.

Figure 90 *Adobe Media Encoder dialog window*

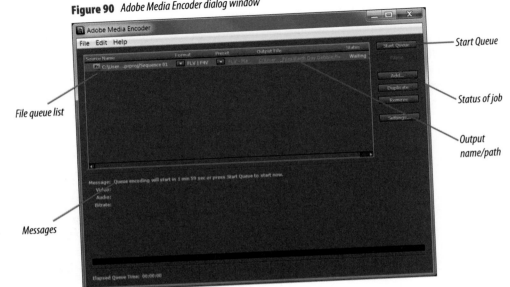

File queue list

Messages

Start Queue

Status of job

Output name/path

Tips to Consider before Compressing

- Edit your video for any unnecessary content to make it shorter.
- Work with raw footage whenever possible.
- Limit special effects and any unnecessary camera work with shaky movements and zooming.
- Consider your audience:
  - Work with appropriate frame dimensions based on your audience, for example, what is the type of Internet connection that most have.
  - Choose an appropriate frame rate based on the processing speed of your audience's computer.
- Preview the file on a system comparable to that of your intended audience, whenever possible.

If you wish to bypass the Adobe Media Encoder you can simply click the Export button instead. The Export button again uses the export settings that have been designated in the Export Settings dialog box. An Encoding dialog box launches to provide a status of the approximate time it will take to export the file, as shown in Figure 91.

Figure 91 *Viewing the Encoding Sequence dialog box*

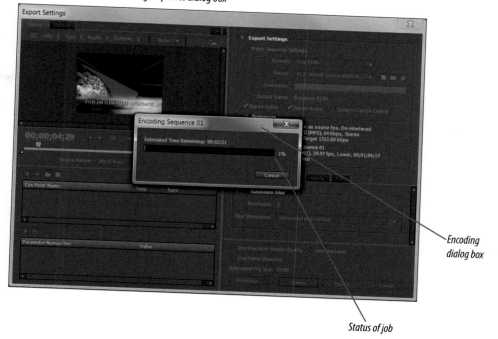

Encoding dialog box

Status of job

QUICK TIP

The MPEG-2 file format is the compression standard for DVD video. When the Adobe Dynamic Link command is used to export directly to Adobe Encore, the MPEG-2 file format is the one utilized, therefore we will be exporting all of our projects as the MPEG-2 file format to facilitate the creation of the Electronic Portfolio later in Chapter 7.

Working with Adobe Media Encoder

Adobe Media Encoder is a stand-alone encoding application used by Premiere Pro, to export your movie to a format appropriate for movies. To start Adobe Media Encoder, you may need to look in a subfolder if you have installed the Creative Suite. Click File on the Application bar, and then click Add Premiere Pro Sequence. Navigate to the project file you wish to encode. Default presets are available, or click the Preset link to access the Export dialog box. Once a sequence is exported and in the queue, you can minimize the Adobe Media Encoder and continue to work in Adobe Premiere Pro while the Media Encoder continues to render in the background.

Export a movie for the Web

1. Open your Earth Day your name.prproj file, if necessary.

2. Click **Sequence 01** on the Project panel to select it.

   A sequence needs to be selected before you export the movie.

3. Click **File** on the Application bar, point to **Export**, then click **Media**.

4. In the Export Settings dialog box make the following selections on the right side of the dialog box: Format: **FLV|F4V**; Preset: **FLV- Match Source Attribute (Medium Quality)**; Output Name: **Earth Day Your Name**.

   When you click Output Name to name your file, the Save As dialog box opens prompting you to name your file and browse to a new location.

   Note that an estimate is given for the file size at the bottom of the Export Settings dialog box, as shown in Figure 92.

5. Click **Export**.

   The Encoding dialog box launches to let you see the status of the file being saved.

6. Save your project file and leave it open for the next exercise.

You exported the Earth Day project as FLV/F4V format for viewing on the Web.

Figure 92 *Export Settings for the web*

Format

Preset

Output Name

Estimated File Size

Creating a Video Montage in Adobe Premiere CS5

Figure 93 *Export settings for the computer and to be put on a DVD*

Format

Preset

Output Name

Estimated
File Size

Figure 94 *Adobe Media Encoder dialog box*

Stop Queue

Pause

Preview

Progress

Export a movie for playback on a computer

1. Open your Earth Day your name.prproj file, if necessary.

2. Select **File** on the Application bar, point to **Export**, then click **Media**.

3. In the Export Settings dialog box, make the following selections: Format: **MPEG2**; Preset: **NTSC DV High Quality**; Output Name: **Earth Day Your Name**, as shown in Figure 93.

4. Click **Queue**.

   The Adobe Media Encoder is launched with the settings you have designated in the Export Settings dialog box.

5. Click **Start Queue**.

   The project is being saved with the settings you have designated as shown in Figure 94.

6. Close the project file.

You exported your project to be viewed on a computer and later to be put on a DVD in your Electronic Portfolio in Chapter 7.

Create a new project and explore the workspace.

1. Start Premiere Pro. Create a new project titled America the Beautiful your name, with a sequence and save it to your Data Files folder.
2. Change the workspace to Effects.
3. Change the workspace to Audio.
4. Change the workspace to Editing.
5. Save your project file, and leave it open.

Import assets.

1. Using the Media Browser, navigate to the drive and folder where your Data Files are located.
2. Import Subtle Storm - 60.mp3 into the Project panel.
3. Create a new bin and title it U.S. Pictures.
4. Open the U.S. Pictures bin as a dockable panel.
5. Import scenic16.jpg through scenic.32.jpg into the U.S. Pictures bin from your Data Files folder.
6. Click the Icon View button on the U.S. Pictures bin and rearrange the images as you would like them to be placed on the sequence.
7. Close the U.S. Pictures bin.
8. Save your project file and leave it open.

Work with the Timeline panel and sequences.

1. Be sure the Current-time Indicator (CTI) is at the beginning of the Timeline.
2. Open the U.S. Pictures bin as a dockable panel.
3. Select all the images in the bin.
4. Click the U.S. Pictures panel options button, then click Automate to Sequence.

5. In the Automate To Sequence dialog box, click the Ordering list arrow, click Sort Order, then click OK.
6. Close the Scenic Pictures bin.
7. Be sure the CTI is at the beginning of the sequence.
8. Zoom in on the Timeline to see the clips easily.
9. Open the Subtle Storm - 60.mp3 file in the Source Monitor.
10. Target the audio track by clicking in the header area and the source track. (Hint: Be sure the video track is no longer targeted.)
11. Click the Overlay button on the Source Monitor to place the audio file on the sequence.
12. Select the first two clips in the sequence.
13. Click Edit on the Application bar, then click Ripple Delete.
14. Press the Play-Stop Toggle button on the Program Monitor to view the contents of the Timeline.
15. Drag the CTI on the Timeline panel left and right to preview the sequence on the Program Monitor.
16. Save your project file and leave it open.

Apply video transitions and work with motion effects.

1. Change the workspace to the Effects workspace.
2. Be sure the CTI is at the beginning of the sequence; zoom in on the Timeline panel so you can easily see the transitions between the clips.
3. Expand the Video Transitions bin on the Effects panel.
4. On the Effects panel, type page in the Contains box.
5. Drag Page Peel to the cut line between the first and second clip on the sequence, place as a Center at Cut.

6. Click the Page Peel transition on the sequence where you just placed it.
7. Click and drag the CTI over the transition to preview it on the Program Monitor.
8. On the Effect Controls panel, click the Show Actual Sources check box to select it.
9. Click the Northeast to Southwest edge selector and preview again.
10. Click the Page Peel transition between the first and second clip on your sequence.
11. Click Edit on the Application bar, then click Copy.
12. On the Timeline panel, move the CTI to the cut line between the third and fourth clip to paste the transition.
13. Target the Video 1 track.
14. Click Edit on the Application bar, then click Paste.
15. Continue pasting the copied transition over the remaining cut lines in the sequence.
16. Preview the changes on the Program Monitor.
17. Be sure the CTI is at the beginning of the sequence.
18. Select the first clip in your sequence.
19. Expand the Opacity properties on the Effect Controls panel.
20. Click the Toggle animation button to add a keyframe.
21. Highlight the Current time display, type 010, then press [Enter] (Win) or [return] (Mac).
22. Click the Add/Remove Keyframe button to add another keyframe.
23. Press [Page Down] to move the CTI to the end of the clip, and then add a third keyframe.
24. Highlight the Current time display, type 320, then press [Enter] (Win) or [return] (Mac).

Creating a Video Montage in Adobe Premiere CS5

25. Click the Add/Remove Keyframe button to add another keyframe.

26. Click the Go to Previous Keyframe button repeatedly until you return to the first keyframe.

27. Click the Opacity value, 100.0%, then type 0.

28. Click the Go to Next Keyframe button repeatedly until you return to the last keyframe, then change its Opacity to 0%.

29. Return the CTI to the beginning of the Timeline and preview the transition on the Program Monitor, as shown in Figure 95.

30. Drag the second keyframe to the right and drag the third keyframe to the left to fade the image more slowly.

31. Preview the clip again to see how the effect has changed.

32. Return the CTI to the beginning of the sequence.

33. Expand the Motion properties on the Effect Controls panel.

34. Click the Toggle Animation button to the left of Position and Scale to activate keyframes.

35. Move to the end of the clip and add another keyframe for both Position and Scale.

36. Return to the first keyframe, and change the Scale setting to 300%, and the Position settings to: 346.0, 436.0.

37. Preview on the Program Monitor.

38. Return the CTI to the beginning of the sequence.

39. Click the Toggle Animation button to the left of Rotation to activate keyframes.

40. Move to the end of the clip, then add another keyframe to Rotation.

41. Go to the first keyframe, then change the Rotation setting to -15 degrees.

42. Preview on the Program Monitor.

43. Move the CTI to the beginning of the second clip.

44. Activate keyframes for Position, Scale, and Rotation.

45. Add keyframes at the end of the clip for Position, Scale, and Rotation, and return the CTI to the first keyframe on the clip.

46. Click the Transform button on the Effect Controls Panel. (*Hint*: Adjust the Select Zoom Level on the Program Monitor if you cannot see the transform box.)

47. On the Program Monitor position, scale and rotate the clip using your own settings.

48. Apply various motion effects (fade, zoom, pan, rotate) to each of the clips on the Video track. You do not need to apply each effect to every image. Be creative.

49. Preview your project on the Program Monitor and render as needed.

50. Save your project file and leave it open.

Design and insert titles.

1. Create a new bin on the Project panel, name it **Titles for Project**, then open it in the Project panel.

2. Click File on the Application bar, click Import, navigate to the drive and folder where your Data Files are stored, click America Text.txt, and then click Open.

3. Open the America Text.txt file in Notepad.

4. Click File on the Application bar, point to New, and then click Title.

5. Type **Nelson** in the Name text box of the New Title dialog box, then click OK.

6. Verify that the Show Background Video button is selected and set the Background Video Timecode to 00;00;09;25 on the Timeline.

7. Copy the Gaylor Nelson quote from the America Text file you should have opened in Notepad and paste the text into the Title panel using the Type tool.

8. Select the text with the Selection tool, apply the Tekton White 45 title style, then resize the text to fit in the window.

9. Close the Nelson title.

10. Drag the title to the sequence so it is placed to the right of the CTI on the Video 2 track.

11. Place the CTI at 00;00;56;00.

12. Click Title on the Application bar, point to New Title, then click Default Roll.

13. Type **Credits** in the Name text box of the New Title dialog box, then click OK.

14. Copy the Song and Photography credits from the America Text file that you should have open in Notepad, and paste it into the Title panel using the Type tool.

15. Select the text with the Selection tool and apply the Minion Pro Black 89 title style to the Rolling Quotes title.

16. Change the font size to 32.0.

17. On the Title Properties panel, adjust the Leading to 50.0 to create more spacing between the lines of text.

18. Click the Roll/Crawl Options button on the Title panel.

19. Specify the following options in the Roll/Crawl Options dialog box: Preroll: **5**; Ease-In: **5**; Ease-Out: **5**; Postroll: **5**.

20. Move the text box approximately one inch below the inner rectangle, then close the Rolling Quote.

21. Close the Credits title.

Creating a Video Montage in Adobe Premiere CS5

22. Drag the title to the sequence so it is placed to the right of the CTI on the Video 2 track.
23. Move the CTI to the beginning of the sequence.
24. Click Title on the Application bar, point to New Title, then click Based on Template.
25. Expand the General category, then expand Woodland.
26. Select Woodland upper3rd, name it **Title**, then click OK.
27. Using the Type tool, replace Outdoors Title with: **America the Beautiful** and replace Woodland Subtitle with **Your Name**. (*Hint:* You will need to resize America the Beautiful to fit.)
28. Close the title you are working on named Title.
29. Drag the Title clip to the Video 2 sequence above scenic1.jpg.
30. Preview the project on the Program Monitor.
31. Save your project file and leave it open.

Export a movie.

1. Select the sequence on the Project panel.
2. Click File on the Application bar, point to Export, then click Media.
3. In the Export Settings dialog box, make the following selections: Format: **FLV|FV**; Preset: **FLV- Match Source Attribute (Medium Quality)**; Output Name: **America the Beautiful Your Name**.
4. Click Queue.
5. Return to Premiere Pro.
6. Select File on the Application bar, point to Export, then click Media.
7. In the Export Settings dialog box, make the following selections: Format: **MPEG2**; Preset: **NTSC DV High Quality**; Output Name: **America the Beautiful Your Name**.
8. Click Queue.
9. Return to the Adobe Media Encoder.
10. Click Start Queue.
11. Close the project file.

Figure 95 *Working with Motion Effects*

Creating a Video Montage in Adobe Premiere CS5

A local travel agency has contacted your advertising firm to create an ad to help advertise a new trip they are promoting called the Tour of Italy! They have a very low budget and can only afford to use still images and music but have heard you specialize in video montages. They would like you to create an eye-catching video montage highlighting this new vacation destination.

The agency has provided the beginning Premiere Pro project file, which includes bins that have already been created and an audio file already? imported. The Pictures bin has 15 images of Italy already imported and ready to use. There is a Titles bin with titles available to be used in the project, including the credits, the travel agency information, and the tour announcement. They plan to run this ad on television and on the Internet, and therefore need you to supply the final version in FLV|F4V and MPEG2 formats.

1. Open Italy.prproj from your Data Files folder, then save it as **Italy your name**.
2. Open the Pictures bin and organize the images using a storyboard. Once you have the images in the order you like, automate them to the sequence on the Video 1 track. (*Hint*: Remove the check mark in the Apply Default Audio Transition check box, and leave the check mark in the Apply Default Video Transition check box.)
3. Place the audio track below the images on the Audio 1 track so that the audio aligns with the images.

(*Hint*: Be careful that your clips on the Video track do not shift to the right when you place your audio track.)
4. Place the titles on the Video 2 track. Place the Intro title over your first clip. Place the other three titles where you think appropriate.

5. Preview your project on the Program Monitor, then compare the first frame of your project to the example shown in Figure 96 as a possible solution.
6. Export your movie to the FLV|F4V and the MPEG2 formats.

Figure 96 *Program Monitor showing first frame*

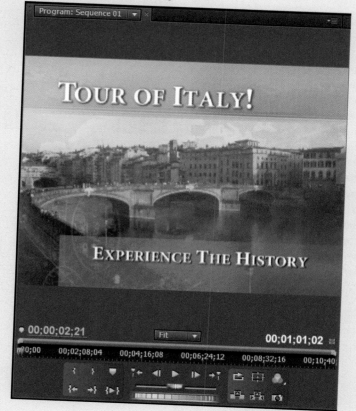

Creating a Video Montage in Adobe Premiere CS5

You have been asked to complete the work on a video montage for the San Antonio Visitors Center, who would like to feature the San Antonio Missions, one of the city's historical attractions, on their Web site. You will apply the Ken Burns Effect (Pan and Zoom) to the images on the Video 1 track in the sequence.

1. Open SA Missions.prproj, from your Data Files folder, then save it as **SA Missions your name**.

2. Preview the movie on the Program Monitor to familiarize yourself with the project's current assets. Currently, there are no motion effects. Notice the images have been placed without transitions to allow you more room on the Timeline to add your own effects.

3. Reset the workspace to the Effects workspace.

4. Create at least two keyframes for each clip. You will be adjusting the Position and Scale properties to create the Pan and Zoom Motion effects.

5. Compare your keyframes and Program Monitor to the example shown in Figure 97.

6. Preview your project on the Program Monitor. When you are pleased with your results, save your project.

7. Export your movie to the FLV|F4V format.

Figure 97 *Effect Controls panel and Program Monitor showing sample motion effects*

Your history teacher has heard about the work you are doing in your multimedia class and wants you to incorporate your knowledge of Adobe Premiere Pro into a project for his class. You are currently studying the history of the United States space program. He would like you to gather images from the NASA images Web site (www.nasaimages.org) and make a two-minute video montage. Be sure to read the "Terms" at the bottom of the Web site and cite your sources correctly. Resize images, if necessary, once placed on your sequence using the Scale property. You may also want to use the Pan and Zoom effect on some images to emphasize certain areas of a photograph or just to add motion to an image.

Descriptions are included with the pictures on the NASA Web site; use this information to create titles for your pictures to describe the images. (*Hint*: You may want to create a text file while you are downloading the images that you can later reference when creating the titles.)

Your teacher would also like you to include background music while the images are playing. Since there will be descriptions on the images that will need to be read while the video is being viewed, he would prefer the music be instrumental. Audio clips are available in the Audio Clips folder on the resource disc that came with this book, if you cannot find your own audio file from the Internet.

Note: If given an option to download either a low- or a high-resolution image, choose to download the low-resolution version. Create a folder to save your images in your Data Files folder.

1. Create a new Premiere Pro Project and sequence and save it as **Space Program your name**.
2. On the Project panel, create bins to organize the images you downloaded, and to save your titles in.
3. Import your assets into the appropriate areas of the Project panel; compare your Project panel to the example shown in Figure 98.
4. Arrange your assets and place them on the sequence. (*Hint*: Consider whether you want a default transition between the clips if you are going to be working with the Pan and Zoom effect extensively.)
5. Apply the Pan and Zoom effect as you feel appropriate.
6. Create title descriptions for your images that you will place on the Video 2 track. (*Hint*: You may want to create your Intro title and Credit title as clips on the Video 1 track since you are placing descriptions on each picture. You will need to use the Insert command to shift the images to the right to place the Intro title at the beginning of the sequence. Remember to lock your Audio 1 track if you have already placed your music clip.)
7. Render and preview your project on the Program Monitor and make any changes before you export your project.
8. When you are finally satisfied with your work, export your video to the MPEG2 format, so that it can be viewed on a computer and later be added to your electronic portfolio.

Figure 98 *Sample Project panel showing assets*

Creating a Video Montage in Adobe Premiere CS5

2

WORKING IN ADOBE
AFTER EFFECTS CS5

Explore the After Effects workspace

Create an on-screen graphic

Create a production logo

Create a title sequence

2 WORKING IN ADOBE AFTER EFFECTS CS5

Adobe After Effects CS5 is a development tool for adding animated text, digital motion graphics, and realistic visual effects to video. After Effects is a **nonlinear editing system** that works with layers much like those you may have used in other Adobe programs such as Premiere Pro, Photoshop, and Illustrator. Nonlinear editing is the ability to access any frame in a video in order to make changes to it. Changes can include removing sections of the video, creating fades, or adding transitions. It is analogous to cutting, pasting, and formatting text in a word processor.

Adobe Dynamic Link provides integration between After Effects and Premiere Pro and Encore as long as you have installed these applications as part of the Creative Suite 5 Production Premium or the Creative Suite 5 Master Collection. Dynamic Link is a command on the File menu that allows you to import Premiere Pro sequences into the Project panel in After Effects and use them as layers. Any changes made to the sequence in Premiere Pro are automatically updated in the composition in After Effects without the need to render. A **composition** is the container that holds all the references for the movie. You can also dynamically link After Effects compositions to Premiere Pro as clips, or to Encore as projects.

In this chapter, we will be creating a digital on-screen graphic, a production logo, and a title sequence using After Effects CS5. Each of these projects is essentially working with motion graphics for which After Effects is the ideal editing program.

A **digital on-screen graphic** is a logo overlaid on a portion of the television viewing area to identify the channel, much like a watermark. The use of this graphic is also to help minimize copyright infringement. The digital on-screen graphic has expanded to included clocks, temperatures and the score bug during athletic events. In the United Kingdom and New Zealand, it is known by the acronym **DOG**; in the United States and Canada, it is referred to as a **bug**.

Movie and television production companies use a **production logo** at the beginning of a theatrical movie or at the end of a television program or movie to brand what they produce. It is referred to as either an opening or closing logo. Production logos can even be found in many video games.

A **title sequence** is shown at the beginning of a movie or television program to provide title and credit to the actors.

Explore the After Effects
WORKSPACE

What You'll Do

In this lesson, you will start After Effects, examine the panels that make up the After Effects workspace, and learn how to change and customize the workspace.

Exploring the After Effects Workspace

After Effects has a customizable workspace with several default workspaces available, similar to Premiere Pro. The main window, comprising the various panels, is called the **application window**. The **workspace** is the arrangement of the panels. Figure 1 shows the default workspace which is called **Standard**.

The workspace can be changed by selecting a preformatted workspace or by rearranging the panels to your individual preference. Preformatted workspaces can be changed using the Workspace command on the Window menu or by making a selection from the drop-down menu on the **Tools panel**.

Each panel has a tab with the panel name. Panels can be moved by clicking and dragging panel tabs. As you drag the panel, an area becomes highlighted; this is called the **drop zone**, and provides a visual reference to where the panel can be placed.

If you wish to save a **customized workspace**, you may do so by selecting **New Workspace** on the Workspace menu or from the dropdown menu on the Tools panel.

A basic workflow in After Effects for creating a project follows six steps:

1. Import and organize footage.
2. Create compositions and arrange footage into layers.
3. Add various effects to layers.
4. Animate elements on layers.
5. Preview work on the Composition panel.
6. Export the final composition.

The panels you will use most often are:

Project panel: The Project panel organizes the references to all of the assets for the project. Assets can include video clips, digital images, and audio clips. In After Effects, assets are referred to as **footage**. The Project panel also lists compositions, which explain how you want to use the footage.

Timeline panel: The Timeline panel is where footage may be added to a composition in components called **layers** and is represented as a bar graph.

Figure 1 *Standard workspace*

Composition panel: The Composition panel represents layers spatially. The Composition panel displays compositions at the location of the Current-time Indicator (CTI) on the Timeline panel.

Showing Rulers and Grids

After Effects provides the option to display grids, rulers, guides, and safe margins. These options can be found on the View menu or by clicking the Choose grid and guide options button on the Composition panel. Using these options can be very beneficial when working with the drawing tools to determine the size of the shapes you are creating. It is important to understand that the grid, guides, and margins do not render for previews or for final output.

The various default settings for the grid, rulers, guides, and safe margins can be modified in the Grids & Guides section of the Preferences dialog box, as shown in Figure 2. Various colors and line styles can be selected based on personal preference to make the grid and guides easier to see. Spacing options on the grid can also be changed to provide greater detail to assist in the drawing and placement of objects. The unit of measurement is the pixel, 1/72nd of an inch.

The grid and guide features work in much the same way as in other Adobe applications. To create a guide you drag from the ruler, to reposition the guide you drag it with the

Figure 2 *Grids & Guides section of the Preferences dialog box*

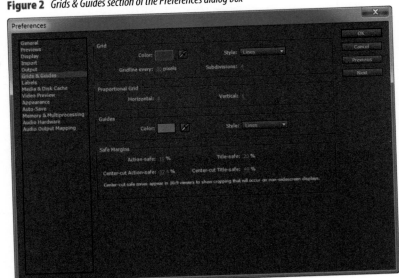

Selection tool. Locking guides prevents them from being moved. Guides can be cleared or hidden from view when you no longer need them.

Viewing area safe zones, or margins, are designed to ensure that certain content is not missed when being played on television screens. The **safe zone** is broken down into two areas: **title safe zone** and **action safe zone**. Programs like After Effects and Premiere Pro provide the option of turning on safe margin guides during editing.

As shown in Figure 3, the inner margin is the title safe zone and the outer margin is the action safe zone. Television stations that use a digital on-screen graphic place it just inside the title safe area to ensure that it will be visible on all television displays.

Figure 3 *Safe margin guides*

Title safe area   Action safe area

Start Adobe After Effects and explore the workspace

1. Click **Start** 🪟 on the Application bar, point to **All Programs**, then click **Adobe After Effects CS5**. (Win) or open the Finder from the dock and click Applications from the sidebar, click the **Adobe applications folder**, then click **Adobe After Effects CS5** (Mac).

   You may need to look in a subfolder if you have installed the Production Premium or Master Collection Suite. The Welcome to Adobe After Effects window appears as shown in Figure 4. This window allows you to open an existing project, create a new composition, see recent projects, and view the Tip of the Day.

   TIP Pressing and holding [Ctrl][Alt][Shift] (Win) or ⌘ [option][Shift] (Mac) while starting After Effects restores default preference settings.

2. Click the **Close button** 🗙 on the Welcome to Adobe After Effects window.

   An untitled project appears in the Standard workspace as shown in Figure 5.

3. Click **Window** on the Application bar, then point to **Workspace**.

   You will see a variety of preformatted workspaces that are available. Note the check mark next to Standard; the check mark indicates the workspace you are currently viewing.

   (continued)

Figure 4 *Welcome to Adobe After Effects window*

Figure 5 *New untitled project*

Tools panel

Info panel

Project panel

Preview panel

Composition panel

Timeline panel

Working in Adobe After Effects CS5

Figure 6 *Displaying the grid*

Choose grid and guide options button

Grid option

4. Click **Animation**.

   The Smoother, Wiggler, and Motion Sketch panels are added to the workspace on the right. These three panels are important when working with animation.

5. Continue to click through the various workspaces and notice how the window changes each time.

6. When you have finished looking at the various workspaces, switch back to the **Standard** workspace.

TIP After selecting Standard, you may want to click Reset "Standard" on the Workspace menu to ensure that the workspace has been reset properly.

7. Leave Adobe After Effects open for the next exercise.

You started Adobe After Effects CS5 and explored the workspace.

Work with the grid and guides

1. Open **GridPractice.aep** from your Chapter 2 Data Files folder.

2. Click the **Choose grid and guide options button** 🔲 on the bottom of the Composition panel, then click **Grid** as shown in Figure 6.

3. Click **Edit** on the Application bar (Win) or click **After Effects** (Mac), point to **Preferences**, then click **Grids & Guides**.

(continued)

4. Click the **Color box** to open the Grid Color dialog box, then click in the large color space to change the color to a **bright yellow** as shown in Figure 7.

5. Click **OK** in the Grid Color dialog box, then click **OK** in the Preferences dialog box.

   The grid line colors on the Composition panel have changed to bright yellow and are easier to see.

6. Click **View** on the Application bar, then click **Show Rulers**.

   Rulers are shown in the pixel unit of measure at the top and to the left of the Composition panel.

   (continued)

Figure 7 *Customizing the color of the grid*

Color box

Where you click will be the new color

Figure 8 *Creating a ruler guide*

Left ruler

Top ruler

Cursor

7. Position the mouse pointer over the **left ruler**, click and drag to the grid to create a vertical guide, then release the mouse pointer when it is approximately at the 300 px mark, as shown in Figure 8.

   Once the mouse pointer is over a ruler, it changes into a double-headed arrow.

   TIP The Info panel shows the location of the guide as you drag it.

8. Repeat this process from the top ruler to create a horizontal guide anywhere on the Composition panel.

   Guides can be moved by clicking and dragging them. To remove a guide, drag it back onto the ruler.

9. Click **View** on the Application bar, then click **Lock Guides** to keep guides from being moved or selected accidentally.

10. Close After Effects.

In this lesson, you showed the grid and rulers and customized the color of the grid. You also placed two guides on the Composition panel and locked them.

Create an
ON-SCREEN GRAPHIC

What You'll Do

In this lesson, you will create a digital on-screen graphic or bug.

Creating a Composition

A **project** in After Effects is a single file that stores **compositions** and references to footage used in the project. **Footage**, what we referred to as digital assets in Premiere Pro, may include video, audio, animation, still images, text, Photoshop and Illustrator files, and even Premiere Pro project files.

The project file must contain at least one composition. A **composition** is the container that holds all the references for the movie. A composition may also be referred to as a **comp** within After Effects; it has its own timeline and layers, as shown in Figure 9.

Each layer can only have one footage item, which then can be manipulated in space and time. A composition is similar to a sequence in Premiere Pro or a movie clip in Flash Professional.

Composition settings are independent of the project settings and if you create multiple compositions, you can create different settings for each composition. For most composition settings, the presets should be acceptable. For our purposes, while working on projects in this book, we will use the NTSC DV and the NTSC DV Widescreen presets. It is always a good idea

Figure 9 *Composition layers and timeline*

Composition

Layers

Timeline

to make the composition settings match the footage. Fortunately, if you do not know the information for your footage you can simply drag the footage to the Create a new Composition button on the Project panel or drag it to the Timeline panel and After Effects will create the composition for you with the appropriate settings. As shown in Figure 10, video footage about air pollution in Beijing was imported into the Project panel, then dragged to the Timeline panel where a composition was automatically created with the default name of the footage and in this case, a custom preset and a duration of 8.03 seconds.

The Composition panel, as shown in Figure 11, displays the layers of footage at the Current-time Indicator (CTI) on the Timeline panel. You can use the Composition panel as a visual preview of the footage on the Timeline, similar to the Program Monitor in Premiere Pro.

Figure 10 *Composition settings created based on footage*

Footage   Composition Settings

Figure 11 *Composition panel sample preview of Timeline*

Composition panel   Current time

Working with Footage

The Project panel is where the compositions and footage items are listed, as shown in Figure 12. After Effects supports practically every format for common file types of video, audio, and still images. A complete list can be found in After Effects Help. Files are not directly imported into the Project panel; instead a reference link to each source file is created. Therefore, if you delete, move, or change the name of a file you are referencing, the link will become broken. If a link becomes broken, the name of the source file will appear in italics on the Project panel, and the File Path column will identify the path as missing, as shown in Figure 13. If the source file is still available, double-click the reference on the Project panel and restore the link by selecting the file again.

You can create folders on the Project panel to store and organize footage. You can embed folders within folders. If you have a folder selected when you choose the Import command, the footage will be placed in that folder. To reveal a folder's contents you simply click the expand arrow to the left of the folder icon. You can also choose the Import Folder option on the Import File dialog box, as shown in Figure 14. The imported folder will become a folder on the Project panel.

Color labels are assigned to footage items by default to represent different types of media,

Figure 12 *Project panel showing sample footage*

Project panel

Composition

Footage

Folders

Figure 13 *Example of missing footage*

Missing footage

Missing in file path

Figure 14 *Import File dialog box*

Folders

Import Folder button

for example, video clips are assigned the color Aqua. Color labels are also assigned to compositions and layers. You can change the default colors in the Labels section of the Preferences dialog box, as shown in Figure 15. The labels allow you to sort by color on the Project panel, or to select all layers with the same label color on either the Project panel or the Timeline panel, as shown in Figure 16.

After Effects projects can become quite large, and the Timeline can become quite long. If you are unable to locate a piece of footage on the Timeline, right-click (Win) or [Control]-click (Mac) the footage on the Project panel, click Reveal in Composition, then select the instance you are looking for. You can also use the Search box on the Project panel and on the Timeline panel to search for footage. As you begin to type in the Search box, the filter process begins and items that do not meet the criteria become hidden. After you find the item you are looking for, click the X on the Search box to clear it.

Creating a Layer

Layers are similar to tracks in Premiere Pro. Without layers, a composition would be empty. When we use the term layers in After Effects, we are referring to the layers on the Timeline panel, not on the Layer panel. The Layer panel in After Effects is similar to the Source Monitor in Premiere Pro; it is the panel where you can view source footage. One very important thing to remember is that a layer in After Effects can only have one footage item (movie, still image, audio, text)

as its source and every layer has properties that are unique to that particular layer.

There are several types of layers in After Effects. There are layers that are created to

hold items created within After Effects such as text layers and shape layers. There are audio and video layers based on the type of footage that has been placed on them.

Figure 15 *Labels section of the Preferences dialog box*

Labels

Label default colors

Figure 16 *Selecting layers based on label color*

Shape layers selected based on label color

Lesson 2   Create an On-Screen Graphic

Finally, there are special function layers that are also created within After Effects for cameras, lights, null objects, guide layers, and adjustment layers. Layers that are created without using source footage are called **synthetic layers**.

There are three panels that allow you to work with layers, the Timeline panel, the Composition panel, and the Layer panel. (We will use the Layer panel in later chapters as we continue to explore After Effects.)

The Timeline panel is where you can change layer properties by using keyframes, in a manner very similar to how we used them in Premiere Pro. Every layer by default begins with the Transform group of properties, as shown in Figure 17. All layer properties can change the layer over time, meaning they are **temporal**. Some layer properties also have the ability to move, or add motion across composition space, meaning they are **spatial**.

Opacity is an example of a property that is a temporal property. It is temporal because the layer does not move; the property causes the layer to fade in or fade out which is an effect that occurs over a period of time. Position is a property that shows movement of a layer, the layer is moved at different keyframes to indicate motion over a period of time. Therefore, position is an example of a property that is both temporal and spatial. (*Note*: Since all properties are temporal, if a property is spatial it is also temporal.)

On the Timeline panel, you can change a layer's starting time, length of time, and its stacking order. After Effects automatically numbers the layers based on the position of the layer in the stacking order, as shown in Figure 18. If the stacking order changes, the numbers assigned to each layer are updated to keep the numbering in numerical order. All layers are placed at the top of the stacking

Figure 17 *Transform group properties*

Transform group

Default settings

Figure 18 *Layers on the Timeline panel*

Timeline panel

Search box

Label colors

Layer #

Zoom Out button

Zoom In button

Timeline

order by default when created. However, a footage item can be dragged to the Timeline panel in the position of the stack where you want it to be placed.

The Composition panel is where you preview the changes you have made to a layer, and the layers in context with other layers; otherwise known as the **composition**. This is also where you can manually modify layers.

Adding Layer Effects

Effects can be found on the Effects & Presets panel or on the Effect menu. To apply an effect to a selected layer, double-click the effect you wish to apply. The Effect Controls panel opens and the effect you applied and its properties become active, as shown in Figure 19.

As a layer is modified and animated, properties are added, and the properties are organized into property groups. The Effects property group is added to the Layer properties on the Timeline panel, as shown in Figure 20. You can edit these properties either on the Timeline panel or on the Effect Controls panel.

Working with Animation Presets

An **animation preset** is a collection of animation settings that includes keyframes and effects that you have applied to a layer. Creating an animation preset allows you to apply the same settings to another layer in the composition or even in another After Effects project.

Figure 19 *Effect Controls panel*

Figure 20 *Viewing the Effects property group*

After Effects also includes a large library of animation presets. You can browse the available animation presets in the Effects & Presets panel or in Adobe Bridge. To preview the animation presets in Adobe Bridge, click Animation on the Application bar then select Browse Presets.

Making a Movie

A **movie** is the name given to a file that is created by rendering a composition. **Rendering** is the process of compiling a composition into its final output from all of its layers and settings. The preferred way to render and export movies from After Effects is by using the Render Queue panel.

The Render Queue panel is used to render compositions, adjust render settings, apply output module settings, name the file, adjust the file location if necessary, and monitor the rendering process, as shown in Figure 21. When a composition is added to the Render Queue it becomes a **render item**, and its status is listed as Queued. Clicking the Render button in the upper-right corner of the Render Queue panel begins the rendering process for all the items listed in the queue with the status Queued in the order they are listed. The status changes to Done when the process is complete. A render item remains in the Render Queue where it can be duplicated and added as a render item in the queue with the same settings or different settings until it is removed.

Just as we did with Premiere Pro, we will be saving to the MPEG-2 file format and the FLV format.

Figure 21 *Render Queue panel*

Render Queue panel

Output Module

Status

Output To

Render button

A Note About Special Function Layers

A **null object** is an invisible layer that can have all the properties of a visible layer; you can then apply those properties to other layers. Null object layers are often used as control layers when working with animations because they are often easier to select and see than when working with a camera or light layer. We will work with this type of layer in later chapters.

The **guide layer** can help you position and edit elements by providing a visual reference in the Composition panel; guide layers are created from existing layers. By default, guide layers do not become part of the final output.

An **adjustment layer** affects all layers that fall below it in the stacking order; therefore, adjustment layers are useful if you want to apply the same effect to many layers at the same time.

Figure 22 *Composition Settings dialog box*

Preset

Name

Duration
value

Create a composition

1. Press and hold [**Ctrl**][**Alt**][**Shift**] (Win) or ⌘ [**option**][**Shift**] (Mac), then start Adobe After Effects CS5 to reset the default preference settings.

2. Click **OK** in the warning dialog box in response to: "Are you sure you want to delete your preferences file?"

   Premiere deletes the old preferences file and creates a new one using default settings. Resetting the default preference settings will remove the bright yellow grid setting we applied in the last lesson.

3. Click the **Close button** 🗵 on the Welcome to Adobe After Effects window, if necessary.

4. Click **File** on the Application bar, click **Save As**, type **BUG your name** in the File name text box, navigate to the drive and folder where your Data Files are located, then click **Save**.

5. Click **Composition** on the Application bar, then click **New Composition**.

   The Composition Settings dialog box opens.

   TIP You can also press [Ctrl][N] (Win) or ⌘ [N] (Mac) to create a new composition.

6. Type **BUG** in the Composition Name text box.

7. Click the **Preset list arrow**, then click **NTSC DV**, the default preset.

8. Change the Duration value to **0;00;07;00** by typing **700** (7 seconds), press [**Tab**], compare your dialog box to Figure 22, then press [**Enter**] (Win) or [**return**] (Mac).

(continued)

Pressing [Enter] (Win) or [return] (Mac) after typing 700 will close the Composition Settings dialog box. If you need to edit the composition settings further, click Composition on the Application bar then select Composition Settings.

9. A new composition named BUG appears on the Project panel, Composition panel, and Timeline panel, as shown in Figure 23.

10. Save your project and leave it open for the next exercise.

You started a new After Effects project and created a new composition.

Import footage

1. Open the Bug your name project file, if necessary.

2. Click **File** on the Application bar, point to **Import**, then click **File**.

3. Navigate to the drive and folder where your Data Files are stored, click **us_11.jpg**, then click **Open**.

   The file appears on the Project panel, as shown in Figure 24.

TIP   Be sure the JPEG Sequence check box is not checked to keep files in a possible sequence from being imported by mistake.

4. Save your project and leave it open for the next exercise.

You imported footage into the Project panel.

Figure 23   *New composition*

Project panel

Composition panel

Timeline panel

Figure 24   *Project panel showing imported footage*

Selected footage preview

Imported footage file

Figure 25 *Shape Layer 1 added to Timeline panel*

Shape Layer 1

Figure 26 *Drawing a rectangle*

Drawing a rectangle

Selected rectangle

Create a shape layer

1. Open the Bug your name project file, if necessary.

2. Click the **Choose grid and guide options button** on the Composition panel, then click **Title/Action Safe**.

3. Repeat Step 2 to select **Grid**, then **Rulers**.

4. Click the **Timeline panel** to select it.

5. Click **Layer** on the Application bar, point to **New**, then click **Shape Layer**.

   A new layer named Shape Layer 1 is added to the BUG composition on the Timeline panel, as shown in Figure 25.

   TIP You can also right-click the Timeline panel, point to New, then click Shape Layer to create a new shape layer.

6. Click the **Rectangle tool** on the Tools panel, then draw a rectangle near the bottom-left corner of the title safe area of the Composition panel, as shown in Figure 26.

   Your rectangle size and location may differ slightly from the figure.

7. With the rectangle still selected, click the **Fill color box** on the Tools panel, type **113355** in the # text box, then click **OK**.

   The # text box in the Text Color dialog box refers to the Hex color code which represents color in the RRGGBB form. RR represents the intensity of the color red, GG the intensity of the color green, and BB the intensity of the color blue. Color intensity is represented by a hexadecimal number from 00 to FF.

8. Click the **Stroke Width value** on the Tools panel, then drag the pointer to **0 px**.

(continued)

9. Click **Effect** on the Application bar, point to **Perspective**, then click **Bevel Edges**.

   The Effect Controls panel becomes active to show the Bevel Edges effect.

10. On the Effect Controls panel, change the Edge Thickness value to **0.05**.

11. Click **Effect** on the Application bar, point to **Stylize**, then click **Color Emboss**.

    The Color Emboss effect is added to the Effect Controls panel.

12. On the Effect Controls panel, change the Relief value to **2.00**, as shown in Figure 27.

13. Deselect the rectangle by clicking away from it on the Composition panel, then click the **Selection tool** on the Tools panel.

TIP You can also press [V] on the keyboard to select the Selection tool.

14. Save your project and leave it open for the next exercise, then compare your Composition panel to Figure 28.

You displayed the grid, rulers, and Title/Action Safe margins. Next, you created a new shape layer on the Timeline panel, drew a rectangle, and applied effects to it.

Create a text layer

1. Open the Bug your name project file, if necessary.

2. Click **Window** on the Application bar, point to **Workspace**, then click **Text**.

   The workspace changes to the Text workspace. The Character and Paragraph panels are included in the Text workspace, as shown in Figure 29.

   (continued)

Figure 27 *Effects added to Effect Controls panel*

Bevel Edges — Edge Thickness — Color Emboss — Relief

Figure 28 *Rectangle with Bevel Edges and Stylize Color Emboss effects*

Rectangle with effects applied

Figure 29 *Text workspace*

Text workspace — Character panel — Paragraph panel

Working in Adobe After Effects CS5

Figure 30 *Entering text on the Composition panel*

Selected
Horizontal
Type tool

Typed text

Figure 31 *New name of the text layer*

Name of Text layer

3. Right-click the **Timeline panel**, point to **New**, then click **Text**.

   A Text layer named Text 1 is added to the Timeline panel. The Horizontal Type tool becomes selected on the Tools panel. A red cursor appears in the center of the Composition panel.

4. Type **News 6**, then press [**Ctrl**][**Enter**] (Win) or ⌘ [**return**](Mac) on the main section of the keyboard to exit text-editing mode.

   Selection handles appear around the text so that it may now be formatted, as shown in Figure 30. The Horizontal Type tool remains selected on the Tools panel. The name of the Text layer has changed to News 6 to reflect the text that has been typed on the layer, as shown in Figure 31.

   TIP Pressing [Enter] on the numeric keyboard will also exit text-editing mode.

5. On the Character panel make the following selections: Font: **Verdana**; Font style: **Bold**; Fill color: **White (#FFFFFF)**; Font size: **30 px**.

   TIP If the text is no longer selected, click the Selection tool ▶ on the Tools panel, then click News 6 on the Composition panel to select it.

6. Save your project and leave it open for the next exercise.

You changed the workspace to the Text workspace and created a text layer. You then typed text on the Composition panel and used the Character panel to format the text.

Lesson 2   Create an On-Screen Graphic

Add a layer effect to text

1. Open the Bug your name project file, if necessary.

2. Set the workspace to the **Text** workspace, if necessary.

3. On the Effects & Presets panel type "**drop shadow**" in the Search box.

4. Press [**V**] to access the Selection tool , then click **News 6**.

5. Double-click **Drop Shadow** on the Effects & Presets panel.

   The Drop Shadow effect is applied to the News 6 text. The Effect Controls panel becomes active and displays the properties for the Drop Shadow effect.

6. Drag the **News 6** text over the rectangle, as shown in Figure 32.

   The News 6 text is above the rectangle because the News 6 text layer is above the Shape 1 layer on the Timeline panel. The text layer was created after the shape layer so it is one level higher in the stacking order.

7. Save your project and leave it open for the next exercise.

You applied the Drop Shadow effect to the News 6 text then moved the text over the rectangle.

Place footage in a composition

1. Open the Bug your name project file, if necessary.

2. Click the **Project panel tab**, then drag **us_11.jpg** from the Project panel to the center of the Composition panel, as shown in Figure 33.

   (continued)

Figure 32 *Placing the text over the rectangle*

Text placed inside rectangle

Figure 33 *Placing footage on the Composition panel*

Large "X"

Working in Adobe After Effects CS5

Figure 34 *us_11.jpg moved to #2 in stacking order*

Stacking order

Figure 35 *Changing the stacking order of layers on the Timeline panel*

White rectangle

Selected layer
being moved

Black line

As you drag the footage, you will see a large X, which represents the item being dragged. When you drag an item from the Project panel to the Composition panel, a new layer is automatically created at the top of the stacking order. The us_11.jpg layer is above the other layers on the Timeline panel. We need to correct the stacking order.

3. Click **Layer** on the Application bar, point to **Arrange**, then click **Send Layer Backward**.

   You should now be able to see "News 6". The us_11.jpg layer should now be #2 in the stacking order, as shown in Figure 34.

4. On the Timeline panel, click the **Shape Layer 1 layer**, then drag it above the us_11.jpg layer, as shown in Figure 35.

   You will see a white rectangle, which represents the layer being dragged, and a black line indicating where the layer will be relocated to when you release the mouse pointer.

5. Click the **Choose grid and guide options button** ⊞ on the Composition panel, then turn off the Title/Action Safe, Grid, and Rulers options.

   (continued)

6. Compare your screen to Figure 36.

7. Save your project and leave it open for the next exercise.

You placed footage into the composition and then rearranged the stacking order of layers on the Timeline panel.

Apply an animation preset

1. Open the Bug your name project file, if necessary.

2. Verify that the Current-time Indicator (CTI) is placed at **0;00;00;00** on the Timeline.

TIP With the Timeline panel selected, press [Home] to return the (CTI) to 0;00;00;00 and [End] to jump to the end of the duration of the composition. The [Home] key equivalent is [FN]+left arrow and the [End] key equivalent is [FN]+down arrow (Mac).

3. Click the **Selection tool** on the Tools panel, then click the **News 6 text**.

TIP If you have trouble selecting the text, click the Text layer on the Timeline panel.

4. Click **Animation** on the Application bar, then click **Browse Presets**.

   This will open Adobe Bridge, as shown in Figure 37.

5. Adjust the size of the thumbnails, if necessary, by dragging the slider at the bottom of the window.

6. Double-click the **Text folder**.

7. Double-click the **Animate In folder**.

8. Click **Center Spiral** to preview it on the Preview panel.

(continued)

Figure 36 *Completed BUG*

Title/Action Safe, Grid, and Rulers turned off

Stacking order

Figure 37 *Adobe Bridge Presets window*

Preview

Preset folders

Adjust size of thumbnails

Figure 38 *Animate In presets*

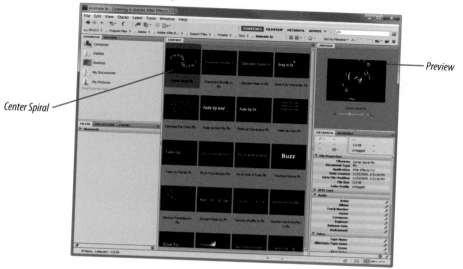

Center Spiral

Preview

Figure 39 *Placing a preset in After Effects*

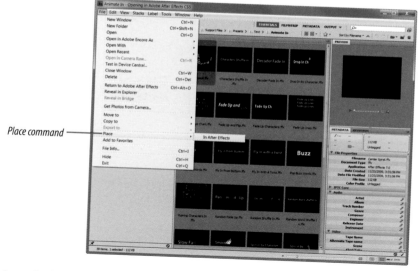

Place command

9. Preview some other "Animate In" effects, as shown in Figure 38.

10. Click **Character Shuffle In**, click **File** on the Application bar, point to **Place**, then click **In After Effects**, as shown in Figure 39.

This will apply the Character Shuffle In preset to the selected News 6 text.

11. Click the **Play/Pause button** ▶ on the Preview panel to preview the effect on the Composition panel.

The preview will play slowly the first time because it is rendering the file. Click the Play/Pause button again to see it in real time.

12. Save your project and leave it open for the next exercise.

You added a preset animation to the News 6 text, then played the animation on the Preview panel.

Make a movie

1. Open the Bug your name project file, if necessary.

2. Click the **Composition panel** to select the BUG composition.

   The composition needs to be selected before you will be able to add it to the Render Queue.

3. Click **Composition** on the Application bar, then click **Add to Render Queue**.

   The Render Queue panel appears at the bottom of the workspace, as shown in Figure 40.

4. Click **Lossless with Alpha**, next to Output Module on the Render Queue panel.

   The Output Module Settings dialog box opens, as shown in Figure 41.

5. Click the **Format list arrow**, click **MPEG2**, then click **OK**.

   Leave the Include Project Link check box checked. This will assist with compatibility when we import our MPEG2 files into Encore in a later chapter.

6. Click the text to the right of the **Output To** heading on the Render Queue panel.

   The Output Movie To dialog box opens, allowing you to name the movie and choose a location to save it in.

7. Name the movie **BUG Final your name**, save it in your Data Files folder, then click **Save**.

   (continued)

Figure 40 *Render Queue panel*

Render Queue panel

Output Module

Output To   File name   Render button

Figure 41 *Output Module Settings dialog box*

Include Project Link check box

Format list arrow

Figure 42 *Watching BUG Final in Windows Media Player*

Text is in motion ————

8. Click the **Render button** on the Render Queue panel.

   The rendering process begins. A status bar displays the approximate time remaining. Depending on the size, quality, complexity, and output method this could take seconds or hours. You will not be able to continue to work in After Effects until the process has completed. An audio alert indicates when the rendering process is complete.

9. Double-click **BUG Final your name.mpeg** to open your project in a digital media player, such as Windows Media Player, to see your movie.

   Your screen should resemble Figure 42.

10. Close the project.

You exported the movie to MPEG2 format and then watched it in a digital media player, such as Windows Media Player.

Create a
PRODUCTION LOGO

What You'll Do

 In this lesson, you will create a production logo.

Importing Photoshop Text

If you are already familiar with working with Photoshop features, such as formatting text and layer styles, it may be easier for you to prepare your text in Photoshop rather than create it in After Effects. After Effects includes the Photoshop rendering engine; it will import all the attributes of the Photoshop file, as shown in Figure 43. The text and the

Figure 43 *Photoshop file imported with attributes*

Layer styles

Working in Adobe After Effects CS5

attributes will be editable in After Effects. This is also true of working with still images created in Photoshop. For this reason, it is important to organize and name your layers in Photoshop. After Effects recognizes the names of the layers and imports them inside a folder by default, as shown in Figure 44, making it easier for you to work with the layers once they are imported. If you make any edits to the original Photoshop file, the Reload Footage command in After Effects will refresh the layers to reference the current Photoshop file. If you delete a layer, you will see the footage is missing from the Project panel, as shown in Figure 45. You can then make any edits to the layer styles in After Effects.

Figure 44 *Photoshop file imported into the Project panel as a composition*

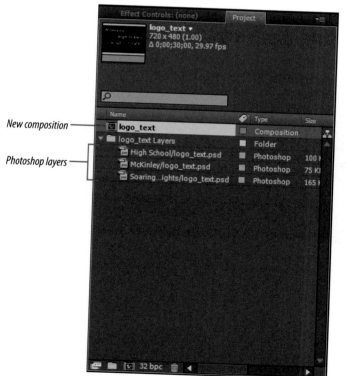

New composition

Photoshop layers

Figure 45 *Photoshop layer deleted*

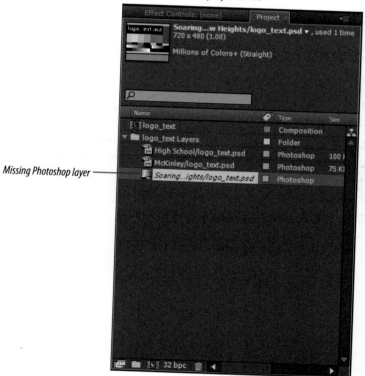

Missing Photoshop layer

You can also convert the Photoshop layer to an After Effects Text layer, as shown in Figure 46. The layer will retain all the attributes it had when it was imported, however it will no longer reference the Photoshop file and you will no longer be able to return to Photoshop to make edits to those layers that have been converted. The text, however, will now be able to be edited on the Composition panel in After Effects.

Formatting Text

When formatting text, it is a good idea to change your workspace to the Text workspace. The Text workspace activates the Character and Paragraph panels on the right side of the application window.

Changes you make on the Character panel affect only the text you have selected. If you select text with the Selection tool while making changes on the Character panel, all the text on that layer will change. If you highlight text with the Text tool, only the highlighted text will change, as shown in Figure 47. If you want to select all of the text on a layer and activate the Text tool, double-click the text layer on the Timeline panel with the Selection tool.

With the Text tool selected, double-click a word to select it, triple-click to select a line of text, and quadruple-click to select a paragraph.

Nesting a Composition

Nesting a composition means to place one composition inside another. The nested composition, sometimes referred to as a **precomposition**, appears as a single layer in the composition in which it is placed, also known as the **master composition**. You can apply effects to the nested composition like any other layer, and you can open the nested

Figure 46 *Photoshop file imported in After Effects*

After Effects Text layer

Figure 47 *Highlighting text*

Formatting changes are only made to highlighted text

Format changes

composition and make changes there as well. Importing Photoshop files encourages us to work with nested compositions. When importing a Photoshop file, selecting the composition option provides greater flexibility in working with Photoshop in After Effects. For instance, layers are preserved and text layers can be converted to editable text. If you choose the footage option, the Photoshop file is imported as a single layer. In addition, nesting is great for repetitive elements such as animated logos so that you can reuse them. You can also think of nesting as a way to organize layers into groups to simplify a composition into manageable parts.

The easiest way to navigate between nested compositions in After Effects is to use the Composition Navigator, as shown in Figure 48. Click the composition name to activate the composition. The directional arrow between the names of the compositions indicates the **downstream** composition to the left and the **upstream** composition to the right. Upstream is another term sometimes used for a nested composition. The composition most upstream is the master composition. Downstream is another term for the composition that contains a nested composition. There can be multiple nestings in a composition; the most downstream composition is referred to as the **root composition**.

Animating Text

There is an entire animation preset library dedicated specifically to text, as shown in Figure 49. The text animation presets were created in an NTSC DV 720x480

Figure 48 *Composition Navigator*

Root composition

Nested composition

Figure 49 *Library of text animation presets*

THE VIDEO COLLECTION

composition using a text layer with the Myriad Pro, size 72-point font. If you use a text animation preset, you may need to adjust the size of the text. Additionally, when using presets from the Fill and Stroke category, the preset may change the colors of your text, and some presets require a stroke or fill in order for the animation to work. Adjustments can be made to the preset using the property settings on the Timeline, as shown in Figure 50.

Figure 50 *Adjusting a text animation preset*

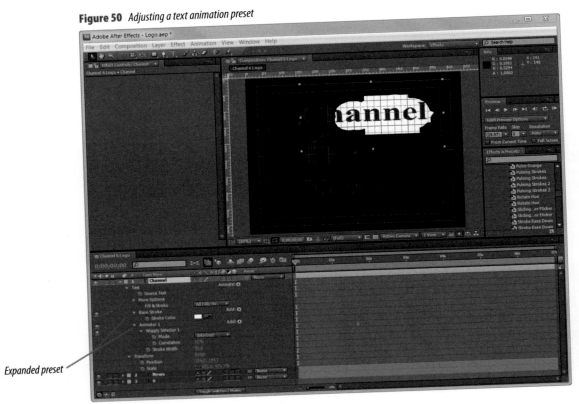

Expanded preset

Figure 51 *Settings for exporting for the Web*

Resize check box ——

Custom menu ——

Export a Production Logo for the Web

The method for exporting a movie is the same for all After Effects projects. However, when saving a file for the Web, the file extension that needs to be chosen is FLV.

In the Output Module Settings dialog box, the Resize option needs to be selected to reduce the size of the video from 720 x 480 px to a more manageable screen size, as shown in Figure 51. The Custom menu provides the Web Video 320 x 240 option, which we will use for the exercises in this book.

Import Photoshop text and convert it to editable text

1. Open Production Logo.aep, then save it as **Logo your name**.

2. Click **File** on the Application bar, then click **Import**.

3. Navigate to the location where you store your Data Files, then click **Channel 6 Logo.psd**.

4. Leave the default settings in the Import File dialog box so that your Import File dialog box matches Figure 52, then click **Open**.

   Another dialog box appears, as shown in Figure 53.

5. Click the **Import Kind list arrow**, click **Composition**, then click **OK**.

   This option will allow us to edit the text that was created in Photoshop. Notice that there is now another composition on the Project panel titled Channel 6 Logo, as shown in Figure 54, and a folder with the various Photoshop layers.

   (continued)

Figure 52 *Import settings for importing Photoshop file*

Figure 53 *Choosing Composition from the Import Kind menu*

Figure 54 *New composition based on Photoshop footage*

Working in Adobe After Effects CS5

Figure 55 *Channel 6 Logo composition*

Production Logo
composition

Channel 6 Logo
composition

6. Double-click **Channel 6 Logo** on the Project panel to make it active on the Timeline panel and on the Composition panel, then compare your screen to Figure 55.

The Channel 6 Logo composition has three layers that were preserved from Photoshop during the import process when the composition option was selected. Each individual layer appears on the Timeline panel.

(continued)

7. Click the **Channel layer** on the Timeline panel, click **Layer** on the Application bar, then click **Convert to Editable Text**.

   The layer is converted to an editable After Effects text layer, as shown in Figure 56, and is no longer a Photoshop file.

8. Right-click the **News layer**, then click **Convert to Editable Text**.

9. Convert Layer 3 to editable text.

   All three layers on the Channel 6 Logo composition are text layers, as shown in Figure 57.

10. Close the Channel 6 Logo composition.

11. Save your project and leave it open for the next exercise.

You imported a Photoshop file as a composition, then converted the Photoshop layers to After Effects text layers so the text would be editable.

Figure 56 *Photoshop layer converted to editable text*

Editable text

Figure 57 *Converted text layers on the Channel 6 Logo composition*

Figure 58 *Channel 6 Logo composition nested in Production Logo composition*

Channel 6 Logo composition

Channel 6 Logo composition

Channel 6 Logo composition

Figure 59 *Composition Navigator*

Composition Navigator

Nest a composition

1. Open the Logo your name project file, if necessary.

2. Click the **Production Logo composition** to activate it on the Timeline panel.

3. Drag the **Channel 6 Logo** composition from the Project panel to the **Production Logo composition** so that it is in the Layer 1 position, as shown in Figure 58.

   We are nesting one composition inside the other. This will allow us to switch between the two compositions, and continue to format the text so that we will be able to preview our formatting changes while we work. The Composition Navigator bar appears on the Composition panel when there is more than one composition, as shown in Figure 59.

(continued)

4. Click the **Composition Navigator list arrow**, then click **Channel 6 Logo** to switch to the Channel 6 Logo composition.

   The Channel 6 Logo composition appears on the Composition panel, as shown in Figure 60.

5. Save your project and leave it open for the next lesson.

You nested a composition and navigated between compositions using the Composition Navigator on the Composition panel.

Format text

1. Open the Logo your name project file, if necessary.

2. Verify that the Channel 6 Logo composition is active on the Composition panel, and that the Text workspace is in place.

3. Click the **Selection tool** on the Tools panel, then click **Channel** on the Composition panel, as shown in Figure 61.

(continued)

Figure 60 *Channel 6 Logo composition*

Composition
Navigator
list arrow

Channel 6 Logo

Figure 61 *Channel selected with Selection tool*

Channel
selected with
Selection tool

Figure 62 *Activating the Stroke Color button*

Stroke Color button

Figure 63 *Formatting the stroke using the Character panel*

Stroke width

Figure 64 *Previewing the changes to the Production Logo composition*

Production Logo composition

Stroke color added to Channel

4. On the Character panel, click the **Stroke Color button**, as shown in Figure 62, to bring it in front of the Fill Color button.

   The Text Color dialog box opens. Because the Stroke Color button is in front of the Fill Color button on the Character panel, the color you choose will be applied to the stroke or border of the text characters.

   TIP Double-click the Fill Color button to bring it in front of the Stroke Color button and open the Text Color dialog box, and vice versa.

5. Click **White (#FFFFFF)**, then click **OK**.

6. Change the Stroke width to **0.5 px** as shown in Figure 63.

7. Click the **Composition Navigator list arrow**, then click **Production Logo** to preview the changes to "Channel" in front of the video footage, as shown in Figure 64.

8. Return to the Channel 6 Logo composition on the Composition panel.

(continued)

9. Make the same color and stroke width changes to the stroke for the "6" and the "News" text, then compare your Composition panel to Figure 65.

TIP You can format both items at the same time by pressing and holding [Shift] as you select them, then make your formatting selections on the Character panel.

10. Click the **Selection tool** 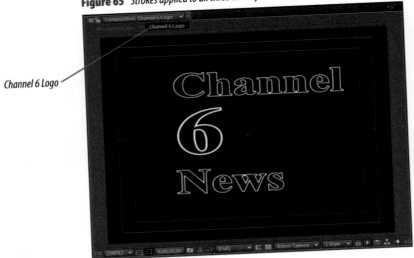 on the Tools panel, press and hold [**Shift**], click **Channel**, click **6**, click **News**, click the **Character panel options button** , then click **Small Caps**.

11. With the text layers still selected on the Composition panel, click **Window** on the Application bar, then click **Align**.

    The Align panel opens.

12. Click the **Align Layers to list arrow**, click **Composition**, then click the **horizontal center alignment button** , as shown in Figure 66.

(continued)

Figure 65 *Strokes applied to all three text layers*

Channel 6 Logo

Figure 66 *Align panel*

Align Layers to menu

Horizontal center alignment

Figure 67 *Edited text layers*

Figure 68 *Preview of Production Logo with animated text*

13. Preview your changes on the Production Logo composition panel, as shown in Figure 67.

14. Save your project and leave it open for the next exercise.

Using the Character panel, you edited text by adding a stroke and changing the font style to small caps. You also worked with the Align panel to align the text so that it is horizontally centered.

Animate text

1. Open the Logo your name project file, if necessary.

2. Activate the **Channel 6 Logo** composition on the Composition panel, then change the workspace to **Effects**.

3. Click the **Selection tool** on the Tools panel, select all three text layers then place the CTI at **0;00;00;00**.

4. Click the **Effects & Presets panel options button**, then click **Browse Presets**.

   Adobe Bridge launches the Presets preview.

5. Double-click the **Text folder**, then double-click **Lights and Optical**.

6. Right-click **Bubble Pulse**, point to **Place**, then click **In After Effects**.

   The Bubble Pulse animated preset is applied to all three text layers.

7. Select the **Production Logo composition** on the Composition panel, click the **Play/Pause button** on the Preview panel to play the composition, then compare your preview to Figure 68.

TIP Select Composition Preview RAM Preview if the preview is running to slow.

(continued)

8. Save your project and leave it open for the next exercise.

You added an animated preset to the three text layers and then previewed the composition.

Export a production logo for the Web

1. Open your Logo your name project file, if necessary.

2. Use the Composition Navigator to select the **Production Logo composition**.

We need to select the Production Logo composition because it is the root composition; the root composition is the one that is exported.

3. Click **Composition** on the Application bar, then click **Add to Render Queue**.

4. Click **Lossless with Alpha** next to Output Module on the Render Queue panel.

5. In the Output Module Settings dialog box make the following selections: Format: **FLV**; check the **Resize check box**; Custom: **Web Video, 320 x 240**, as shown in Figure 69.

We are selecting the FLV (Flash Video) file format since we are planning on using this for the Web.

6. Click the text to the right of the Output To heading on the Render Queue panel.

(continued)

Figure 69 *Output settings for Web*

Check Resize

Figure 70 *Logo Final file*

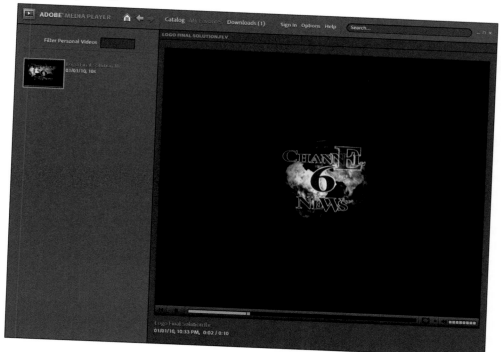

7. Name your movie **Logo Final your name**, select your Data Files folder, then click **Save**.

8. Click the **Render button** on the Render Queue panel.

9. Open Logo Final your name.flv to see your movie, as shown in Figure 70.

10. Close the project.

You exported your movie for the Web using the FLV file format.

Create a
TITLE SEQUENCE

What You'll Do

In this lesson, you will create a title sequence.

Working with Keyframes

We worked with keyframes in Premiere Pro when we customized motion effects on the Effect Controls panel. Keyframes work much the same way in After Effects.

You can work with keyframes in either layer bar mode or Graph Editor mode. Layer bar mode is the default displayed on the Timeline panel. The duration of a layer is shown as a bar with its keyframes aligned vertically with their properties, as shown in Figure 71. Graph Editor mode shows keyframes in value and speed graphs, as shown in Figure 72. We will be using layer bar mode. A keyframe

marks the point in time when you specify a change in value to a layer property such as position, scale, or opacity. Refer to Table 2-1 for more transform property shortcut keys. If you do not specify at least two keyframes when you change a value to a property, that value will remain for the duration of the layer.

To activate keyframes on a specific property, the stopwatch icon on the Timeline needs to be selected, as shown in Figure 73. Once the keyframes are activated, the keyframe navigator is displayed. The keyframe navigator includes the Go to next and Go to

Figure 71 *Layer bar mode*

Working in Adobe After Effects CS5

previous keyframe buttons and the Add or remove keyframe at current time button. The yellow diamond on the Timeline represents the selected keyframe. If you click the Add or remove keyframe button, a keyframe will be either added or removed at the location of the CTI. You can then quickly jump between keyframes with the Go to next and previous keyframe buttons. The keyframe navigator is specific to each layer property.

Keyframes can be deleted by selecting them and pressing [Delete], or to remove all the keyframes for a layer property, click the stopwatch button for that property. When you click the stopwatch, the value of the property will default to the value at the location of the CTI.

In the previous lesson, keyframes were created when we used animation presets. Keyframes will be created automatically when we create motion paths in this lesson.

Working with Motion Paths

When you animate properties that include the ability to be changed over space as well as time, the movement is shown as a **motion path**. A motion path is a series of dots; each dot indicates the position of the layer at each frame. The number of dots indicates the relative speed of the layers: the closer the dots, the slower the speed; the farther apart, the faster the speed.

Figure 72 *Graph Editor mode*

Figure 73 *Working with keyframes*

Add or remove keyframe at current time button

Go to previous keyframe button

Go to next keyframe button

Inactive stopwatch

Active stopwatch

Selected keyframe

A path consists of two parts, **segments** and **vertices** (plural for **vertex**), as shown in Figure 74. A **segment** is the line or curve that connects the vertex. Motion paths can be modified using the Selection tool, the Add Vertex tool, and the Delete Vertex tool. The Selection tool allows you to move an existing vertex point, or to activate the direction handles and reshape the path, as shown in Figure 75. The Add and Delete Vertex tools allow you to add or delete vertex points to make adjustments that are more detailed to your motion path as needed.

After Effects includes the Motion Sketch panel, as shown in Figure 76, which will record a motion path for you. You first click the Start Capture button on the Motion Sketch panel; recording begins when you click the layer on the Composition panel. The recording ends when you release the mouse button or the composition duration ends. The Motion Sketch panel records the position of the layer and the speed at which you draw, and generates a Position keyframe at each frame.

When working with the Motion Sketch panel, it is important to note that you are not able to adjust the start time of the recording. Keyframes will be generated at the beginning of the Timeline. If you have set keyframes for other properties, those generated by the Motion Sketch panel are not affected.

A few options can be adjusted on the Motion Sketch panel including:

Capture speed at: If the capture speed is set to 100%, the playback speed matches what was recorded. If the capture speed is greater than 100%, the recording will play back slower than what was recorded.

Smoothing: Smoothing eliminates unnecessary keyframes from the motion path; a higher value will create a smoother curve, but a value that is too high will cause you to lose the shape of the curve.

Figure 76 *Motion Sketch panel*

Figure 75 *Adjusting a direction handle on a motion path*

Figure 74 *Motion path*

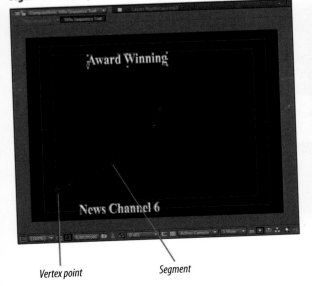

Vertex point   Segment

Vertex point   Direction handle

Working in Adobe After Effects CS5

Show: The Wireframe view displays a wireframe view of your layer while you are sketching, and the Background view displays a static view of the contents of the frame when you begin sketching.

Trimming Layers

There may be times when you do not want to use all of the frames in a movie clip. In addition, and quite often, you will not want a text or shape layer's duration to be the same length as the composition. Trimming a layer is a way to change the duration of a layer.

On the Timeline panel, layers are represented by a duration bar. The **In point** marks the beginning of the layer, and the **Out point** marks the end. The span between the In point and the Out point is called the **duration**. The **layer duration bar** is the bar that extends between the In point and the Out point, as shown in Figure 77. Changing the In and Out points on the Layer panel or the Timeline panel is called **trimming**.

Trimming a layer does not affect the source footage or the original source file.

Trimming or extending the layer on the Timeline panel with keyboard shortcuts is probably the quickest and easiest way to adjust the duration of layers. Place the CTI where you want to set the In or Out point. To set the In point at the current time, press [Alt][[] (Win) or [option][[] (Mac). To set the Out point at the current time, press [Alt][]] (Win) or [option][]] (Mac).

Figure 77 *Examples of In and Out points*

In point

Layer duration bar

Out point

Once you have adjusted the duration of the various layers, After Effects has an automated process for arranging them that may prove beneficial. The Sequence Layers keyframe assistant automatically arranges layers based on the order that you select, as shown in Figure 78.

The Sequence Layers command is just one of the several Keyframe Assistant options designed to work with keyframes. Another example is Easy Ease, which creates smooth transitions in and out of a keyframe by adjusting the speed of change

as motion advances toward and retreats from a keyframe. Variations of Easy Ease are Easy Ease In and Easy Ease Out, which automatically adjusts the influence in/out of a keyframe. The Keyframe Assistant command is found on the Animation menu.

Figure 78 *Example of sequencing layers*

In points vary

Layer duration bars staggered

Out points vary

Figure 79 *Selecting multiple text layers*

Current time
display at 4
seconds

Layers #1—#6
selected

CTI at 4 seconds

Figure 80 *Trimmed text layers*

Trimmed layers

Trim layers

1. Open Title Sequence.aep, then save it as **Title Sequence your name**.

   Notice that there are two compositions already created, Title Sequence, and Title Sequence Text.

2. Use the Composition Navigator to select the **Title Sequence Text composition**.

   We will be working with the text layers in the Title Sequence Text composition.

3. Click the **Current time display** on the Timeline panel, type **400**, then press [**Enter**] (Win) or [**return**] (Mac).

   The CTI moves to the 4-second mark on the time ruler.

4. On the Timeline panel, using the **Selection tool**, select **Text Layer #1**, then [Shift]-click **Text Layer #6**, as shown in Figure 79.

5. Press [**Alt**][[]] (Win) or [**option**][[]] (Mac) to trim the layers to the CTI at 4 seconds, as shown in Figure 80.

   Notice that Layer 7 did not change because it was not selected.

6. Save your project and leave it open for the next exercise.

You trimmed text layers 1 through 6 on the Title Sequence Text composition.

Create a motion path

1. Open the Title Sequence your name project file, if necessary.

2. Select the **Title Sequence Text composition** on the Composition panel, then verify that the CTI is at 0;00;00;00.

3. Change the workspace to **Minimal**.

4. Click **Window** on the Application bar, then click **Motion Sketch**.

5. Click **Window** on the Application bar, click **Preview**, then drag the **Preview panel** so it is below the Motion Sketch panel, as shown in Figure 81.

6. Turn on the Title/Action Safe margins.

7. Click the **Selection tool** on the Tools panel, then click **Award Winning** on the Composition panel.

8. On the Motion Sketch panel choose the following settings: Capture speed at: **50%**; Smoothing: **20**; Wireframe check box: **Check**, as shown in Figure 82.

(continued)

Figure 81 *Minimal workspace with Motion Sketch & Preview panels*

- Motion Sketch panel
- Minimal workspace
- Preview panel

Award Winning
Late Breaking
National   Local
Sports   Weather
News Channel 6

Figure 82 *Motion Sketch panel*

- Smoothing
- Capture speed
- Wireframe

Motion Sketch
Capture speed at: 50 %
Smoothing: 20
Show: ✓ Wireframe
☐ Background
Start:
Duration:
Start Capture

Working in Adobe After Effects CS5

Figure 83 *Drawing a path with the Motion Sketch panel*

Path

Bounding
box of
text

9. Click the **Start Capture button** on the Motion Sketch panel, click **Award Winning** on the Composition panel, then drag the text around the panel in an arc until you reach the bottom-left corner, just inside the Title Safe margin, as shown in Figure 83.

The text layer and the bounding box disappear during the recording process. You will see a bounding box representing the size of your text layer and a path while you are dragging. Recording will stop when you release the mouse button.

10. Repeat this procedure for Layers 2 through 6 using the same settings on the Motion Sketch panel.

(continued)

Lesson 4   Create a Title Sequence

Placing the CTI at 4 seconds will allow you to see the ending positions for the text layers as you work, as shown in the example in Figure 84. This will help you with the placement of the text so there is no overlap.

11. Return the CTI to **0;00;00;00**, then select the **Title Sequence composition**.

12. Preview the Title Sequence composition by clicking the **Play/Pause button** on the Preview panel.

    You should see the preview of the animated text with the Seattle skyline.

13. Save your project and leave it open for the next exercise.

In this lesson, you placed the text on a motion path.

Modify the Scale property

1. Open the Title Sequence your name project file, if necessary.

2. Select the **Title Sequence Text composition**, then verify that the CTI is at **0;00;00;00**.

3. Reset the workspace to the **Effects** workspace.

TIP You may need to select Reset "Effects" on the Workspace menu.

4. Select **Text layers #1** through **#7**, then press **[S]**.

    Pressing [S] filters the Scale property on all of the selected layers. See Table 2-1 for more Transform shortcuts.

    (continued)

Figure 84 *Previewing end position of text*

CTI

TABLE 2-1: TRANSFORM SHORTCUTS
[P] Position
[S] Scale
[R] Rotation
[T] Opacity
[U] Properties with keyframes or expressions
[UU] Reveals only properties that have been modified
[Shift] —Select a shortcut, reveals more than one property

Working in Adobe After Effects CS5

Figure 85 *Working with the Scale property*

Toggle Animation button

Add or remove keyframe at current time button

Scale

Keyframe

Figure 86 *Setting a beginning and ending keyframe*

Go to previous keyframe button

Add or remove keyframe at current time button

End keyframe

5. Click the **Toggle Animation button** on the Timeline to activate keyframes for Scale, as shown in Figure 85.

6. Drag the **CTI** to 4 seconds, then create a keyframe for each Text layer by clicking the **Add or remove keyframe at current time button**, as shown in Figure 86.

7. Click the **Go to previous keyframe button**, while leaving all the layers still selected.

(continued)

8. To the right of Scale on the Timeline panel, change 100.0% to **50.0%**, then compare your window to Figure 87.

   The proportions are linked so you only need to change one of them. All the text layers change size.

9. With all the text layers still selected, press **[S]** to close the Scale property.

10. Return the CTI to **0;00;00;00**, then select the **Title Sequence composition**.

11. Preview the Title Sequence composition by clicking the **Play/Pause button** on the Preview panel.

12. Save your project and leave it open for the next lesson.

You changed the Scale property for all of the text layers.

Arrange layers over time

1. Open the Title Sequence your name project file, if necessary.

2. Select the **Title Sequence Text composition**, if necessary, then verify that the CTI is at **0;00;00;00**.

3. Click the **Selection tool** on the Tools panel, press and hold **[Shift]**, then click **Text layer #1** through **Text layer #6** on the Timeline panel.

4. Click **Animation** on the Application bar, point to **Keyframe Assistant**, then click **Sequence Layers**.

(continued)

Figure 87 *Preview after changing scale*

Scale

Figure 88 *Sequence Layers dialog box*

Overlap ——
Duration ——
Transition ——

The Sequence Layers dialog box opens, giving you the option to overlap the layers, choose a transition type, and set the length of a transition. If you do not choose to overlap the layers, the other selections become inactive and your layers will be arranged one right after the other with no overlap.

TIP To leave a gap between your layers, click the Overlap check box and enter a negative number in the Duration field.

5. Make the following settings in the Sequence Layers dialog box: Overlap: **check mark**; Duration: **0;00;02;00**; Transition: **Cross Dissolve Front and Back Layers**, then compare your dialog box to Figure 88.

6. Click **OK**.

The Layers are arranged across time based on their selection order, as shown in Figure 89. The motion paths we created with each of the individual layers in the last exercise moved with their Text layer to its new position in time.

7. Click **Composition** on the Application bar, then click **Composition Settings**.

The Composition Settings dialog box opens. The duration is currently 0;00;30;00. We need to adjust the duration of the composition to match that of the Title Sequence composition.

8. Change the Duration setting to **0;00;13;05**.

The Title Sequence Text composition will now match the duration of the Title Sequence composition.

(continued)

Figure 89 *Layers arranged across time*

9. Compare your Timeline panel to Figure 90.

10. Return the CTI to **0;00;00;00**, then select the **Title Sequence composition**.

11. Preview the Title Sequence composition by clicking the **Play/Pause button** ▷ on the Preview panel.

12. Save your project and leave it open for the next exercise.

You arranged Text layers 1 through 6 over time, and modified the duration of the Title Sequence Text composition. You then previewed your changes on the Title Sequence composition panel.

Modify a motion track

1. Open your Title Sequence your name project file, if necessary.

2. Select the **Title Sequence Text composition**, then verify that the CTI is at **0;00;00;00**.

3. Verify that the workspace is set to Minimal, with the Motion Sketch and Preview panels displayed.

4. Move the CTI to **0;00;03;00** so that you can see the motion path that was previously created, then compare your screen to Figure 91.

5. Click the **Selection tool** ▨ on the Tools panel, then click **Late Breaking** on the Composition panel.

Figure 90 *Title Sequence Text composition*

Composition duration shortened

Figure 91 *Motion path for Text layer 2*

Vertex

Segment

Motion path

Time display

Figure 92 *Adjusting a motion path*

Selected vertex

Direction handle

Figure 93 *Adding more vertices*

6. Click a **vertex**, as shown in Figure 92.

   Direction handles appear so that you can adjust the curvature of the arc.

7. Click and hold the **Pen tool** ▣ on the Tools panel, then click the **Add Vertex tool** ▣.

   The Add Vertex tool allows you to add additional points on the path that you have already drawn to create more detail, as shown in Figure 93.

8. Return the CTI to **0;00;00;00**, then select the **Title Sequence composition**.

9. Preview the Title Sequence composition by clicking the **Play/Pause button** ▣ on the Preview panel.

10. Save your project as an MPEG2 file, named **Title Sequence Final your name**.

In this lesson, you modified a motion path, and saved your project as an MPEG 2 movie file.

Explore the After Effects workspace.

1. Click Start on the Application bar, point to All Programs, then click Adobe After Effects CS5. (Win) or open the Finder from the dock and click Applications from the sidebar, click the Adobe applications folder, then click Adobe After Effects CS5 (Mac).
2. Click the Close button in the Welcome dialog box.
3. Click Window on the Application bar, point to Workspace, then click Effects.
4. Click Window on the Application bar, point to Workspace, then click Minimal.
5. Click Window on the Application bar, point to Workspace, then click Standard, to change the workspace back to Standard.

Create a composition & import footage.

1. Click Composition on the Application bar, then click New Composition.
2. Click the Preset list arrow, then click NTSC DV.
3. Change the Duration value to 0;00;07;00 by entering 700. (*Hint*: Pressing [Enter] (Win) or [return] (Mac) after entering 700 will close the Composition Settings dialog box.)
4. Click File on the Application bar, point to Import, then click File.
5. Import us_10.jpg from your Data Files folder. (*Hint*: Be sure that the JPEG Sequence check box is not checked.)
6. Drag us_10.jpg to the Composition panel to add the footage to the Timeline panel.
7. Click File on the Application bar, click Save As, type **Digital Graphic your name**, then click Save.
8. Save the file to your Data Files folder and leave it open.

Create layers and add effects and presets.

1. Click the Choose grid and guide options button on the Composition panel, then click Title/Action Safe.
2. Repeat Step 2 to select Grid, then Rulers.
3. Select the Timeline panel.
4. Click Layer on the Application bar, then click New Shape.
5. Press and hold the Rectangle tool on the Tools panel, click the Rounded Rectangle tool, then draw a rounded rectangle with a fill color of #FA8E1C, and a stroke color of #953C01, and a width of 2 px, in the bottom-left corner of the title safe area on the Composition panel. (*Note*: Draw the rectangle approximately 5 grid squares wide and 3 grid squares tall.)
6. With the rounded rectangle still selected, click Effect on the Application bar, point to Perspective, then click Bevel Edges.
7. On the Effect Controls panel, modify the Edge Thickness to .05.
8. With the rounded rectangle still selected, click Effect on the Application bar, point to Stylize, then click Color Emboss.
9. Click the Choose grid and guide options button, then click Grid to remove the check mark.
10. Click Window on the Application bar, point to Workspace, then click Text.
11. Right-click the Timeline panel, then click New Text.
12. Type: **News 6**, press [Enter] (Win) or [return] (Mac), then type **Nighttime** on the Composition panel.
13. Click the Selection tool on the Tools panel, then select the text on the Composition panel.

14. On the Character panel make the following selections: Font: Verdana; Font style: Bold; Fill color: White; Font size; 12 px; Stroke color: Black; Stroke width: 1 px.
15. Click the All Caps button on the Character panel, then click the Center text button on the Paragraph panel. Change the workspace to Effects.
16. Move the News 6 Nighttime text above the rounded rectangle.
17. On the Effects & Presets panel search for the "drop shadow" effect.
18. With the Text layer still selected, double-click the drop shadow effect to apply the effect. (*Hint*: Remove the search from the search box by clicking the X.)
19. Click Animation on the Application bar, then click Browse Presets.
20. Open the Curves and Spins folder inside the Text folder and select Newton.ffx.
21. Click the Play/Pause button on the Preview panel to preview the effect in the Composition panel.
22. Right-click on Netwon.ffx, point to Place, then click In After Effects.
23. Save your project and leave it open.

Make a movie.

1. Select the Digital Graphic composition, click Composition on the Application bar, then click Add to Render Queue.
2. Click Lossless with Alpha, next to Output Module on the Render Queue panel.
3. Click the Format list arrow, then click MPEG2.

4. Click the text to the right of the Output To heading on the Render Queue panel, name your movie **Digital Graphic Final your name**, then save it in your Chapter 2 Data Files folder.

5. Click the Render button on the Render Queue panel to render the movie.

6. Open Digital Graphic Final your name.mpeg, to see your movie, as shown in Figure 94.

7. Close your project.

Figure 94 *Completed Skills Review Part 1*

Import Photoshop text.

1. Open Nighttime.aep, then save it as **Nighttime your name** in your Chapter 2 Data Files folder.
2. Change the workspace to Text.
3. Import the Nighttime Logo.psd footage to the Project panel. (*Hint*: Leave the default settings on the Import File dialog box, Import As: Footage; and leave the Photoshop Sequence check box deselected.)
4. In the Nighttime Logo.psd dialog box make the following selection: Import Kind: Composition.
5. Double-click Nighttime Logo on the Project panel to open the composition in its own Timeline and Composition panels.
6. Shift-click to select all the Photoshop layers, right-click, then select Convert to Editable Text.
7. Save your project and leave it open for the next step.

Format text.

1. With the Selection tool, select Nighttime on the Composition panel.
2. On the Character panel, double-click the Stroke button to bring it forward and activate it.
3. Click White (#FFFFFF) in the Text Color dialog box, then click OK.
4. Change the Stroke width to 0.5 px.

5. Make the same changes to the stroke on "6" and on "News".
6. Select Nighttime, 6, and News by using the [Shift]-click method, click the Character panel options button, then click Small Caps.
7. With all the text layers still selected, change the Font size to 13 px.
8. Save your project and leave it open for the next step.

Trim layers

1. With the Nighttime Logo composition, still active, Shift-click to select all the text layers.
2. Click the Current time display, type **300**, then press [Enter] (Win) or [return] (Mac).
3. Click the Selection tool, click Text Layer #1 on the Timeline panel, press and hold [Shift], then click Text Layer #3.
4. Press [Alt][]] to trim the layers to the location of the CTI at 3 seconds.
5. Save your project and leave it open for the next step.

Create a motion path.

1. Verify that the Nighttime Logo composition is still active, and that the CTI is at 0;00;00;00.
2. Drag Skyline.jpg to the Timeline panel so it is layer #4. (*Note*: We will be using this footage while we draw

our motion path to help us with placement; we will delete it from Nighttime Logo composition when we are finished.)
3. Change the workspace to Minimal.
4. Select Window on the Application bar, then click Motion Sketch.
5. Select Window on the Application bar, click Preview, then drag the Preview panel below the Motion Sketch panel.
6. Turn on Title/Action Safe margins.
7. Click Nighttime on the Composition panel.
8. On the Motion Sketch panel enter the following: Capture speed at: 50%; Smoothing: 20; Background check box: Check.
9. On the Motion Sketch panel, click the Start Capture button, click Nighttime on the Composition panel, then drag the text around the panel in an arc from the bottom-left corner around to the right so the text settles in the upper-left corner just inside the Title Safe margin. (*Hint*: Create the appearance of the text rising from behind the buildings.)
10. Repeat this procedure, keeping the same settings on the Motion Sketch panel for Layers 2 and 3.
11. Preview the Nighttime Logo composition by clicking the Play/Pause button on the Preview panel.
12. Save your project and leave it open for the next step.

Modify a motion track.

1. Verify that the Nighttime Logo composition is still active.
2. Move your CTI to 3 seconds so you can see the motion path that was created in the last step, and the text layers.
3. Click Nighttime on the Composition panel with the Selection tool.
4. Click a vertex, then make adjustments to the curves as you think appropriate.
5. If needed, use the Add/Delete Vertex tool to make additional adjustments to the Nighttime layer.
6. Repeat this process to Layer 2 and 3 as needed.
7. Select Layer 4 then press [Delete].
8. Preview the Nighttime Logo composition by clicking the Play/Pause button on the Preview panel.

Animate text.

1. Verify that the Nighttime Logo composition is still active, then change the workspace to Effects.
2. Select all three text layers and be sure the CTI is at 0;00;00;00.
3. Click the Effects & Presets options button, then click Browse Presets.
4. Double-click the Text folder, double-click the Organic folder, right-click Insects.ffx, then click Place In After Effects.

5. Click the Play/Pause button on the Preview panel to play the composition, return the CTI to 0;00;00;00 when you have finished previewing.
6. Save your project and leave it open for the next step.

Arrange layers over time.

1. Select Nighttime from the Composition Navigator, if necessary, then verify that the CTI is at 0;00;00;00.
2. On the Timeline panel click Text layer #1, press and hold [Shift], then click Text layer #3.
3. Click Animation on the Application bar, point to Keyframe Assistant, then click Sequence Layers.
4. Choose the following settings: Overlap: check mark; Duration: 0;00;01;00; Transition: Off.
5. Click OK.
6. Click Composition on the Application bar, then click Composition Settings.
7. Change the Duration to 0;00;07;00.
8. Select Title Sequence on the Composition Navigator.
9. Drag the Nighttime composition to the Timeline panel to the #1 position in the stacking order.
10. Drag the Nighttime composition to the Timeline panel again, to the #2 position in the stacking order.
11. [Shift]-click Layer #1, then click Layer #2.
12. Click Animation on the Application bar, point to Keyframe Assistant, then click Sequence Layer.

13. Click OK in the Sequence Layers dialog box. (Note: We do not want the layers to overlap so we are not making any selections.)
14. Save your project and leave it open for the next step.

Export production logo for the web.

1. Select Title Sequence on the Composition Navigator.
2. Click Composition on the Application bar, then click Add to Render Queue.
3. Click on Lossless with Alpha, next to Output Module on the Render Queue panel.
4. In the Output Module Settings dialog box make the following selections: Format: FLV; Resize: check mark; Custom: Web Video, 320 x 240; Audio Output: check mark.
5. Click the text to the right of the Output To heading on the Render Queue panel.
6. Name the movie **Nighttime Final your name**, save it in your Chapter 2 Data Files folder, then click Save.
7. Click the Render button on the Render Queue panel.
8. Open Nighttime Final your name.flv, to see your movie, as shown in Figure 95.
9. Close your project.

Figure 95 *Completed Skills Review Part 2*

You and a coworker just completed attending training in After Effects. Your boss has asked that you collaborate on a small demo movie showing off some of the text animation presets that are available. So far your movie has a composition and text layers named after an animation preset. You are expected to complete the project for the staff meeting.

1. Open Demo.aep, then save it as **Animation Preset Demo your name**.

2. Format the text on each text layer using the Character panel and layer styles.

3. Browse the animation presets to find the animation preset named for each text layer.

4. Apply the appropriate animation preset to the appropriate text layer. (*Hint*: Be sure the CTI is at 0;00;00;00 when you apply the preset.)

5. Trim the duration of the layers based on the length of the effect. (*Hint*: Press UU to see keyframes and help you decide where to place the Out point.)

6. Adjust the sequence of the layers so that the text does not all play at the same time, as shown in Figure 96. (*Hint*: Use the Sequence Layers command that can be found under Keyframe Assistant.)

7. Add the Demo Composition to the Render Queue and export the movie as an MPEG2 named **Animation Preset Demo Final your name**.

Figure 96 *Completed Project Builder 1*

The elementary school principal in your district has heard about your video production class. They are planning a video to be presented at their annual awards ceremony in the spring and would like you to design a creative opening title sequence for the video that would be appropriate for elementary age students. She thinks that using many colorful shapes with vibrant music would be fantastic. She would like the video to last 25 seconds and include the name of the school and some slogans.

1. Create an After Effects project titled **Elementary Title Sequence**, with a composition with the default preset NTSC DV, and duration of 30 seconds. (*Note*: Select a background color of your choice.)
2. Create a minimum of five shape layers with your choice of shapes and colors and apply layer styles.
3. Create a text layer for the name of the school with your choice of formatting and layer styles. The name of the school is **Holmes Elementary School**.
4. Create a text layer for each of the following slogans with your choice of formatting and layer styles, as shown in Figure 97:
   - Believe & Succeed
   - Catch the Spirit
   - Knowledge is Power

5. Apply animation effects with motion paths and animation presets.
6. Adjust the duration of the various layers and sequence the layers to vary the timing of the layers.
7. Export the movie to the MPEG2 video format with the name **Elementary Title Sequence Final your name**.

Figure 97 *Completed Project Builder 2*

Your video production teacher has asked you to create an animated production logo for your own video production company. He would like you to place this logo at the end of all the video projects you create while working through this book.

1. Come up with a creative title for your production company.
2. Create a composition with the NTSC DV Preset and Duration of 15 seconds, and the background color of your choice.
3. Obtain at least one good quality still image or video that works well with the theme of your production company.
4. Include a background audio clip. You may download one from the Internet, or look in the Audio folder that can be found with the resource files provided with this book. (*Note*: Be sure to check the terms of use regarding any media you may download to use with your project.)
5. Import your footage and create layers with the footage.
6. Create a text layer with the name of your production company, as shown in Figure 98.
7. Format your text, apply layer styles, and animate your text.
8. Add a shape layer to place behind the text, and add effects to the shape of your choice to enhance its look.
9. Your animated production logo should be exported so it is available for both MPEG2 and FLV formats; name your file after the name of your production company.

Figure 98 *Portfolio Project*

CHAPTER 3

EDITING A MUSICAL SCORE IN
ADOBE SOUNDBOOTH CS5

1. Explore the Soundbooth workspace
2. Work with sound effects
3. Work with scores

CHAPTER 3
EDITING A MUSICAL SCORE IN ADOBE SOUNDBOOTH CS5

Adobe Soundbooth CS5 is an entry-level audio editing application designed to be easy to learn for those who are not sound professionals. Soundbooth is compatible with most stand-alone audio files such as MP3, WAV, and WMA as well as video/audio files such as AVI, MPEG2, and FLV.

Soundbooth allows you to edit audio, create voiceovers, and produce royalty-free musical scores from a music library that you can customize.

In this chapter, we will explore the Soundbooth workspace, import and play audio files, work with scores, and save them as the Soundbooth ASND format. The ASND file format provides maximum flexibility in editing and sharing files with Premiere Pro and After Effects.

TOOLS YOU'LL USE

Explore the
SOUNDBOOTH WORKSPACE

What You'll Do

In this lesson, you will start Soundbooth, create a new project, and explore the workspace.

Exploring the Soundbooth Workspace

Adobe Soundbooth, like Premiere Pro and After Effects, includes a number of preformatted, customizable workspaces that optimize the arrangement of panels for particular tasks. When you select one of the preformatted workspaces, the current workspace is adjusted accordingly. Figure 1 shows the default workspace for Soundbooth, which is called Default.

Soundbooth has the following preformatted workspaces available:

Default—The Default workspace is designed to optimize audio editing by providing a large view of the Editor panel.

Edit Audio to Video—The Video and Markers panels are adjusted above the Editor panel so that you can synchronize audio and video.

Edit Score to Video—The panels are arranged to facilitate working with a musical score to synchronize the music to the video.

Find Sound Effects and Scores—The Resource Central panel is activated so that you can search for royalty-free sound effects and scores that are available for download. Some are fee based and are indicated by a $ sign.

Meta Logging—The Metadata panel is expanded to help you quickly edit properties for files, clips, and speech transcripts.

The workspace can be changed by selecting a default workspace or by rearranging the panels to your individual preference. Default workspaces can be changed using the Workspace command on the Window menu or by making a selection from the drop-down menu on the Tools panel.

Panels can be moved by clicking and dragging **panel tabs**. As you drag the panel, an area becomes highlighted; this is called the **drop zone**, and provides a visual reference to where the panel can be placed.

If you wish to save your customized workspace, you may do so by selecting New Workspace on the Workspace menu or from the drop-down menu on the Tools panel.

Understanding Sound

Soundbooth is designed for the non-musical professional to edit and create musical scores. However, an understanding of some fundamental digital audio concepts will help you as you work with Soundbooth.

Sound is created by a vibration in the air created by an object that causes the air

Figure 1 *Default workspace*

Tools panel

Files panel

Tasks panel

History panel

Workspace drop-down menu

Editor panel

pressure to change. This vibration eventually reaches the eardrum causing it to vibrate, which is then interpreted as sound. The object could be vocal cords, guitar strings, drums—anything that we interpret as making sound.

Sound is represented in a **waveform**, the waves being created by the air pressure, much like the way the wind creates waves in the water. The line at its high point, caused by higher pressure, is called the **crest**. Lower pressure is represented at its lowest point

and is called the **trough**. When there is no air pressure, the sound wave is at zero, indicated by the red zero line, as shown in Figure 2. Several properties describe sound waveforms that you will be working with in

Figure 2 *A sample waveform on the Editor panel*

Crest

Zero line

Trough

Cycle

Soundbooth. Refer to Figure 3 as you read the definitions that follow. **Amplitude** is the change in pressure from crest to trough; high-amplitude waveforms are loud and low-amplitude waveforms are quiet. The number of cycles per second measured in hertz is called **frequency**. The position of the waveform in the cycle is measured in 360°, and is called the **phase**. The start point is 0° phase, the crest is 90° phase, the halfway point is 180° phase, 270° phase is the trough, and the end point is 360° phase. A **wavelength** is the distance measured between any two points, at the same degree on the phase in inches or centimeters. Waveforms, and their properties, can be seen and edited on the Editor panel in Soundbooth in the waveform display. The waveform is displayed on the Editor panel when you open an audio file in Soundbooth or when you double-click an audio clip on the Files panel.

The waveform will be either displayed with one or two channels. If you see two channels displayed one above the other,

Figure 3 *Waveform measurements*

the audio file was recorded in **stereo** to give the sense of spatial placement of sound from two sound sources. If you only see one channel, the audio file is called a monophonic signal or **mono**, and contains only one sound source.

Cleaning Up Audio

Audio frequency components are shown in the spectral frequency display, or **spectral display**, as shown in Figure 4. The x-axis measures time and the y-axis measures frequency. The display can be activated by clicking the Spectral Frequency Display button on the Tools panel; it appears below the waveform display on the Editor panel. The colors in the spectral display represent amplitude from bright yellow to dark blue. Bright yellow represents high amplitude,

Figure 4 *Spectral frequency display*

Editor panel

Waveform display

Spectral frequency display

and is located near the bottom of the display; dark blue represents low amplitude and is located near the top of the display. The spectral display is used for removing unwanted noise, such as clicks, hums, coughs, and other artifacts, known as **frequency-space editing**.

You can use the spectral display to identify and select noise. Bright vertical bars that extend from the top to the bottom are usually clicks and crackles. Light red clouds that extend across the top of the display are usually hissing noises, as shown in Figure 5.

The Noise command on the Processes menu can be used to remove noises like hisses and hums that remain constant in the background. Select a noise with the Rectangular Marquee tool in the spectral display to generate a sample for Soundbooth.

Figure 5 *Identifying noises in the spectral frequency display*

Hissing noises

Clicks and Crackles

Working with Preferences

You can use a wide range of audio input devices, such as microphones and tape decks, and output devices such as headphones and speakers. If you are having trouble with any devices, check in the Audio Hardware section of the Preferences dialog box and refer to Adobe Help for more information for your particular device.

To increase performance, Soundbooth creates cache files for each audio and video file it opens. In the Media section of the Preferences dialog box, you can modify the location of the folder that is created to hold the cache files, clean the media cache database to get better performance, and delete cache files to save disk space, as shown in Figure 6. If you would like to change the location of where these files are being saved, click Browse in the Media Cache Files section of the dialog box, then choose a new location.

The **Media Cache Database** is a file that records the locations of all related media and cache files. To remove references to files that are no longer in use, click the Clean button. To change the location where this file is saved, click Browse.

When an audio file is imported into an Adobe application, in most cases it is converted or conformed to match the sample rate of your project. Conforming the audio file results in two files being created—a PEK (.pek) and a CFA (.cfa) file—that are managed by the Media Cache Database. These are Adobe proprietary file extensions.

The **Delete Temporary .pek Files** button will remove PEK files that are generated to display audio waveforms. This reference file contains the necessary information for the associated Waveform display.

The **Delete Temporary .cfa Files** button will remove large conformed files that are created when audio files are opened that use a compressed format or an unsupported sample rate.

The PEK and CFA files work hand in hand and if deleted, will automatically regenerate when they are needed for that specific Soundbooth Multitrack File.

Adobe video applications have the option to insert a unique document ID automatically into each imported file. These IDs ensure that each application uses the same cached previews and conformed audio files, therefore preventing unnecessary rendering and conforming. The **Metadata section** in the Preferences dialog box is where you find this option. Check the Write XMP IDs to Files on Import check box in the Metadata section to activate this feature.

The selection you make is identified by color. Then, choose Capture Noise Print on the Processes menu to create a **noise print**, or sample. You can then clean up the audio using the noise print by selecting the Reduce Noise command on the Processes menu. This will open the Noise dialog box. The **Reduction** setting in the Noise dialog box sets the amplitude of the **noise floor**. The noise floor is the level of amplitude representing the near-constant background noise that you have identified and are trying to remove. Lower values should be used on audio with loud and quiet passages, higher values can be used on those clips that have a narrow range. Audio that falls below the noise floor will be dropped, or not heard. This can be adjusted with the **Reduce By** setting. You can preview the settings you choose in the Noise dialog box before processing the file.

Also on the Processes menu are Remove Clicks & Pops and the Remove Rumble commands. You do not need to capture a sample before using these two menu commands. The Remove Clicks & Pops command removes audio artifacts, subtle clips, and loud pops. The Remove Rumble command removes microphone handling sounds and traffic noises.

Figure 6 *Media section of the Preferences dialog box*

Media section

Media Cache Files

Media Cache Database

Delete Temporary .pek Files

Delete Temporary .cfa Files

Editing a Musical Score in Adobe Soundbooth CS5

Figure 7 *Edit Audio to Video workspace*

Video panel

Editor panel

Edit Audio to Video workspace

Start Adobe Soundbooth CS5 and explore the workspace

1. Click **Start** on the Application bar, point to **All Programs**, then click **Adobe Soundbooth CS5** (Win) or open the Finder from the dock, click **Applications** from the sidebar, click the **Adobe applications folder**, then click **Adobe Soundbooth CS5** (Mac).

   You may need to look in a subfolder if you have installed the Video Collection or Master Collection.

   TIP Pressing and holding [Shift][Ctrl] (Win) or [Shift] ⌘ (Mac) while starting Soundbooth restores default preference settings.

2. Click **Window** on the Application bar, point to **Workspace**, then click **Edit Audio to Video**.

   As shown in Figure 7, the workspace changes to the Edit Audio to Video workspace. The Video panel becomes active at the top of the workspace and the Editor panel relocates to the bottom of the workspace.

3. Continue to click through the various workspaces and notice how the window changes each time.

4. Return the workspace to the Default workspace.

   TIP After selecting Default, you may want to click Reset "Default" on the Workspace menu to ensure that the workspace has been reset properly.

5. Leave Adobe Soundbooth open for the next exercise.

You started Soundbooth CS5 and explored the workspace.

Remove background noise

1. Open Soundbooth, if necessary, then verify that the workspace is set to Default.
2. Click **File** on the Application bar, point to **Import**, then click **Files**.

   The Import Files dialog box opens.
3. Navigate to the drive and folder where you store your Data Files, click **PopeyetheSailorMan**, then click **Open**.

   The PopeyetheSailorMan audio file is imported into the Files panel, as shown in Figure 8.
4. Double-click **PopeyetheSailorMan** on the Files panel.

   The audio file is opened on the Editor panel, and is seen on two tracks because it is a stereo file.
5. Click the **Spectral Frequency Display button** on the Tools panel to activate the spectral display on the Editor panel, as shown in Figure 9.
6. Click the **Play button** on the Editor panel to hear the audio file.

   The audio file starts with a crackling noise at the beginning; we will select that portion of the audio and use the Capture Noise Print and Noise processes to remove the artifact.
7. Click the **Rectangular Marquee tool** on the Tools panel, then select a small portion of the area of the spectral frequency display where you heard the crackling noise, as shown in Figure 10.

   We are creating a sample of the noise to create a noise print. This will help us to better remove the crackling noise from the larger area in the next step.

   (continued)

Figure 8 *Imported audio file on Files panel*

Files panel

Audio file

Figure 9 *Spectral frequency display*

Waveform display

Spectral frequency display

Two identical channels

Two identical channels

Editing a Musical Score in Adobe Soundbooth CS5

Figure 10 *Capturing a noise sample*

Selection

Figure 11 *Applying the Noise process*

Noise dialog box

Reduction slider

Preview button

Reduce By slider

8. Click the **Tasks panel tab**, click **Clean Up Audio**, then click the **Capture Noise Print button** on the panel.

9. Using the Rectangular Marquee tool [image], select the entire area where you heard the crackling noise at the beginning of the audio clip.

10. On the Tasks panel, click the **Noise button**.

    The Noise dialog box opens. Notice that the Use Captured Noise Print check box is checked.

11. Drag the **Reduce By slider** towards the Light side of the scale to **25.2%**, click the **Preview button**, then compare your screen to Figure 11.

TIP Clicking the green power button in the Noise dialog box allows you to preview the original audio file for comparison.

12. Drag the **Reduction slider** towards the Aggressive side of the scale to **90%**, then click the **Preview button**.

    Your settings may vary, based on your captured noise print.

TIP Leave the Preview button selected as you adjust the sliders in the Noise dialog box; the audio will continue to play as you make adjustments.

13. Click **OK** when you are satisfied with your results.

14. Click **File** on the Application bar, click **Save As**, navigate to the drive and folder where you store your Data Files, name the file **PopeyeRestored**, click **Save**, then click **Save** in the MP3 Compression Options dialog box.

15. Click the **Spectral Frequency Display button** [image] on the Tools panel to deactivate the spectral frequency display on the Editor panel.

You imported an audio file and removed a background artifact noise.

Work with SOUND EFFECTS

What You'll Do

Working with Multitrack Files

A **multitrack file** is a Soundbooth document that allows you to mix audio files and scores together to create soundtracks for videos that you can then import into Premiere Pro or After Effects. The file extension for a Soundbooth document is .asnd.

Soundbooth has the ability to import a video file to use as a reference while mixing a soundtrack. Only one video track can be created in a multitrack file, and it appears at the top of the Editor panel. The Video panel becomes active when you create this track for previewing the video clip with the audio as you work. You can create a track by dragging a video clip to an audio track from the Files panel, or by clicking the Tracks list arrow on the Editor panel and selecting Add Video Track.

Multitracks appear on the Editor panel, and you can quickly switch between audio clips by selecting the drop-down menu on the Editor panel, as shown in Figure 12. Tracks are named Audio 1, Audio 2, and Audio 3 and so on, by default. Tracks can be renamed by clicking the current name and typing a new name. If you have several

audio tracks, it is helpful to assign them descriptive names so that you can easily keep track of where your sound effects or audio clips are located.

Audio clips on the Files panel can be placed on an audio track by dragging them to the Editor panel. If you drag to the empty area below an existing track, a new

Figure 12 *Editor panel*

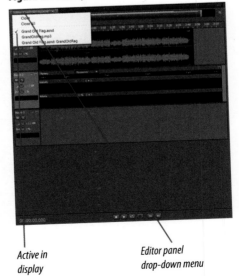

Active in display

Editor panel drop-down menu

Editing a Musical Score in Adobe Soundbooth CS5

track will be created. To insert a clip at a specific time, place the CTI where you would like the audio clip to be inserted, point to Insert on the Edit menu, then click File. The clip will be placed at the location of the CTI. The file will also be placed on the Files panel if it is not already there. Files that are part of the multitrack are placed under the multitrack file on the Files panel, as shown in Figure 13.

Adjusting the length or duration of an audio clip is as simple as clicking and dragging, as shown in Figure 14. When you place the pointer at the edge of a clip the cursor changes into a red "E"; if you are on the right side of the clip the "E" is backwards. Click and drag the "E" icon to adjust the length of the clip.

Saving a Multitrack File

While you are working on a soundtrack by performing edits and syncing it to video, you should keep it in the Soundbooth **ASND** file format. The ASND format allows you to add effects, adjust fades, and store history snapshots. History snapshots allow you to restore previous edits. You can also import ASND files directly into Premiere Pro and After Effects and access them from those applications for editing.

When you are done editing your file and ready to save it for playback or for use in other devices you need to do what is called a **mix down**. This process combines all of your audio tracks and outputs them together. This is accomplished using the Export Multitrack Mixdown command. You will then need to decide which audio file format is your best option.

The **MP3** file format is one of the most widely used file formats for portable media players and Web-based audio. MP3 has a highly compressed file size to make downloads faster, but also results in poorer quality. Use the MP3 file format when saving for the Web or portable media players.

Windows Waveform or WAV is the standard, uncompressed audio format for the Windows operating system. Audio Interchange File Format or AIF is the standard, uncompressed audio file format

Figure 13 *Multitrack file*

Multitrack file

Source files

Video track

Video panel

Figure 14 *Trimming a clip*

Red E icon

for the Mac OS. These file formats should be used when you plan to share your files with other applications or for burning to discs.

You have the option to save the entire file or a selected range. You also have the option to add the saved file to the Files panel. The WAV file format provides additional options regarding compression that the AIF file format does not.

Exploring Resource Central

The Resource Central panel, or simply Resource Central, in Soundbooth provides instant access to product related news, tutorials, sound effects, and scores, as shown in Figure 15. Internet access is required to use Resource Central. The sound effects and scores that you download using Resource Central are all royalty-free. You have the ability to preview audio clips before you choose to download them.

The News tab on the Resource Central panel provides links to information about Adobe digital video applications and Soundbooth specifically. A Soundbooth CS5 Feature Tour is available, along with a Production Premium Feature Tour to explain the highlights of all the digital video applications. Descriptions are provided with each link. The number of results found and pages available are identified to help guide you through the results, as shown in Figure 16. A Refresh button is available at the upper-right corner of the panel; when clicked, it lists all new topics first.

The Sound Effects tab has a library of categories that can be viewed via a drop-down menu. Categories range from Ambience and Animals, to Cartoons and

Figure 15 *Resource Central panel*

Resource
Central
panel

Sound Effects
tab selected

Figure 16 *News tab*

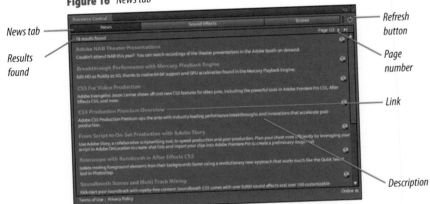

News tab

Results
found

Refresh
button

Page
number

Link

Description

Editing a Musical Score in Adobe Soundbooth CS5

Crashes, to Science Fiction and Sports. There are nearly 10,000 sound effects available for download. You also have the ability to search for a sound effect in the search box. Type a keyword in the search box then press [Enter] (Win) or [return] (Mac) to activate the search. To clear the search contents, click the X on the far right of the search box.

The Scores tab provides genres of music including Jazz, Rock and Pop, Blues and Country, and Urban. Additionally, categories such as Ambient, World, and Environment are included to comprise the 80-plus royalty-free scores available to download and customize, as shown in Figure 17.

Downloading from Resource Central

Soundbooth shows a status bar when you download files from Resource Central. In addition, to help keep track of the resources you have downloaded, a check mark is added to the right of the filename and the icons to the left of the filename change in appearance. The Music Notes icon becomes active and the Download button becomes inactive, as shown in Figure 18.

During installation, Soundbooth creates a folder titled Soundbooth-3.0 (en-US) with folders to save your downloads from the Sound Effects and Scores panels. There is also a folder created for media cache files, as shown in Figure 19.

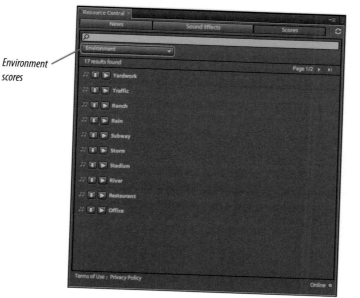

Figure 17 *Scores tab*

Environment scores

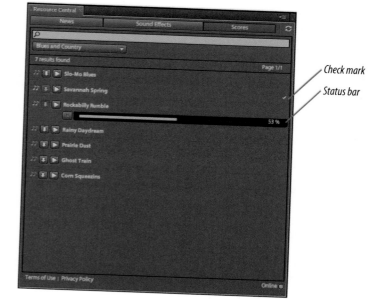

Figure 18 *Downloading a score*

Check mark

Status bar

Sound effect files are saved as WAV files; they need to be imported into the Files panel when you want to use them. Scores are downloaded as Zip files, as shown in Figure 20, and need to be imported in the Score library on the Scores panel before they can be used. This is done by clicking the Import Scores to Score Library button on the Scores panel and navigating to the Scores folder. Once you have installed your scores, the Zip file is no longer needed and can be deleted. Once scores are installed in the Score library, they cannot be removed.

Figure 19 *Soundbooth-3.0 (en-US) folder*

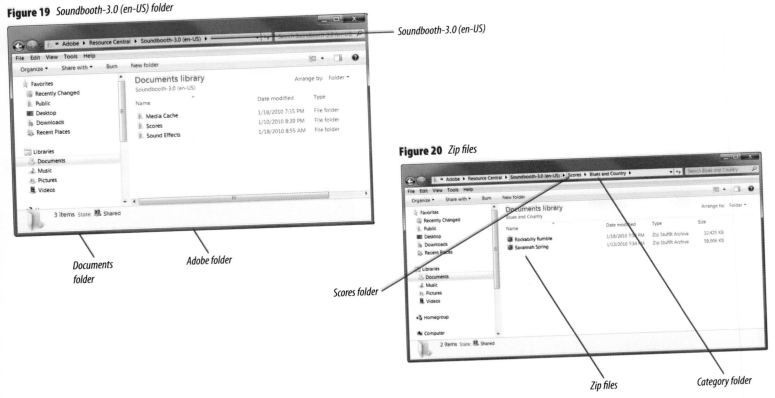

Soundbooth-3.0 (en-US)

Documents folder

Adobe folder

Figure 20 *Zip files*

Scores folder

Zip files

Category folder

Editing a Musical Score in Adobe Soundbooth CS5

Figure 21 *Adobe Soundbooth CS5 What's New download*

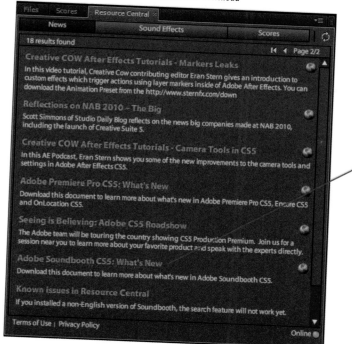

Adobe
Soundbooth CS5:
What's New

Explore the News tab

1. Open Soundbooth, if necessary.

2. Click the **Workspace list arrow** on the Tools panel, then click **Find Sound Effects and Scores**.

   The Resource Central panel appears in the workspace.

3. Click the **News tab** on the Resource Central panel, locate, then click **Adobe Soundbooth CS5 What's New?**, as shown in Figure 21.

   Your Web browser opens and takes you to Adobe TV Web site to preview a video about new features in Adobe Soundbooth CS5.

4. Preview the video, then close your Web browser when you are done to return to Soundbooth.

5. Click the Refresh button ⊚ to refresh the News panel.

6. Continue to browse the News panel and view any additional stories that interest you.

7. Leave Soundbooth open for the next exercise.

You explored the News tab on the Resource Central panel and viewed a resource online.

Find and download sound effects

1. Open Soundbooth, if necessary, then verify that the Find Sound Effects and Scores workspace is active.

2. Click the **Sound Effects tab** on the Resource Central panel, type **volcano** in the Search box as shown in Figure 22, then press [**Enter**] (Win) or [**return**] (Mac).

3. Click the **Play button** ▶ next to Explosion Volcano 02 to preview the audio clip.

   The Play button and Pause button icons toggle between the play and pause functions.

4. Click the **Play button** ▶ next to **Explosion Volcano 01** to preview the audio clip.

5. Click the **Download button** ⬇ next to **Explosion Volcano 02** to download the sound effect, then repeat this process for **Explosion Volcano 01**.

   You will see a status bar showing the progress of the download and a check mark on the panel to confirm that it has been downloaded, as shown in Figure 23.

6. Click ⬛ on the Search box to remove the search parameters.

7. Leave Soundbooth open for the next exercise.

You searched for sound effects and downloaded sound effects from Resource Central.

Figure 22 *Searching for sound effects*

Search box

Figure 23 *Downloading a sound effect*

Check mark

Status bar

Editing a Musical Score in Adobe Soundbooth CS5

Figure 24 *Import Files dialog box*

Resource Central folder

Sound Effects folder

Figure 25 *Sound effects on the Files panel*

Files panel

Import file

Audio files

Create a multitrack file

1. Open Soundbooth, if necessary.
2. Reset the workspace to **Default**.
3. Click **File** on the Application bar, point to **Import**, then click **Files**.
4. Click the **Libraries folder**, double-click the **Documents folder**, double-click the **Adobe folder**, then double-click the **Resource Central folder** (Win) or click **Macintosh HD** from the sidebar, click the **Users folder**, click the **Shared folder**, click the **Adobe folder**, then click the **Resource Central folder** (Mac).
5. Double-click the **Soundbooth-3.0 (en-US) folder**, then double-click the **Sound Effects folder** (Win) or click the **Soundbooth-3.0 (en-US) folder**, then click the **Sound Effects folder** (Mac).

   The Adobe folder normally resides in the Documents folder for those using Windows, as shown in Figure 24.
6. Press and hold [**Shift**], click **Explosion Volcano 01**, click **Explosion Volcano 02**, then click **Open**.

   Explosion Volcano 01 and Explosion Volcano 02 appear on the Files panel, as shown in Figure 25.
7. Click the **Import file button** 🖼 on the Files panel, navigate to the drive and folder where you store your Data Files, click **Volcano.flv**, then click **Open**.

(continued)

The Volcano.flv movie clip is added to the Files panel. This will allow you to view the movie clip at the same time you are adjusting the sound effects so that you are able to place them more accurately.

8. Click **File** on the Application bar, point to **New**, then click **Multitrack File**.

   A new Untitled Multitrack 1 file is created on the Files panel and on the Editor panel.

9. Right-click the **Untitled Multitrack 1 file** on the Files panel, as shown in Figure 26, click **Save "Untitled Multitrack 1" As** on the pop-up menu, navigate to the drive and folder where you store your Data Files, name it **Volcano your name**, then click **Save**.

   The file is saved as an Adobe Sound Document.

10. Leave Soundbooth open for the next exercise.

You imported files, created a multitrack file, and saved a Soundbooth ASND document.

Create a video and an audio track

1. Open Volcano your name, if necessary, then verify that the Default workspace is active.

   The Volcano your name multitrack file should be open on the Editor panel.

2. Click and drag **Volcano.flv** from the Files panel to the beginning of the Audio 1 track on the Editor panel.

   The audio track is automatically converted to a video track. The video preview has become active on the Video panel, as shown in Figure 27.

3. Drag **Volcano.flv** to **00:00:00.000**, if necessary.

   (continued)

Figure 26 *Saving a multitrack file*

Untitled Multitrack 1

Menu

Untitled Multitrack 1

Figure 27 *Creating a video track*

Parts of multitrack

Video track

Video panel

Figure 28 *Adding clips to a multitrack*

Parts of multitrack

Name a track

Video track

Audio track

Figure 29 *Naming a track*

Named track

4. Click and drag **Explosion Volcano 01.wav** from the Files panel to the Audio 1 track on the Editor panel, as shown in Figure 28.

The Audio 1 track moves below the newly created video track.

5. Adjust the audio clip as needed so that it is also at **00:00:00.000**.

6. Click **Audio 1** in the upper-left corner of the track controls in the Audio 1 track, then type **Explosion 1**, as shown in Figure 29.

Renaming a track allows you to identify its content easier.

7. Click the **Play button** on the Editor panel to preview the sound effect with the movie clip.

TIP Press [Home] (Win) or [FN] + left arrow (Mac) to return the CTI to 00:00:00.000.

8. Select **File** on the Application bar, then click **Save** to save the Volcano your name multitrack file.

9. Leave Soundbooth open for the next exercise.

You created a new video track, then placed an audio file on an audio track and renamed it. Finally, you previewed the Soundbooth document.

Adjust the length of an audio clip

1. Open Volcano your name, if necessary, then verify that the workspace is set to Default.

The Volcano your name multitrack file should be open on the Editor panel, and the CTI should be at 00:00:00.000.

2. Drag **Explosion Volcano 01** from the Files panel to the Audio 2 track on the Editor panel.

(continued)

3. Adjust the placement of the audio clip so that it begins to play after the first explosion ends, as shown in Figure 30.

4. Rename the Audio 2 layer **Explosion 2**.

The Explosion 2 audio track is much too long; we will need to trim its length to match that of the video clip track.

5. Hover the mouse pointer over the right edge of the audio clip on the Explosion 2 track, then drag the clip to the left until the right edge lines up with the video clip on the video track, as shown in Figure 31.

The mouse pointer should resemble a backwards red E as you drag.

6. Save your file and leave Soundbooth open for the next exercise.

You added an additional audio track and trimmed the length of the audio clip.

Export an MP3 file

1. Open Volcano your name, if necessary, then verify that the workspace is set to Default.

The Volcano your name multitrack file should be open on the Editor panel, and the CTI should be at 00:00:00.000.

2. Click **File** on the Application bar, point to **Export**, then click **Multitrack Mixdown**.

The Export Multitrack Mixdown dialog box opens.

3. Navigate to the drive and folder where you store your Data Files, then name the file **Volcano Sound Effects your name**.

(continued)

Figure 30 *Placing Explosion Volcano 02 audio clip*

End of sound on
Explosion 1

Figure 31 *Trimming the Explosion Volcano 02 audio clip*

"E" pointer

Figure 32 *MP3 Compression Options dialog box*

Figure 33 *Volcano Sound Effects MP3*

4. Click the **Save as type list arrow** (Win) or **Format drop-down arrow** (Mac), click **MP3 (*.mp3)**, then click **Save**.

    The MP3 Compression Options dialog box opens.

5. Accept the default options as shown in Figure 32.

    The video does not export; it was only used as a reference for editing.

6. Click **Save**.

    The newly generated MP3 file opens on the Editor panel, as shown in Figure 33.

7. Click **File** on the Application bar, then click **Close All** to close all the files that are open on the Files and Editor panels.

8. Leave Soundbooth open for the next exercise.

You saved the volcano sound effects file as an MP3 file.

Work with SCORES

In this lesson, you will work with scores and create a soundtrack.

Working with the Scores Panel

The Scores panel maintains a library of installed score templates, commonly referred to as **scores**, that are downloaded from Resource Central. Score template files (SBST) determine the parts and parameters that make up a score. The parts and parameters are what Soundbooth makes very easy to customize to create soundtracks for video projects.

The Scores panel has a Genre drop-down menu that lists the genres of music that have been imported. The Scores panel is also referred to as the Score library since it houses the catalog of scores. You have the option to show all the scores available, or to sort the various genres, as shown in Figure 34. (Your menu may vary from that shown in the figure.)

To import a score into the Score library, click the Import Scores to Score Library button on the Scores panel. You will need to navigate to the Scores folder, which is inside the Resource Central folder, as shown in Figure 35. Scores are downloaded as Zip files and need to be extracted. Once they are extracted into the Score library, the Zip file is no longer needed and can be deleted. If the genre of the score is new to the library, it will be added to the drop-down menu automatically.

To place a score in a multitrack file you can either drag it from the Scores panel to the Editor panel, or click the Add Score to Multitrack button on the Scores panel. The score will be placed at the location of the CTI. If you want to replace

Figure 34 *Scores panel*

Genre drop-down menu

More Scores at Resource Central link

Import Scores to Score Library button

Start Score Preview button

Add Score to Multitrack button

Replace Score in Multitrack button

Name	BPM	Time Signa...
✓ All		
My	125	4/4
Ou	Ambient	120	4/4
Ro	Country	110	4/4
Sa	Rock-Pop	143	4/4
Upt...	95	4/4

Figure 35 *Navigating to the Scores folder*

Resource Central folder

a score, select the score that you want to replace on the Editor panel and click the Replace Score in Multitrack button on the Scores panel.

Adjusting the Score's Duration

Each score is created in parts: an intro, an end (outro), and parts in the middle. On the Properties panel, there are many options for adjusting the duration of a score. You can choose whether to leave an intro and outro when adjusting the length,

leave only the intro, leave only the outro, or remove them both. If you decide to leave both the intro and outro as parts of the score, the parts in between will be adjusted or dropped completely.

Notice in Figure 36, three different scores are used to demonstrate what happens when a predefined duration is used to shorten the length of an audio clip and how the parts in the middle are adjusted. The Audio 1 track has a clip that consists of four parts that are adjusted between the intro and the outro

in 58 seconds. On the Audio 2 track, only the intro was enabled and there are three parts in 59 seconds. Finally, on the Audio 3 track, neither the intro nor the outro was left in place and there are only two parts in 60 seconds.

The duration of a score can be adjusted using the default durations provided on the Variation drop-down menu, or by setting a custom clip duration if you know the exact length of your video clip. Audio clips can also be adjusted on the Editor panel by

Figure 36 *Intro and Outro options*

Editing a Musical Score in Adobe Soundbooth CS5

positioning the pointer over the right edge of the score and dragging to the left. (*Note:* If you have imported your video, you can adjust the length of the audio clip to match the length of the video clip by matching the end of the clips.)

Changing the Mood of the Score

Once you have set the duration of your score, the next thing you want to work on is the mood of the music. The mood of the music can be changed by adjusting the parameters. Every score has at least two parameters, Intensity and Volume. Parameters can be adjusted using sliders on the Properties panel, or dynamically on the Editor panel using keyframes.

The Properties panel, as shown in Figure 37, shows a sample Soundbooth Score Clip.

Figure 37 *Properties panel*

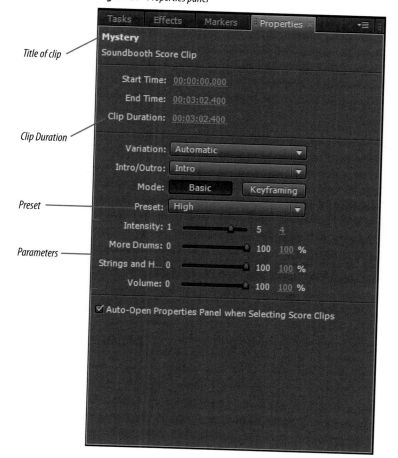

This clip has the following parameters: Intensity, More Drums, Strings and Horns, and Volume. Presets are available to make automatic adjustments on a scale from High to Low; a variety of options are shown in Figure 38. Notice the sliders adjust to varying degrees as the preset is modified. You can also adjust the sliders manually. These settings allow you to change the mood of the score by increasing or decreasing any of these parameters. Every score is different and adjusting these parameters will affect each score in a unique way.

By default, the Intensity and Volume parameters are the only parameters set to Show. In order to view the additional parameters on the Editor panel, click the Parameter menu and select Show All, or just the specific parameters you would like to view, as shown in Figure 39.

Keyframes work much the same way in Soundbooth as they do in Premiere Pro and

Figure 38 *Examples of modifying presets*

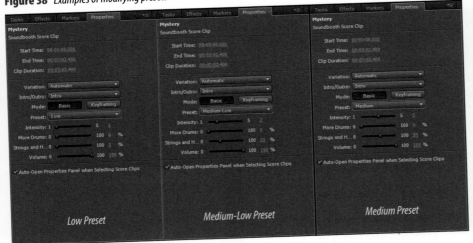

Low Preset

Medium-Low Preset

Medium Preset

Figure 39 *Viewing parameters on the Editor panel*

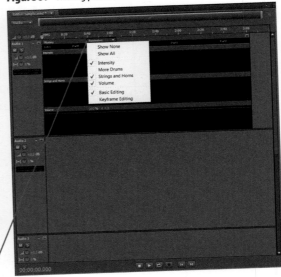

Parameters menu

Editing a Musical Score in Adobe Soundbooth CS5

in After Effects. To activate keyframes, you first need to click the Keyframing button on the Properties panel. The Add/Remove keyframe button becomes active. Next, you need to click the parameter where you would like to apply keyframes, as shown in Figure 40.

Each parameter has its own **parameter line** where the keyframes will be added. As in the other applications, keyframes are placed at the location of the CTI. Adjustments to the keyframes can be made along the parameter line by either dragging a keyframe up or down

to change the value of the parameter, or right or left to change the time position.

A Hold keyframe is created by default, as shown in Figure 40. A **Hold keyframe** creates an abrupt change in value at each keyframe that is created, and is represented by a

Figure 40 *Setting keyframes on the parameter line*

Selected keyframe

Add/Remove keyframe button

Keyframing button

Parameter line

Hold keyframe

square. Hold keyframes can be converted into Linear keyframes. **Linear keyframes** create a gradual change in value from one keyframe to the next. A Linear keyframe is represented by a diamond. Figure 41 shows a comparison between the two types of keyframes. The type of keyframe can be changed by right-clicking the keyframe and choosing either Hold or Linear. If you want to change all of the keyframes at once, select one keyframe, right-click, and then choose Select All Keyframes. Right-click again to make your selection.

QUICK TIP

If you are not in the Find Sound Effects and Scores workspace and you click the More Scores at Resource Central link on the Scores panel, the Scores tab of the Resource Central panel will become activated without changing the workspace.

Figure 41 *Hold keyframes and Linear keyframes*

Example of Linear keyframes

Example of Hold keyframes

Figure 42 *Downloading a score*

Status bar

Figure 43 *Resource Central panel showing score is downloaded*

TBD#1 activated

Check mark

Download scores in Resource Central

1. Open Soundbooth, if necessary, then verify that the Find Sound Effects and Scores workspace is active.

2. On the Resource Central panel, click the **Scores tab**, then click **Ambient** on the drop-down menu, if necessary.

3. Click the **Play button** next to Out of Time to preview the audio clip, then click the **Pause button** to stop the preview.

4. Click the **Download buton** next to Out of Time to download the score to the Scores panel.

   A status bar shows the progress of the download, as shown in Figure 42.

5. On the Resource Central panel, click the **Scores tab**, then click **Blues and Country** on the drop-down menu.

6. Scroll down in the panel, click the **Play button** next to Slo-Mo Blues to preview the audio clip, then click the **Pause button** to stop the preview.

7. Click the **Download button** next to Savannah Spring to download the score to the Scores panel.

   The Savannah Spring score has been copied to your computer, as indicated by the check mark added to the Resource Central panel, and the Music Notes icon which has become active, as shown in Figure 43.

8. Leave Soundbooth open for the next exercise.

You downloaded a score from the Resource Central panel.

Import a score to the Score library

1. Open Soundbooth, if necessary, then verify that the Find Sound Effects and Scores workspace is active.

2. Click the **Import Scores to Score Library button** on the Scores panel to import the Savannah Spring score into the Score library.

   The Import Scores to Score Library dialog box opens.

3. Click the **Libraries folder** as shown in Figure 44, double-click the **Documents folder**, double-click the **Adobe folder**, then double-click the **Resource Central folder** (Win) or click **Macintosh HD** from the sidebar, click the **Users folder**, click the **Shared folder**, click the **Adobe folder**, then click the **Resource Central folder** (Mac).

4. Double-click the **Soundbooth-3.0 (en-US) folder**, double-click the **Scores folder**, double-click the **Blues and Country folder**, click the **Savannah Spring Zip file** as shown in Figure 45, then click **Open** (Win) or click the **Soundbooth-3.0 (en-US) folder**, click the **Scores folder**, click the **Blues and Country folder**, click the **Savannah Spring Zip file**, then click **Open** (Mac).

   The audio file is extracted and installed in Soundbooth. The Zip file can now be deleted. Once you install scores in Soundbooth, you will not be able to remove them.

5. Click the **Start Score Preview button** on the Scores panel to preview the score.

(continued)

Figure 44 *Navigating to the Scores folder*

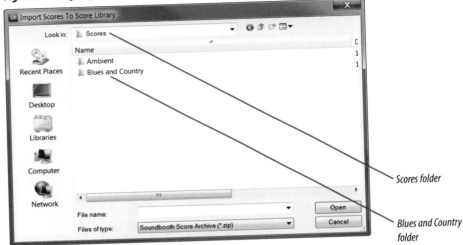

Scores folder

Blues and Country folder

Figure 45 *Selecting the Zip file*

Zip file

Blues and Country folder

Editing a Musical Score in Adobe Soundbooth CS5

Figure 46 *Activating the Scores panel*

Scores panel

Genre drop-
down menu

Figure 47 *Placing a score on a multitrack*

Selected score

Add Score to
Multitrack
button

Score on
multitrack

6. Click the **Import Scores to Score Library button** on the Scores panel to import the Out of Time score into the Score library.

7. Navigate to the Scores folder, double-click the **Ambient folder**, click the **Out of Time Zip file**, then click **Open**.

8. Leave Soundbooth open for the next exercise.

You imported the Savannah Spring score into the Score library.

Adjust the duration of a score

1. Open Soundbooth, if necessary.

2. Reset the current workspace to Default, and verify that the CTI is placed at **00:00:00.000**.

3. Click **File** on the Application bar, point to **New**, then click **Multitrack File**.

4. Click **Window** on the Application bar, then click **Scores**.

   The Scores panel becomes active in front of the Files panel, as shown in Figure 46. (*Note*: The Scores panel in the figure may appear differently than yours because of the scores that are installed.)

5. Select **Savannah Spring** on the Scores panel, then click the **Add Score to Multitrack button** on the Scores panel.

   The Opening File dialog box launches briefly and the score is placed at the location of the CTI, as shown in Figure 47.

6. Preview the score by clicking the **Play button** on the Editor panel.

(continued)

7. On the Properties panel, click the **Variation drop-down menu**, then click **30 Seconds**, as shown in Figure 48.

   The length of the score is automatically adjusted to approximately 30 seconds. These standard durations are set by the template creator and may not be exact.

   TIP On the number pad of your keyboard, press [+] to zoom the tracks in or [-] to zoom the tracks out on the Editor panel.

8. Preview the score by clicking the **Play button** ▷ on the Editor panel.

9. Save the Soundbooth document as **Savannah Spring Mix your name**.

10. Leave Soundbooth open for the next exercise.

You placed a score on a multitrack at the location of the CTI, and then you adjusted its duration.

Modify the score's Intensity parameter

1. Open Savannah Spring Mix your name, if necessary.

2. Reset the current workspace to Default, and verify that the CTI is placed at **00:00:00.000**.

3. Click **View** on the Application bar, then click **Zoom Out Full** to zoom out on the Audio 1 track.

   TIP The shortcut key for Zoom Out Full is [\].

4. Drag the **CTI** to **00:00:04.032**, then click the **Add/Remove keyframe button** 🔽 to the right of the Intensity parameter on the Editor panel to add a keyframe at the CTI, as shown in Figure 49.

   A Hold keyframe is added to the parameter line.

   (continued)

Figure 48 *Adjusting the duration of a score*

Shortened clip

Variation

Figure 49 *Adding keyframes*

Add/Remove keyframe button

Hold keyframe

Intensity parameter

Editing a Musical Score in Adobe Soundbooth CS5

Figure 50 *Adding additional keyframes*

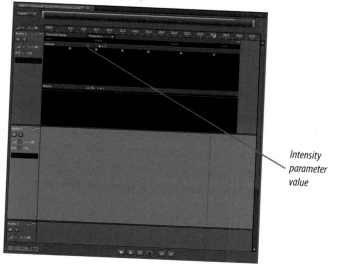

Intensity parameter value

Figure 51 *Final figure after adjusting Hold keyframes*

1

3

2

5. Place additional keyframes at the following times: **00:00:08.011**, **00:00:12.099**, **00:00:16.089**, **00:00:21.130**, and **00:00:26.172**, as shown in Figure 50.

6. Click the **Go to previous keyframe button** ◀ five times until the CTI returns to the first keyframe; the time display should be 00:00:04.032.

7. Click the **Hold keyframe** so that it turns yellow, then press ↓ three times.

   The Intensity parameter value drops from five down to two.

8. Click the **Go to next keyframe button** ▶ two times until the CTI is placed at 00:00:12.099.

9. Click the **Hold keyframe** and press ↓ two times.

   The Intensity parameter value changes to three.

10. Click the **Go to next keyframe button** ▶ two times until the CTI is placed at 00:00:21.130.

11. Click the **Hold keyframe**, then press ↓ four times so that your screen resembles Figure 51.

    The Intensity parameter value changes to one.

12. Click the **Play button** ▶ on the Editor panel to preview the score.

13. Save your Soundbooth document and leave it open for the next exercise.

You adjusted the intensity of a score by adding Hold keyframes.

Change Hold keyframes to Linear keyframes

1. Open the Savannah Spring Mix your name Soundbooth document, if necessary.

2. Reset the current workspace to Default, and verify that the CTI is placed at **00:00:00.000**.

3. Right-click one of the keyframes located under the Intensity parameter, then click **Select All Keyframes**.

   All of the keyframes for the Intensity parameter are selected, as shown in Figure 52.

4. Verify that the keyframes are still selected, right-click one of the keyframes again, then click **Linear**.

   All of the Hold keyframes are converted to Linear keyframes, as shown in Figure 53.

5. Press the **Play button** ▶ on the Editor panel to preview the score.

6. Save your Soundbooth document and leave it open for the next exercise.

You converted all of the Hold keyframes to Linear keyframes.

Modify a parameter specific to a score

1. Open Savannah Spring Mix your name, if necessary.

2. Reset the current workspace to Default, and verify that the CTI is placed at **00:00:00.000**.

3. Select the Audio 2 track, then select the Out of Time score on the Scores panel.

4. Click the **Add Score to Multitrack button** on the Scores panel.

   The Out of Time score is placed on the Audio 2 track.

(continued)

Figure 52 *Selecting all keyframes*

All keyframes are selected

Figure 53 *Changing all Hold keyframes to Linear keyframes*

Linear keyframe

Editing a Musical Score in Adobe Soundbooth CS5

Figure 54 *Duration of Out of Time score*

Duration
of score

Figure 55 *Second and fourth keyframes changed to 55% value*

Figure 56 *Keyframes changed to Hold keyframes*

Hold keyframe

Linear keyframe

5. Adjust the Variation to 30 Seconds on the Properties panel.

   The Out of Time score's duration should now be a close match to the score that is on the Audio 1 track, as shown in Figure 54.

6. Click the **Out of Time Parameters drop-down menu**, then click **Strings**.

   The Strings parameter becomes activated.

7. Create keyframes at the following times: **00:00:01.923**, **00:00:07.978**, **00:00:15.037**, **00:00:22.621**, and **00:00:27.663** by placing the CTI at each of those times and clicking the **Add/Remove keyframe button** 🔸.

8. Click the **Go to next keyframe button** ◁ or the **Go to previous keyframe button** ▷ until the CTI is on the **2nd keyframe**, click **100%** to the left of the keyframe navigator, type **55%**, then press **[Enter]** (Win) or **[return]** (Mac).

9. Repeat this step for the **4th keyframe**, as shown in Figure 55.

   This is a percentage of the modifier value for the parameter on a scale of 100%.

10. Press the **Play button** ▷ on the Editor panel to preview the score.

11. Change all the keyframes to Hold keyframes, as shown in Figure 56.

12. Press the **Play button** ▷ on the Editor panel to preview the score.

13. Save your Soundbooth document, then exit Soundbooth.

You added another score to the multitrack file and you customized the Strings parameter specific to a score.

Start Adobe Soundbooth CS5 and explore the workspace

1. Click Start on the Application bar, point to All Programs, then click Adobe Soundbooth CS5 (Win) or open the Finder from the dock, click Applications from the sidebar, click the Adobe applications folder, then click Adobe Soundbooth CS5 (Mac).
2. Click Window on the Application bar, point to Workspace, then click Edit Audio to Video.
3. Continue to click through the various workspaces and notice how the window changes each time.
4. Return the workspace to the Default workspace.

Remove background noise.

1. Click File on the Application bar, point to Import, then click Files.
2. Navigate to the drive and folder where you store your Data Files, click GrandOldRag, then click Open.
3. Double-click GrandOldRag on the Files panel.
4. Click the Spectral Frequency Display button on the Tools panel to activate the spectral display on the Editor panel.
5. Click the Play button on the Editor panel to hear the audio file.
6. Use the Rectangular Marquee tool to select a small portion of the area of the spectral display where you heard the crackling noise.
7. Click the Tasks panel tab, click Clean Up Audio, then click the Capture Noise Print button on the panel.
8. Using the Rectangular Marquee tool, select the entire area where you heard the crackling noise at the beginning of the audio clip.
9. On the Tasks panel, click Noise.
10. Adjust the Reduction slider towards the Aggressive side of the scale, then click the Preview button.
11. Adjust the Reduce By slider towards the Light side of the scale, then click the Preview button.
12. Click OK when you are satisfied with the results.
13. Click File on the Application bar, click Save As, navigate to the drive and folder where you store your Data Files, name the file **GrandOldRagRestored**, then click Save.
14. Click the Spectral Frequency Display button on the Tools panel to deactivate the spectral display.

Explore the News tab.

1. Click the Workspace list arrow on the Tools panel, then click Find Sound Effects and Scores.
2. Click the News tab.
3. Click the Refresh button to refresh the News panel.
4. Browse the News panel and view at least one story that interests you.
5. Close the Web browser and return to Soundbooth.

Find and download a sound effect.

1. Click the Sound Effects tab, type **plane** in the search box, then press [Enter] (Win) or [return] (Mac).
2. Click the Play button next to Ambience Countryside Planes Over Head 01 to preview the audio clip.
3. Click the Play button next to Transportation Flyby 04 to preview that audio clip.
4. Click the Download button next to Ambience Countryside Planes Over Head 01 to download the sound effect.
5. Click the X to remove the search parameters from the search box.

Set up a multitrack file.

1. Reset the workspace to Default.
2. Click File on the Application bar, point to Import, then click Files.
3. Click the Libraries folder, double-click the Documents folder, double-click the Adobe folder, then double-click the Resource Central folder (Win) or click Macintosh HD from the sidebar, click the Users folder, click the Shared folder, click the Adobe folder, then click the Resource Central folder (Mac).
4. Double-click the Soundbooth-3.0 (en-US) folder, double-click the Sound Effects folder. (*Note*: if you are on a Mac you will only need to single-click.)
5. Select Ambience Countryside Planes Over Head 01.wav, then click Open.
6. Click the Import file button on the Files panel, navigate to your Data Files folder, select airplane.m2v, then click Open.
7. Right-click the Untitled Multitrack 1 file on the Files panel, select Save "Untitled Multitrack 1" As, navigate to the drive and folder where you store your Data Files, name it **Airplane your name**, then click Save.

Create a video and audio track.

1. Drag the airplane.m2v file from the Files panel to the Audio 1 track on the Editor panel.
2. Drag the Ambience Countryside Planes Over Head 01 file from the Files panel to the Audio 1 track on the Editor panel.
3. Click Audio 1 in the upper-left corner of the track controls on the Audio 1 track, then type **Overhead**.
4. Click the Play button on the Editor panel to preview the sound effect with the movie clip.

Adjust the length of an audio clip.

1. Move the CTI to approximately 00:00:08.838.
2. Hover the pointer over the left edge of the audio clip on the Overhead track, then drag the clip to the CTI.
3. Return the CTI to 00:00:00.000.
4. Select the Ambience Countryside Planes Over Head 01 audio clip, then drag it to the CTI.
5. Hover the pointer over the right edge of the audio clip on the Overhead track and drag until the right edge lines up with the video clip on the Video track.
6. Compare your Overhead track to Figure 57.

7. Click the Play button on the Editor panel to preview the sound effect with the movie clip.

Save your video for use in other applications.

1. Choose File on the Application bar, point to Export, then click Multitrack Mixdown.
2. Navigate to the drive and folder where you store your Data Files, name the file **Airplane Sound Effects your name**, click the Save as list arrow, save the file as an MPEG2 with the Preset: NTSC DV High Quality.

3. Click File on the Application bar, then click Close All to close all the files that are open on the Files and Editor panels.

Download scores in Resource Central.

1. Open Soundbooth, if necessary, then verify that the Find Sound Effects and Scores workspace is active.
2. Click the Scores tab in Resource Central, then choose Rock and Pop from the drop-down menu.
3. Click the Play button next to Uptown to preview the audio clip, then click the Pause button to stop the preview. (*Hint*: You may need to search through different pages to locate the Uptown score.)
4. Go to Page 2, click the Download button next to Lost Highway to download the score to the Scores panel.

Import scores.

1. Click the Import Scores to Score Library button on the Scores panel to import the score into the library.
2. Click the Libraries folder, double-click the Documents folder, double-click the Adobe folder, then double-click the Resource Central folder (Win) or click Macintosh HD from the sidebar, click the Users folder, click the Shared folder, click the Adobe folder, then click the Resource Central folder (Mac).
3. Double-click the Soundbooth-3.0 (en-US) folder, double-click the Scores folder, click the Lost Highway Zip file, then click Open (*Note*: Mac users will only need to single-click).
4. Click the Starts Score Preview button on the Scores panel to preview the score.

Adjusting the duration of a score.

1. Reset the current workspace to Default, then verify that the CTI is placed at 00:00:00.000.

Figure 57 *Overhead track*

Right edge of audio clip

Editing a Musical Score in Adobe Soundbooth CS5

THE VIDEO COLLECTION CS5/SOUNDB…

2. Click File on the Application bar, point to New, then click Multitrack File.
3. Click Window on the Application bar, then click Scores.
4. Select Lost Highway on the Scores panel, then click Add Score to Multitrack button on the Scores panel.
5. Preview the score by clicking the Play button on the Editor panel.
6. On the Properties panel, select the Variation drop-down menu, then choose 32 Seconds.
7. Preview the score by clicking the Play button on the Editor panel.
8. Save the Soundbooth document as **Lost Highway Mix your name**, then leave it open for the next step.

Modify the score's Intensity parameter.

1. Verify that the CTI is placed at 00:00:00.000.
2. Select View on the Application bar, then click Zoom Out Full to zoom out on the Audio 1 track.
3. Drag the CTI to 00:00:03.575, then click the Add/Remove keyframe button to the right of the Intensity parameter to add a keyframe at the CTI.
4. Place additional keyframes at the following times: 00:00:08.112, 00:00:14.941, 00:00:20.991, and 00:00:26.675.
5. Click the Go to previous keyframe button four times until the CTI returns to the first keyframe; the time display should be 00:00:03.575.
6. Click the Hold keyframe so that it turns yellow, then press ↓ three times.
7. Click the Go to next keyframe button two times until the CTI is placed at 00:00:14.941.
8. Click the Hold keyframe, then press ↓ once.
9. Click the Go to next keyframe button two times until the CTI is placed at 00:00:26.675.

10. Click the Hold keyframe, then press ↓ three times.
11. Press [Home] (Win) or [FN] + left arrow (Mac), then click the Play button to preview the score.

Change hold keyframes.

1. Right-click one of the keyframes located under the Intensity property, then click Select All Keyframes.
2. Right-click one of the keyframes again, then click Linear.
3. Press the Play button to preview the score.
4. Save the Soundbooth document and leave it open for the next step.

Modify a parameter specific to a score.

1. Select the Parameters list arrow, then click Guitar.
2. Create keyframes at the following times: 00:00:02.475, 00:00:08.158, 00:00:15.720, 00:00:23.008, and 00:00:28.600.
3. Change the second and fourth keyframes to 35%.
4. Press the Play button to preview the score.
5. Change all the keyframes to Hold keyframes, then compare your keyframes to Figure 58.
6. Press the Play button to preview the score.
7. Export the Multitrack Mixdown file as a Windows Waveform with the default settings.
8. Name the file **Lost Highway Mix Final your name**.

Figure 58 *Completed Skills Review*

You are working on a history project about Martin Luther King, Jr. and plan on incorporating a speech you were able to locate online at the John F. Kennedy Presidential Library & Museum. The speech is considered part of the National Archives and therefore part of the public domain, so you do not need to worry about copyright, or altering the file. Robert Kennedy gave the speech on April 4, 1968 in Indianapolis, Indiana about the assassination of Martin Luther King, Jr., and the audio needs to be cleaned up before you feel you can use it in your project.

Figure 59 *Completed Project Builder 1*

1. Working in the Default workspace, import the file **rfkonmlkdeath45454.mp3** into the Files panel.
2. Double-click **rfkonmlkdeath45454.mp3** on the Files panel to open it on the Editor panel.
3. Click the Spectral Frequency Display button.
4. Click the Play button to preview the audio clip.
5. On the Tasks panel, click Clean Up Audio to expand that portion of the panel.
6. Click the Clicks & Pops button.
7. Click the Preview button and adjust the slider during playback. (*Hint*: Click the Power button to hear the audio without the changes.)
8. Click OK when you are satisfied with the results.
9. Click the Noise button and adjust the slider during playback.
10. Click OK when you are satisfied with the results, then compare your screen to Figure 59.
11. Save the file as an MP3 titled **RFK Speech your name**.

Editing a Musical Score in Adobe Soundbooth CS5

The elementary school principal in your district loves the video you created for the school's annual awards ceremony in the spring. She has asked you to add some vibrant music to the title sequence to complete the project for her.

1. Open Elementary Title Sequence Final from the drive and folder where your Data Files are stored.
2. Reset the workspace to Find Sound Effects and Scores.
3. Locate an appropriate score, then download and import it into the Scores panel.
4. Reset the workspace to Default.
5. Create a multitrack file and add your video and score to tracks.
6. Save the multitrack file as **Elementary Title Sequence with Music your name**.
7. Edit the score's duration to match the length of the title sequence, then edit the score's parameters.
8. Export the Multitrack Mixdown file as an MPEG2 file with the Preset: NTSC DV High Quality named **Elementary Title Sequence with Music your name**.

Figure 60 *Completed Project Builder 2*

Your Video Production teacher has found an old Charlie Chaplin video titled "The Kid Auto Race in Venice" from 1914. Charlie Chaplin introduces his famous tramp character in this silent film. He arrives at an auto race for children that is being filmed and he is constantly getting in the way. He annoys the director, the camera operator, and the public.

Your teacher thinks this film would be an excellent opportunity for you to demonstrate the skills you have learned in Soundbooth during this chapter. After watching the film, he would like you to replace the existing soundtrack with one you feel is appropriate and add sound effects to the film. Finally, he would like you to export it as an MPEG2 file with the NTSC DV High Quality preset.

Figure 61 *Sound effects for Charlie Chaplin film*

1. Open the Soundbooth file titled Charlie Chaplin, then rename the file **Chaplin Soundtrack your name**.
2. Preview the film before beginning your project.
3. Explore Resource Central for scores and sound effects to use for this film, compare your sound effects search to Figure 61.
4. Organize your audio clips onto separate tracks.
5. Edit the score's duration to match the length of the video clip, then edit the score's parameters as appropriate to address the mood of the film.
6. Remember to preview as you work.
7. When you are satisfied with your work, export your file as an MPEG2 with the Preset: NTSC DV High Quality named **Chaplin Soundtrack Final your name**.

Editing a Musical Score in Adobe Soundbooth CS5

4

CREATE A DOCUMENTARY USING PREMIERE PRO AND SOUNDBOOTH CS5

Transfer and import video

Edit Video

Work with Advanced Editing & Video Effects

Edit Audio in Soundbooth

CREATE A DOCUMENTARY USING PREMIERE PRO AND SOUNDBOOTH CS5

In this chapter, working with the film concept of the documentary, we will learn how to edit video in Premiere Pro and integrate our knowledge of Soundbooth to bring life to our documentary with audio.

A **documentary** is a broad category used to describe videos that are meant to "document" history. This may be done through the use of video footage or still images. We will be incorporating video footage filmed from a reenactment propaganda footage from World War II using staged reenactments, still photos, archival NASA footage, and audio from primary sources.

Transfer and
IMPORT VIDEO

What You'll Do

In this lesson, you will transfer file-based video and import it into Premiere Pro.

Transferring File-Based Video

To work with video in Premiere Pro, you need to remove it from your video camera. Bringing footage into a Premiere Pro project may first involve capturing, digitizing or transferring video files depending on the source of the video. If you are using a camcorder that uses tape, or you want to get video from a VHS video, then you need to capture and digitize your footage. **Capturing** occurs when you connect a live video camera or an analog tape device, such as a camcorder or VCR that uses videotape, and you then record the video from the source to a hard disk. The process of converting the analog video to digital form is called **digitizing**, and is done so that a computer can process and store it.

Premiere Pro does have the ability to capture and digitize video if a video capture card and a device are installed in the computer. Premiere Pro saves digitized footage to the designated location as files. For more information about capturing video from an external device, refer to the Adobe Premiere Pro Help.

Importing video is different from capturing video. Digital video cameras that do not use video tape are called **tapeless** or **file-based**. These cameras record video and audio into specific formats with a folder structure specific to the manufacturer such as P2 cards, XDCAM cartridges, SxS cards, RED R3D, or DVDs. Typically, these video cameras record directly to a hard disk, a DVD, or flash memory media as they are recording. Therefore, these files are already digital, therefore no capturing or digitizing is necessary to work with them in Premiere Pro. The XDCAM, RED, P2, AVCHD and HD clips can be mixed and matched on a timeline sequence without rendering.

If you are working with video that has been saved on **file-based media**, it is possible to edit the assets on that particular media by attaching the camera to the computer. The computer will then recognize the camera as an external drive allowing you to work directly with the files. However, it is suggested that a copy of the tapeless media or file-based media folder containing the video and all related files and subfolders be copied to a local hard disk to improve performance. AVCHD (advanced video codec high definition) is a format developed by Sony and Panasonic for recording and playback of high definition video, and is used in their tapeless video cameras which record directly to either an SD memory card or a hard disk drive. The **AVCHD** file-based media creates a BDMV folder with subfolders, BACKUP, CLIPINF, PLAYLIST and STREAM, as shown in Figure 1. XDCAM EX media creates a BPAV folder with subfolders, and a DVD has a VIDEO_TS folder with subfolders, and if it exists, the contents of the AUDIO_TS folder.

It is important to keep the file structure of the original file-based media when making your copy.

Importing Video from a File-Based Media Source

Once you have transferred video files from your file-based media you then need to import the files into Premiere Pro to make them available to be used, just as we did with the still images in Chapter 1. Using the Media Browser is the recommended method for importing files that have been transferred from file-based media because of the file structure associated with them.

The Media Browser not only allows you to locate your files more quickly by allowing you to see the structure of your drives and folders but it filters through the folders and files for you by displaying only the video clips, as shown in Figure 2.

Creating a Sequence for AVCHD Video Footage

A sequence may contain different types of assets with different file formats. Premiere Pro performs best, if the sequence parameters are set to match the settings for most of the assets that are in the sequence. Therefore, when creating a sequence, use a

Figure 1 *BDMV folder system*

BDMV folder

Subfolders and files

Figure 2 *Viewing file-based media on the Media Browser*

AVCHD file-based media

preset that conforms to the specifications of your original assets to preserve editing quality. The preset you choose sets the frame and pixel aspect ratios for the sequence. For that reason, it is important to choose a preset that most closely matches the parameters of your asset. If necessary, you can customize the preset so that its settings match the asset exactly by clicking the General tab in the New Sequence dialog box. Most settings cannot be modified after the sequence is created so it is extremely important to make sure the settings are accurate.

If you do not know the parameters for the footage you are working with, Premiere Pro has a command called "Get Properties for" that allows you to retrieve that information from either an external clip, as shown in Figure 3 or a clip that is on the Project panel, as shown in Figure 4.

Figure 3 *Viewing the parameters of an external clip*

Image Size

Frame Rate

Pixel Aspect Ratio

External clip

Figure 4 *Viewing the parameters for a clip on the Project panel*

File on Project panel

The clip in Figure 3 came from an AVCHD file-based media source, which can be identified in the file path name. The parameter settings are Image Size: 1440 x 1080; Frame Rate: 29.97; and Pixel Aspect Ratio: 1.333.

Once you have identified the parameters of the clip, you can open the New Sequence dialog box and begin looking through the presets for a match, as shown in Figure 5. The AVCHD presets do not have any presets that match the parameters as closely as the HDV presets. The HDV 1080p30 preset matches the parameters for the AVCHD file-based media source.

Figure 5 *HDV preset*

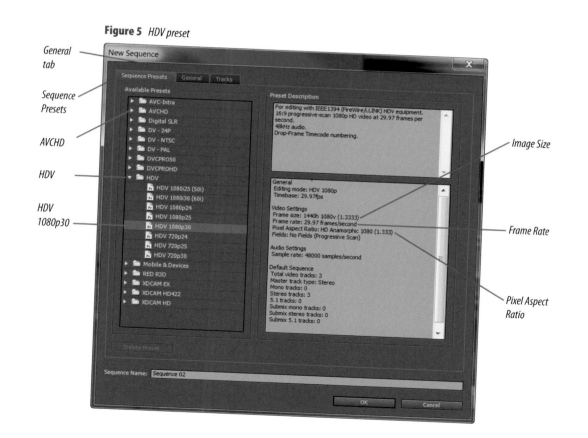

Transfer tapeless video

1. Before starting Premiere Pro, navigate to the location where your Data Files are stored, then locate the Video Clips folder in the Navigation pane, as shown in Figure 6.

   Your Video Clips folder may be in a different location than that in the figure.

2. Open the Video Clips folder, select **AVCHD-AirShow**, click **Organize** on the Toolbar, then click **Copy** (Win) or select the **AVCHD-Airshow** folder, click **Edit** on the Application bar, then click **Copy** (Mac).

   The AVCHD-AirShow folder and its contents, which was recorded from a hard disk camcorder, are copied.

   (continued)

Figure 6 *Locating the Video Clips folder*

Windows File Explorer

Toolbar

Organize

Navigation pane

Video Clips folder

Create a Documentary Using Premiere Pro and Soundbooth CS5

Figure 7 *Copy of AVCHD-AirShow in Chapter 4 Data Files folder*

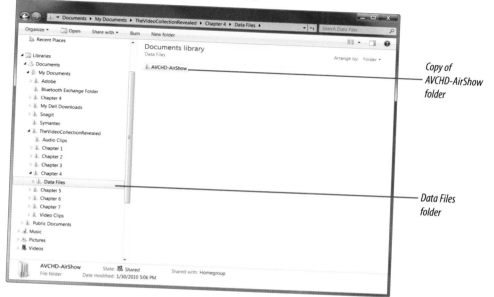

Copy of
AVCHD-AirShow
folder

Data Files
folder

3. Select the **Data Files folder** for the Chapter 4
using the Navigation pane (Win) or Sidebar (Mac),
click **Organize** on the Toolbar, then click **Paste**.

This will place a copy of the AVCHD-AirShow
folder and its contents to your Chapter 4 Data
Files folder, as shown in Figure 7.

*You copied AVCHD digital files that were recorded from a hard
disk camcorder to your Data Files folder.*

24p Workflows in Premiere Pro

Footage that is captured from a video camcorder or by film transfer at approximately 24 non-interlaced (progressive) frames per second (fps) is referred to as 24p footage. Each frame is built from progressive lines giving it the appearance of a motion-picture film. Premiere Pro has a 24p sequence preset to edit 24p footage; your footage is then captured as usual. To complete the process for playback and keep the motion-picture film effect, Premiere Pro uses a method referred to as a pulldown scheme to convert the footage for playback on standard NTSC devices at 29.97 fps.

There are two alternate 24p pulldown schemes: Interlaced Frame and Repeat Frame. The scheme may be selected when creating the sequence, or changed in an existing sequence.

Create a sequence for AVCHD video footage

1. Start Premiere Pro, then click **New Project** in the Welcome to Adobe Premiere Pro dialog box.

   The New Project dialog box opens.

2. Click **Browse**, navigate to the drive and folder where your Data Files are stored, then click **OK**.

3. Name the project **Airshow your name**, then click **OK**.

   The New Sequence dialog box opens. We will be importing the AVCHD-AirShow video we transferred in the previous exercise.

4. Click the **expander arrow** in front of **HDV**, select **HDV 1080p30**, as shown in Figure 8, then click **OK**.

   The footage was shot in high definition at 29.97 fps and a frame size of 1440 x 1080. Even though the footage is AVCHD, this is the closest available preset.

5. Save your project file and leave it open for the next exercise.

You created a sequence for AVCHD video footage.

Figure 8 *Choosing an HDV preset*

HDV expander arrow

HDV 1080p30

29.97 fps

1440 x 1080

Working with Audio

Premiere Pro has nearly as many options for editing sound as it does video. You can edit tracks, add effects and mix together mono, stereo, or 5.1 surround channels. A sequence of clips can contain any combination of mono, stereo, or 5.1 (three front audio channels on the left, center, and right, two rear or surround audio channels on the left and right, and a low-frequency effects audio channel) audio. There are effects in the Effects control panel for each specific channel format.

When editing audio, it sometimes becomes difficult to get the In and Out points exactly in the correct location. Digital audio is not divided into frames like video, but into audio samples and occur far more frequently than frames. The time ruler can be changed from the default Timecode display to Audio Time Units. This time ruler is available in the Source and Program Monitors and the Timeline panel and can be selected from the panel menu.

As you work with different aspects of audio editing in Premiere Pro, a more advanced feature is to map channels of audio tracks before you add a clip to a Timeline sequence using the Source Channel Mappings command. Mapping allows you to decide exactly which channel multichannel tracks go to, giving you better control over stereo or 5.1 surround.

Figure 9 *Locating the Data Files folder on the Media Browser*

Media Browser panel

Chapter 4 folder

Data Files folder

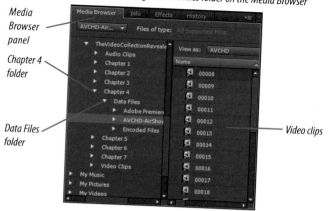

Video clips

Figure 10 *Clip 00029 imported into Project panel*

00029 video clip

Import video from a file-based source

1. Open Airshow your name, if necessary.

2. On the Media Browser panel, locate your Data Files folder for Chapter 4, then double-click the **AVCHD-AirShow folder**, as shown in Figure 9.

   View as option on the Media panel automatically changes to AVCHD, filtering the folder leaving only the video clips listed on the right side of the panel.

3. Double-click **00015**.

   The clip is opened on the Source Monitor for previewing; it is not imported into the Project panel.

4. Click the **Play-Stop Toggle button** ▶ on the Source Monitor to preview the clip.

5. Click the **Source Monitor drop-down menu** then click **Close**.

   The video clip is closed.

6. Select **clip 00029**, click **File** on the Application bar, then click **Import from Media Browser**.

   The clip is imported into the Project panel, as shown in Figure 10.

7. Save and close your project file.

You imported video from a file-based source.

Edit VIDEO

What You'll Do

In this lesson, you will edit video using the Source Monitor and the Timeline panel.

Trimming Clips on the Source Monitor

As you have already seen, you can preview clips on the Source Monitor. The Source Monitor can also be used for trimming clips. **Trimming** clips is an editing procedure in which you define In and Out points for a video clip. The **In point** defines the first frame that is to be included in a sequence and the **Out point** defines the last frame. Trimming clips is useful when you want to show part of a video clip, not all of it. Trimming a clip does not alter the original clip on the Project panel.

In and Out points are created on the Source Monitor by using the CTI on the time ruler and the Set In Point and Set Out Point buttons. These buttons are located just below the time ruler on the Source Monitor. There are additional controls to help navigate the In and Out points. The Play In to Out button previews the clip on the Source Monitor from the set In and Out points. In addition, there are two buttons to quickly navigate to the In and Out points: Go to In Point and Go to Out Point, as shown in Figure 11.

Figure 11 *Source Monitor*

Set Out Point button

Set In Point button

Go to In Point button

Go to Out Point button

Play In to Out button

Overlay button

Insert button

Create a Documentary Using Premiere Pro and Soundbooth CS5

Placing Trimmed Clips in a Sequence

Once a clip is trimmed, it can be placed in a sequence on the Timeline. Clips that have been placed in a sequence on the Timeline panel can also be viewed on the Source Monitor. Double-click the clip in the sequence if you would like to view it on the Source Monitor. If the clip has been trimmed, the In and Out points will still be set and can be seen in the Duration display, as shown

in Figure 12. The shaded area between the In and Out points on the time ruler on the Source Monitor is called the In/Out Grip and can be dragged to adjust the location of both In and Out points at the same time. **Tick marks** and numbers are displayed along the time ruler and are based on the timecode display.

The Source menu, on the Source Monitor tab, lists any open clips, and can be accessed by clicking the Source drop-down menu, as shown

in Figure 13. Clips opened from a sequence are identified by their sequence name, clip name, and starting time in the sequence. Clips opened from the Project panel are identified by their file name. The Source menu also provides options to clear either the selected clip or all the clips from the Source Monitor.

The Insert and Overlay buttons are used to place video clips from the Source Monitor into selected tracks at the location of the CTI.

Figure 12 *A trimmed clip opened from a sequence*

Clip name

New In point

New Out point

Figure 13 *Source menu*

Source menu

Selected clip

Click arrow to display menu

File opened from sequence

File opened from Project panel

These buttons are available in the lower portion of the Source Monitor. The Insert button shifts the contents of the selected track to the right, as shown in Figure 14. This is referred to as an **insert edit**. If you have clips on more than one track, and Sync Lock is enabled, the contents of the other tracks will also shift to the right by the length of the inserted clip, as shown in Figure 15. The Sync Lock feature retains the relationship between clips in multiple tracks. As you begin to use advanced editing techniques and make a change to one clip,

Figure 14 *Insert button with Sync Lock disabled*

Disabled Sync Lock

Inserted clip

Figure 15 *Insert button with Sync Lock enabled*

Enabled Sync Lock

Gap created because of Sync Lock

Inserted clip

Create a Documentary Using Premiere Pro and Soundbooth CS5

Premiere Pro will keep your edits in place by adjusting the other clips on the Timeline. Keep in mind, video can have an audio component linked to it.

The Overlay button places the clip from the Source Monitor over the existing clip replacing what is already there for the duration of the placed clip, as shown in

Figure 16. Sync Lock does not affect the other tracks when using the Overlay button, as shown in Figure 17. Using the Overlay button is referred to as an **overlay edit**.

Figure 16 *Overlay button with Sync Lock disabled*

Disabled Sync Lock

Overlayed clip

Figure 17 *Overlay button with Sync Lock enabled*

Enabled Sync Lock

Overlayed clip

Trimming on the Timeline Panel

Editing can also be done on the Timeline panel directly on the sequence by using tools from the Tools panel. If you want to trim a video clip's In point or Out point, use the Selection tool. When the cursor is placed over the left edge of a clip, the cursor's appearance changes to the Trim-in icon, as shown in Figure 18, and the Trim-out icon, as shown in Figure 19. When it is placed on the right edge, click and drag to trim the clip. A tool tip displays the number of frames that are being trimmed; a negative number when dragging the clip from the right, a positive number when dragging from the left.

Using the Ripple Edit Tool

The Ripple edit tool can be used to adjust the cut between two clips; this edit is called a **ripple edit**. A ripple edit can move the cut point either backward or forward in time (if the clip has frames available). The clip adjacent to the cut line adjusts accordingly, either shifting to the left or to the right by the amount of the ripple edit to compensate.

A ripple edit is performed by positioning the Ripple edit tool at the cut line in the Timeline panel and dragging either left or right.

Figure 18 *Using the Trim-in icon on the Timeline panel*

Trim-in icon

Tool tip

Figure 19 *Using the Trim-out icon on the Timeline panel*

Trim-out icon

Tool tip

Create a Documentary Using Premiere Pro and Soundbooth CS5

Rearranging Clips on the Timeline Panel

Once you have trimmed your clips you may decide to rearrange their order. A **rearrange edit** allows you to click and drag a clip to a new location in the sequence. When you release the clip in place, the existing clips automatically shift to make room for the clip you are placing, as shown in Figure 20. A rearrange edit is performed by pressing and holding [Ctrl][Alt] (Win) or ⌘[option] (Mac) while clicking and dragging the clip and releasing the mouse button once the clip is in the new location.

Creating Custom Keyboard Shortcuts

Premiere Pro allows you to assign your own custom keyboard shortcuts to almost any menu command, button, or tool. This allows you the flexibility to assign shortcuts to commands that currently do not have shortcuts, or reassign shortcuts to match other software you currently use and already have memorized.

Premiere Pro does not have keyboard shortcuts to trim clips on a sequence like After Effects does. However, you can create your own keyboard shortcuts in the Keyboard Customization dialog box which can be found on the Edit menu. You can then quickly create In and Out points at the location of the CTI using your newly created keyboard shortcuts.

Figure 20 *Using a rearrange edit*

Where clip will be placed

Number of frames clip is being moved

Rearrange edit icon

Slip and Slide Tools

Two more editing tools are the Slip tool and the Slide tool. By dragging a clip's In or Out point with the Slip tool, you can change a clip's starting and ending frames without changing its duration or affecting adjacent clips. In a single action the slip edit moves a clip's In and Out points forward or backward by the same number of frames.

A slide edit moves a clip while trimming adjacent clips to compensate for the change. With the Slide tool, as you drag a clip to the left or right, the Out point of the previous clip and the In point of the next clip are trimmed by the number of frames the clip has been moved. The duration of the clip that is being adjusted remains unchanged.

Trim video on the Source Monitor

1. Open Pearl Harbor Reenactment.prproj from your Data Files folder, then rename it **Pearl Harbor Documentary your name**.

2. Click the **Workspace list arrow** on the Tools panel, then click **Editing**.

   If the Editing workspace is already selected, choose Reset Current Workspace to be sure the workspace is set to the Editing workspace default settings.

3. Double-click **AirshowVideo1.m2v** on the Project panel.

   The video footage opens on the Source Monitor.

4. Click the **Play-Stop Toggle button** ▶ to preview the video clip.

   You will notice the footage needs editing.

5. Turn on **Safe Margins** ⊞ in both the Source and Program Monitors, if they are not already activated.

6. Drag the **CTI** on the Source Monitor until the timecode display reads **00;00;02;25**, then click the **Set In Point button** , as shown in Figure 21.

7. Drag the **CTI** until the timecode display reads **00;00;05;16**, then click the **Set Out Point button** , as shown in Figure 22.

8. Click the **Play In to Out button** ▶▶ to preview the trimmed clip on the Source Monitor.

   At the beginning of the clip, the plane enters the safe margins. We need to adjust the start time of the clip.

   (continued)

Figure 21 *Setting an In point*

New In point

Set In Point button

Figure 22 *Setting an Out point*

New Out point

Set Out Point button

Play In to Out button

Create a Documentary Using Premiere Pro and Soundbooth CS5

Figure 23 *Dragging the In/Out Grip*

Moving two
tick marks
left

In/Out Grip

Figure 24 *Using the Trim-out icon to adjust the Out point*

Timecode
display

Trim-out
icon

9. Drag the **In/Out Grip** on the Source Monitor to the left two tick marks to move the In point to the left, as shown in Figure 23.

    The In/Out Grip is the shaded area between the In and Out points you set earlier. (*Note*: the new In point is now 00;00;02;16.)

10. Click the **Play In to Out button** ▶ to preview the trimmed clip on the Source Monitor.

    The Out point moved as a result of dragging the In/Out Grip earlier, so we need to adjust the Out point without moving the In point.

11. Hover your mouse over the Out point, then drag the right edge of the clip using the **Trim-out icon** until the timecode display reads **00;00;05;20**, as shown in Figure 24.

12. Click the **Play In to Out button** ▶ to preview the trimmed clip on the Source Monitor.

13. Click the **Insert button** ▣ on the Source Monitor to place the trimmed clip in the sequence on the Timeline panel.

    You may want to zoom in on the sequence to get a better look at the clip.

TIP Press [Alt] (Win) or [option] (Mac) and use the scroll wheel on your mouse to zoom in and out on the Timeline panel. **Note**: Be sure to have the Timeline panel selected first.

14. Press the [**Spacebar**] to preview the clip on the Program Monitor.

15. Save your project file and leave it open for the next exercise.

You created In and Out points on a video clip and then made adjustments to them on the Source Monitor, and finally you placed a trimmed video clip on a sequence.

Edit a clip on the Timeline panel

1. Open Pearl Harbor Documentary your name, if necessary.

2. Drag **AirshowVideo2.m2v** to the Video 1 track directly after the AirshowVideo1 video clip on the Timeline panel, as shown in Figure 25.

3. Press the [**Page Down**] key to move the CTI to the beginning of the AirshowVideo2 video clip.

4. Press the [**Spacebar**] to preview the video clip on the Program Monitor.

   We will be trimming the clip on the Timeline panel to show the two planes flying in from the right side of the viewing area.

5. Click the **Selection tool** on the Tools panel, then place the cursor over the left edge of the AirshowVideo2 video clip.

6. Once the Trim-in icon appears, drag the left edge to the right until the tool tip displays **+00;00;09;09**, as shown in Figure 26.

   The Program Monitor will preview the video clip as you drag the Trim-in icon to the right; we want to trim the clip just before the planes appear.

   (continued)

Figure 25 *Dragging AirshowVideo2.m2v to the Video 1 track*

AirShowVideo2.m2v

AirShowVideo2.m2v

Figure 26 *Trimming a clip from the left on the Timeline panel*

Current time in clip

Plane

Trim-in icon

Tool tip display

Create a Documentary Using Premiere Pro and Soundbooth CS5

Figure 27 *Removing space between video clips*

Ripple Delete

Figure 28 *Trimming a clip from the right on the Timeline panel*

Plane

Current time in clip

Trim-out icon

Tool tip display

7. Point the cursor to the blank space between the two video clips on the Video 1 track, right-click, then click **Ripple Delete**, as shown in Figure 27.

 The AirshowVideo2 video clip is shifted to the left removing the gap.

TIP Pressing the [Delete] key on a gap also performs the Ripple Delete command.

8. Press the [**Page Down**] key to move the CTI to the end of the AirshowVideo2 video clip.

 We will now trim the clip from the right side.

9. Place the cursor over the right edge of the AirshowVideo2 video clip, once the Trim-out icon appears, drag the right edge to the left until the tool tip displays -**00;00;14;06**, as shown in Figure 28.

 We want to trim the clip to the point when the plane disappears out of the viewing area.

10. Press [**Spacebar**] to preview the sequence on the Program Monitor.

11. Save your project file and leave it open for the next exercise.

You trimmed a video clip from the left and right on the Timeline panel.

Create keyboard commands to set In and Out points

1. Open Pearl Harbor Documentary your name, if necessary.

2. Click **Edit** on the Application bar, then click **Keyboard Customization**.

   The Keyboard Customization dialog box opens, as shown in Figure 29.

3. Scroll down to Trim In Point to CTI, click in the **Shortcut area** to the right, then press [[] (left bracket), as shown in Figure 30.

   In After Effects, we used the keyboard shortcut [Alt][[] to trim clips. This same shortcut key is not available in Premiere Pro. Instead, we will simply use the left and right brackets without the [Alt].

4. Click in the **Shortcut area** to the right of the Trim Out Point to CTI and type a []] then click **OK**.

5. Save your project file and leave it open for the next exercise.

Figure 29 *Keyboard Customization dialog box*

Figure 30 *Creating a keyboard shortcut*

Shortcut area

Type] here

Create a Documentary Using Premiere Pro and Soundbooth CS5

Figure 31 *Trimming a video clip using a keyboard shortcut*

Trimmed at CTI

Use the CTI to set In and Out points

1. Open Pearl Harbor Documentary your name, if necessary.

2. Drag **AirshowVideo3.m2v** after the AirshowVideo2.m2v video clip on the Video 1 track.

3. Preview the AirshowVideo3.m2v video clip, then move the CTI to the beginning of the video clip.

   We will just need to trim the right end of the clip.

4. Drag the **CTI** to **00;00;06;06**.

   The plane has left the viewing area to the right.

5. Press [ ]] on your keypad, then compare your screen Figure 31.

   The right bracket key (]) is the keyboard shortcut we created in the last exercise to set an Out point at the location of the CTI.

6. Press [**Spacebar**] to preview the sequence on the Program Monitor.

7. Save your project file and leave it open for the next exercise.

You trimmed a clip on the Timeline panel at the CTI using a keyboard shortcut.

Applying the Fast Color Corrector Effect

The Fast Color Corrector effect can be found under the Color Correction bin in the Effects panel and is recommended for making straightforward color corrections that preview quickly in the Program monitor. This effect adjusts a clip's color using hue and saturation controls. In addition, levels controls are available to adjust shadows, midtones, and highlights of an image. A color wheel is used when making adjustments to the Hue and Balance controls.

Trim a video clip with the Ripple Edit tool

1. Open Pearl Harbor Documentary your name, if necessary.

2. Drag **AirshowVideo4.m2v** after the AirshowVideo3.m2v video clip on the Video 1 track.

3. Preview the AirshowVideo4.m2v video clip, then drag the **CTI** to the beginning of the video clip.

   This video clip is primarily of the smoke. We want to trim the clip to get footage that has been zoomed in and is not shaky.

4. Click the **Ripple Edit tool** ◄►► on the Tools panel.

   TIP Press [B] on the keypad to activate the Ripple Edit tool.

5. Place the cursor on the left edge of the **AirshowVideo4.m2v** video clip, then drag the **Ripple Edit icon** to the right until the tool tip display shows **+00;00;10;29**, as shown in Figure 32.

6. Click the **Selection tool** ► on the Tools panel, place the CTI at **00;00;13;06**, then press []], to create a Trim out point, as shown in Figure 33.

7. Press [**Spacebar**] to preview the sequence on the Program Monitor.

8. Save your project file and leave it open for the next exercise.

You edited a video clip using the Ripple Edit tool.

Figure 32 *Working with the Ripple Edit tool*

Last frame of outgoing clip

Preview of clip being trimmed

Ripple Edit icon

Tool tip display

Figure 33 *Creating a Trim Out point*

Trim Out point at CTI

Figure 34 *Setting a Trim Out point*

Timecode display

Trim Out point

Figure 35 *Placing a clip with the Insert button*

AirshowVideo5.m2v
video clip

Use the Insert button to place a trimmed clip

1. Open Pearl Harbor Documentary your name, if necessary.

2. Double-click **AirshowVideo5.m2v** on the Project panel.

3. Click the **Play-Stop Toggle button** ▶ on the Source Monitor to preview the video clip.

   This video clip shows two planes flying in from both directions and needs to be trimmed from the right.

4. Drag the **CTI** until the timecode display reads **00;02;32;00**, then click the **Set Out Point button** 〕 on the Source Monitor, as shown in Figure 34.

TIP You can click Step Forward � or Step Back ◀▌ to adjust the timecode display if you are having trouble getting the image in the frame exactly where you want it.

5. On the Timeline panel, place the CTI at the end of the AirshowVideo4.m2v video clip.

   The timecode display should be 00;00;13;06.

6. Click the **Insert button** 🔛 on the Source Monitor.

   The trimmed AirshowVideo5.m2v video clip is placed at the location of the CTI on the Video 1 track, as shown in Figure 35.

7. Press [**Spacebar**] to preview the sequence on the Program Monitor.

8. Save your project file and leave it open for the next exercise.

You placed a trimmed clip from the Source Monitor using the Insert button.

Use the Overlay button to place a trimmed clip

1. Open Pearl Harbor Documentary your name, if necessary.

2. Open AirShowVideo6.m2v on the Source Monitor and preview the video clip.

   This video clip shows a plane flying in from the left and needs to be trimmed from both sides.

3. Drag the **CTI** until the timecode display reads **00;00;25;05**, then click the **Set In Point button** on the Source Monitor.

4. Drag the **CTI** until the timecode display reads **00;00;29;00**, then click the **Set Out Point button** on the Source Monitor, as shown in Figure 36.

5. On the Timeline panel, place the CTI at the end of the AirshowVideo3.m2v video clip.

   The timecode display should be 00;00;06;06.

6. Click the **Overlay button** on the Source Monitor to place the video clip on the Timeline panel, as shown in Figure 37.

   This replaces a segment of the AirshowVideo4.m2v video clip with AirShowVideo6.m2v at the location of the CTI and extends the length of the AirshowVideo6 video clip leaving the remaining portion of the AirshowVideo4 video clip.

7. Press [**Spacebar**] to preview the sequence on the Program Monitor.

8. Save your project file and leave it open for the next exercise.

You placed a trimmed clip from the Source Monitor using the Overlay button.

Figure 36 *Setting In and Out points*

In Point

Out Point

Figure 37 *Using the Overlay button*

AirshowVideo6.m2v

AirshowVideo4.m2v

Create a Documentary Using Premiere Pro and Soundbooth CS5

Figure 38 *Adjusting the Timeline panel zoom level*

Zoom slider

Figure 39 *Performing a rearrange edit*

Rearrange icon

Figure 40 *New order of video clips*

Lesson 2   Edit Video

Perform a rearrange edit

1. Open Pearl Harbor Documentary your name, if necessary.

2. Using the Zoom Slider, zoom in on the Timeline panel so that you can see all of your video clips at the same time, as shown in Figure 38.

3. Click the **Selection tool** on the Tools panel, click **AirshowVideo3.m2v**, press and hold [**Ctrl**] [**Alt**] (Win) or ⌘ [**option**] (Mac), drag the video clip in front of **AirshowVideo1.m2v**, then release the mouse button.

   When you press [Ctrl][Alt] (Win) or ⌘ [option] (Mac), the rearrange icon appears as shown in Figure 39. A tool tip appears when you hover over a video clip displaying the clip's name, start and end time, and duration.

4. Using the rearrange edit technique, reorder the video clips on the Video 1 track so that they are arranged as follows: AirshowVideo3.m2v, AirshowVideo5.m2v, AirshowVideo1.m2v, AirshowVideo6.m2v, AirshowVideo2.m2v, and AirshowVideo4.m2v, as shown in Figure 40.

5. Press [**Spacebar**] to preview the sequence on the Program Monitor.

6. Save your project file and leave it open for the next exercise.

You rearranged video clips on a sequence using the rearrange edit technique.

Work with Advanced Editing & VIDEO EFFECTS

What You'll Do

In this lesson, you will use advanced editing techniques and apply effects to video clips.

Working with the Razor Tool

If you need to remove a portion of a clip that is not either at the beginning or at the end, you can use the **Razor tool** to split the clip at the point where you click the Razor tool pointer. The point that you split the clip is called the **cut point**. A tool tip appears to indicate the In and Out points of the clip and its duration, as shown in Figure 41. Mark as many cut points as needed then simply select the cut portion that you do not want and press [Delete] on your keyboard. To remove the gap that is left between the remaining clips use the **Ripple Delete** command; this will shift the clips to the left removing the empty space. If you have clips on more than one track the Ripple Delete command will not be available unless you disable the Sync Lock and lock the track you are not applying the Ripple Delete command to, as shown in Figure 42.

Figure 41 *Using the Razor tool*

Trim-in icon

December7th.m2v
Start: 00;00;01;09
End: 00;00;07;01
Duration: 00;00;05;23

Tool tip

Create a Documentary Using Premiere Pro and Soundbooth CS5

The **Go to Gap** command is a convenient way to jump between gaps and to find gaps that are very short and may be difficult to see. This command can be used on a sequence or on a specific track if multiple tracks are being used.

Rearranging Clips Using the Program Monitor

The Program Monitor can also be used to edit video clips much the same way clips are edited on the Source Monitor. When editing clips on the Program Monitor the clips being referenced are those already placed on the Timeline panel.

The **Extract button** on the Program Monitor removes a specified area of the sequence marked with In and Out points without leaving a gap in its place. The **Lift button** works in a similar manner to the Extract button removing a specified area of the sequence however, the Lift button does leave a gap in its place.

In both cases, the frames that are removed from the sequence are copied to the system clipboard and can then be placed at the location of the CTI with the Paste or Paste Insert command. The **Paste** command behaves like an Overlay edit, and the **Paste Insert** command behaves like an Insert edit.

Nesting a Sequence

Just as we nested compositions in After Effects, you can **nest** sequences within sequences to create complex groupings. Sequences can be created with different presets, or the same presets and be nested inside one another. However, you cannot nest a sequence inside itself. Nesting sequences can be used as a time-saving technique. You can simply nest a sequence you want to repeat so you only need to create it once. Nesting sequences can also be used as an organizational tool. If your movie is getting too large, either with many layers or with a long duration, you can break it down into manageable parts with sequences. You can then assemble the final movie in its own sequence.

A nested sequence appears as a single linked clip and can be treated as such; you can select, trim, move and apply effects to it. You can also open a nested sequence on the Source Monitor where you can set In and Out points just as you would with any other clip. If you double-click a nested sequence on

Figure 42 *Using the Ripple Delete command*

Disabled Sync Lock

Locked track

Ripple Delete

Cuts in clip

the Timeline panel, it will open the source of the sequence and become the active sequence on the Timeline panel, as shown in Figure 43.

A nested sequence will add an empty audio track to the Timeline even when your sequence has no audio associated with it. The **Drag Video Only** icon on the Source Monitor will allow you to nest the sequence without the empty audio track. The Drag Video Only is not a button; it is an icon that provides a place to click when you begin to drag. You click the Drag Video Only icon to initiate the dragging of the clip from the Source Monitor.

Using Keyboard Shortcuts to Preview a Sequence

Most of the playback controls on the Program Monitor have keyboard equivalents. When the Timeline panel is selected you can use the keyboard shortcuts to preview your sequence on the Program Monitor more efficiently.

You have already used the [Spacebar] to toggle between Play and Stop. You can also press [L] to play and [K] to stop. To play a sequence in reverse, press [J]. To increase the speed in which the sequence is playing, press [L] or [J] to play it forward or backward respectively. If you want to advance or retreat one frame, press and hold [K] and then press either [L] or [J] respectively. In order to play the sequence in slow motion, press and hold the [Shift] key and then press either [L] or [J] to play it forward or backward respectively.

A list of keyboard shortcuts can be found in the Help file by pressing [F1].

Applying Video Effects

In Chapter 1 you used the standard Motion effects to create panning and zooming effects on still images. Premiere Pro has many additional effects available which include the ability to change the exposure or color of footage, distort images, or to remove the background.

Figure 43 *Opening a nested sequence*

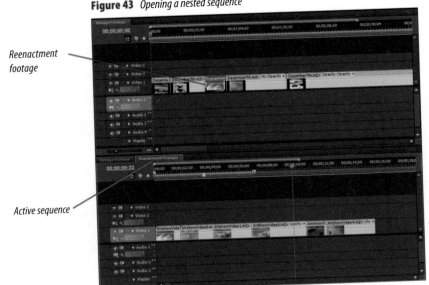

Reenactment footage

Active sequence

Create a Documentary Using Premiere Pro and Soundbooth CS5

In this chapter, we will be modifying the color of a video clip to black and white and adjusting the lighting effects to make the clip appear darker. The Black & White effect from the Image Control category removes color from a clip and changes it to black and white. There are no controls available for this effect.

Lighting Effects can be found in the Adjust category and can use up to five lights to produce creative effects. The properties that can be manipulated include Lighting Type, Direction, Intensity, Color, Lighting Center, and Lighting Spread. These properties can be manipulated directly on the Program Monitor by clicking the Transform icon on the Effect Controls panel.

You can apply any number of effects to a clip by selecting the effect on the Effects panel and dragging the effect icon to a clip on the Timeline panel. Adjustments are made on the Effect Controls panel, as shown in Figure 44. Not all effects will have parameters that can be adjusted.

Working with Transitions

We learned about video transitions in Chapter 1 and will be using them again as we apply them between cuts in video clips. Transitions are used to piece together two clips that have been cut. Transitions are often used to indicate a change in location, a change in the rate of the action, or simply the passage of time. Another reason to use transitions is to smooth out minor video or audio errors, which could appear more prominent with just a cut, but which may be less obvious with a well-placed transition such as a dissolve.

There are many transitions to choose from, but most professionals only use simple cuts and crossfades. Using too many transitions can be distracting and can affect the flow of the video. Try and keep transitions as smooth and as unnoticeable as possible; transitions should not call attention to themselves.

Consider the following when you choose a transition:

- Does the transition fit with the story you are trying to tell?
- Do the clips work well together with the transition?
- Is the transition confusing?
- What do you hope to achieve with the transition?

Figure 44 *Effect Controls panel*

Effect without adjustments

Effect with adjustments

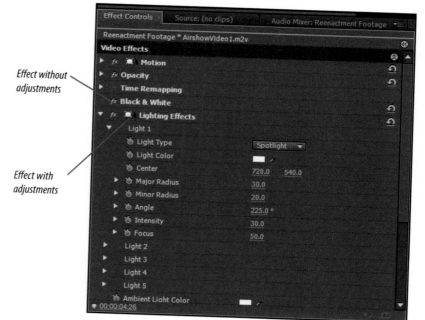

Create a new sequence

1. Open Pearl Harbor Documentary your name, if necessary.

2. Click **File** on the Application bar, click **Import**, navigate to your Data Files folder, select **December7th.m2v**, then click **Open**.

   We will need to look at the properties of this video clip to determine its parameters before we can create the sequence.

3. On the Project panel, right-click (Win) or [Ctrl]-click (Mac) the **December7th.m2v video clip**, then click **Properties**.

   The Properties window opens, as shown in Figure 45 showing the parameters needed to identify and customize a preset to create a sequence.

4. Click **File** on the Application bar, point to **New**, then click **Sequence**.

   The New Sequence dialog box opens.

5. Click the **expand arrow** in front of **HDV** then select **HDV 1080p30**, as shown in Figure 46.

   Look in the Preset Description; you will notice we do not need to customize the preset.

6. In the Sequence Name box, type **Vintage Footage**.

   The new sequence appears on the Project panel.

   (continued)

Figure 45 *Properties for the December7th.m2v video clip*

Image Size

Frame Rate

Pixel Aspect Ratio

Figure 46 *HDV 1080p30 sequence preset*

Frame Rate

Image Size

Pixel Aspect Ratio

HDV 1080p30

Sequence Name

Figure 47 *Project window with the new Vintage Footage sequence*

Reenactment sequence

Vintage Footage sequence

Figure 48 *Making a razor cut*

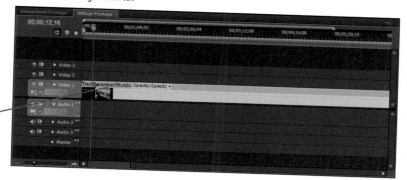

Razor cursor

7. Right-click **Sequence 01** on the Project panel, click **Rename**, type **Reenactment Footage**, then compare your screen to Figure 47.

8. Save your project file and leave it open for the next exercise.

You imported a video clip and identified its properties so you could create a new sequence.

Use the Razor tool to edit video

1. Open Pearl Harbor Documentary your name, if necessary.

2. Drag the **December7th.m2v video clip** to the Vintage Footage sequence on the Timeline panel, then preview the clip on the Program Monitor.

   We are going to edit this video clip to use with the video of the Pearl Harbor reenactment that we have already edited.

3. Place the CTI at **00;00;12;16** on the Timeline panel, then click the **Razor tool** on the Tools panel.

4. As shown in Figure 48, place the cursor where the CTI overlaps the video clip, then click.

   The appearance of the cursor changes to that of a razor when over a clip. The clip is cut into two parts. We will continue to move through the video clip making razor cuts.

TIP You can also access the Razor tool by pressing [C].

(continued)

5. Make razor cuts at the following durations: **00;02;06;15**, **00;02;24;15**, **00;04;42;04**, **00;05;51;04**, **00;07;27;20**, **00;09;02;25**, **00;10;19;19**, **00;12;30;18**, **00;16;12;16**, and **00;17;10;29**, then compare your sequence to Figure 49.

We will now remove the clips we do not need.

6. Click the **Selection tool** on the Tools panel, select the clip with the Start time 00;00;12;16, as shown in Figure 50, then press [**Delete**].

This clip should be the second cut clip in the sequence. Hover the mouse pointer over the clip to see a tool tip displaying the start and end points of the clip. You may need to zoom in on the sequence to see the video clips.

7. Delete the clips with the following start times from the sequence: **00;02;24;15**, **00;05;51;04**, **00;09;02;25**, **00;12;30;18**, and **00;17;10;29**, then compare your Timeline panel to Figure 51.

8. Save your project file and leave it open for the next exercise.

You edited a video with the Razor tool to remove unwanted sections of the footage.

Figure 49 *Sequence with the razor cuts*

Razor cuts

Figure 50 *Selecting a clip to delete*

Start time

Figure 51 *Sequence after video clips deleted*

Gaps from deleted clips

Figure 52 *Using the Go to Gap command*

CTI at beginning
of Out point

First gap

Figure 53 *Using the Ripple Delete command*

Ripple Delete
command

Selecting a gap

Remove gaps between video

1. Open Pearl Harbor Documentary your name, if necessary.

   There is a lot of space between the remaining video clips that we now need to remove.

2. Verify that the Vintage Footage sequence is active on the Timeline panel, and that the CTI is at **00;00;00;00**.

3. Click **Sequence** on the Application bar, point to **Go to Gap**, then click **Next in Sequence**.

   The CTI jumps to the beginning of the Out point of the first video clip, which marks the beginning of the first gap, as shown in Figure 52.

   Because we have only one track in our sequence, we can choose Next in Sequence. If we were using multiple tracks and would need to distinguish between which tracks we were on, then we would choose Next in Track.

   TIP The gaps in this sequence are rather large and easy to see. The Go to Gap command is good to use to find hard-to-see gaps to verify that there will be no gaps in your final footage.

4. Click the **gap**, click **Edit** on the Application bar, then click **Ripple Delete**, as shown in Figure 53.

   The gap is removed from the track and the remaining clips shift to the left.

   (continued)

Lesson 3   Work with Advanced Editing & Video Effects

5. Select the remaining gaps on the sequence and then remove them using the Ripple Delete command so that your Timeline resembles Figure 54.

6. Save your project file and leave it open for the next exercise.

You used the Ripple Delete command to remove gaps left behind from the Razor tool.

Rearrange a clip using the Program Monitor

1. Open Pearl Harbor Documentary your name, if necessary.

2. Press [**Spacebar**] to preview the Vintage Footage sequence on the Program Monitor.

   The first cut video clip needs to be moved to the end of the sequence after the attack has taken place.

3. Place the CTI at **00;00;00;00**, then click the **Set In Point button** on the Program Monitor.

4. Press [**Page Down**], then click the **Set Out Point button** on the Program Monitor.

   Notice the color change on the Timeline panel to show the location of the In and Out points that were just set on the Program Monitor, as shown in Figure 55.

5. Click the **Extract button** on the Program Monitor.

   The first cut video clip is removed from the sequence without leaving a gap, as shown in Figure 56.

6. Verify that the Timeline panel is active, press [**End**] to move the CTI to the end of the sequence, click **Edit** on the Application bar, then click **Paste**.

(continued)

Figure 54 *Sequence with all gaps removed*

Figure 55 *Specified area of a sequence when setting In and Out points on the Program Monitor*

Specified area of a sequence

Create a Documentary Using Premiere Pro and Soundbooth CS5

Figure 56 *Removed clip with no gap left*

Figure 57 *Searching for a transition*

Cross

Contains field

The extracted clip is placed at the location of the CTI.

TIP You can also use [Ctrl][V] (Win) or ⌘ [V] (Mac) to paste the video clip.

7. Save your project file and leave it open for the next exercise.

You used the Extract button on the Program Monitor and the Paste command to change the location of a video clip in the sequence.

Apply transitions between video clips

1. Open Pearl Harbor Documentary your name, if necessary.

We will add transitions to smooth out the choppiness created by the cut points in the video.

2. Verify that the Vintage Footage sequence is active on the Timeline panel.

3. Change the current workspace to Effects.

4. Drag the **CTI** to **00;00;17;29**.

TIP Remember that you can use the [Page Up] and [Page Down] keys to jump to the beginning and end of a clip on a track.

5. Type **Cross** in the Contains field on the Effects panel.

Entering the keyword *Cross* filters out transitions that have the word cross in it, as shown in Figure 57. We will be using the Cross Dissolve transition.

6. Click the **Cross Dissolve transition** on the Effects panel, click **Sequence** on the Application bar, then click **Apply Video Transition**.

The Cross Dissolve transition is placed at the location of the CTI, as shown in Figure 58.

(continued)

Lesson 3   Work with Advanced Editing & Video Effects

TIP The keyboard shortcut to place the selected transition at the location of the CTI is [Ctrl][D] (Win) or ⌘[D] (Mac).

7. Place the Cross Dissolve transition at each of the remaining cut points in the sequence: **00;06;20;16**, **00;03;02;04**, **00;05;22;03**, and **00;06;20;16**, as shown in Figure 59.

TIP Another way to place the selected transition at the end of each clip is to press [Page Down] and then press [Ctrl][D] (Win) or ⌘[D] (Mac).

8. Place the Dip to Black transition on the last clip in the sequence as an End at Cut transition as shown in Figure 60.

   This will fade the last video clip to black at the end of the sequence.

9. Press [**Spacebar**] to preview the clip on the Program Monitor.

10. Save your project file and leave it open for the next exercise.

You applied a Cross Dissolve transition on the cut lines to remove the choppiness that occurred because of the previous editing.

Nest a sequence

1. Open Pearl Harbor Documentary your name, if necessary.

2. Reset the current workspace to Editing, then verify that the Vintage Footage sequence is active on the Timeline panel.

3. Right-click the **Reenactment Footage sequence** on the Project panel, then click **Open in Source Monitor**, as shown in Figure 61.

   The sequence opens on the Source Monitor where it can be previewed and edited.

   (continued)

Figure 58 *Placing a transition at the CTI*

Cross Dissolve transition

Figure 59 *Cross Dissolve transition between all cut points*

Cross Dissolve transition

Figure 60 *Placing a Dip to Black transition*

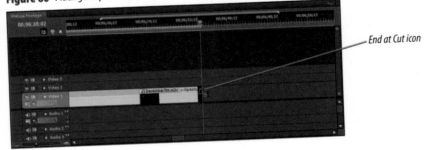

End at Cut icon

Figure 61 *Previewing a sequence on the Source Monitor*

Reenactment
Footage sequence

Vintage
Footage sequence

Figure 62 *Previewing a sequence using keyboard shortcuts*

First frame
of sky

Location of CTI

4. Drag the **CTI** to **00;00;35;00**.

   We will preview the clip for just a few seconds. At the point where the sailor is looking up at the sky and then planes start to appear in the sky, but they are very faint. This would be a good place to insert the Reenactment Footage.

5. Press [**Shift**][**L**] on the keyboard to play the sequence at a slow speed, press [**K**] to stop the sequence from playing, then press [**Shift**][**J**] to play the sequence in reverse at a slow speed.

6. Leave the CTI where you can still see the sailor for the next step.

   We want the CTI to be placed at the exact point where the sailor disappears and the sky appears.

7. Press and hold [**K**], then continue to press [**L**] until you see the first frame of the sky on the Program Monitor, as shown in Figure 62.

8. Click the **Razor tool** on the Tools panel, then click at the location of the CTI to make a cut.

   We are now ready to insert the Reenactment Footage sequence at the location of the cut that was just created.

9. Click the **Insert button** on the Source Monitor to place the Reenactment Footage sequence at the location of the CTI.

   Notice the Reenactment Footage sequence has an empty audio track that was also inserted, as shown in Figure 63.

10. Click **Edit** on the Application bar, then click **Undo**.

    The sequence is removed from the Timeline panel. We need to place the sequence without the empty audio track.

    (continued)

11. Press and hold [**Ctrl**] (Win) or ⌘ (Mac), then click and drag the **Drag Video Only icon** ▐ to the location of the CTI to place the Reenactment Footage sequence, as shown in Figure 64.

The sequence is placed without the empty audio track.

12. Press [**Spacebar**] to preview the clip on the Program Monitor.

13. Save your project file and leave it open for the next exercise.

You used keyboard shortcuts to preview a sequence on the Timeline panel and then inserted a sequence using the Drag Video Only icon after creating a razor cut.

Apply a video effect

1. Open Pearl Harbor Documentary your name, if necessary.

2. Reset the current workspace to Effects, then verify that the Vintage Footage sequence is active on the Timeline panel.

The Reenactment Footage needs to be made black and white.

3. Place the CTI at the beginning of the Reenactment Footage clip on the Timeline panel.

4. Click the **expand arrow** in front of Video Effects on the Effects panel, and then click the **expand arrow** in front of Image Control.

The categories of Video Effects are displayed and the Image Control video effects are also displayed.

(continued)

Figure 63 *Inserting the Reenactment Footage sequence using the Insert button*

Reenactment Footage sequence

Empty audio track

Figure 64 *Dragging video only to sequence with Insert edit command*

Last and first frame and insert point

Drag Video Only icon

Insert icon

Figure 65 *Applying a Black & White video effect*

Black & White preview

Black & White video effect

Black & White video effect

Drag Black & White effect here

Figure 66 *Applying the Lighting Effects*

Lighting Effects

Light Type drop-down menu

Lighting Effects

Ambience Intensity

5. Click **Black & White** on the Effects panel, then drag it on top of the Reenactment Footage clip on the Timeline panel.

   As shown in Figure 65, the footage is converted to black and white as shown on the Program Monitor and the Black & White video effect is added to the Effect Controls panel. The effect is a little too bright, so we will make adjustments to it in the next step.

6. Click the **expand arrow** in front of **Adjust**, then drag **Lighting Effects** on top of the Reenactment Footage clip on the Timeline panel.

   This is the second video effect applied to the Reenactment Footage clip.

7. On the Effect Controls panel, click the **expand arrow** in front of **Lighting Effects**, and again in front of **Light 1**, select the **Light Type drop-down menu**, then click **None**.

8. Click the **expand arrow** in front of Ambience Intensity then drag the **slider** to **34.1**, as shown in Figure 66.

   This modifies the appearance of the video footage so that it fits in better with the Vintage Footage sequence with its black and white appearance.

9. Press [**Spacebar**] to preview the clip on the Program Monitor.

10. Save your project file and leave it open for the next exercise.

You changed the appearance of a video clip to black and white through the use of video effects.

Edit Audio
IN SOUNDBOOTH

What You'll Do

 In this lesson, you will repair an audio file in Soundbooth and then edit the file in Premiere Pro.

Editing an Audio Source File in Soundbooth

If you have either the Master Collection or Production Premium Suite installed, which includes Soundbooth, you can apply the **Edit in Adobe Soundbooth** command to an audio clip from Premiere Pro, as shown in Figure 67.

When editing an audio clip in Soundbooth you have three options. The **Edit Source file** option makes changes to the actual source, and any references made to the source file in Premiere will be updated when the file is saved in Soundbooth. The audio file remains open in Soundbooth until you close it. You can easily swap between applications while

Figure 67 *Edit in Adobe Soundbooth*

Edit in Adobe Soundbooth command

working on the file to preview your changes in Premiere Pro while you work.

This option can be chosen when the source clip is selected on the Timeline panel or on the Project panel. The **Render and Replace** option renders a new audio clip that is edited in Soundbooth and replaces it with the original clip on the Timeline panel; the original source clip remains untouched on the Project panel. The new file that is created appears on the Premiere Pro Project panel. The **Extract Audio** option can only be chosen when the audio clip is selected on the Project panel. A copy of the audio file is created from the source clip and appears on the Project panel and then opens in a new Soundbooth file.

Working with Audio Transitions

Transitions are also available for audio in Premiere Pro to add a fade-in or fade-out effect. There are three types of **crossfades**: Constant Gain, Constant Power, and Exponential Fade, as shown in Figure 68. Crossfades are audio transitions that fade in or fade out an audio clip. A crossfade is created between two adjoining clips on the same audio track. A fade-in or fade-out effect is created by placing a crossfade transition on either end of a single clip.

The **Constant Gain** crossfade can sound abrupt because it changes the audio at a constant rate in and out as it transitions between clips, as shown in Figure 69. The **Constant**

Power crossfade is the default transition. It is analogous to the Dissolve transition between video clips because of the way that it creates a smooth, gradual transition between audio clips. The Constant Power transition works by decreasing the audio slowly and then more quickly towards the end of the transition on the first clip and then when it reaches the second clip it increases the audio quickly at first and then more slowly toward the end of the transition, as shown in Figure 70. The **Exponential Fade** transition fades out the first clip and fades up the second clip.

Converting Speech to Text

Either Premiere Pro or Soundbooth can convert the spoken word in an audio file

Figure 68 *Audio transitions*

Crossfades

Figure 69 *Constant Gain crossfade*

Constant Gain

Figure 70 *Constant Power crossfade*

Constant Power

into text transcripts. Text transcripts can be used to create closed captioning, or as a way to quickly navigate through video or audio clips by searching on the spoken work. In both applications, the Metadata panel is used to initiate the transcription process and to display the transcript when the process is complete. An **XMP metadata file** is generated and shared between all of the Video Suite applications when the transcript is created. **Metadata** includes the text transcript and can also include any additional information, for example the title, author, camera model, and date and time the video or image was taken. Metadata appears on the Metadata panel.

Not all the transcribed words are accurate, and the accuracy depends on the clearness of the speaker and the quality of the audio. The tools in Soundbooth can be used to clean up the audio before initiating the Convert to Speech option. Generally, the transcription that is generated is useful enough to aide in searching for keywords. However, transcripts can be edited where errors were made in the transcription process if a more accurate transcript is required. If you have a reference script available, you can refer to that file during the transcription process to get a more accurate transcription.

In Premiere Pro, you can convert the spoken word to written text by clicking the Analyze button in the Speech Analysis section of the Metadata panel. The Analyze Content dialog box opens, as shown in Figure 71. There are two quality options in the dialog box; the default is set to High (slower) so the Media Encoder will move at a slower pace as it passes through the audio clip. If you have more than one speaker in the audio clip that you wish to have identified, check the box next to Identify Speakers. Once you click OK, the Media Encoder launches, placing the request in the queue, as shown in Figure 72.

Figure 71 *Analyze Content dialog box*

Quality

Figure 72 *Adobe Media Encoder*

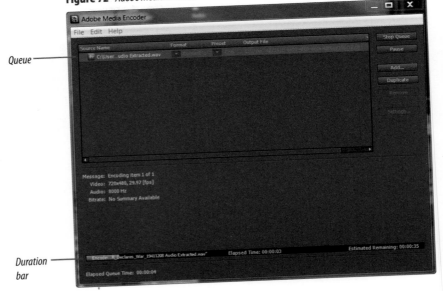

Queue

Duration bar

Create a Documentary Using Premiere Pro and Soundbooth CS5

When the Media Encoder has finished, you can close the application and return to your project in Premiere Pro. The transcript then appears in the Speech Analysis portion of the Metadata panel, as shown in Figure 73. Having the text available in Premiere Pro allows you to navigate through a clip by selecting keywords or phrases. When a word is highlighted on the Metadata panel, the CTI navigates to that location of the clip. This allows you to quickly jump to a location in a video or audio clip and set In and Out points for the clip, as shown in Figure 74.

If you are going to edit your source file in Soundbooth from Premiere Pro to convert your audio file to a text transcript, you will need to export the speech analysis to generate the XMP metadata file, so that when you return to your project the text transcript will appear on the Metadata panel in Premiere Pro.

Figure 73 *Metadata panel with transcribed text*

Metadata panel

Transcribed text

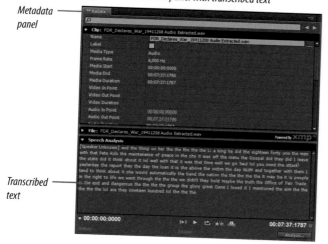

Figure 74 *In and Out points and transcribed text*

In point

Out point

Import an audio file and preview

1. Open Pearl Harbor Documentary your name, if necessary.

2. Reset the current workspace to Editing, then verify that the Vintage Footage sequence is active on the Timeline panel.

3. On the Media Browser, locate your Data Files folder for Chapter 4, as shown in Figure 75.

4. Click **FDR Speech**, press and hold [**Shift**], click **History Pearl Harbor**, right-click, then click **Import**.

   Both audio files are imported into the Project panel, as shown in Figure 76.

   (continued)

Figure 75 *Locating the Data Files folder for Chapter 4 in the Media Browser*

Media Browser

Data Files folder

Figure 76 *Audio files imported into Project panel*

Project panel

Audio files

Create a Documentary Using Premiere Pro and Soundbooth CS5

Figure 77 *Dragging only the audio to a new audio track*

Drag Audio Only

New audio track being created

5. Double-click **FDR Speech** to open it on the Source Monitor, then click the **Play button** to preview the audio clip.

   You will notice there are some areas of the speech that have scratchy noises that need to be cleaned up in Soundbooth.

6. Click the **Drag Audio Only icon** then drag the **FDR Speech** to the audio track, as shown in Figure 77.

   An Audio 4 track is created for this audio file because the FDR Speech audio clip is mono and the other tracks are formatted for stereo.

7. Save your project file and leave it open for the next exercise.

You imported audio files, previewed a file on the Source Monitor, and finally dragged the audio clip to an audio track.

Clean up an audio source file in Soundbooth

1. Open Pearl Harbor Documentary your name, if necessary.

2. Click the **FDR Speech audio clip** on the Timeline, click **Edit** on the Application bar, click **Edit in Adobe Soundbooth** and then click **Edit Source File**.

   Soundbooth opens with the FDR Speech file active on the Editor panel.

(continued)

3. In Soundbooth, choose the Default workspace, then click the **Spectral Frequency Display button** 🔲 on the Tools panel to show the spectral display on the Editor panel.

   Looking at the spectral display, we can quickly determine that there are areas we can remove at the very beginning and at the end of the speech, indicated by the black area, as shown in Figure 78.

4. Click the **Time Selection tool** 🔲 on the Tools panel, highlight the areas indicated in Figure 78, then press [**Delete**].

   The unwanted areas from the audio file are removed; your Editor panel should look similar to Figure 79.

5. Click **File** on the Application bar, then click **Save**.

   The FDR Speech audio clip that we opened from Premiere Pro for editing in Soundbooth is saved.

6. Close Soundbooth, then return to the open project file in Premiere Pro.

7. Keep the file open for the next exercise.

You removed the unwanted areas at the beginning and the end of the FDR Speech in Soundbooth.

Edit an audio clip on the Timeline panel

1. Open Pearl Harbor Documentary your name, if necessary.

2. Open the FDR Speech audio clip, if it is not already open on the Source Monitor.

   The edits made in Soundbooth have transferred to the audio file in Premiere Pro.

3. Click the **Play button** ▶ on the Source Monitor to preview the FDR Speech audio file.

(continued)

Figure 78 *Areas to be removed*

Area that can be removed

Area that can be removed

Figure 79 *Edited source FDR Speech source file*

Create a Documentary Using Premiere Pro and Soundbooth CS5

Figure 80 *Viewing the waveform on the audio track*

Expand arrow   Waveform

Figure 81 *Deleting applause*

Applause

Figure 82 *Shortening the duration of the audio clip*

Lesson 4   Edit Audio in Soundbooth

4. Click the **expand arrow** on the Audio 4 track, as shown in Figure 80.

   The waveform now becomes visible. You will notice the audio clip is much longer than the video. We can correct this by removing some of the applause from the speech. The applause is recognizable in the waveform as large portions of green where the waves are not distinguishable.

5. Click the **Razor tool** on the Tools panel, make cuts at the following durations: **00;04;45;18**, **00;04;56;00**, **00;05;11;08**, **00;05;38;28**, **00;06;01;25**; **00;06;11;07**; **00;06;41;26**, and **00;06;53;15**.

   Your cut lines may vary slightly based on the edits made in Soundbooth.

6. Use keyboard shortcut keys to preview the audio clip and make any necessary modifications to the locations of the cuts.

   We will leave the first round of applause when the President is introduced.

7. Lock the Video 1 track, click the **Selection tool** on the Tools panel, right-click between the cut lines, then click **Ripple Delete** to delete the applause using Figure 81 as a guide.

8. Drag the **CTI** to **00;06;23;27**, place the cursor at the right edge of the FDR Speech audio clip and using the **Trim-out icon**, drag the clip to the CTI, then compare your Figure to 82.

   Your time may vary. Place the CTI where the President stops speaking.

9. Save your project file and leave it open for the next exercise.

You edited an audio clip on the Timeline panel using the Razor tool, and removed gaps using the Ripple Delete command.

Convert speech to text

1. Open Pearl Harbor Documentary your name, if necessary.

2. Click the **History PearlHarbor audio clip** on the Project panel, click **Edit** on the Application bar, point to **Edit in Adobe Soundbooth**, then click **Edit Source File**.

   Soundbooth opens with the History PearlHarbor audio clip active on the Editor panel.

3. Change the workspace to Meta Logging.

4. Click the **expand arrow** in front of **Speech Analysis**, as shown in Figure 83, then click the **Analyze Speech button** on the Metadata panel.

5. Accept the default settings in the Speech Analysis Options dialog box, then click **OK**.

   The Analyzing speech dialog box opens to begin the transcription, as shown in Figure 84.

6. Click **File** on the Application bar, point to **Export**, then click **Speech Analysis**.

7. Click **File** on the Application bar, then click **Save**.

8. Close Soundbooth to return to your open project file in Premiere Pro.

9. Open the History PearlHarbor audio clip on the Source Monitor.

10. Click **Window** on the Application bar, then click **Metadata**.

    The Metadata panel opens.

    (continued)

Figure 83 *Metadata panel*

Meta Logging workspace

Metadata panel

Speech Analysis

Analyze Speech button

Figure 84 *Analyzing speech dialog box*

Duration

Figure 85 *Moving the Metadata panel*

Metadata panel

Speech Analysis

Figure 86 *Highlighting a word in the Speech Analysis to adjust the CTI*

CTI

Highlighted word

11. Move the Metadata panel to the bottom left of the application window, as shown in Figure 85, then click the **expand arrow** in front of Speech Analysis.

12. Look through the passage for the part that reads: "the the these pollutants".

   The transcription has some errors in it. Your transcription may vary. The last statement said by the commentator just after where FDR's speech is played in the clip should be, "the day that will live in infamy became only the first of many as the United States entered the most devastating global conflict in modern history."

13. Click on the first **the** in the statement.

   The CTI moves to the location of the text you highlight in the Metadata panel, as shown in Figure 86.

14. Click the **Play-Stop Toggle button** ▶ on the Source Monitor to preview the History PearlHarbor audio clip from this point.

   Notice the transcription does not match the spoken word. We will trim the audio clip from this point in the next step to use at the end of our video.

15. Save your project file and leave it open for the next exercise.

You opened an audio clip from Premiere Pro in Soundbooth, converted the speech to text, returned to Premiere Pro and used the Metadata panel to find text and navigate the CTI to that location.

Edit an audio clip on the Source Monitor

1. Open Pearl Harbor Documentary your name, if necessary.

2. Open History PearlHarbor on the Source Monitor.

   We will be editing this audio file on the Source Monitor and then placing it on the Audio 4 track.

3. Set the Current-time display on the Source Monitor to **00;01;51;16**.

4. Click the **Set In Point button** .

5. Set the Current-time display on the Source Monitor to **00;02;02;15**.

6. Click the **Set Out Point button** , then compare your Source Monitor to Figure 87.

   The Video 1 track should still be locked, and your CTI should still be at 00;06;24;00.

7. Click in the **header** of the Audio 4 track.

   This targets the track by highlighting it and preparing it for the Insert command, as shown in Figure 88.

8. Click the **Insert button** on the Source Monitor.

   The trimmed clip is placed at the location of the CTI on the Timeline panel, as shown in Figure 89.

9. Save your project file and leave it open for the next exercise.

You edited an audio clip on the Source Monitor and then placed it on the audio track.

Figure 87 *Setting In and Out points on the Source Monitor*

In point

Out point

Figure 88 *Targeting the Audio track*

Target track

Figure 89 *Trimmed audio clip inserted from Source Monitor*

Create a Documentary Using Premiere Pro and Soundbooth CS5

Figure 90 *Placing an audio transition*

Center at Cut alignment icon

Figure 91 *Preview of sample title on Video 2 track*

Preview of sample title

Apply an audio transition

1. Open Pearl Harbor Documentary your name, if necessary.

2. Reset the workspace to Effects, click the **Source menu** on the Source Monitor, then click **Close All**.

3. Preview the transition between the last FDR Speech audio clip and the History PearlHarbor audio clip.

   The FDR Speech audio clip needs to fade into the History PearlHarbor audio clip.

4. Click the **expand arrow** in front of **Audio Transitions**, then click the **expand arrow** in front of **Crossfade**.

5. Drag the **Constant Power transition** from the Effects panel and drop it between the last FDR Speech audio clip and the History PearlHarbor audio clip with a Center at Cut alignment, as shown in Figure 90.

   The Constant Power audio transition is analogous to the Dissolve transition used in video.

6. Create a Default Still Title, place it on the Video 2 track to title your documentary, and give yourself credit. One example is provided in Figure 91.

   It is not necessary to provide credits for the clips used in this project; they are all public domain and therefore have no restrictions for their use. The Reenactment footage was filmed by the author and is provided for use as a part of this project.

7. Save and export your movie with the MPEG2 format using the NTSC DV High Quality Preset.

You applied an audio transition between audio clips and exported your final movie with the MPEG2 format.

Transfer tapeless video.

1. Without starting Premiere Pro, navigate to the drive and folder where your Data Files are stored for Chapter 4.
2. Select AVCHD-Glassworks, click Organize on the Toolbar, then click Copy.
3. Select the Data Files folder for Chapter 4 using the Navigation pane, click Organize on the Toolbar, then click Paste.

Create a sequence for AVCHD video footage.

1. Start Premiere Pro, then click New Project in the Welcome to Adobe Premiere Pro dialog box.
2. Click Browse, navigate to your Data Files folder, then click OK.
3. Name the project **Glassworks your name**, then click OK.
4. Click the expander arrow in front of HDV, select HDV 1080p30, then click OK.

Import video from a file-based source.

1. On the Media Browser panel, locate the Data Files folder for Chapter 4, then double-click the AVCHD- Glassworks folder.
2. Double-click 00003.
3. Click the Source menu on the Source Monitor, then click Close.
4. Select clip 00001, click File on the Application bar, then click Import from Media Browser.
5. Save and close your project file.

Trim video on the Source Monitor.

1. Open Kennedy SpaceDocumentary.prproj, then rename it **Kennedy Space Documentary your name**.
2. Select Workspace on the Application bar, then choose the Editing workspace.
3. Double-click **space1.m2v** on the Project panel.
4. Click the Play-Stop Toggle button to preview the video clip.
5. Turn on Safe Margins in both the Source and Program Monitors, if they are not already activated.
6. Drag the CTI until the timecode display reads 00;14;35;05, then click the Set In Point button on the Source Monitor.
7. Drag the CTI until the timecode display reads 00;18;48;04, then click the Set Out Point button on the Source Monitor.
8. Click the Play In to Out button to preview the trimmed clip on the Source Monitor.
9. Drag the In/Out Grip to the left two tick marks to move the In point to the left.
10. Click the Play In to Out button to preview the trimmed clip on the Source Monitor.
11. Hover your mouse over the Out point, then drag the right edge of the clip with the Trim-out icon until the timecode display reads 00;19;18;02.
12. Click the Play In to Out button to preview the trimmed clip on the Source Monitor.
13. Click the Insert button to place the trimmed clip in the sequence on the Timeline panel.
14. Press [Spacebar] to preview the clip on the Program Monitor.

Edit a clip on the Timeline panel.

1. Drag space2.m2v to the Video 1 track on the Timeline panel.
2. Press the [Page Down] key to move the CTI to the beginning of the space2 video clip.
3. Press [Spacebar] to preview the video clip on the Program Monitor.
4. Click the Selection tool on the Tools panel, then place your cursor over the left edge of the space2 video clip. Once the Trim-in icon appears, drag the left edge to the right until the tool tip displays +00;06;32;02.
5. Point your cursor to the blank space between the two video clips on the Video 1 track, right-click, then click Ripple Delete.
6. Press [Page Down] to move the CTI to the end of the space2 video clip.
7. Place your cursor over the right edge of the space2 video clip. Once the Trim-out icon appears, drag the right edge to the left until the tool tip displays -00;00;26;17.
8. Press [Spacebar] to preview the sequence on the Program Monitor.
9. Save your project file and leave it open for the next step.

Create keyboard commands to set In and Out points.

1. Click Edit on the Application bar, then choose Keyboard Customization. (*Hint*: These keyboard shortcuts have already been created and may already be set on your computer, unless your computers are restored to factory settings.)
2. Click the Set drop-down menu, then click Custom.
3. Scroll down to Trim In Point to CTI, click in the Shortcut area to the right, then press [[].
4. Click the Shortcut area to the right of the Trim Out Point to CTI, press []], then click OK.

Use the CTI to set In and Out points.

1. Drag space3.m2v after the space2.m2v video clip on the Video 1 track.
2. Preview the space3.m2v video clip and move the CTI to the beginning of the video clip.
3. Move the CTI to 00;08;18;19.
4. Press [[] on your keyboard, to create a Trim in point.
5. Move the CTI to 00;08;44;22.
6. Press []] on your keyboard, to set a Trim out point.
7. Press [Spacebar] to preview the sequence on the Program Monitor.
8. With the Selection tool, click the gap in front of space3.m2v, then press [Delete].

Trim a video clip with the Ripple Edit tool.

1. Drag space4.m2v after the space3.m2v video clip on the Video 1 track.
2. Preview the space4.m2v video clip, then move the CTI to the beginning of the video clip.
3. Click the Ripple Edit tool on the Tools panel.

4. Place your cursor over the left edge of the space4.m2v video clip, then drag the Ripple Edit icon from the left edge to the right until the tool tip displays +00;04;35;15.
5. Click the Selection tool on the Tools panel, place the CTI at 00;06;45;24, then press []] to create a Trim Out point.
6. Press [Spacebar] to preview the sequence on the Program Monitor.

Use the Insert button to place a trimmed clip.

1. Open space5.m2v on the Source Monitor and preview the video clip.
2. Set the Source Monitor timecode display to read 01;11;00;11, then click the Set In Point button on the Source Monitor.
3. Set the Source Monitor timecode display to read 01;11;48;02, then click the Set Out Point button on the Source Monitor.
4. On the Timeline panel, place the CTI at the end of the space4.m2v video clip.
5. Click the Insert button on the Source Monitor.
6. Press [Spacebar] to preview the sequence on the Program Monitor.
7. Set the Source Monitor timecode display to read 01;04;14;22, then click the Set In Point button on the Source Monitor.
8. Set the Source Monitor timecode display to read 01;04;39;18, then click the Set Out Point button on the Source Monitor.
9. On the Timeline panel, place the CTI at the end of the space5.m2v video clip.
10. Click the Insert button on the Source Monitor.

Use the Overlay button to place a trimmed clip.

1. Open space6.m2v on the Source Monitor and preview the video clip.
2. Set the Source Monitor timecode display to read 01;15;33;17, then click the Set In Point button on the Source Monitor.
3. Set the Source Monitor timecode display to read 01;19;53;29, then click the Set Out Point button.
4. On the Timeline panel, place the CTI at the end of the second space5.m2v video clip.
5. Click the Overlay button on the Source Monitor to place the video clip on the Timeline panel.

Perform a rearrange edit.

1. Use the Zoom Slider to adjust the Timeline panel so that you can see all of your video clips at the same time.
2. Click the Selection tool, click the first space5.m2v, press and hold [Ctrl][Alt] (Win) or ⌘ [option] (Mac), drag the video clip in front of space2.m2v, then release the mouse button.
3. Using the rearrange edit technique, reorder the video clips on the Video 1 track so they are arranged as follows: space1.m2v, space5.m2v, space5.m2v, space2.m2v, space4.m2v, space3.m2v, space6.m2v.
4. Press [Spacebar] to preview the sequence on the Program Monitor.

Create a new sequence.

1. Click File on the Application bar, click Import, navigate to your Data Files folder for Chapter 4, select apollo launch.m2v, then click Open.

2. On the Project panel, right-click the apollo launch. m2v video clip, then click Properties.
3. Click File on the Application bar, then click New Sequence.
4. Click the expand arrow in front of DV-NTSC, then click Standard 48kHz.
5. In the Sequence Name box, type **Launch**.
6. Right-click Sequence 01 on the Project panel, click Rename, then type **Apollo Flight**.
7. Save your project file and leave it open for the next step.

Use the Razor tool to edit video.

1. Drag the apollo launch.m2v video clip to the Launch sequence on the Timeline panel, then preview the clip on the Program Monitor.
2. Place the CTI at 00;02;07;17 on the Timeline panel, click the Razor tool on the Tools panel, place the cursor over the point of the CTI, then click the video clip.
3. Make razor cuts at the following durations: 00;03;37;14, 00;08;12;02, 00;08;34;22, 00;13;59;29, and 00;16;40;00.
4. Select the clip with the Start time 00;02;07;17, then press the [Delete] key.
5. Delete the clips with the following start times from the sequence: 00;03;37;14, 00;08;34;22, and 00;16;40;00.

Remove gaps between video.

1. Verify that the Launch sequence is active on the Timeline panel, with the CTI at 00;00;00;00.
2. Click Sequence on the Application bar, point to Go to Gap, then click Next in Sequence.

3. Click the gap, click Edit on the Application bar, then click Ripple Delete.
4. Select the remaining gaps on the sequence and remove them with the Ripple Delete command.

Rearrange a clip using the Program Monitor.

1. Press [Spacebar] to preview the Launch sequence on the Program Monitor.
2. Place the CTI at 00;00;00;00, click the Set In Point button on the Program Monitor, press [Page Down], then click the Set Out Point button.
3. Press the Extract button on the Program Monitor.
4. Press [End] to move the CTI to the end of the sequence, click Edit on the Application bar, then click Paste.

Apply transitions between video clips.

1. Change the current workspace to Effects.
2. Move the CTI to the location of the first cut point.
3. Type **Cross** in the Contains field on the Effects panel.
4. Click the Cross Dissolve transition on the Effects panel, click Sequence on the Application bar, then click Apply Video Transition.
5. Place the Cross Dissolve transition at the remaining cut points in the sequence.
6. Press [Spacebar] to preview the clip on the Program Monitor.

Nest a sequence.

1. Reset the current workspace to Editing with the Apollo Flight sequence active on the Timeline panel.
2. Right-click the Launch sequence on the Project panel, then click Open in Source Monitor.

3. Drag the CTI on the Timeline panel to 00;00;00;00.
4. Click the Insert button on the Source Monitor to place the Launch sequence at the location of the CTI.
5. Click Edit on the Application bar, then click Undo.
6. Press and hold [Ctrl] (Win) or [⌘] (Mac), then click and drag the Drag Video Only icon to place the Launch sequence at the location of the CTI.
7. Press [Spacebar] to preview the clip on the Program Monitor.

Apply a video effect.

1. Reset the current workspace to Effects with the Apollo Flight sequence active on the Timeline panel.
2. Place the CTI at the beginning of the Launch clip on the Timeline panel.
3. Click the expand arrow in front of Video Effects on the Effects panel, then click the expand arrow in front of Color Correction.
4. Drag Tint on top of the Launch clip on the Timeline panel.
5. On the Effect Controls panel, adjust the Amount to value to 70.0%.
6. Press [Spacebar] to preview the clip on the Program Monitor.
7. Save your project file and leave it open for the next step.

Import an audio file and preview.

1. Reset the current workspace to Editing with the Apollo Flight sequence active on the Timeline panel.
2. On the Media Browser, locate your Data Files folder for Chapter 4.
3. Click Kennedy Space, press and hold [Shift], click Kennedy Rice, right-click, then click Import.

4. Double-click Kennedy Rice to open it on the Source Monitor then click the Play button to preview the audio clip.
5. Click the Drag Audio Only icon, then drag Kennedy Rice to the audio track at the beginning of the sequence.

Clean up an audio source file in Soundbooth.

1. Click the Kennedy Rice audio clip on the Timeline panel, click Edit on the Application bar, point to Edit in Soundbooth, then click Edit Source File.
2. In Soundbooth, choose the Default workspace, then click the Spectral Frequency Display button on the Tools panel to show the spectral display.
3. Use the Rectangular Marquee tool to take a sample at approximately 00;10;20;837, where there is a bright vertical line.
4. In the Clean up Audio panel, click the Capture Noise Print button, click the Noise button, then click OK.
5. Click File on the Application bar, then click Save.
6. Close Soundbooth to return to your open project file in Premiere Pro.

Edit an audio clip on the Timeline panel.

1. Click the Play button on the Source Monitor to preview the Kennedy Rice audio file.
2. Click the expand arrow on the Audio track where the Kennedy Rice audio file is located.
3. Using the Razor tool make cuts at the following durations: 00;10;57;26, 00;11;03;12, 00;11;44;01, 00;11;48;21, 00;12;01,07, 00;12;09;10, 00;05;26;21, 00;05;37;29, 00;08;40;01, 00;08;48;17, 00;09;14;04,

00;09;21;17, 00;13;07;21, 00;13;12;27, 00;13;21;09, 00;14;21;09, 00;14;27;13, 00;16;03;06, 00;16;12;26, 00;16;52;22, 00;17;00;23, and 00;17;32;21.
4. Lock the Video 1 track and using the Selection tool, right-click between the cut lines, then click Ripple Delete to delete the applause.

Convert speech to text.

1. Click the Kennedy Space audio clip on the Timeline panel, click Edit on the Application bar, point to Edit in Soundbooth, then click Edit Source File.
2. Change the workspace to Meta Logging.
3. Click the expand arrow in front of Speech Analysis, then click the Analyze Speech button on the Metadata panel.
4. Accept the default settings in the Speech Analysis Options dialog box, then click OK.
5. Click File on the Application bar, point to Export, then click Speech Analysis.
6. Click File on the Application bar, then click Save.
7. Close Soundbooth and return to your open project file in Premiere Pro.
8. Open the Kennedy Space audio clip on the Source Monitor.
9. Select Window on the Application bar, then click Metadata.
10. Move the Metadata panel to the bottom left of the application window, then click the expand arrow in front of Speech Analysis.
11. Look through the passage for the part that reads: "I believe that this nation"; your analysis may vary.
12. Click the "I" in the statement.

Edit an audio clip on the Source Monitor.

1. Open Kennedy Space on the Source Monitor.
2. Set the Current-time display on the Source Monitor to 00;03;03;12.
3. Click the Set In Point button.
4. Set the Current-time display on the Source Monitor to 00;04;14;11.
5. Click the Set Out Point button.
6. Click in the header of the Audio track where the Kennedy Rice audio file is located.
7. Click the Insert button on the Source Monitor.
8. Reset the workspace to Effects, then close all on the Source Monitor.
9. Preview the transition between the Kennedy Rice audio clip and the Kennedy Space audio clip.

Apply an audio transition.

1. Click the expand arrow in front of Audio Transitions, and again in front of Crossfade.
2. Drag the Constant Power transition and drop it between the last Kennedy Rice audio clip and the Kennedy Space audio clip with a Center at Cut alignment.
3. Create a Default Still Title, place it on the Video 2 track to title your documentary, and give yourself credit. Figure 92 shows one sample.
4. Save and export your movie with the MPEG2 format.

Figure 92 *Completed Skills Review*

Create a Documentary Using Premiere Pro and Soundbooth CS5

The Chamber of Commerce has announced that they are having their first annual air show to coincide with the 4th of July celebrations to honor America and our military. They have contacted your advertising firm to create a 20-second commercial using some footage they have shot at another air show.

The Chamber has provided the beginning Premiere Pro project file, which includes the video clips they would like you to edit into the 20-second spot. They own the footage, therefore no credits are necessary. They plan to run this ad on television and on the Internet, and therefore, need you to supply the final version in FLV|F4V and MPEG2 formats.

1. Open Chamber.prproj, then save it as **Chamber Commercial your name**.
2. Preview the various video clips on the Source Monitor to decide how you will compose your 20-second spot.
3. Trim the video clips using the techniques you have learned in this chapter.
4. Add a title announcing this as the **First Annual 4th of July Air Show**.
5. Export your movie to the FLV|F4V and MPEG2 formats.

Figure 93 *Sample Project Builder 1*

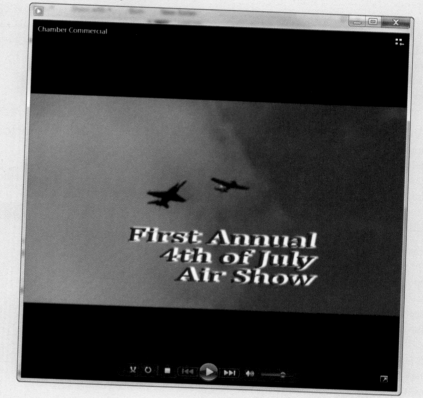

Create a Documentary Using Premiere Pro and Soundbooth CS5

Your speech teacher is doing a unit on famous speeches and the phrases that have become a part of our everyday lives: Martin Luther King Jr.'s "I have a dream", Douglas MacArthur's "Old soldiers never die", Ronald Reagan's "Tear down this wall", and Lou Gehrig's "Today I consider myself the luckiest man on the face of the earth".

You have decided to use your knowledge of Soundbooth and your Internet shrewdness to compile an audio compilation of 10 of your favorite phrases from famous speeches using the Metadata panel and the Analyze Speech button to transcribe the speech and share with your speech teacher.

1. Research and download 10 famous speeches from the Internet that are in the public domain.
2. Open Soundbooth and import the files into the Files panel.
3. Change the workspace to Meta Logging. (*Hint*: This makes the Metadata panel easily accessible.)
4. Open the first audio file on the Editor panel, then click the Analyze Speech button on the Metadata panel.
5. Repeat this process for the other nine audio clips.
6. Create a new multitrack file, then place the 10 edited clips on the multitrack.
7. Use the information in the transcription to locate the phrase in the speech, edit the audio clips, and add transitions.
8. Export your Multitrack Mixdown as an MP3 file titled **Great Speech Phrases your name**.

Figure 94 *Sample Project Builder 2*

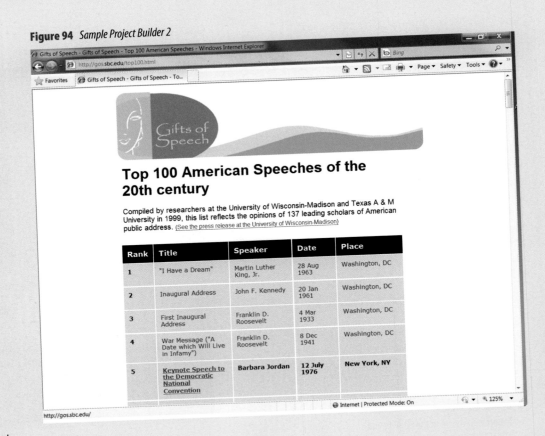

Gifts of Speech - Gifts of Speech - Top 100 American Speeches - Windows Internet Explorer

http://gos.sbc.edu/top100.html

Favorites | Gifts of Speech - Gifts of Speech - To...

Top 100 American Speeches of the 20th century

Compiled by researchers at the University of Wisconsin-Madison and Texas A & M University in 1999, this list reflects the opinions of 137 leading scholars of American public address. (See the press release at the University of Wisconsin-Madison)

Rank	Title	Speaker	Date	Place
1	"I Have a Dream"	Martin Luther King, Jr.	28 Aug 1963	Washington, DC
2	Inaugural Address	John F. Kennedy	20 Jan 1961	Washington, DC
3	First Inaugural Address	Franklin D. Roosevelt	4 Mar 1933	Washington, DC
4	War Message ("A Date which Will Live in Infamy")	Franklin D. Roosevelt	8 Dec 1941	Washington, DC
5	Keynote Speech to the Democratic National Convention	Barbara Jordan	12 July 1976	New York, NY

http://gos.sbc.edu/

Internet | Protected Mode: On   125%

Your history teacher was quite impressed with the video montage you created about the Space Program. He heard that you are now able to edit audio and video. Utilizing your new skills, he would like you to create a documentary about the holocaust using information from the United States Holocaust Memorial Museum (http://ushmm.org). There are plenty of materials that can be found by choosing Collections and Archives under the Research link.

You will need to trim and combine video clips with appropriate transitions and create an audio narration with audio files you are able to find at this Web site.

In addition, your instructor would like you to do the following:

1. Place an appropriate title at the beginning of the documentary.
2. Provide credits for the sources used in your documentary.
3. Make the documentary at least 20 minutes in length.
4. Place the Production Company Logo (created in Chapter 2) at the end of your documentary.
5. Export to the MPEG2 format with the NTSC DV High Quality Preset.

Figure 95 *Portfolio Project*

5 DEVELOP A PSA & COMMERCIAL USING PREMIERE PRO & AFTER EFFECTS CS5

CHAPTER

1. Edit a public service announcement
2. Edit a commercial for television
3. Edit a commercial developed for the Internet

DEVELOP A PSA & COMMERCIAL
USING PREMIERE PRO & AFTER EFFECTS CS5

In this chapter, we will work with the film concept of the commercial and the public service announcement (PSA) like those that you see on television or the Internet. You will continue to use the editing techniques you have learned in Premiere Pro and will learn advanced techniques in After Effects to add special effects to a commercial and a PSA.

A **commercial** is a short film broadcast for the public interest as a marketing device to raise awareness of a consumer product, service, or issue. **Public service announcements (PSAs)** are intended to modify public attitudes by raising awareness about specific issues. The most common topics of PSAs are health and safety. A typical PSA is part of a public awareness campaign to inform or educate the public about an issue such as smoking or compulsive gambling.

Edit a Public Service
ANNOUNCEMENT

What You'll Do

In this lesson, you will edit a public service announcement by using advanced techniques in After Effects and creating a voice over in Premiere Pro.

Working with the Cartoon Effect

The Cartoon effect in After Effects creates a stylized effect that resembles vector art by simplifying and smoothing the shading and colors in an image and adding strokes to the edges between features. You may have seen this technique a few years ago in the Charles Schwab television commercials and the full-length movie *A Scanner Darkly*. The result can produce an image that may resemble a sketch or a cartoon, as shown in Figure 1.

The Cartoon effect is in the Stylize category on the Effects & Presets panel. Figure 2 shows the default Cartoon settings applied to video footage. A good rule of thumb when working with the Cartoon effect is to

Figure 1 *Example of Cartoon effect*

Resembles a sketch

Resembles a cartoon

begin with the Fill properties. The Shading Steps and Shading Smoothness properties simplify the shading and coloring in the image, a process known as **posterization**, creating a more cartoon-like effect. The Shading Smoothness property can overrule the Shading Steps settings if the Shading Smoothness value is placed too high, returning the image to a more realistic look. The Detail Radius and Detail Threshold properties work with blurs and soften the image. The Edge properties determine what is considered an edge and how strokes are applied to edges. The Width property is the thickness that is added to an edge, like a thin pencil or a thick marker. Softness is the transition between the edge's stroke and the surrounding colors. Opacity can reduce the appearance of the stroke that is applied to the edge.

Each property has an expand arrow which when clicked reveals a slider, as shown in Figure 3. This may provide greater flexibility when making adjustments on the various properties. It is also a good practice to try different combinations of settings as you work with the effect.

Working with the Levels Effect

After applying the Cartoon effect, it may need a little help to look more cartoon-like. The Cartoon effect relies heavily on color and contrast to detect the edges of the objects or people in the footage. Most footage does not have enough color and contrast for the Cartoon effect to work effectively. The Levels effect, which helps to create contrast, will almost always be necessary.

Figure 2 *Cartoon effect with default settings*

Cartoon effect

Preview of effect

Figure 3 *Revealing the slider*

Expand arrow

Slider

The Levels effect, once applied, needs to be moved above the Cartoon effect so that it is applied to the footage first and therefore will aid the Cartoon effect in picking up contrast.

Apply the Levels effect after you've worked with the Cartoon effect. The Cartoon effect works with the color and contrast of the footage; this will help you make the proper levels adjustments while being able to preview the effect as it is applied with the Cartoon effect.

The Levels effect displays a **histogram**, a chart that represents the changes of color from dark to light in the image, as shown in Figure 4. (*Note*: You may need to expand the Effect Controls panel if you are unable to see the entire histogram.) The left side of the histogram shows how much black (or even dark gray) is in the image, and the right side how much white. The triangles at the bottom of the histogram are Input controls that adjust the contrast of the image. The triangle on the left is the Input Black control and on the right is the Input White control. The center triangle is the Gamma control, which adjusts the midtones. Dragging the Gamma control to the left will increase the brightness of the image, dragging to the right will reduce the brightness.

As you work with the histogram controls, you will notice the values for the Input Black, Input White, and Gamma adjust as you move the controls. A slider is also available, as shown in Figure 5, by clicking the expand arrow for these properties.

Figure 4 *Levels effect histogram*

Figure 5 *Levels effect histogram with sliders*

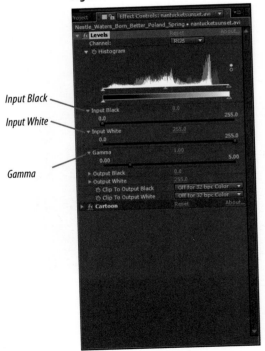

Develop a PSA & Commercial Using Premiere Pro & After Effects CS5

Working with the Hue/Saturation Effect

The Hue/Saturation effect is another color correction effect, which will add to the overall Cartoon effect. This effect is based on the color wheel. Adjusting the color, or hue, represents one rotation around the wheel. Adjusting the saturation, or intensity of the color, represents a move across the radius of the circle. The Master Hue color wheel and Master Saturation setting change the overall hue and saturation of the image, as shown in Figure 6. The value above the color wheel indicates the number of degrees of rotation around the wheel from the original color. A positive value means the wheel was rotated in a clockwise rotation, a negative value indicates a counterclockwise rotation.

Working with the Channel Mixer Effect

The Channel Mixer effect, in the Color Correction category, is another option that allows more subtle shading for the overall Cartoon effect. Unlike Hue/Saturation, which makes overall changes to the image, the Channel Mixer effect works on specific color channels.

An example of how the Channel Mixer effect works on an image by using a simple red square is shown in Figure 7. The true color red is shown in the upper-left square and the Red-Red, Green-Red, and Blue-Red property values are all set to 50 for comparison. When the Red-Red value is reduced to 50, half of the red is removed from the red channel making the color darker. When green is added to the red in the Green-Red channel

by changing the value to 50, the red appears orange. Finally, when we change the value to 50 in the Blue-Red channel, the color appears pink.

The color on the left is the input color. The color on the right is the output color, before any effects are applied. As you adjust the color by raising the value (a positive number) you add the input color. If you reduce the value (a negative number) you remove the input color.

Each channel also has a constant value abbreviated as *Const*. This channel increases the constant color with every other color combination in that color channel. For example, a Blue-Const setting of 100 saturates the blue channel by adding 100 percent blue.

Figure 6 *Hue/Saturation effect*

Master Hue color wheel   Default settings

Modified settings

Figure 7 *Channel Mixer Red property*

True Red   Blue-Red 50

Red-Red 50   Green-Red 50

Figure 8 shows a comparison between two images with the default Channel Mixer settings on the left and with some of the color channels modified on the right. As you can see, a more subtle effect is obtained using the Channel Mixer than when applying the Hue/Saturation effect. In this case, in the red channel, red was added to the green channel and subtracted from the blue channel. In the case of the green channel, green was added to the red channel and removed from the blue channel and in addition, the Green-Const value was adjusted to a value of 12, adding 12 percent green to

all of the green channels. Finally, in the blue channel blue was added to the green channel.

Importing an After Effects Project to Premiere Pro

Adobe Dynamic Link is a feature available between Premiere Pro, After Effects, and Encore if installed as part of the Creative Suite Production Premium or Master Collection. A change made in an After Effects composition that is dynamically linked in a Premiere Pro project is updated

immediately. The same is true for a change to a Premiere Pro sequence that is dynamically linked to an After Effects composition. Therefore, it is unnecessary to render or save changes for the updates to take place between applications.

Dynamic links are created when a file is imported from one of the programs into another. The files appear with a unique icon and label color, as shown in Figure 9. In this figure, an After Effects file named PSA/PSA Solution was imported into Premiere Pro.

Figure 8 *Channel Mixer effect*

Default settings   *Modified settings*

Figure 9 *File with dynamic link*

Dynamic link icon

Develop a PSA & Commercial Using Premiere Pro & After Effects CS5

The colorful file icon indicates the dynamic link established.

You can link an existing After Effects composition into a Premiere Pro project by clicking Dynamic Link on the File menu, and then clicking the Import After Effects Composition command. If the After Effects project has multiple compositions, you will have the option to choose one or more of the compositions, as shown in Figure 10.

To make changes to the linked composition in this example, you would select the composition on the Project panel or Timeline panel and choose the Edit Original command. This will launch After Effects with the composition active in After Effects; you will then be able to switch between the two applications to view changes.

Like any other asset, dynamic links may become unlinked. This happens if a file has been moved or renamed. If you need to relink a dynamic link, as shown in Figure 11, right-click the dynamic link and choose Link Media. The Link Media to dialog box opens,

Figure 10 *Import After Effects Composition dialog box*

Compositions available for import

After Effects project file

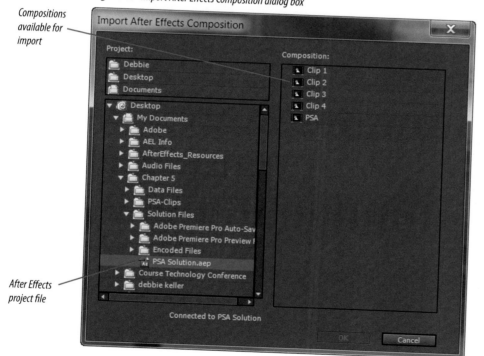

Figure 11 *Missing dynamic link*

Missing link

as shown in Figure 12, allowing you to locate the missing file.

Dynamically linked files can be manipulated like any other asset. They may be previewed on the Source Monitor, trimmed, and placed on the Timeline panel. As with other assets, the linked files may also be edited on the Timeline panel and may be unlinked from associated audio tracks if needed.

Creating a Voice Over in Premiere Pro

You can record audio directly into Premiere Pro to an audio track in a new sequence or to an audio track in an existing sequence.

The recording (wav file) is saved to your project folder, and an audio clip is added to the sequence in your project and to the Project panel.

On the Audio Mixer panel you will need to indicate which audio track you want to record to by enabling the track, as shown

Figure 12 *Link Media to dialog box*

Name of file

in Figure 13. The red microphone icon indicates the Audio 1 track has been enabled for recording. The trumpet icon indicates the other tracks are muted. It is important to remember to turn down your speakers while you are recording to prevent feedback and echo. While you are recording, you can preview the video on the Program Monitor to assist with timing.

There are two steps in the recording process; you first need to click the Record button, which will then begin to blink; then, when you are ready to record, click the Play-Stop Toggle button to begin recording. To stop the recording process, click the Play-Stop Toggle button again. The audio clip will then appear on the Project panel and at the location of the CTI on the audio track.

Figure 13 *Audio Mixer panel*

Enabled track for recording

Apply the Cartoon effect

1. Open the PSA.ae file from the drive and folder where you store your Data Files, then save it as **PSA your name**.

   Notice there are five compositions already created: Clip 1, Clip 2, Clip 3, Clip 4, and PSA.

   TIP If you see an error that four clips are missing, click OK and re-link the missing footage with the clips found in the PSA-Clips folder.

2. Right-click **Ban044.mov** on the Project panel, point to **Replace Footage**, then click **File**.

3. Navigate to the PSA-Clips folder, click **Ban044.mov**, then click **Open**.

   The other three clips should update automatically.

4. Use the Composition Navigator to select **Clip 1**, as shown in Figure 14.

   The Cartoon, Levels, and Hue/Saturation effects have already been applied to this clip as an example for you to preview.

5. Use the Composition Navigator to select **Clip 2**, then verify that the Effects workspace is in place.

   We will be applying the Cartoon effect to Clip 2.

   You may need to select the Timeline panel and move the CTI to the 00;00;00;00 position to activate the video footage on the Composition panel.

6. Click the **Selection tool** on the Tools panel, then click the **video footage** on the Composition panel.

7. Click **Effect** on the Application bar, point to **Stylize**, then click **Cartoon**.

(continued)

Figure 14 *Example of Cartoon effect applied to Clip 1*

Levels effect

Cartoon effect

Clip 1 composition

Hue/Saturation effect

Figure 15 *Cartoon effect applied to Clip 2*

Cartoon effect

Clip 2 composition

Develop a PSA & Commercial Using Premiere Pro & After Effects CS5

Figure 16 *Shading Steps and Shading Smoothness properties modified in Clip 2*

Shading
Steps

Shading
Smoothness

Figure 17 *Softness, Detail Radius, and Threshold modified in Clip 2*

Detail Radius

Detail
Threshold

Softness

The Cartoon effect is added to the Effect Controls panel with the default settings, as shown in Figure 15.

8. Click the **Fill expand arrow**, then click the **Shading Steps** and **Shading Smoothness expand arrows**.

The sliders become visible for the Shading Steps and Shading Smoothness properties.

9. Adjust the Shading Steps value to **4.5** and the Shading Smoothness value to **60.5**, then compare your screen with Figure 16.

The Shading Steps property sets the level of posterization in the color fill areas. A higher Shading Smoothness value blends the colors together with more gradual transitions.

10. Click the **Edge expand arrow**, then change the Softness value to **73.8**.

The transition between the edge's stroke and surrounding colors is softened.

11. Change the Detail Radius value to **9.0** and the Detail Threshold value to **8.4**, then compare your screen to Figure 17.

The Detail Radius setting applies a blur to the image and the Detail Threshold setting removes some of the detail.

12. Save your project and leave it open for the next exercise.

You applied the Cartoon effect to Clip 1 in the PSA file and then customized the effect.

Customize the Cartoon effect

1. Open the PSA your name.ae file, if necessary.

2. Use the Composition Navigator to select **Clip 3**, then verify that the Effects workspace is in place.

   You may need to select the Timeline panel and move the CTI to 00;00;00;00 to activate the video footage on the Composition panel.

3. Click the **Selection tool** on the Tools panel, then click the **video footage** on the Composition panel.

4. Right-click the **Composition panel**, click **Effect**, point to **Stylize**, then click **Cartoon**.

   The Cartoon effect is added to the Effect Controls panel with the default settings.

5. Click the **expand arrow** in front of **Fill**, then click the **Shading Steps** and **Shading Smoothness expand arrows**.

6. Drag the **Shading Steps slider** to the right and to the left to see how it affects the video footage on the Composition panel.

7. Drag the **Shading Smoothness slider** to the right and to the left to see how it affects the video footage.

   You may want to go back and forth between changing the Shading Steps value and the Shading Smoothness value to see how the details can change as a result, then compare your screen to Figure 18.

8. Change the Shading Steps value to **4.2**, then change the Shading Smoothness value to **80.0**.

9. Click the **Edge expand arrow**, then expand the following properties: Softness, Detail Radius, and Detail Threshold.

   (continued)

Figure 18 *Shading Steps and Shading Smoothness values for Clip 3*

Shading Steps Value 4.2

Shading Smoothness Value 80.0

Develop a PSA & Commercial Using Premiere Pro & After Effects CS5

Figure 19 *Cartoon effect values modified for Clip 3*

Detail Radius
value 2.7

Detail Threshold
value 16.1

Softness
value 57.6

Edge
Enhancement
value 28.0

Edge Contrast
value 0.51

Figure 20 *Searching for the Cartoon effect*

Cartoon
in search
field

10. Click the **Advanced expand arrow**, then expand the following properties: Edge Enhancement and Edge Contrast.

    The sliders become visible for each of these properties. You will work with adjusting these values to fine tune the Cartoon effect further.

11. Drag the **sliders** to the left and right for the following parameters: Softness, Detail Radius, Detail Threshold, Edge Enhancement and Edge Contrast.

    You can switch between properties and change values to see the effect.

12. Change the following values to: Softness: **57.6**; Detail Radius: **2.7**; Detail Threshold: **16.1**; Edge Enhancement: **28.0**; and Edge Contrast: **0.51**, then compare your screen to Figure 19.

13. Save your project and leave it open for the next exercise.

You applied the Cartoon effect to Clip 3 in the PSA file, and then customized it.

Search for the Cartoon effect

1. Open the PSA your name.ae file, if necessary.

2. Use the Composition Navigator to select **Clip 4**.

    You may need to select the Timeline panel and move the CTI to 00;00;00;00 to activate the video footage on the Composition panel.

3. Click the **Selection tool** ▶ on the Tools panel, then click the **video footage** on the Composition panel.

4. Type **Cartoon** in the search field on the Effects & Presets panel, as shown in Figure 20.

(continued)

The search feature filters the Cartoon effect on the Effects & Presets panel, showing only the Cartoon effect under the Stylize category.

5. Select the **Cartoon effect** on the Effects & Presets panel, then drag it to the Composition panel, as shown in Figure 21.

   You will see an X indicating that you are placing the effect on the video footage, and the Cartoon effect appears on the Effect Controls panel.

6. Enter the following values: Shading Steps: **4.0**; Shading Smoothness: **60.0**; Softness: **75.2**; Edge Enhancement: **7.0**; Detail Radius: **5.0**; and Detail Threshold: **12.4**, as shown in Figure 22.

7. Save your project and leave it open for the next exercise.

You searched for the Cartoon effect on the Effects & Presets panel and applied the effect to Clip 4 in the PSA file.

Figure 21 *Applying the Cartoon effect*

Figure 22 *Cartoon effect values modified for Clip 4*

Detail Radius value 5.0

Detail Threshold value 12.4

Shading Steps value 4.0

Shading Smoothness value 60.0

Softness value 75.2

Edge Enhancement value 7.0

Develop a PSA & Commercial Using Premiere Pro & After Effects CS5

Figure 23 *Levels effect applied to Clip 4*

Levels effect —

Figure 24 *Moving the Levels effect above the Cartoon effect*

Drop line —

Rectangle —

Apply the Levels effect

1. Open the PSA your name.ae file, if necessary.

2. Use the Composition Navigator to select **Clip 2**.

3. Click the **Selection tool** 🔲 on the Tools panel, then click the **video footage** on the Composition panel.

4. Click **Effect** on the Application bar, point to **Color Correction**, then click **Levels**.

   The Levels effect is used for improving the contrast in an image, which is very important for the Cartoon effect to be effective. The Levels effect is added to the Effect Controls panel, as shown in Figure 23.

5. Drag the **Levels effect** above the Cartoon effect on the Effect Controls panel.

   A white rectangle appears around the effect you are moving and a black drop line shows you where the effect will be placed when you release the mouse button, as shown in Figure 24. The Levels effect is moved above the Cartoon effect so that it is applied to the image before the Cartoon effect and therefore will influence the Cartoon effect.

   (continued)

6. On the Effect Controls panel, drag the **Input Black control** to the right, just before the pink line begins, until the Input Black value is **12.0**, as shown in Figure 25.

   The Input controls are the triangles directly underneath the histogram: the black on the left, the gray in the middle, and the white on the right.

TIP You may need to resize the Effect Controls panel so that it is wide enough to see the entire width of the histogram display and the Input controls.

7. Drag the **Input White control** to the left, of the yellow lines just before the green until the Input White value is **210.0**.

8. Drag the **Input Gray control** to the left to adjust the shadows until the Gamma value is **1.07**, as shown in Figure 26.

9. Save your project and leave it open for the next exercise.

You applied and customized the Levels effect using the Input controls on the histogram to Clip 2 to improve the Cartoon effect.

Customize the Levels effect

1. Open the PSA your name.ae file, if necessary.

2. Use the Composition Navigator to select **Clip 3**, then verify that you can see the video footage on the Composition panel.

3. Click the **Selection tool** ![Selection tool icon] on the Tools panel, then click the **video footage** on the Composition panel.

4. Right-click the **Composition panel**, click **Effect**, point to **Color Correction**, then click **Levels**.

(continued)

Figure 25 *Adjusting the Input Black control*

Black Input control

Input Black value

Figure 26 *Customizing the Levels effect on Clip 2*

White Input control

Gray Input control

Black Input control

Input Black value

Input White value

Gamma value

Develop a PSA & Commercial Using Premiere Pro & After Effects CS5

Figure 27 *Customized Levels values for Clip 3*

Input Black value 11.5

Input White value 201.5

Gamma value 1.37

Figure 28 *Customized Levels values for Clip 4*

Input Black value 21.0

Input White value 217.0

Gamma value 1.11

5. Drag the **Levels effect** above the Cartoon effect on the Effect Controls panel.

6. Click the **expand arrows** in front of **Input Black**, **Input White**, and **Gamma**.

   The sliders become visible for each of the Input values.

7. Adjust the Input White slider by dragging it to the right and the Input Black slider by dragging it to the left.

   You are trying to improve the contrast in the image.

8. Drag the **Input White slider** to **201.5**, then drag the **Input Black slider** to **11.5**.

9. Drag the **Gamma slider** to the left and right to adjust the shadows.

10. Drag the **Gamma slider** to **1.37**, then compare your image to Figure 27.

11. Use the Composition Navigator to select **Clip 4**, then verify that you can see the video footage on the Composition panel.

12. Locate and drag the **Levels effect** above the Cartoon effect on the Effect Controls panel.

13. Enter the following values: Input Black: **21.0**; Input White: **217.0**; and Gamma: **1.11**, as shown in Figure 28.

14. Save your project and leave it open for the next exercise.

You applied and customized the Levels effect using the slider controls to adjust the Input Black, Input White, and Gamma levels to Clip 3 and Clip 4 to improve the Cartoon effect.

Apply the Hue/Saturation effect

1. Open the PSA your name.ae file, if necessary.

2. Use the Composition Navigator to select **Clip 2**, then verify that you can see the video footage on the Composition panel.

3. Click the **Selection tool** on the Tools panel, then click the **video footage** on the Composition panel.

4. Click **Effect** on the Application bar, point to **Color Correction**, then click **Hue/Saturation**.

   The Hue/Saturation effect is added to the Effect Controls panel, as shown in Figure 29.

5. On the Effect Controls panel, click the **Master Hue dial**, then drag it counterclockwise until you reach the value **0x -40.0°**, as shown in Figure 30.

   TIP Dragging the dial counterclockwise produces a negative number, dragging clockwise produces a positive number.

   (continued)

Figure 29 *Hue/Saturation effect applied to Clip 2*

Hue/Saturation effect

Figure 30 *Adjusting the Master Hue in Clip 2*

Master Hue value

Develop a PSA & Commercial Using Premiere Pro & After Effects CS5

Figure 31 *Adjusting the Master Saturation in Clip 2*

Master Saturation value

Figure 32 *Customizing the Hue/Saturation effect on Clip 4*

Master Hue value

Master Saturation value

Master Lightness value

6. Drag the **Master Saturation slider** until the value is **49**, as shown in Figure 31.

   The footage is brighter.

7. Use the Composition Navigator to select **Clip 4**, then verify that you can see the video footage on the Composition panel.

8. Locate and apply the Hue/Saturation effect.

9. Change the following values: Master Hue: **0x +11.0°**; Master Saturation: **-6**; and Master Lightness: **1**, as shown in Figure 32.

10. Save your project and leave it open for the next exercise.

You applied and customized the Hue/Saturation effect to correct the colors and shadows of the Cartoon effect applied to Clip 2 and Clip 4.

Apply the Channel Mixer effect

1. Open the PSA your name.ae file, if necessary.

2. Use the Composition Navigator to select **Clip 3**, then verify that you can see the video footage on the Composition panel.

3. Click the **Selection tool** 🠆 on the Tools panel, then click the **video footage** on the Composition panel.

4. Right-click the **Composition panel**, click **Effect**, point to **Color Correction**, then click **Channel Mixer**.

(continued)

5. On the Effect Controls panel, change the following values for the Channel Mixer effect: Red-Green: **20**; Red-Blue: **15**; Green-Red: **10**; Green-Blue: **-15**; Blue-Red: **-10**; and Blue-Green: **10**, as shown in Figure 33.

   The Channel Mixer effect is much more subtle than the Hue/Saturation effect, and is able to work on specific channels of color by adding red to the footage and removing some of the blues and greens.

6. Save your project and leave it open for the next exercise.

You applied and customized the Channel Mixer effect to Clip 3.

Import an After Effects composition into Premiere Pro

1. Open the PSA.prpoj file, then save it as **PSA your name**.

2. Click **File** on the Application bar, point to **Adobe Dynamic Link**, then click **Import After Effects Composition**.

   The Import After Effects Composition dialog box opens.

3. Locate the PSA your name After Effects project file, select the **PSA composition**, as shown in Figure 34, then click **OK**.

   The linked After Effects composition appears on the Project panel.

   (continued)

Figure 33 *Customizing the Channel Mixer effect on Clip 3*

Channel Mixer

Figure 34 *Import After Effects Composition dialog box*

Import After Effects Composition dialog box

PSA composition

PSA project file

Develop a PSA & Commercial Using Premiere Pro & After Effects CS5

Figure 35 *Previewing the After Effects composition on the Source Monitor*

PSA After Effects
composition

4. Double-click the **PSA After Effects composition** on the Projects panel to preview the composition on the Source Monitor as shown in Figure 35.

5. Click the **Drag Video Only icon** 🎬 on the Source Monitor, then place the After Effects composition on the Video 1 track.

   The After Effects composition is placed on the video track without the audio track, as shown in Figure 36.

6. Click the **Play-Stop Toggle Button** ▶ on the Program Monitor to preview the sequence.

7. Save your project and leave it open for the next exercise.

You imported the After Effects project into Premiere Pro and placed it onto a sequence.

Figure 36 *Placing the After Effects composition on the Video 1 track*

PSA After Effects
composition

Create a voice over in Premiere Pro

1. Open the PSA your name.prproj file, if necessary.

2. Open the PSA Script.txt file.

   You will be reading the text into a microphone to record this into your PSA project. You may want to print the file.

3. Make sure your microphone is plugged into the microphone jack, then verify that your microphone is working.

   Check your computer's documentation if you are not sure how to record with your microphone.

4. Click the **Audio Mixer panel options button** ▦, then click **Meter Input(s) Only**.

   This activates the sound meter and will allow you to see the input levels of your microphone.

5. On the Audio Mixer panel, under the Audio 1 track, click the **Enable track for Recording button** 🎙 and the **Solo Track button** 🎙, as shown in Figure 37.

   This enables the Audio 1 track for recording and will place the wav file that is generated automatically at the location of the CTI on that track when you have finished recording.

6. Click the **Record button** 🔴 on the Audio Mixer panel.

   The Record button begins to blink.

7. Verify that the CTI is at 00;00;00;00.

   The video will play on the Program Monitor while you are reading the script.

(continued)

Figure 37 *Audio Mixer panel*

Solo Track button

Enable Track for Recording button

Record button
Play-Stop Toggle button

Develop a PSA & Commercial Using Premiere Pro & After Effects CS5

Figure 38 *Recording voice over*

Sound Meter

Record button active

Play-Stop Toggle button toggled to Stop

Figure 39 *Audio clips from voice over*

8. Click the **Play-Stop Toggle button** ▶ on the Audio Mixer panel, as shown in Figure 38, then read the PSA script.

If you make a mistake, you can undo your last action and return to Step 6.

9. Click the **Play-Stop Toggle button** ▶ on the Audio Mixer panel when you have finished recording.

The audio clip appears on the selected audio track and on the Project panel, as shown in Figure 39. The wav file is also saved to the location of the project file.

10. Preview your project on the Program Monitor.

If you are not happy with your recording, you can delete the track from the audio track and the Project panel and record it again. Keep in mind, copies of each of your recordings will still be saved in your projects folder.

11. Export your final project to the **MPEG-2** video format, then exit Premiere Pro.

You created a voice over narration in Premiere Pro to describe your PSA.

Edit a Commercial
FOR TELEVISION

What You'll Do

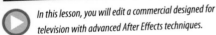

In this lesson, you will edit a commercial designed for television with advanced After Effects techniques.

Creating an After Effects Composition in Premiere Pro

There may be times when you are working in Premiere Pro and decide that you would like to add a special effect to a sequence in After Effects. You can create a new After Effects composition in Premiere Pro, and it becomes dynamically linked. Select the clips in the sequence that you want in the composition, choose the Adobe Dynamic Link command, and then select Replace with After Effects

Composition. If After Effects is already open, it will create a new composition in the existing project. If After Effects is not open, the Save As dialog box will open prompting you to name the After Effects project file.

The new After Effects project file with the composition is created based on the sequence settings in Premiere Pro and inherits all of its settings, as shown in Figure 40. The new After Effects project file replaces the clips on the sequence with the dynamic link, as

Figure 40 *Creating a composition from clips in Premiere Pro*

Dynamic link to Premiere Pro

Clips and transitions from Premiere Pro

Develop a PSA & Commercial Using Premiere Pro & After Effects CS5

shown in Figure 41. (*Note*: The composition duration is set to 30 seconds by default when you create a dynamically linked After Effects composition.)

Stabilizing Motion in Mocha for After Effects

After Effects includes a standalone application called Mocha that records

tracking data for use in After Effects compositions. **Tracking data** records the motion of a defined area of footage and creates keyframes for the Transform properties, which then can be exported and used in After Effects. One use for tracking data is to stabilize footage to remove a camera shake from a handheld camera during filming.

Mocha opens with a splash screen that provides you with one of two options, as shown in Figure 42. You can either open the manual or you can start the program. Once you click Start, you need to begin a project by importing footage to work with.

When using Mocha, it is recommended to import only the part of the clip that needs editing. Tracking unnecessary data

Figure 41 *Composition dynamically linked*

Dynamic link to After Effects

Figure 42 *Mocha for After Effects workspace*

Splash screen

Start

can be quite time consuming. A **spline** is a selection tool used to track motion on a plane and can be used to determine position, scale, rotation, shear and perspective. Mocha has two splines, an X-spline and a Bezier spline. An **X-spline** works better for tracking, especially if your motion involves perspective. A **Bezier spline** is versatile and is the industry standard.

To track data, you first need to draw an X-spline, as shown in Figure 43. The Create X-Spline Layer tool does a better job of tracking than the Create Bezier Layer tool, and it is not necessary to be very accurate in drawing the spline. The tracking technology discards the pixel movement that does not

conform to the majority of the motion within the X-spline.

On the Track tab, found in the lower portion of the Mocha workspace, there is an area where you can define the type of motion the tracker will be working with, large motion or small motion. Small motion is used for tracking small jitters and camera shakes. The Perspective option is used when you are tracking an image that has perspective and you would like to attach another image to, for example when placing an alternate image on a billboard or on a cellphone display.

Once you have drawn the spline and set the motion parameter, it is time to track

the spline. Just below the Mocha work area, which is referred to as the **canvas**, are the Track controls. You can either track the footage frame-by-frame or click the Track Forwards button and let Mocha track all the frames. In the upper-right corner of the workspace is a tracking status bar to let you monitor the progress. You can stop tracking at any time if you see your spline going off track and you would like to make adjustments.

Once the tracking is complete, it is a good idea to click the Surface button on the View Controls panel. The Surface button activates the surface box, as shown in Figure 44. The **surface box** is used as a

Figure 43 *Drawing an X-spline to track motion*

Drawing a spline

Figure 44 *Selecting a reference point to stabilize*

Surface box

Develop a PSA & Commercial Using Premiere Pro & After Effects CS5

reference point, and needs to be resized and positioned as a stabilizing center. The final step is to export a copy of the tracking data to be used in After Effects, by selecting the Export Tracking Data button. The Export Tracking Data dialog box launches, as shown in Figure 45. You need to select the Format drop-down arrow and choose the After Effects Transform Data option to get a copy of the correct data. You will then have the option to copy the data or to save it as a txt file.

Pasting the Tracking Data into After Effects

Once you copy the tracking data from Mocha, you return to After Effects to paste it in order to place the keyframes for the Transform properties. These keyframes represent the tracked motion of the footage. The tracking data that is created in Mocha consists of many keyframes; therefore, it is a good idea to use a Null Object layer for pasting this data, as shown in Figure 46. Tracking data is pasted at the location of the CTI. The position keyframes will need to be removed and reset manually to

keep the footage from moving out of the Composition panel.

A Null Object layer is an invisible layer that has all the properties of a visible layer. You assign the Null Object layer as a parent layer. The other layer is referred to as the child layer. The transform properties of the child layer become relative to the parent layer. A layer can only have one parent, but a parent layer can have a number of child layers. Parenting is assigned on the Timeline panel under the Parent column by using the drop-down menu.

Figure 45 *Export Tracking Data dialog box*

Format for tracking data

Figure 46 *Pasting tracking data*

Null Object layer

Parent layer   Tracking data

Creating 3D Text

The Shatter effect is an effect that is applied to give the illusion of exploding images, but it can also be customized to create 3D text. To create 3D text, you need three layers. The first layer is a Text layer, which will be referenced by the Shatter effect text. The second layer is a Solid layer and is where you choose the text color. (The text color can always be changed later by selecting the layer and choosing Solid Settings on the Layer menu.) The last layer is a Camera layer, which is used to create a camera to get different views of the Solid layer. Figure 47 shows the Shatter effect applied to the Solid layer.

To customize the Shatter effect and make the text 3D, you need to customize some settings on the Effect Controls panel, as shown in Figure 48. The Rendered View option allows you to preview the final output. Under the Shape property, you can customize the pattern to reference the text on the text layer if you are not using a pattern and want to display text.

A Camera layer allows you to view 3D objects from any angle by moving and rotating a camera around the scene to get different views of a 3D object. The camera preset is the type of camera named according to the focal length of the lens. All cameras are based on the behavior of a 35mm camera with a different lens. The Camera System option allows you to reference a Camera layer rather than working with the camera within the Shatter effect, providing more flexibility.

Figure 47 *Applying the Shatter effect*

Shatter effect

Three required layers

Develop a PSA & Commercial Using Premiere Pro & After Effects CS5

You must disable the Strength and Gravity values in the Shatter effect if you do not want to see the text explode.

Animating 3D Text with the Orbit Camera Tool

By adjusting the location of the camera, the 3D text and Light layer will follow the camera. You will need to use the Orbit Camera tool to adjust the camera; you do not need to be on the Camera layer when making adjustments. The Orbit Camera tool is found below the Unified Camera tool on the Tools panel, or can be retrieved by pressing the letter [c] on the keyboard. Pressing [c] repeatedly will cycle through the four camera tools. By creating an initial keyframe on the Position property, each time you move the CTI and make changes to the position of the camera in the Composition panel, a keyframe will automatically be created.

Working with a Light Layer

The Light layer can be used to add lighting effects and cast shadows on the footage. The Light layer needs to be placed above the layer that you want the light to shine on. There are different types of lights to choose from: parallel, spot, point, and ambient. The **parallel** type is approximating the light from a source like that of the sun. The **spot** type gives off light that is constrained by a cone, like a flashlight or spotlight. The **point** type is

Figure 48 *Creating 3D text with the Shatter effect*

Pattern is set to Custom

unconstrained like a bare light bulb. Finally, the **ambient** type has no source but simply contributes to the overall brightness and casts no shadows.

The light can be adjusted on the Composition panel, as shown in Figure 49. Three colored arrows at the tip of the cone represent the x, y, and z planes, and can be adjusted by dragging any of these arrows. The distance of the cone from the text can be modified by selecting the cross hairs. As you move the lighting, you will notice the light and shadows move across the text.

Enhancing 3D Text

After creating 3D text using the Shatter effect, you may want to enhance the appearance of your text. Effects can be added to the Solid layer. There are many effects to choose from. Two options are the CC Light Sweep effect and the Color Emboss effect.

The Color Emboss effect works like the Emboss effect without overriding the original colors of the image the effect is being applied to. The **Relief** setting controls

the maximum width of the highlighted edges, and the **Contrast** setting determines the sharpness of the image.

The **CC Light Sweep effect** creates a light reflection along the layer, as shown in Figure 50. By adding a keyframe to the Center control on the Timeline panel, you can adjust the light reflection at various durations and animate the CC Light Sweep effect.

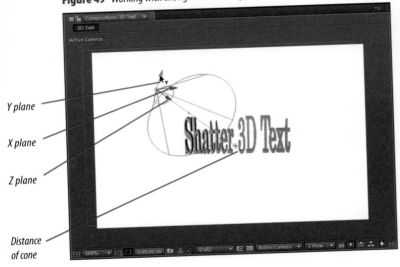

Figure 49 *Working with the light on the Composition panel*

Y plane

X plane

Z plane

Distance of cone

Figure 50 *Applying the CC Light Sweep effect*

Develop a PSA & Commercial Using Premiere Pro & After Effects CS5

Figure 51 *Save As dialog box*

Figure 52 *New composition in After Effects*

Linked layer

Composition

Create an After Effects composition in Premiere Pro

1. Start Premiere Pro, open the Glassworks Commercial.prproj project file, then save it as **Glassworks Commercials your name**.

2. Preview the video clip on the Program Monitor.

   We will use Adobe Dynamic Link to work with this file between Premiere Pro and After Effects to remove the camera shake in the video when the man is molding the glass on the table and then add some 3D animated text. We will first create a new After Effects composition.

3. Click the **Selection tool** [icon] on the Tools panel, then select the **Blown Glass clip** on the sequence.

4. Click **File** on the Application bar, point to **Adobe Dynamic Link,** then click **Replace After Effects Composition**.

   The Save As dialog box opens, as shown in Figure 51.

5. Name your project **Glassworks Dynamic Link your name**, then click **Save**.

   TIP Save the file to the same location as your Premiere Pro project file.

   Adobe After Effects launches with the composition created and active, as shown in Figure 52.

6. Click the **Timeline panel**, click **Layer** on the Application bar, point to **New**, then click **Null Object**.

   A Null Object layer is created above the Blown Glass.avi layer on the Timeline panel. We will be using this layer later to place the tracking data.

(continued)

7. On the Timeline Panel, on the Blown Glass.avi layer, click the **Parent drop-down arrow**, then click **2. Null 1**.

   The Null Object layer is assigned as the parent to the Blown Glass.avi layer.

8. Click **File** on the Application bar, point to **Import**, then click **File**.

   The Import File dialog box opens. We will import a Photoshop file to create a frame around the video.

9. Locate the Frame.psd file located in the Glassworks-Clips folder, verify the **Import As** drop-down menu is set to **Footage**, then click **Open**.

   The Frame.psd dialog box opens.

10. Accept the default settings, then click **OK**.

11. Drag **Frame.psd** from the Project panel to the Timeline panel above the Null 1 layer, then compare your screen to Figure 53.

12. Click the **Premiere Pro icon** on the taskbar (Win) or dock (Mac) to return to Premiere Pro.

    The After Effects composition is dynamically linked in the Premiere Pro project, as shown in Figure 54.

13. Save Glassworks Commercial your name and then close the file.

14. Save Glassworks Dynamic Link your name and leave it open for the next exercise.

You created a new After Effects composition from Premiere Pro and dynamically linked it to Premiere Pro.

Figure 53 *Setting up the Glassworks dynamic link composition*

Frame.psd layer

Null Object layer

Null Object layer assigned as parent

Figure 54 *Linked composition in Premiere Pro*

Linked composition

Linked composition

Figure 55 *Starting Mocha for After Effects CS5*

Start

Figure 56 *New Project dialog box in Mocha*

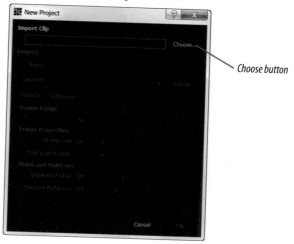

Choose button

Track motion in Mocha for After Effects

1. Start After Effects, then open the Glassworks Dynamic Link.ae file, if necessary.

2. Minimize the After Effects window.

   We will be working with Mocha for After Effects first to track the motion of a portion of the Glassworks video where the camera shakes, and will return to After Effects later.

3. Click **Start** on the Application bar, point to **All Programs**, then click **Mocha for After Effects CS5** (Win) or open the Finder from the dock and click **Applications** from the sidebar, select the **Applications folder**, select **Adobe After Effects CS5**, then click **Mocha for After Effects CS5** (Mac).

   You may need to look in a subfolder if you have installed the Creative Suite.

4. Click **Start** on the Mocha splash screen, as shown in Figure 55.

   The Mocha workspace opens. We will need to begin a new project.

5. Click **File** on the Application bar, then click **New Project**.

   The New Project dialog box opens, as shown in Figure 56.

(continued)

6. Click **Choose** in the New Project dialog box, click the **Blown Glass.avi** file inside the Glassworks-Clips folder, as shown in Figure 57, then click **Open**.

The Choose a file dialog box closes and brings you back to the New Project dialog box.

7. Type **1050** in the first Frame Range text box, type **1110** in the second Frame Range text box, as shown in Figure 58, then click **OK**.

These are the frame numbers which will import the time frame of the video clip from 35 to 37 seconds where the camera shakes.

(continued)

Figure 57 *Choose a file dialog box*

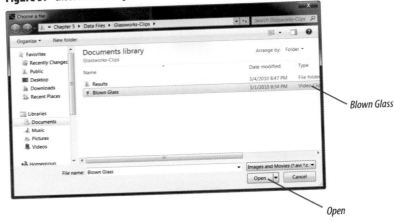

Blown Glass

Open

Figure 58 *Entering the frame range*

Frame Range

OK

Develop a PSA & Commercial Using Premiere Pro & After Effects CS5

Figure 59 *Selecting what to track*

Point

Auto-closed
shape

Spline

Figure 60 *Motion section of Track tab*

Tracking status

Surface button

Track controls

Shear

Small Motion

8. Click the **Create X-Spline Layer Tool** on the Tools panel, then, using Figure 59 as a guide, click in the upper-left corner, click in the upper-right corner, the lower-right corner, and the lower-left corner, then right-click to auto-close the shape.

9. On the Track tab, under Motion, click the **Shear check box** to deselect it, then click the **Small Motion option button**, as shown in Figure 60.

Since we are tracking the camera shaking we do not have to worry about shear or perspective, therefore we need to deselect Shear. The camera shaking is a small motion and for that reason we need to select the Small Motion option.

TIP Motion track settings work in a hierarchical order. When you deselect Shear, Perspective is automatically deselected.

(continued)

10. In the Transport controls section, click the **Track Forwards button** .

The program is now tracking the movement of the video clip, and the status can be viewed in the upper-right corner of the Mocha workspace.

TIP If the spline moves out of the viewing area, you will need to click the Stop Tracking button and readjust the spline. Click the Go to Previous Frame button if necessary.

11. If necessary, click the **Go to In point button** to return to the first frame on the Timeline.

12. On the View Controls panel, click the **Surface button** .

The surface box appears, as shown in Figure 61.

13. Resize the surface box to fit on the wall above the man's right shoulder, as shown in Figure 62.

This will be the point we will use as the stabilizing point of reference for the video clip.

(continued)

Figure 61 *Surface box*

Surface box

Figure 62 *Resized surface box*

Resized surface box

Figure 63 *Export Tracking Data dialog box*

Format list arrow

14. On the Parameters panel, click the **Export Tracking Data button**.

    The Export Tracking Data dialog box opens.

15. Click the **Format list arrow**, point to **After Effects Transform Data [anchor point, position, scale and rotation]**, as shown in Figure 63, then click **Copy to Clipboard**.

    A copy of the keyframes that were generated in Mocha are created and are ready to be pasted into After Effects.

16. On the Tools panel, click the **Save the project button**.

17. Click **File** on the Application bar, then click **Exit** to close Mocha.

18. Return to Glassworks Dynamic Link.ae in After Effects and leave it open for the next exercise.

You created tracking information for a portion of the Blown Glass video clip and copied the tracking data.

Paste the tracking data into After Effects

1. Select the **Null Object layer**.

   We will place the tracking data we copied from Mocha on this layer.

2. Click the **Current Time**, type **3500**, then press [**Enter**] (Win) or [**return**] (Mac).

   The CTI moves to the 35 second mark on the Timeline, which matches the first frame of the movie clip we worked with in Mocha.

3. Click **Edit** on the Application bar, then click **Paste**.

   The tracking data is pasted at the location of the CTI on the Null Object layer.

4. Click the **expand arrow** on the Null Object layer.

   Notice that the Null 1 layer is the Blown Glass.avi layer's parent.

5. Click the **Transform expand arrow**.

   The Transform properties for the layer are displayed, as shown in Figure 64, and all of the properties are selected.

6. Click **Transform** above the list of properties to deselect the multiple selections.

   We will be working with the Position property.

7. Click the **Toggle Animation button** in front of Position.

   The keyframes that were created in Mocha are removed; we need to customize the Position property.

(continued)

Figure 64 *Expanded Transform properties on Null Object layer*

Null layer

Develop a PSA & Commercial Using Premiere Pro & After Effects CS5

Figure 65 *Adjusting Position using Null Object layer*

Moving position reference

X-value

Cursor

Y-value

8. Click the **Play/Pause button** [▶] on the Preview panel to preview the stabilized video clip.

 The footage moves in and out of the frame. We need to make corrections with the Position property on the Null Object layer.

9. Return the CTI to **0;00;35;00**, select the Position property then click the **Toggle Animation button** [⏱] in front of Position.

 We will adjust the position using a reference on the Null Object layer.

10. Place the cursor over the X-value and when it becomes a pointing finger, drag the **cursor** to the left to move the image left until your value is approximately **134.8**. Adjust the Y-value to an approximate value of 91.5 to move the image upward.

 You will see a red line appear on the Composition panel representing the position reference, as shown in Figure 65.

11. Drag the **CTI** to **0;00;37;00**, then change the Position property to bring the image into the frame using a Y-value of approximately **122.6** (Note: it is not necessary to adjust the X-value.).

 The keyframe was created automatically on the Timeline.

12. Click the **Play/Pause button** [▶] on the Preview panel to preview the stabilized video clip.

13. Save Glassworks Dynamic Link your name and leave it open for the next exercise.

You pasted the tracking data from Mocha for After Effects onto a Null Object layer and made some minor adjustments to the Position property to remove camera jitter from the video footage.

Create 3D text

1. Open the Glassworks 3D Text file, and then save it as **Glassworks 3D Text your name**.

   The composition and the first Text layer have already been created.

2. Click **Layer** on the Application bar, point to **New**, then click **Solid**.

   The Solid Settings dialog box opens, as shown in Figure 66.

3. In the Name box, type **Text Color**, click the **color picker**, select a dark red color, then click **OK**.

   The Solid layer appears above the Text layer on the Timeline panel.

   TIP If you wish to change the color, click Layer on the Application bar with the Solid layer selected, then click Solid Settings.

4. Type **Shatter** on the Effects & Presets panel search field, drag the **Shatter preset** onto the Text Color layer, then compare your screen to Figure 67.

5. Expand the Shatter effect on the Effect Controls panel, click the **View drop-down arrow**, then click **Rendered**.

   This shows a preview of the final effect.

6. Click the **Shape expand arrow**, click the **Pattern list arrow**, then click **Custom**.

   We will now apply the Custom shape to the Text layer that we created earlier.

   (continued)

Figure 66 *Solid Settings dialog box*

Name

Color picker

Figure 67 *Applying the Shatter effect*

Shatter effect

Render property

Shatter effect

Text Color shape layer

Figure 68 *Customizing settings for Shatter effect*

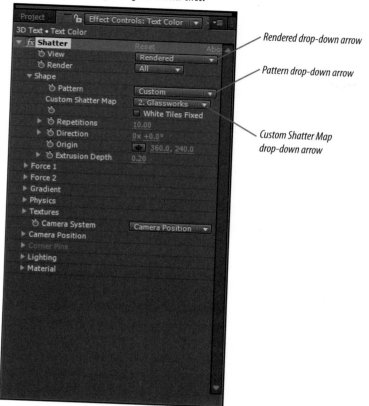

Rendered drop-down arrow

Pattern drop-down arrow

Custom Shatter Map drop-down arrow

7. Click the **Custom Shatter Map drop-down arrow**, then click **2. Glassworks**, as shown in Figure 68.

   The text we created is now referenced to the Shatter effect, so we no longer need to view the Text layer that was created earlier.

8. On the Timeline panel, to the left of Layer 2, click the **Video Switch button** 👁 on Layer 2.

9. Click the **Play/Pause button** ▶ on the Preview panel to preview the 3D text.

   We are using the Shatter effect to create 3D text, but we do not want it to shatter so we will need to make changes to some settings.

10. Click the **expand arrow** in front of **Force 1**, **Force 2**, and **Physics**, change the Strength and Gravity values to **0.00**, then collapse these properties when you have finished.

    Changing these values to 0.00 will remove the Shatter effect for the duration of the video.

11. Click the **Play/Pause button** ▶ on the Preview panel to preview the 3D text.

    You can no longer see the 3D effect. We will add camera and lighting layers in the next step.

12. Save Glassworks 3D Text your name and leave it open for the next exercise.

You created 3D text for the Glassworks commercial.

Animate 3D text with a Camera layer

1. Open the Glassworks 3D Text your name, if necessary, then verify that the CTI is at **00;00;00;00**.

2. Right-click the **Timeline panel**, click **New**, then click **Camera**.

   The Camera Settings dialog box opens.

3. Click the **Preset list arrow**, click **35mm**, then click **OK**, as shown in Figure 69.

   This preset will behave like a 35mm camera with a standard lens.

4. Select the **Text Color layer** on the Timeline panel, then, on the Effect Controls panel, click the **Camera Position drop-down menu**, then click **Comp Camera**.

   This references the Camera layer we created. If we do not reference the Camera layer when we make adjustments to our camera, the text will not move.

5. Click and hold the **Unified Camera tool** on the Tools panel, then click the **Orbit Camera tool**.

6. Click **Glassworks** on the Composition panel, drag to the left and down, then compare your image to Figure 70.

   Your figure may vary.

   (continued)

Figure 69 *Camera Settings dialog box*

Preset

OK

Figure 70 *Adjusting the camera with the Orbit Camera tool*

Orbit Camera tool

Figure 71 *Adjusting the light with the Selection tool*

Z plane

7. Click the **Text Color layer**, then, on the Effect Controls panel, change the Extrusion Depth to **1.00**.

   This increases the thickness of the text.

8. Right-click the **Timeline panel**, point to New, then click **Light**.

   The Light Settings dialog box opens.

9. Accept the default settings in the Light Settings dialog box, then click **OK**.

   We will move the light on the Composition panel to add a spot light and brighten the text.

10. Click the **Selection tool** ▶ on the Tools panel, move the light to the upper-left area of the Composition panel, then compare your screen to Figure 71.

    Notice as you hover the mouse over the different colored arrows, letters pop up to tell you which plane you will be moving the lighting on, x, y, or z.

11. Click the **Text Color layer** and then, on the Effect Controls panel, click the **Lighting expand arrow**, click the **Light Type list arrow**, then click **First Comp**.

    First Comp references the Lighting layer we created.

(continued)

12. Click the **Camera layer**, press the letter [**P**], then click the **Toggle Animation button** ⏱.

    This creates a keyframe on the Camera layer for position. Keyframes are automatically created at the location of the CTI when position settings are changed.

13. Click the **Orbit Camera tool** 🔄 on the Tools panel, drag the **CTI** to **0;00;01;00**, then adjust the Glassworks text on the Composition panel so it appears as shown in Figure 72.

    The light will automatically follow the camera, and your text will be animated.

14. Make additional adjustments with the Orbit Camera tool 🔄 at 2 seconds, 3 seconds, 4 seconds, and 5 seconds.

15. Click the **Play/Pause button** ▷ on the Preview panel to preview the 3D text.

16. Save Glassworks 3D Text your name and leave it open for the next exercise.

You animated the 3D text by adding a Camera layer and a Light layer for the Glassworks commercial.

Figure 72 *Adjusting the Glassworks text at 1 second*

Develop a PSA & Commercial Using Premiere Pro & After Effects CS5

Figure 73 *Adding the Color Emboss effect*

Color Emboss effect

Figure 74 *Adding the CC Light Sweep effect*

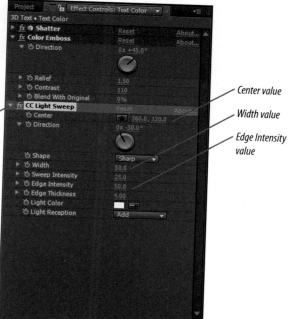

CC Light Sweep

Center value

Width value

Edge Intensity value

Enhance 3D text

1. Open the Glassworks 3D Text your name file, if necessary.

2. Select the **Text Color layer**, place the **CTI** at **00;00;00;00**, then collapse the Shatter effect on the Effect Controls panel.

3. Click **Effect** on the Application bar, point to **Stylize**, then click **Color Emboss**.

   The Color Emboss effect is added to the Effect Controls panel below the Shatter effect, as shown in Figure 73.

4. Change the Relief value to **1.50** and the Contrast value to **110**.

5. Click **Effect** on the Application bar, point to **Generate**, then click **CC Light Sweep**.

   The CC Light Sweep effect is added to the Effect Controls panel below the Color Emboss effect, as shown in Figure 74.

6. Set the Width value to **25.0** and the Edge Intensity value to **25.0**.

   This softens the effect of the light.

7. Click the **Toggle Animation button** in front of Center to create a keyframe.

(continued)

8. Click the **Effect Control point**, as shown in Figure 75, on the Composition panel to move the location of the light.

9. Make additional adjustments with the Effect Control point at 2 seconds, 3 seconds, 4 seconds, and 5 seconds.

10. Save the Glassworks 3D Text your name project, then close After Effects.

You made enhancements to the 3D text for the Glassworks commercial.

Figure 75 *Adjusting the Effect Control point*

Effect Control point

Figure 76 *Import After Effects Composition dialog box*

3D Text composition

Import an After Effects composition

1. Start Premiere Pro, then open the Glassworks Commercial your name file.

2. Verify that the workspace is set to Editing and that the CTI is at 00;00;00;00.

3. Click **File** on the Application bar, then click **Import**.

   The Import dialog box opens.

4. Locate the Glassworks 3D Text your name file, then click **Open**.

   The Import After Effects Composition dialog box opens.

5. Select the **3D Text composition** as shown in Figure 76, then click **OK**.

   This will dynamically link the After Effects composition.

6. Double-click the **3D Text/Glassworks 3D Text** linked composition on the Project panel to open the file on the Source Monitor.

7. Click the **Drag Video only icon** on the Source Monitor, then drag to the Video 2 layer at the location of the CTI.

   This is the beginning of a television commercial.

8. Preview your project on the Program Monitor.

9. Save your project, export your final project to the MPEG-2 video format without audio, then close Premiere Pro.

You imported your 3D Text After Effects file into your Premiere Pro project and exported your project to the MPEG-2 video format.

Edit a Commercial
DEVELOPED FOR THE INTERNET

What You'll Do

In this lesson, you will edit a commercial that is designed to be published on the Internet. You will also learn animation techniques in After Effects.

Animating with the Puppet Pin Tool

The Puppet tools are used to add natural motion to raster images and vector graphics. This can include still images, shapes, and text characters as well as imported Photoshop and Illustrator files.

The Puppet Pin tool works by deforming parts of an image. A **deform pin** is a type of pin that you can place or move with the Puppet Pin tool. It is best to plan ahead before using the Puppet Pin tool. For example, you may want to remove an image from its background, and if possible, divide different parts of the image onto separate layers, as shown in Figure 77.

When the first deform pin is placed a mesh is created, which is divided into triangles. Each part of the mesh is linked with pixels in

Figure 77 *Using the Puppet Pin tool*

Puppet Pin tool

Deform pin

Puppet Pin tool cursor

Selected deform pin

Puppet effect

the image, so the image will move with the mesh. The mesh changes shape to conform to the movement of the image based on the location of the deform pin(s).

Similar to using Motion Sketch as we did in a previous chapter, you can sketch the motion path of the deform pins as well. When you have the Puppet Pin tool selected, the Record Options setting becomes available. The Speed setting sets the ratio of the speed to the recorded motion. If the speed is set at 100%, the motion will play back at the speed it was recorded. If the speed is less than 100%, the motion will play back faster. The Smoothing setting will remove unnecessary keyframes that are created and make a smoother motion. When you are ready to record, press and hold [Ctrl] (Win) or ⌘ (Mac) as you click and drag a deform pin. Recording will stop when you release the mouse button.

Customizing the Particle Playground Effect

The **Particle Playground effect** is used to animate an object by reproducing it randomly, such as a flock of birds. The Particle Playground effect can be used to duplicate a vector graphic that was animated with the Puppet Pin tool, as shown in Figure 78. The Particle Playground generates three kinds of particles: dots, layers, or text

Figure 78 *Particle Playground effect*

Particle Playground effect

characters. There are four particle generators; they are the four properties listed at the top of the Particle Playground effect on the Effect Controls panel: Cannon, Grid, Layer Exploder, and Particle Exploder. By default, Cannon is the only generator active but you may have all of them active if you choose. However, you can only specify one kind of particle per particle generator. By default, dot particles are created. The movement of the particles is determined by the settings under Gravity, Repel, Wall, and Property Mapper settings.

The controls we will be using are Cannon, Layer Map, and Gravity. The Cannon controls create particles in a continuous stream from a single point.

Position: The Position control specifies the x and y coordinates from which particles are created.

Barrel Radius: The Barrel Radius control sets the size of the barrel radius; a negative value creates a circular barrel and a positive value creates a square barrel.

Particles per Second: The Particles per Second control specifies how often particles will be created. A value of zero results in no particles being created; a high value increases the density of the particle stream. Keyframes can be set on the Timeline for this control to set the value to zero when you may not want particles created.

Direction: The Direction control sets the angle that the particles are fired from.

Direction Random Spread: The Direction Random Spread control specifies how much a particle direction deviates from the cannon direction.

Velocity: The Velocity control specifies the initial speed in pixels per second the particles fire from the cannon.

Velocity Random Spread: The Velocity Random Spread control specifies the amount of random velocity of particles; a higher value results in more variation in velocity.

By default, the Particle Playground creates dot particles, as shown in Figure 79. The Layer Map controls replace the dots with a layer of your choosing in the composition.

Use Layer: The Use Layer control specifies the layer you want to use as the particles.

Time Offset Type: The Time Offset Type control specifies how you want to use the frames of a multiframe layer. For our example, we show a butterfly flapping its wings. If we were to leave the default

Figure 79 *Particle Playground effect default dot particles*

Develop a PSA & Commercial Using Premiere Pro & After Effects CS5

setting of Relative and the Time Offset at zero, all of the butterflies would be flapping their wings at the same time; they would be synchronized. For simplicity, let us just consider the random options.

Relative Random: The Relative Random control starts playing the layer from a frame chosen at random. The frame is chosen from within a range between the current time of the effect layer and the Random Time Max you specify.

Absolute Random: The Absolute Random control starts playing the layer from a frame chosen at random. The frame is chosen from a range between zero to the Random Time Max you specify.

Time Offset: The Time Offset control specifies the frame to start playing sequential frames from the layer.

The Gravity controls accelerate particles in the direction of gravity.

Force: The Force control specifies the force of gravity. A positive value increases the force; a negative value reduces the force.

Direction: The Direction control specifies the angle along which gravity pulls; the default is 180°, simulating the real world.

Here is a summary of the other properties in the Particle Playground effect:

The **Grid generator** works like the Cannon generator, except that it creates particles in a continuous stream from a set of grid intersections.

The **Layer Exploder** and **Particle Exploder** generator creates new particles based on a layer. The Particle Exploder then has the ability to explode a particle into more new particles.

The **Repel control** specifies how nearby particles repel or attract each other, simulating adding a positive or negative magnetic charge to each of the particles. The **Wall control** creates an area restricting where the particles can move.

The **Property Mapper** control gives you the ability to control specific properties by using a layer map.

Working with a Pre-Composed Layer

If you want to group some or all of the layers in a composition, you can pre-compose those layers into a new composition. Pre-composing the layers keeps all of the attributes that were applied to the layers and replaces the layers with a new single layer nested composition, as shown in Figure 80.

Figure 80 *Pre-composed layers*

Before

After

One benefit of creating a pre-composed layer is that you can apply Transform properties, such as Scale, to the pre-composition and all of the layers in the pre-composed layer will be affected by the transformation.

Placing Text on a Path

After Effects has the ability to place text on a path just as you can in Photoshop and Illustrator. However, in After Effects, you have the ability to animate the text once it is placed on the path. The path is created with the Pen tool. To create text on a path, you must first select the text on the Composition panel before you select the Pen tool. This will draw the path as a mask, which will make the stroke transparent when you attach the text to the path. Once you have selected the Pen tool, the RotoBezier check box needs to be checked. The **RotoBezier** option makes paths easier to draw and makes the curves smoother.

Once you have drawn a path for your text, like the one shown in Figure 81, expand the Text controls on the Timeline panel. The Path Options control should now be an option if you successfully drew a mask. Select the Path drop-down menu and choose Mask 1, and your text will align to the path.

Animating Text on a Curved Path

Once you have created text on a path, you may want to animate it. To animate text

Figure 81 *Placing type on a path*

Develop a PSA & Commercial Using Premiere Pro & After Effects CS5

on a path, you can adjust the text with the properties found under the Path Options property group on the Timeline panel. The Path Options properties allow you to specify a path and to alter the way individual characters appear on the path. Text can appear perpendicular to the path, aligned left or right, reversed, or the First or Last Margins adjusted to a specific location, as shown in Figure 82. Keyframes can be created for any of these properties to animate text along a path. For example, select the First Margin control on the Timeline panel, click the Time-vary stopwatch to activate keyframes, then point to the text on the path on the Composition panel, as shown in Figure 83. As you move the CTI and adjust the text on the path, another keyframe will automatically be created.

Figure 82 *Path Options controls*

Figure 83 *Adjusting text on a path*

Path Options

Mask 1

Adjustment cursor

Animate with the Puppet Pin tool

1. Open Hummingbird Insurance.ae from the drive and folder where your Data Files are stored, then save it as **Hummingbird Insurance your name**.

   The file has compositions already created and it is dynamically linked to Premiere Pro.

2. Click the **Composition Navigator**, then click **hummingbird**.

3. Click the **hummingbird composition** on the Timeline panel.

   Three layers in this composition make up the hummingbird, the body and the two wings.

4. Select the **Left Wing layer**, click the **Puppet Pin tool** on the Tools panel, point to the **tip of the wing**, then click to place a deform pin, as shown in Figure 84.

5. Click to place two more deform pins on the left wing near the body, one towards the head and the other in the bright green area, as shown in Figure 85.

   These two deform pins will help stabilize the wing when we create the animation to look like it is flapping.

   (continued)

Figure 84 *Placing a deform pin*

Deform pin

Figure 85 *Placing deform pins to stabilize*

Deselected deform pin

Selected deform pin

Develop a PSA & Commercial Using Premiere Pro & After Effects CS5

Figure 86 *Animating the left wing*

Puppet Sketch tool

Keyframes generated

Figure 87 *Placement of deform pins on the right wing*

Deform pins

6. Verify that the **CTI** is at **00;00;00;00**, select the deform pin at the tip of the wing, then press and hold [**Ctrl**] (Win) or ⌘ (Mac) while dragging the tip of the wing up and down until the CTI reaches the end of the Timeline.

   Pressing and holding [Ctrl] (Win) or ⌘ (Mac) activates the Puppet Sketch tool, which looks like a stopwatch. Keyframes are automatically recorded as you move the deform pin up and down, as shown in Figure 86.

7. Click the **Play/Pause button** ▶ on the Preview panel to preview the animation.

8. Click the **Video button** 👁 on Left Wing layer to hide the hummingbird's left wing.

   We will be adding deform pins to the Right Wing layer and hiding the left wing will make it easier to see the right wing.

9. Select the **Right Wing layer**, click the **Puppet Pin tool** 📌 on the Tools panel, if necessary, then place three deform pins at each corner of the wing, as shown in Figure 87.

   (continued)

10. Click **Record Options** on the Tools panel.

    The Puppet Record Options dialog box opens, as shown in Figure 88.

11. Change the Speed value to **50%** and the Smoothing value to **20**, then click **OK**.

    If the speed value is set to less than 100%, the motion will play back faster than it was recorded. Setting a higher smoothing value will remove keyframes as the motion is created.

12. Click the **deform pin** at the tip of the wing, then press and hold [**Ctrl**] (Win) or ⌘ (Mac) while dragging the tip of the wing up and down until the CTI reaches the end of the Timeline.

13. Click the **Video button** 👁 on Left Wing layer.

14. Click the **Play/Pause button** ▷ on the Preview panel to preview the animation.

15. Save Hummingbird Insurance your name and leave it open for the next exercise.

You animated the wings of the hummingbird with the Puppet Pin tool.

Figure 88 *Puppet Record Options dialog box*

Speed value

Smoothing value

Figure 89 *Working with the Particle Playground effect*

Particle Playground

Bird Particles layer

Customize the Particle Playground effect

1. Open the Hummingbird Bird Insurance your name.ae project file, if necessary, then select the **Effects workspace**.

2. Click the **Commercial composition** on the Timeline panel, then click the **Play/Pause button** ▶ on the Preview panel to preview the animation.

   A Solid layer has been created with the Particle Playground effect (the random red dots) already applied, as shown in Figure 89.

3. Drag the **CTI** to **0;00;05;00**, then select the **Bird Particles layer**.

   Using the Particle Playground effect, we will be duplicating the hummingbird we animated earlier.

4. Click the **Cannon expand arrow**, then change the following values: Barrel Radius: **25**; Particles Per Second: **3**; Direction: **-90x +0.0°**; Direction Random Spread: **360.00**; Velocity: **200.00**; and Velocity Random Spread: **100.00**.

   These values determine how far apart the birds will fly, how often they will appear, and at what speed and direction.

   (continued)

5. Click the **Gravity expand arrow**, then change the Force value to **7**.

   This will slow the speed of the birds.

6. Click the **Layers Map expand arrow**, click the **Use Layer drop-down menu**, then click **2.hummingbird**.

7. Click the **Time Offset Type drop-down menu**, click **Relative Random**, then change the Random Time Max setting to **2.40**.

   Your settings should match those shown in Figure 90.

   The hummingbird layer is assigned to the Particle Playground effect and the red dots are replaced with the hummingbird. The Relative Random setting brings in the birds at random intervals.

8. Click the **Play/Pause button** on the Preview panel to preview the animation.

9. Save Hummingbird Insurance your name and leave it open for the next exercise.

You customized the Particle Playground effect to create multiple hummingbirds that you animated earlier.

Figure 90 *Particle Playground effect modified settings*

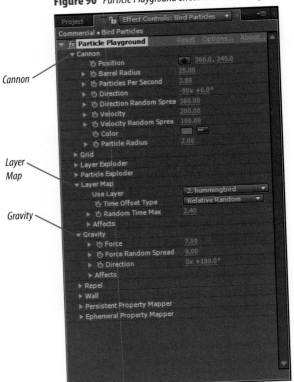

Figure 91 *Pre-compose dialog box*

New composition name

Figure 92 *Changing the Scale property*

New composition

Create a pre-compose layer

1. Open the Hummingbird Bird Insurance your name.ae file, if necessary.

2. Select the **hummingbird composition** on the Composition panel, then select the **Left Wing**, **Right Wing**, and **hummingbird layers** on the Timeline panel.

   You will create a pre-compose layer from these three layers.

3. Click **Layer** on the Application bar, then click **Pre-Compose**.

   The Pre-Compose dialog box opens, as shown in Figure 91.

4. In the New composition name text box, type **Whole Hummingbird**, then click **OK**.

   The layers are grouped inside the new composition and are now more manageable. The Whole Hummingbird layer appears on the Timeline.

5. Press [**S**] on the keyboard to reveal the Scale property, then change the value to **50.0%**, as shown in Figure 92.

6. Select the **Commercial composition** on the Composition panel, then click the **Play/Pause button** ▶ on the Preview panel to preview the animation.

   The hummingbirds are now smaller.

7. Save Hummingbird Insurance your name and leave it open for the next exercise.

You created a pre-compose layer using the three hummingbird layers, and used it to scale the Particle Playground effect.

Place text on a path

1. Open the Hummingbird Bird Insurance your name.ae file, if necessary.

2. Select the **Text Composition** on the Composition panel, click the **Selection tool** ![selection tool] on the Tools panel, then select the text on the Composition panel.

3. Click the **Pen Tool** ![pen tool] on the Tools panel, then check the **RotoBezier check box** on the Tools panel.

   You are going to draw a curved path to attach the text.

4. Click in the lower-left area of the Composition panel.

   A **vertex**, which is represented by a yellow square, appears each time you click the mouse button.

5. Using Figure 93 as a guide, move the cursor in an upward direction, then click again where the second vertex appears in the figure, then move the mouse again and this time press and hold the mouse button while you click to create a curved line.

6. Using Figure 94 as a guide, continue to draw the curved line until you get to the edge of the viewing area, holding the mouse button for the creation of each vertex.

   Your curved path may vary from the figure.

   (continued)

Figure 93 *Drawing with the Pen tool*

Create a curved line

Figure 94 *Curved line*

Develop a PSA & Commercial Using Premiere Pro & After Effects CS5

Figure 95 *Attaching text to a path*

Mask 1

Figure 96 *Text attached to a path*

7. On the Timeline panel, expand the Text layer (Hummingbird Insurance here when you need us.), then expand the Text property.

8. Click the **Path Options expand arrow**, click the **Path drop-down menu**, then click **Mask 1**, as shown in Figure 95.

 Your text should now be attached to the curved path, as shown in Figure 96.

9. Save Hummingbird Insurance your name and leave it open for the next exercise.

You created a curved path and attached text to the path.

Animate text on a curved path

1. Open the Hummingbird Insurance your name.ae file, if necessary.

2. Select the **Text composition**, then expand the Path Options property if necessary.

3. Verify that the CTI is at **00;00;00;00**, then click the **Toggle Animation button** 🕐 in front of First Margin to activate keyframes.

4. Place keyframes at **8 seconds** and **14 seconds** by clicking the **Add or remove keyframe at current time button** 🔷.

5. Return to the first keyframe.

6. Click the **Selection tool** ▶ on the Tools panel, point to the red rectangle to the left of the letter "H" in "Hummingbird" on the yellow path on the Composition panel, then click and drag the text along the path, as shown in Figure 97.

7. Click the **Go to Next Keyframe button** ▶ to jump to the second keyframe, then drag the text along the path as shown in Figure 98.

(continued)

Figure 97 *Adjusting first margin for first keyframe*

Cursor to move text on path

Figure 98 *Adjusting first margin for second keyframe*

Develop a PSA & Commercial Using Premiere Pro & After Effects CS5

Figure 99 *Adjusting first margin for third keyframe*

Figure 100 *Text composition added to Commercial composition*

8. Click the **Go to Next Keyframe button** to jump to the third keyframe, then drag the text along the path as shown in Figure 99.

9. On the Timeline panel, select the **Commercial composition**, then drag the **Text composition** to the top of the stacking order as shown in Figure 100.

10. Click the **Play/Pause button** on the Preview panel to preview the animation.

11. Click **Composition** on the Application bar, click **Add to Render Queue**, set the Output Module as an **FLV** and title your file **Hummingbird Insurance Commercial your name**.

12. Save your project file and close After Effects.

You added motion to text on a curved path and saved your project as an FLV movie for the Internet.

Apply the Cartoon effect.

1. Start After Effects, open the Water Pollution.ae file, and then save it as **Water Pollution your name**.
2. Use the Composition Navigator to select Clip 1, then verify that the Effects workspace is in place.
3. Click the Selection tool on the Tools panel, then click the video footage on the Composition panel.
4. Click Effect on the Application bar, point to Stylize, then click Cartoon.
5. Click the Fill expand arrow, then change the Shading Steps value to 18.0 and the Shading Smoothness value to 65.0.
6. Click the Edge expand arrow, then change the Softness value to 60.0.
7. Change the Detail Radius value to 2.2 and the Detail Threshold value to 50.0.
8. Save your work.

Customize the Cartoon effect.

1. Use the Composition Navigator to select Clip 2, then verify the Effects workspace is in place.
2. Click the Selection tool on the Tools panel, then click the video footage on the Composition panel.
3. Right-click the Composition panel, click Effect, point to Stylize, then click Cartoon.
4. Click the expand arrow in front of Fill, then click the expand arrows in front of Shading Steps and Shading Smoothness.
5. Drag the Shading Steps slider to the right and to the left to see how it affects the video footage on the Composition Panel.

6. Drag the Shading Smoothness slider to the right and to the left to see how it affects the video footage on the Composition Panel.
7. Click the expand arrow in front of the following properties: Edge, and then Softness, Detail Radius, Detail Threshold; Advanced, and then Edge Enhancement, Edge Contrast.
8. Drag the sliders to the left and right for the following properties: Softness, Detail Radius, Detail Threshold, Edge Enhancement, and Edge Contrast.

Figure 101 *Completed Skills Review, Water Pollution PSA*

Search for the Cartoon effect.

1. Use the Composition Navigator to select Clip 3 and verify the Effects workspace is in place.
2. Click the Selection tool on the Tools panel, then click the video footage on the Composition panel.
3. Type **Cartoon** in the search field on the Effects & Presets panel.
4. Select the Cartoon effect on the Effects & Presets panel, then drag it to the Composition panel.
5. Enter the following values: Shading Steps: 4.3; Shading Smoothness: 79.0; Softness: 60.0; Edge Enhancement 1.0; Detail Radius: 6.5; and Detail Threshold: 22.0.

Apply the Levels effect.

1. Use the Composition Navigator to select Clip 1, then verify that you can see the video footage on the Composition panel.
2. Click the Selection tool on the Tools panel, then click the video footage on the Composition panel.
3. Click Effect on the Application bar, point to Color Correction, then click Levels.
4. Drag the Levels effect above Cartoon on the Effect Controls panel.
5. On the histogram, drag the Input Black control to the right, just before the pink line begins so that your Input Black value is 7.0.
6. Drag the Input White control to the left until the Input White value is 244.0.
7. Drag the Input Gray control to the left to adjust the shadows until the Gamma value is 1.02.

Customize the Levels effect.

1. Use the Composition Navigator to select Clip 2, then verify that you can see the video footage on the Composition panel.
2. Click the Selection tool on the Tools panel, then click the video footage on the Composition panel.
3. Right-click the Composition panel, click Effect, point to Color Correction, then click Levels.
4. Drag the Levels effect above the Cartoon effect on the Effect Controls panel.
5. Click the expand arrows in front of Input Black, Input White, and Gamma.
6. Adjust the Input Black slider by dragging it to the right and the Input Black slider by dragging it to the left.
7. Adjust the Gamma slider by dragging it to the left and right to adjust the shadows.
8. Select the Levels effect on the Effects & Presets panel, then drag it to the Composition panel to apply it to the Clip 3 composition.
9. Drag the Levels effect above the Cartoon effect on the Effect Controls panel.
10. Enter the following values: Input Black: **9.0**; Input White: **182.0**; Gamma: **0.79**.

Apply the Hue/Saturation effect.

1. Use the Composition Navigator to select Clip 1, then verify that you can see the video footage on the Composition panel.
2. Click the Selection tool on the Tools panel, then click the video footage on the Composition panel.
3. Click Effect on the Application bar, point to Color Correction, then click Hue/Saturation.

4. Click the Master Hue dial then drag it counterclockwise until you reach the value 0x +337.0°.
5. Drag the Master Saturation slider until the value is 42.
6. Save your project and leave it open for the next step.

Apply the Channel Mixer effect.

1. Use the Composition Navigator to select Clip 2, then verify that you can see the video footage on the Composition panel.
2. Click the Selection tool on the Tools panel, then click the video footage on the Composition panel.
3. Right-click the Composition panel, click Effect, point to Color Correction, then click Channel Mixer.
4. Change the following values: Red-Const: -15; Green-Const: -23; Blue-Const: 31.
5. Double-click the Hue/Saturation effect on the Effects & Presets panel to apply the effect to the Clip 3 composition.
6. Change the following values: Master Hue: 0x -48.0°; Master Saturation: -21; Master Lightness: -20.
7. Save your project, then close After Effects.

Import an After Effects composition into Premiere Pro.

1. Start Premiere Pro, open the Water Pollution.prpoj file, then rename it **Water Pollution your name**.
2. Click File on the Application bar, point to Adobe Dynamic Link, then click Import After Effects Composition.
3. Locate the Water Pollution your name After Effects project file, click the PSA composition, then click OK.
4. Double-click the PSA/Water Pollution After Effects composition on the Project panel to preview the composition on the Source Monitor.

5. Click the Drag Video Only icon on the Source Monitor, then place the After Effects composition on the Video 1 track.
6. Click the Play-Stop Toggle button on the Program Monitor to preview the sequence.

Create a voice over in Premiere Pro.

1. Open the Water Pollution Script.txt file.
2. Make sure your microphone is plugged in to the microphone jack input.
3. Click the Audio Mixer panel options button then click Meter Input(s) Only. On the Audio Mixer panel, under the Audio 1 track, click the Enable Track For Recording button and the Solo Track button.
4. Click the Record button on the Audio Mixer panel.
5. Click the Play-Stop Toggle button on the Audio Mixer panel, then read the Water Pollution script.
6. Click the Play-Stop Toggle button when you have finished recording.
7. Preview your project on the Program Monitor.
8. Export your final project to the MPEG-2 video format.

Create a new After Effects composition in Premiere Pro.

1. Open the Luckenbach Commercial.prproj file, then save it as **Luckenbach Commercial your name**.
2. Preview the video clip on the Program Monitor.
3. Click the Selection tool, then select the Luckenbach clip in the sequence.
4. Click File on the Application bar, point to Adobe Dynamic Link, then click Replace After Effects Composition.

5. Name your project **Luckenbach Dynamic Link your name**, then click Save.
6. Select the Timeline panel, click Layer on the Application bar, point to New, then click Null Object.
7. On the Timeline panel, on the Luckenbach.avi layer, click the Parent drop-down menu, then click 2. Null 1.
8. Click File on the Application bar, point to Import, then click File.

9. Locate the Frame.psd file located in the Luckenbach-Clips folder, then click Open.
10. Drag Frame.psd from the Project panel to the Timeline panel above the Null 1 layer.
11. Click the Premiere Pro icon on the taskbar (Win) or dock (Mac) to return to Premiere Pro, as shown in Figure 102. save, then close the file.

Figure 102 *Luckenbach Commercial*

Track motion in Mocha for After Effects.

1. Minimize the After Effects workspace.
2. Click Start on the Application bar, point to All Programs, then click Mocha for After Effects CS5 (Win) or open the Finder from the dock and click Applications from the sidebar, select the Applications folder, select Adobe After Effects CS5, then click Mocha for After Effects CS5 (Mac).
3. Click Start on the Mocha splash screen.
4. Click File on the Application bar, then click New Project.
5. Click Choose to open the Choose a file dialog box, select the Luckenbach.avi file located in the Luckenbach-Clips folder, then click Open.
6. Type **640** in the first Frame Range text box, then type **756** in the second Frame Range text box.
7. On the Pixel Aspect Ratio drop-down menu select CS4 DV NTSC Anamorphic, then click OK.
8. Select the Create X-Spline Layer tool on the Tools panel, click in the upper-left corner, click in the upper-right corner, the lower-right corner, and the lower-left corner, then right-click to auto-close the shape.
9. In the Track tab, under Motion, click the Shear check box to deselect it, then click the Small Motion option button.
10. In the Transport controls section, click the Track Forwards button.
11. Resize the spline as needed.
12. Click the Surface button on the View Controls panel.
13. Resize the surface box to fit inside the picture above the green pennant.
14. Click the Export Tracking Data button to open the Export Tracking Data dialog box, select the Format drop-down arrow, then click After Effects Transform Data [anchor point, position, scale and rotation].
15. Click the Save the project button.
16. Click File on the Application bar, then click Exit to close Mocha.
17. Return to Luckenbach Dynamic Link.ae in After Effects and leave it open for the next step.

Paste the tracking data into After Effects.

1. Select the Null Object layer.
2. Click the Current time display, type **2110**, then press [Enter] (Win) or [return] (Mac).
3. Click Edit on the Application bar, then click Paste.
4. Click the expand arrow on the Null Object layer.
5. Click the Transform expand arrow.
6. Click Transform, above the list of properties, to deselect the multiple selections.
7. Click the Toggle Animation button in front of Position to remove all of the keyframes.
8. Click the Toggle Animation button in front of Rotation then change the Rotation value to 0x +0.0°.
9. Click the Play/Pause button on the Preview panel to preview the stabilized video clip.
10. Return the CTI to 0;00;21;10 in the Current time display, then click the Toggle Animation button in front of the Position property to create a keyframe.
11. Adjust the Position property to bring the image into the frame, if necessary.
12. Move the CTI to 0;00;22;25 in the Current time display, then adjust the Position property to bring the image into the frame.
13. Move the CTI to 0;00;25;06 in the Current time display, then adjust the Position property to bring the image into the frame.
14. Click the Play/Pause button on the Preview panel to preview the stabilized video clip.
15. Save Luckenbach Dynamic Link your name and leave it open for the next step.

Create 3D text.

1. Open the Luckenbach 3D Text.ae file, then save it as **Luckenbach 3D Text your name**.
2. Click Layer on the Application bar, point to New, then click Solid.
3. In the Name text box type **Text Color**, click the color picker, select a dark green color, then click OK.
4. On the Effects & Presets panel search field, type **Shatter**, then drag the Shatter preset onto the Text Color layer.
5. On the Effect Controls panel, click the View drop-down menu, then click Rendered.
6. Click the expand arrow in front of Shape, click the Pattern drop-down menu, then click Custom.
7. Click the Custom Shatter Map drop-down menu, then click 2. Luckenbach.
8. Click the Video button on Layer 2.

9. Click the Play/Pause button on the Preview panel to preview the 3D text.
10. Click the expand arrow in front of Force 1, Force 2, and Physics, then change the Strength and Gravity values to 0.00.
11. Collapse these properties when you have finished.
12. Click the Play/Pause button on the Preview panel to preview the 3D text.

Animate 3D text with a Camera layer.

1. Right-click the Timeline panel, click New, then click Camera.
2. Click the Preset drop-down menu, click 35mm, then click OK.
3. Select the Text Color layer on the Timeline panel, click the Camera Position drop-down menu, then click Comp Camera.
4. Click the Orbit Camera tool on the Tools panel, click Luckenbach on the Composition panel, then drag to the left and down.
5. Select the Text Color layer, then change the Extrusion Depth to 1.20.
6. Right-click the Timeline panel, point to New, then click Light.

7. Accept the default settings in the Light Settings dialog box, then click OK.
8. Using the Selection tool, move the light to the upper-left area of the Composition panel.
9. Select the Text Color layer, then, in the Effect Controls panel, click the expand arrow in front of Lighting.
10. Click the Light Type drop-down menu, then click First Comp Light.
11. Select the Camera layer, press [P], then click the Toggle Animation button.
12. Move the CTI to 0;00;01;00, click the Orbit Camera tool on the Tools panel, then adjust the Luckenbach text on the Composition panel.
13. Make additional adjustments with the Orbit Camera tool at 2 seconds, 3 seconds, 4 seconds, and 5 seconds.
14. Click the Play/Pause button on the Preview panel to preview the 3D text.

Enhance 3D text.

1. Select the Text Color layer, place the CTI at 00;00;00;00, then collapse the Shatter effect on the Effect Controls panel.

2. Select Effect on the Application bar, point to Stylize, then click Color Emboss.
3. Change the Relief value to 2.10, then change the Contrast value to 120.
4. Click Effect on the Application bar, point to Generate, then click CC Light Sweep.
5. Change the Width value to 25.0, the Sweep Intensity to 10.0 and the Edge Intensity value to 25.0.
6. Click the Toggle Animation button in front of Center to create a keyframe, then click the Effect Control point on the Composition panel to move the location of the light.
7. Make additional adjustments with the Effect Control point at 2 seconds, 3 seconds, 4 seconds, and 5 seconds.
8. Save the Luckenbach 3D Text your name project and close After Effects.

Import an After Effects composition.

1. Start Premiere Pro, open the Premiere Pro project Luckenbach Commercial your name.
2. Verify that the workspace is set to Editing and that the CTI is at 00;00;00;00.
3. Click File on the Application bar, then click Import.

4. Locate the Luckenbach 3D Text your name project file, then click Open.
5. Select the 3D Text composition, then click OK.
6. Double-click the 3D Text/Luckenbach 3D Text linked composition on the Project panel to open the file on the Source Monitor.
7. Click the Drag Video only icon, then drag to the Video 2 layer at the location of the CTI.
8. Preview your project on the Program Monitor.
9. Save your project, export your final project to the MPEG-2 video format without audio, then close Premiere Pro.

Animate with the Puppet Pin tool.

1. Open World Peace.ae, then save it as **World Peace your name**.
2. Select the Dove composition on the Timeline panel.
3. Select the Left Wing layer, click the Puppet Pin tool on the Tools panel, then click the tip of the wing to place a deform pin.
4. Place two more deform pins on the left wing, one on the left near the head and another at the right near the branch.
5. Click the deform pin at the tip of the tip of the wing, then press and hold [Ctrl] (Win) or ⌘ (Mac) while dragging the tip of the wing up and down until the CTI reaches the end of the Timeline.

6. Select the Right Wing layer, click the Puppet Pin tool, if necessary, then click the tip of the wing to place a deform pin.
7. Click to place two more deform pins on the right wing, one near the head and another near the base of the wing near the body.
8. Click the Play/Pause button on the Preview panel to preview the animation.
9. Click Record Options on the Tools panel to open the Puppet Record Options dialog box.
10. Change the Speed value to 50%, change the Smoothing value to 20, then click OK.
11. Click the Selection tool, select the deform pin at the tip of the right wing, then press and hold [Ctrl] (Win) or ⌘ (Mac) while dragging the tip of the wing up and down until the CTI reaches the end of the Timeline.
12. Click the Play/Pause button on the Preview panel to preview the animation.

Customize the Particle Playground effect.

1. Select the Effects workspace.
2. Select the World Peace composition on the Timeline panel, then click the Play/Pause button on the Preview panel to preview the animation.
3. Move the CTI to 0;00;05;00 in the Current time display, then select the Dove Particles layer.

4. Click the expand arrow in front of Cannon, then change the following values: Barrel Radius: 175; Particles Per Second: 4; Direction: 60x +0.0°; Direction Random Spread: 150.00; Velocity: 300.00; Velocity Random Spread: 250.00.
5. Click the expand arrow in front of Gravity, then change the Force value to 6.
6. Click the expand arrow in front of Layers Map, click the Use Layer drop-down menu, then click 2. Dove.
7. Click the Time Offset Type drop-down menu, click Relative Random, then change the Random Time Max value to 2.40.
8. Click the Play/Pause button on the Preview panel to preview the animation.

Work with a pre-compose layer.

1. Select the Dove composition, select the three layers on the Timeline panel, click Layer on the Application bar, then click Pre-Compose.
2. In the New composition name text box, type **Whole Dove**, then click OK.
3. Press [S] to reveal the Scale property, then change the value to 35.0%.
4. Select the World Peace composition, then click the Play/Pause button on the Preview panel to preview the animation.

Place text on a path.

1. Open the Text composition, then select the text on the Composition panel.
2. Select the Pen tool on the Tools panel, then click the RotoBezier check box on the Tools panel.
3. Click in the lower-left area of the Composition panel, move the cursor, click again, move the cursor again and this time hold the mouse button while you click to create a curved line.
4. Continue to draw the curved line until you get to the edge of the viewing area, holding the mouse button for the creation of each vertex.
5. On the Timeline panel, expand the Text layer properties.
6. Click the Path Options expand arrow, click the Path drop-down menu, then click Mask 1.
7. Select the Text composition, then expand the Path Options properties, if necessary.
8. Verify that the CTI is at 00;00;00;00, then click the Toggle Animation button in front of First Margin to activate keyframes.
9. Place keyframes at 15 seconds and 30 seconds by clicking the Add or remove keyframe at current time button.
10. Return to the first keyframe, then drag the text along the path until the text is all the way to the right.
11. Click the Go to Next Keyframe button to jump to the second keyframe, then drag the text along the path until it reaches the middle of the path.
12. Click the Go to Next Keyframe button to jump to the third keyframe, then drag the text along the path and return it to where it began.

13. Select the World Peace composition, then drag the Text composition to the top of the stacking order. An example of the composition is shown in Figure 103.
14. Click the Play/Pause button on the Preview panel to preview the animation.
15. Click Composition on the Application bar, then click Add to Render Queue.
16. Set the Output Module as an FLV and title your file **World Peace Commercial your name**.
17. Save your project file, then close After Effects.

Figure 103 *Completed Skills Review, World Peace Commercial*

Your multimedia instructor would like you to practice your skills with the Cartoon effect on the After Effects project file titled Cartoon practice. The Cartoon effect has already been applied to the footage with the default settings for you.

1. Start After Effects, open Cartoon Practice.ae, then save it as **Cartoon Practice your name.ae**.
2. Set the workspace to Effects.
3. Select the footage on the Composition panel, then make any necessary adjustments to the Cartoon effect on the Effect Controls panel that you feel appropriate.
4. Add the Levels effect to the footage and place it above the Cartoon effect.
5. Make appropriate adjustments to the Levels effect.
6. Add the Hue/Saturation effect to adjust the color.
7. Preview your final composition and save your project. A sample project is shown in Figure 104.
8. Export your project to the FLV file format named **Cartoon Practice your name**.

Figure 104 *Sample Project Builder 1*

Develop a PSA & Commercial Using Premiere Pro & After Effects CS5

A local steakhouse restaurant has contracted you to create a 30-second Internet commercial featuring a sculpture of a longhorn. They would like you to animate the longhorn using the Puppet Pin tool. They would also like you to create some animated 3D text with the name of their restaurant to play above the longhorn for the first 10-seconds of the commercial. For the remaining time they would simply like the address and the phone number of the restaurant featured. Since this will loop on the Internet, they do not want any sound.

A file has been provided titled Longhorn.ae with the necessary compositions already created for you to work with.

1. Open Longhorn.ae, then save it as **Longhorn your name.ae**.
2. Select the Longhorn composition, then using the Puppet Pin tool, animate the four legs on the Longhorn layer.
3. Select the 3D Text composition, select the Text Color layer, and on the Effect Controls panel, modify the Shatter effect to create 3D text. (*Hint*: The text has already been created for you.)

4. Select the Final composition, then drag the Longhorn and 3D Text compositions into this composition to compile the commercial spot. (*Hint*: The layers with the address and phone number are already created.)

5. Preview your Final composition to be sure you have placed the layers in the correct order. A sample project is shown in Figure 105.
6. Save your project and export as an FLV file named **Longhorn Commercial Spot your name**.

Figure 105 *Sample Project Builder 2*

The zoo in your area has contracted you to create a PSA they would like to air on local television and on their Web site bringing public awareness to a campaign about endangered animals. They are providing you with 12 video clips featuring animals they would like included in the commercial. A sample workspace is shown in Figure 106.

Using your skills in Premiere Pro and After Effects, create a 30-second commercial with appropriate text and a voice over from your own research concerning these endangered animals. You will need to export your movie in the MPEG-2 and FLV file formats.

1. Import the video clips into Premiere Pro.
2. Trim clips and combine them on a sequence (needs to be 30 seconds).
3. Use Adobe Dynamic Link to create an After Effects composition from the Premiere Pro sequence.
4. Add special effects of your choosing in After Effects.
5. Add appropriate text either in Premiere Pro or in After Effects.
6. Return to Premiere Pro and add a voice over.
7. Export as an MPEG-2 and FLV.

Figure 106 *Sample Portfolio Project*

CHAPTER 6

WORKING WITH SPECIAL EFFECTS TO ENHANCE VIRAL VIDEOS – ADOBE PREMIERE & ADOBE AFTER EFFECTS CS5

Adjust speed in Premiere Pro

Work with weather effects in After Effects

Animate lips on an animal in After Effects

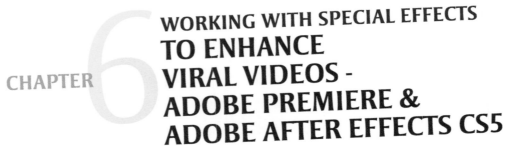

WORKING WITH SPECIAL EFFECTS TO ENHANCE VIRAL VIDEOS - ADOBE PREMIERE & ADOBE AFTER EFFECTS CS5

CHAPTER 6

A **viral video** is a video that gains popularity on the Internet through the process of sharing via Web sites and email. Viral videos have also become a popular means for marketing, showing off new bands and promoting music, and even as instructional aids in education. Special effects are often used to enhance videos that become viral.

In this chapter, we will work with special effects such as adjusting the speed of a clip, adding weather effects footage, and making an animal appear to sing in Premiere Pro and in After Effects.

Adjust Speed IN PREMIERE PRO

What You'll Do

In this lesson, you will use Premiere Pro to adjust the speed of a video clip.

Adjusting Speed in Premiere Pro

Adjusting the speed of a video clip is a popular editing technique. Increasing the speed of a clip is a creative way to indicate the passage of time. Common examples include accelerating the movement of clouds, street traffic, or crowds of people. Decreasing the speed of a clip can enhance emotional and dramatic moments, such as scenes from a wedding or highlights from sporting events.

The playback rate compared to the rate at which the video was recorded is called the **speed**. The speed is identified in percentages. 100% is the recorded playback speed; the speed of a clip can be adjusted to play faster by making the value greater than 100% or slower by making the value less than 100%. Adjusting the speed of a video clip does not adjust the audio and may cause the audio to be out of sync.

Premiere Pro offers the following options to use for adjusting speed: the Time Remapping effect, the Rate Stretch tool, and the Clip Speed/Duration dialog box.

Applying the Time Remapping Effect to a Clip

The Time Remapping effect is used on clips that are on the Timeline panel. This effect can be used to speed up, slow down, play backward, or freeze portions of a video clip. The Time Remapping effect has the flexibility to vary the speed across the duration of an entire clip. You can also ease in or ease out the speed changes.

When the Time Remapping effect is applied to a clip, the clip's appearance changes. The white speed control track at the top of the clip includes the speed keyframes. It is also where you will see left-pointing angle brackets if the clip is set to play in reverse. The rubber band represents 100% speed. The area above the rubber band represents speeds higher than 100%, and the area below the rubber band represents speeds less than 100%. A speed keyframe is created by pressing [Ctrl]-click (Win) or ⌘-click (Mac) at any point on the rubber band. A speed keyframe is identified by a dotted line and a pair of handles in the speed control track,

Working with Special Effects to Enhance Viral Videos - Adobe Premiere & Adobe After Effects CS5

as shown in Figure 1. The rubber band controls the speed of the clip and can be dragged on either side of the keyframe to increase or decrease the speed (the speed on the other side remains the same). Adding keyframes allows the speed to vary, as shown in Figure 2. (*Note:* The duration of the clip will automatically adjust to accommodate the new speed(s). If there is no available space to the right of the clip, and the speed is reduced,

thus increasing the length of the clip, the overall clip duration will remain the same and the adjusted clip will be trimmed where the next clip begins.)

Playing a Clip Backward then Forward

You can play a clip backward then forward by [Ctrl]-dragging (Win) or ⌘-dragging (Mac) a speed keyframe to the place in the clip where you want the backward motion

to end. The Program Monitor displays a split screen; the left frame displays the static frame where the drag was initiated and the right frame previews the reverse playback, as shown in Figure 3. When the mouse button is released to define the segment of backward motion, an additional segment is automatically added to replay the forward motion. Left-pointing angle brackets appear in the speed control track, as shown in

Figure 1 *A Speed keyframe and the rubber band*

Figure 2 *Time Remapping varying speed*

Figure 3 *Playing a clip backward*

Lesson 1   Adjust Speed in Premiere Pro

Figure 4, to indicate which segment of the clip will play in reverse. You can use the Razor tool or the Trim tool to remove the segment of the clip that replays the forward motion if you only want the clip to play in reverse.

Adding a Speed Transition

After creating a speed change using time remapping, you can create a smoother transition between the different speeds.

When you create a speed keyframe, it has two handles joined together on the speed control track. Drag either of these handles left or right to create a transition area, as shown in Figure 5. A blue curve control appears in the middle. Drag either of the handles on the curve control to smooth the transition—the speed change will then ease in and out, creating a smoother transition. The line between two handles is referred to as the **speed ramp**.

Using the Rate Stretch Tool

The Rate Stretch tool is used to change the duration of a clip on the Timeline while simultaneously adjusting the speed to compensate. Using the Rate Stretch tool you can stretch the clip until it fills the gap. Dragging the clip edge to shorten it increases its speed; dragging the clip edge to lengthen it decreases its speed. The clip's In and Out points are not changed, only its speed.

Figure 4 *Left-pointing angle brackets*

Left-pointing angle brackets

Figure 5 *Adjusting speed transitions*

Default speed transition

Blue curve control

Speed keyframe handles

Speed ramp

Control handles

Varying adjustments to the speed transition

You can view the clip's speed by hovering the mouse pointer over the clip until a tool tip appears, as shown in Figure 6.

Adjusting Speed with the Clip Speed/Duration Dialog Box

The Clip Speed/Duration dialog box allows you to enter the desired speed or duration of the clip, as shown in Figure 7. By default

the speed and duration are linked, therefore, if you increase the speed of the clip, the duration will shorten. Click the Link/Unlink icon to change either the speed or duration separately. To play the video backwards, check the Reverse Speed check box. The Maintain Audio Pitch option, when selected, prevents the sound from going up or down in pitch when the speed is adjusted.

The Ripple Edit, Shifting Trailing Clips option, when selected, will shift any existing clips already on the track, either moving them to the left if the speed is increased so the next clip is not trimmed, or to the right if the speed is decreased so there is no gap remaining. Adjusting the playback rate using the Clip Speed/Duration dialog box applies a constant speed across the entire clip.

Figure 6 *Tool tip showing speed*

Tool tip

Figure 7 *Clip Speed/Duration dialog box*

Speed

Duration

Link/Unlink icon

Apply the Time Remapping effect to a clip

1. Open the Speed 1.prproj file from the drive and folder where you store your Data Files, then save it as **Speed 1 your name**.

   The 42.avi video clip has already been added to the Video 1 track for you.

2. Select the Skateboarding sequence to activate the Timeline panel, then click the **Play-Stop Toggle button** on the Program Monitor to preview the clip.

   You will be adjusting the speed of the clip to highlight the action of the skateboarders.

3. Drag the **CTI** to **00;00;00;00**.

4. On the Timeline panel, click the **Clip Effect menu**, point to **Time Remapping**, then click **Speed**, as shown in Figure 8.

   A yellow horizontal rubber band control appears across the center of the clip, as shown in Figure 9.

   TIP Resize the track to get a better view of the rubber band control.

   (continued)

Figure 8 *Selecting Speed from the Clip Effect menu*

Time Remapping   Clip Effect menu   Speed

Figure 9 *Rubber band control*

Time Remapping: Speed   Rubber band control   Track resized for better view

Figure 10 *Activating speed keyframes*

Speed keyframe   White speed-control

Figure 11 *Speed keyframes*

5. [Ctrl]-click (Win) or ⌘-click (Mac) the **rubber band** at the location of the **CTI (00;00;00;00)**.

   Keyframes are activated and a speed keyframe is placed in the white speed control track, as shown in Figure 10.

6. Drag the **CTI** to **00;00;01;15**, then click the **Add-Remove keyframe button** on the Timeline panel.

   This places a speed keyframe.

7. Add additional speed keyframes at the following times: **00;00;03;08**, **00;00;04;19**, **00;00;07;14**, and **00;00;09;27**, then compare your Timeline to Figure 11.

8. Save your project and leave it open for the next exercise.

You applied the Time Remapping effect to a clip and set speed keyframes on a video clip.

Adjust the speed of a clip

1. Open the Speed 1 your name.prproj project file, if necessary.

2. Click the **first rubber band segment** which is between the first and second speed keyframes, then drag in a downward direction until the tool tip reads **25.00%**, as shown in Figure 12.

   The speed of the video clip between the first two speed keyframes will be reduced to 25% of the original speed; the overall duration of the clip is extended as a result.

3. Drag the **CTI** to **00;00;00;00**, then click the **Play-Stop Toggle button** on the Program Monitor to preview the clip.

4. Click the **second rubber band segment**, then drag in an upward direction until the tool tip reads **175.00%**, as shown in Figure 13.

   The speed of the video clip between the second and third speed keyframes will be increased to 175% of the original speed; the overall duration of the clip is reduced as a result.

   (continued)

Figure 12 *Decreasing the speed of a clip*

Tool tip – 25.00%

Figure 13 *Increasing the speed of a clip*

Tool tip – 175.00%

Working with Special Effects to Enhance Viral Videos - Adobe Premiere & Adobe After Effects CS5

Figure 14 *Adjusting the speed of a clip*

5. Make the following adjustments along the rubber band segments: 3rd segment: **15.00%**, 4th segment: **280.00%**, 5th segment: **30.00%** and 6th segment: **165.00%**, then compare your Timeline panel to Figure 14.

6. Drag the **CTI** to **00;00;00;00**, then click the **Play-Stop Toggle button** ▶ on the Program Monitor to preview the clip.

7. Export your video to the FLV|F4V format and name the file **Skateboarding your name**.

8. Close the Speed 1 your name.prproj project file.

You adjusted the speed of a video clip by increasing and decreasing the speed in different sections, then exported the file to the FLV|F4V format for the Internet.

Play a clip backward then forward

1. Open the Speed 2.prproj file from the drive and folder where you store your Data Files, then save it as **Speed 2 your name**.

   The 30.avi video clip has already been added to the Video 1 track for you.

2. On the Timeline panel, click the **Clip Effect menu**, point to **Time Remapping**, then click **Speed**.

3. Resize the Video 1 track to get a better view of the rubber band control.

4. On the Timeline panel, drag the **CTI** to **00;00;06;27**, then **[Ctrl]**-click (Win) or ⌘-click (Mac) the **rubber band** to create a speed keyframe.

5. Drag the **CTI** to **00;00;08;08**, then click the **Add-Remove keyframe button** ◉ on the Timeline panel.

   At the location of this speed keyframe, you will duplicate a portion of the video clip to play it back in reverse.

6. **[Ctrl]**-click (Win) or ⌘-click (Mac) the **second speed keyframe**, then drag to the right until the first portion of the tool tip reads **00;00;09;17**, as shown in Figure 15.

   The Program Monitor shows a split screen. The clip on the right displays the portion of the video clip that is being duplicated. As a result, the location of the speed keyframe has adjusted slightly on the Timeline and is now located at the duration 00;00;08;07. Your time may vary.

   (continued)

Figure 15 *Reversing a portion of a clip*

Portion of clip being reversed in Timeline panel

Tool tip – 00;00;09;17

Figure 16 *Creating a speed transition*

Right half of speed keyframe

Tool tip – 00;00;09;06

Left-pointing angle brackets

Figure 17 *Adjusting the speed transition*

Gray area indicating length of speed transition

Blue curve control

Speed ramp

7. Drag the **CTI** to **00;00;00;00**, then click the **Play-Stop Toggle button** ▶ on the Program Monitor to preview the clip.

8. Save your project and leave it open for the next exercise.

You made a portion of a clip play backwards then forwards.

Add a speed transition

1. Open the Speed 2 your name.prproj project file, if necessary.

2. On the Timeline panel, click and drag the right half of the speed keyframe that is in front of the left point brackets, until the first portion of the tool tip reads **00;00;09;06**, as shown in Figure 16.

   The distance between the left and right halves of the speed keyframe specifies the duration of the speed transition, and is shown by a gray area.

   A blue curve control appears, which is used to adjust the curvature of the speed ramp, as shown in Figure 17.

3. Drag the **CTI** to **00;00;08;23**, verify that the Timeline panel is active, then press [=] (equal sign) repeatedly to zoom in on the gray area while still seeing both sides of the speed keyframe.

(continued)

4. Click the right handle of the blue curve control, then drag either left or right to adjust the speed ramp, as shown in Figure 18.

   This adjusts the curve of the speed ramp, and the speed change will now ease in and out.

5. With the Timeline panel active, press [-] (minus sign) repeatedly to zoom out until you see the entire clip.

   The goal is to see the clip play one time in forward motion and one time in reverse motion.

6. Click the **Razor tool** on the Tools panel, drag the **CTI** to **00;00;10;15** on the Timeline panel, then click the location of the CTI.

TIP You can also press [C] on the keyboard to activate the Razor tool.

7. On the Timeline panel, drag the **CTI** to **00;00;11;25** then click the location of the CTI.

   Cut points have been created on either side of the portion of the clip where the clip replays the forward motion.

8. Click the **Selection tool** on the Tools panel, then click the clip with the cut points as shown in Figure 19.

9. Click **Edit** on the Application bar, then click **Ripple Delete**.

   The selected clip is removed without leaving a gap between clips.

10. Drag the **CTI** to **00;00;00;00**, then click the **Play-Stop Toggle button** on the Program Monitor to preview the clip.

(continued)

Figure 18 *Adjusting the curvature of the speed ramp*

Speed ramp

Adjusting the blue curve control

Figure 19 *Selecting the clip between cut points*

Selected clip

Figure 20 *Using the Rate Stretch tool*

Rate Stretch tool cursor

Figure 21 *Stretching the clip to fill the gap*

Black line

11. Export your video to the FLV|F4V format and name the file **Skateboarding Stunts your name**.

12. Close the Speed 2 your name.prproj project file.

You adjusted the speed ramp between the clips playing forward and reverse, then you trimmed the clip and exported it for the Internet.

Adjust the speed of a clip with the Rate Stretch tool

1. Open the Speed 3.prproj file from the drive and folder where you store your Data Files, then save it as **Speed 3 your name**.

   Three video clips have already been added to the Video 1 track for you: 7.avi, 13.avi, and 22.avi. A gap has been left between clip 13.avi and 22.avi, and the 22.avi clip's speed has been adjusted to 12.00%.

2. Click the **Play-Stop Toggle button** ▶ on the Program Monitor to preview the clip.

3. Click the **Rate Stretch tool** 🔧 on the Tools panel, then point to the right edge of the 13.avi clip on the Timeline.

   The Rate Stretch tool cursor appears, as shown in Figure 20.

   TIP You can also press [X] to active the Rate Stretch tool.

4. Click and drag the right edge of the 13.avi clip to the right to fill the gap, then release the mouse button when you see a vertical black line appear, as shown in Figure 21.

   (continued)

The vertical black line indicates the length the clip will be when the mouse button is released. The cursor will snap to the left edge of the next clip.

5. Click the **Selection tool** on the Tools panel.

6. Drag the **CTI** to **00;00;00;00**, then click the **Play-Stop Toggle button** on the Program Monitor to preview the clip.

The 13.avi clip speed was adjusted to compensate to fill the gap; the speed was reduced to 34.33%, as shown in Figure 22.

7. Save your project and leave it open for the next exercise.

You adjusted the speed of a clip using the Rate Stretch tool, then you exported it for the Internet.

Adjust the speed of a clip with the Clip Speed/Duration dialog box

1. Open the Speed 3 your name.prproj project file, if necessary.

2. On the Timeline panel, right-click the **7.avi clip**, then click **Speed/Duration**.

The Clip Speed/Duration dialog box opens as shown in Figure 23.

3. In the Clip Speed/Duration dialog box change the Speed value to **50%**, click the **Ripple Edit, Shifting Trailing Clips check box**, then click **OK**.

The speed of the clip will be reduced to 50% and the clips on the Video 1 track will shift to allow for the adjustment made to the length of the clip. Next you will create a duplicate of the same clip playing in reverse.

(continued)

Figure 22 *Adjusted speed of clip after using the Rate Stretch tool*

Adjusted speed

Figure 23 *Activating the Clip Speed/Duration dialog box*

Clip Speed/Duration dialog box

Working with Special Effects to EnhanceViral Videos - Adobe Premiere & Adobe After Effects CS5

Figure 24 *Copying and inserting a clip*

Duplicated clip

4. Click the **Selection tool** on the Tools panel, if necessary, then click the **7.avi clip** on the Timeline panel.

5. Click **Edit** on the Application bar, then click **Copy**.

   A copy of the 7.avi clip is created with the 50% speed duration applied to it.

6. Place the **CTI** at the **cut line**, between the 7.avi and 13.avi clips.

7. Click **Edit** on the Application bar, click **Paste Insert**, then compare your sequence to Figure 24.

   A copy of the 7.avi clip is inserted and the other clips in the sequence are shifted to the right.

8. Right-click the second instance of the 7.avi clip on the Timeline panel, then click **Speed/Duration**.

9. In the Clip Speed/Duration dialog box, click the **Reverse Speed check box**.

   This will cause the clip to playback in reverse.

10. Drag the **CTI** to **00;00;00;00**, then click the **Play-Stop Toggle button** on the Program Monitor to preview the clip.

11. Export your video to the FLV|F4V format and name the file **Bike Stunts your name**.

12. Close the Speed 3 your name.prproj project file.

You adjusted the speed of a clip using the Clip Speed/Duration dialog box. You also copied a clip, inserted it in the sequence, and reversed the playback of a clip. Finally you exported the video for the Internet.

Work with Weather Effects
IN AFTER EFFECTS

What You'll Do

In this lesson, you will add lightning and rain effects to a video clip.

Working with Weather Effects

Weather effects are another way to establish mood and setting in a video. After Effects includes effects for creating rain, snow, lightning and fog. In this section, we will explore the CC Rain and Advanced Lightning effects. Once you know how to use these effects, you will be able to explore the others on your own.

Applying the Linear Color Key Effect

The **Linear Color Key effect** uses RGB, hue, or chroma information to create a range of transparency across an image based on a specified color. This will then allow you to place another image below the layer to replace the color that has been removed or **keyed**. For example, you could use this effect to remove the sky from footage so it could be replaced with footage that better suits a rainy day, such as a gray, cloudy sky.

When applied to a clip, the Linear Color Key effect displays two thumbnail images on the Effect Controls panel, as shown in Figure 25. The thumbnail on the left shows the unaltered image and the one on the right shows a preview of the image. The preview of the image can be one of the following choices from the View menu: Final Output, Source Only, or Matte Only. (*Note:* The View menu is located just below the right thumbnail.) The **Final Output** view displays a preview of the keyed area, the **Source Only** view shows the original footage without the key applied, and the **Matte Only** view shows the alpha channel matte to view holes in the transparency.

The **Key Color** menu has the Key Color swatch and the eyedropper available to select the color which will be keyed. The key color can be selected by clicking the **Key Color swatch** or with the **eyedropper** and pointing to a color in the footage on the Composition panel. The **Matching Tolerance** property determines how closely the pixels must match the key color before they become transparent.

A value of 100.0% will make the entire image transparent; whereas a value of 0.0% will make the entire image opaque. The **Matching Softness** property adjusts the softness of the edges between the image and the transparent area. It is suggested that values under 20% usually produce the best results.

To assist in keeping the image opaque, or solid, in the areas where it needs to be, a Photoshop composition can be created and placed below the layer on which the effect is being applied. This method was used in Figure 26. The areas of the footage that were made transparent because of the sky and the buildings being so similar in color were restored.

Working with the CC Rain Effect

The **CC Rain effect** is a self-animating effect that simulates rain. Although the effect is self-animating, keyframes can still be added to customize the effect. The **Amount** property determines how much rain fall. A setting of zero stops the rain. The larger the Amount value, the more rain fall. The **Speed** property changes the rate at which the rain falls.

The angle of the rain can be adjusted with the **Angle** and **Angle Variation** properties. The **Drop Size** property modifies the size of the rain, and the **Opacity** property blends the rain into the footage on which the effect was applied. Finally, the **Source Depth** property gives the illusion that the rain is falling within the footage, not just in front of it.

Using the CC Mr. Mercury Effect

The **CC Mr. Mercury** effect is a particle system that creates ever-changing blobs, which you can make appear like rain drops on a camera lens,

Figure 25 *The Linear Color Key effect*

Unaltered image

Selected View preview

View

Figure 26 *The Linear Color Key comparison*

Original Image

Linear Color Key applied

Linear Color Key applied with Photoshop composition

as shown in Figure 27. The properties can be combined to create blobs that behave realistically, splitting up and rejoining, just like real-world liquid particles. The source layer is used as a reflection map for the particles.

The **Radius X** and **Radius Y** properties determine the size of the blob producer based on the X and Y coordinates. The **Velocity** property determines the speed of the blobs at birth. The higher the setting the faster the blobs move; a setting of zero will keep the blobs stationary.

The **Birth Rate** property determines the number of blobs that are generated at any given point in time. The higher the Birth Rate value the greater the concentration of blobs.

The **Gravity** property determines how quickly the blobs fall; a negative Gravity value causes them to rise. Setting the Gravity value to zero, along with a zero value for the Velocity property, will keep the blobs from moving.

The **Influence Map** property offers a drop-down menu with options that determine the behavior of the blobs as they appear and disappear. For the effect of water on a lens, the Constant Blobs setting maintains a somewhat constant size from the time they appear to the time they disappear.

The **Blob Birth and Death Size** properties determine the size of the blobs when they first appear and just before they disappear.

Creating Lightning with the Advanced Lightning Effect

The Advanced Lightning effect, in the Generate category, creates simulations of electrical discharges. The Advanced Lightning effect does not self-animate like the CC Rain and CC Mr. Mercury effects. The **Conductivity State** property changes the path of the lightning and can be used to animate the effect. It will be necessary to activate keyframes if you want to have some influence over the effect.

The **Lightning Type** property specifies the characteristics of the lightning; the **Direction** and **Outer Radius** properties will change based on this selection.

Figure 27 *An example of the CC Mr. Mercury effect*

Working with Special Effects to Enhance Viral Videos - Adobe Premiere & Adobe After Effects CS5

The **Origin** property determines the point at which the lightning strike begins.

If the Lightning Type is set to Vertical, the Direction and Outer Radius settings are not available.

The **Outer Radius** property determines the distance the lightning travels from the point of origin. This property is enabled when the Lightning Type property is set to Omni or Anywhere.

The **Direction** property indicates which route the lightning will take. It is available if one of the following Lightning types is selected: Direction, Strike, Breaking, Bouncy, and Two-Way Strike.

The **Alpha Obstacle** property specifies the influence of the alpha channel of the layer the Advanced Lightning effect is being applied to. The **alpha channel** represents the transparent areas on the layer. If the Alpha Obstacle value is greater than zero, the lightning attempts

to wrap itself around the solid areas in the layer by moving through the transparent areas. (*Note*: When setting the value greater than zero, it is not always possible to preview the correct results without selecting Full Resolution in the Preview panel.)

The **Composite on Original** option shows the lightning on the footage as shown in Figure 28. If the Composite on Original check box is not selected only the lightning will be visible, as shown in Figure 29.

Figure 28 *Applying the Advanced Lightning effect*

Composite on Original

Figure 29 *Composite on Original option is disabled*

Composite on Original

Apply the CC Rain and Linear Color Key effects

1. Open the Weather 1.ae file from the drive and folder where you store your Data Files, then save it as **Weather 1 your name**.

   The us_5.avi video clip has already been added to the US Capitol composition for you.

2. On the Timeline panel, click the **us_5.mov layer**, click **Effect** on the Application bar, point to **Simulation**, then click **CC Rain**.

   This applies the CC Rain effect to the video footage of the Capitol building and activates the Effect Controls panel, as shown in Figure 30.

3. Click the **Play/Pause button** ▶ on the Preview panel to preview the clip.

   Rain has been added to the video footage with the CC Rain effect, but the appearance does not change throughout the duration of the footage and the sky is too bright for a rainy day.

4. On the Timeline panel, click the **us_5.mov layer**, click **Effects** on the Application bar, point to **Keying**, then click **Linear Color Key**.

   We will begin by removing the sky and replacing it with darker clouds.

5. On the Effect Controls panel, click the **Linear Color Key effect** then drag it above the CC Rain effect, as shown in Figure 31.

6. On the Effect Controls panel, under the Linear Color Key effect, click the **Match colors drop-down menu**, then click **Using Hue**.

   The transparency will be created based on the hue from the specified color. The Selected View

   (continued)

Figure 30 *Applying the CC Rain effect*

CC Rain effect

Figure 31 *Applying the Linear Color Key effect*

Linear Color Key effect

Match colors

Key color swatch

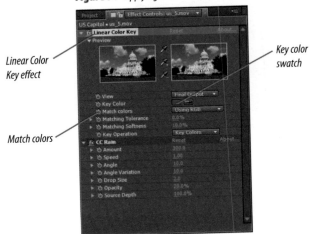

Working with Special Effects to Enhance Viral Videos - Adobe Premiere & Adobe After Effects CS5

Figure 32 *Adjusting settings in the Linear Color Key effect*

Key Color swatch

Figure 33 *Placing the US Capitol Mask composition in the active composition*

Project panel

US Capitol Mask composition

US Capitol Mask composition

preview becomes dark because the default Key Color has been applied to the layer and the color is keyed out.

7. Click the **Key Color swatch**, type **475C82** in the # text box in the Key Color dialog box, then click **OK**.

The Key Color dialog box lets you select a specific color that will be removed from the footage, in this case a light blue, as shown in Figure 32. Holes have been created in the Capitol building because of the Matching Tolerance level, which allows additional pixels that vary from the color selected to be removed. The US Capitol composition will be used to correct any problems with the portions of the building that are transparent, therefore you need only focus on removing the sky and the edges of the Capitol building.

8. On the Effect Controls panel, under the Linear Color Key effect, change the Matching Tolerance value to **0%** and the Matching Softness value to **24.0%**.

These settings will improve the edges around the building by making the edges less transparent.

TIP On the View drop-down menu choose Matte Only, this may help you when creating your transparency area.

9. Click the **Project panel**, click the **US Capitol Mask composition**, then drag it to the US Capitol composition on the Timeline, below the us_5.mov layer.

The US Capitol Mask composition should be 2 in the stacking order, as shown in Figure 33. Notice the holes in the building have been corrected.

(continued)

Lesson 2   Work with Weather Effects in After Effects

10. Click the **Project panel**, click the **Storm Clouds.m2v footage**, then drag it to the US Capitol composition on the Timeline, below the US Capitol Mask composition layer.

The Storm Clouds.m2v footage composition should be 3 in the stacking order, as shown in Figure 34.

11. Click the **Play/Pause button** on the Preview panel to preview the clip.

(*Note*: Color correction techniques learned in an earlier chapter could be applied to the us_5.mov layer to blend the Capitol Building with the storm clouds.)

12. Save your project and leave it open for the next exercise.

You applied the CC Rain effect, keyed out the sky, and replaced the sky with storm cloud footage.

Customize the CC Rain effect

1. Open the Weather 1 your name project file, if necessary, then verify that the Effect Controls panel is visible and that the CTI is at **00;00;00;00**.

2. On the Timeline panel click the **us_5.mov layer**, click the **Effects expand arrow**, then click the **CC Rain expand arrow**.

As adjustments are made on the Effect Controls panel, keyframes will be automatically generated on the Timeline panel allowing you to see them as they are created.

3. On the Effect Controls panel, in the CC Rain effect, click the **Time-Vary stopwatch button** in front of the Amount, Speed, Drop Size,

(continued)

Figure 34 *Placing the Storm Clouds.m2v footage in the active composition*

Storm Clouds.m2v

Storm Clouds.m2v

Figure 35 *Changing the CC Rain default values*

Amount

Speed

Drop Size

Keyframes

Figure 36 *Reducing the CC Rain Amount property to zero*

No rain

Amount value = 0

and Source Depth properties, then change the values as follows: Amount: **260.0**, Speed: **3.5**, Drop Size: **3.5**, and Source Depth: **0.0%**.

Keyframes for the Amount, Speed, Drop Size, and Source Depth properties are activated and a strong rain begins at the beginning of the video footage, as shown in Figure 35.

4. Drag the **CTI** to **00;00;04;00**, and on the Timeline panel, in the CC Rain effect, change the Amount value to **250.0**.

   You will continue to move through the footage reducing the amount of rain, as the clouds begin to clear.

5. Continue to adjust the CTI and the values as follows: At 08 seconds: Amount: **225.0**, Speed: **2.25**, Drop Size: **3.0**, and Source Depth: **100.0%**, and at 12 seconds: Amount: **0**.

   The rain effect is turned off on the last keyframe because the Amount value has been set to zero; the other values do not need to be updated since the rain has been stopped by changing the Amount value, as shown in Figure 36.

6. On the Timeline and the Effect Controls panels, click the **CC Rain collapse arrow** to close the properties.

   It is no longer necessary to have the CC Rain effects expanded in either the Timeline panel or the Effect Controls panel.

7. Click the **Play/Pause button** ▶ on the Preview panel to preview the clip.

8. Save your project and leave it open for the next exercise.

You adjusted the CC Rain effect to change the appearance of the rain as the clouds changed.

Lesson 2   Work with Weather Effects in After Effects

Apply the CC Mr. Mercury effect

1. Open the Weather 1 your name project file, if necessary, then verify that the Effect Controls panel is visible and that the CTI is at **00;00;00;00**.

2. On the Timeline panel, click the **us_5.mov layer**, click **Effect** on the Application bar, point to **Simulation**, then click **CC Mr. Mercury**.

   The CC Mr. Mercury effect is applied to the layer and the effect appears on the Effect Controls panel. You will need to move this effect above the CC Rain effect in order to see the rain that was created earlier.

3. On the Effect Controls panel, click the **CC Mr. Mercury effect**, then drag it above the CC Rain effect, as shown in Figure 37.

   This effect will give the impression of drops of water getting on the camera lens during filming.

4. Click the **Play/Pause button** ▶ on the Preview panel to preview the clip.

   Some adjustments need to be made to the effect to minimize the "blob" effect.

5. On the Effect Controls panel, in the CC Mr. Mercury effect, click the **Time-Vary stopwatch button** 🕙 in front of the Birth Rate property to activate keyframes for the Birth Rate property.

   The Birth Rate keyframe is necessary so the effect can be turned off towards the end of the duration of the footage. A keyframe only needs to be created for the Birth Rate property. The property value adjustments will automatically change over time.

   (continued)

Figure 37 *Applying the CC Mr. Mercury effect*

CC Mr. Mercury

CC Rain

Working with Special Effects to Enhance Viral Videos - Adobe Premiere & Adobe After Effects CS5

Figure 38 *Customizing the CC Mr. Mercury effect*

CC Mr.
Mercury

6. On the Effect Controls panel, make the following changes to the property values for the CC Mr. Mercury effect: Radius X: **164.0**, Radius Y: **78.0**, Velocity: **0.0**, **Birth Rate**: 0.5, Gravity: **0.0**, Influence Map: **Constant Blobs**, Blob Birth Size: **0.25**, and Blob Death Size: **0.32**, as shown in Figure 38.

These adjustments will create drops, keep the drops from moving, slow down the appearance of the drops, and adjust the size of the drops when they are created and when they fade away.

7. Drag the **CTI** to **00;00;12;00**, and on the Effect Controls panel change the Birth Rate property of the CC Mr. Mercury effect to **0.0**, as shown in Figure 39.

This will fade out the appearance of the rain drops.

8. Click the **Play/Pause button** ▶ on the Preview panel to preview the clip.

9. Export your video to the FLV format and name the file **Rain Effects your name**.

10. Close the Weather 1 your name.ae project file.

You made it appear that there were raindrops on the camera lens during filming, and customized the effect so that it would cause the rain to end at the end of the clip.

Work with the Advanced Lightning effect on a logo

1. Open the Lightning 1.ae file from the drive and folder where you store your Data Files, then save it as **Lightning 1 your name**.

The Lightning Logo composition has already been created for you with an Adobe Illustrator document.

(continued)

Figure 39 *Disabling the CC Mr. Mercury effect*

Birth Rate = 0

12 seconds

Lesson 2   Work with Weather Effects in After Effects

2. On the Timeline panel click the **Lightning Logo.ai layer**, click **Effect** on the Application bar, point to **Generate**, then click **Advanced Lightning**.

   The Advanced Lightning effect is applied to the Lightning Logo.ai layer and appears on the Effect Controls panel, as shown in Figure 40.

3. On the Effect Controls panel, click the **Composite on Original check box**.

   The lightning will be composited with the original layer so the contents of the layer are visible with the lightning. When the layer is not selected, only the lightning is visible.

4. Click the **Play/Pause button** on the Preview panel to preview the clip.

   The Advanced Lightning effect does not self-animate as the CC Rain effect did.

5. On the Effect Controls panel, click the **Time-Vary stopwatch button** in front of the Conductivity State property.

   Keyframes only need to be created for the Conductivity State property to animate the lightning. Keyframes can be activated for other properties if you would like to have additional control over the Advanced Lightning effect.

6. Drag the **CTI** to **00;00;13;00**, then change the Conductivity State value to **3.5** on the Effect Controls panel, as shown in Figure 41.

   The Conductivity State setting changes the path of the lightning.

7. On the Effect Controls panel, change the Origin values to **245.0** and **125.0**.

   The Origin values specify the x and y coordinates from where the lightning will strike.

   (continued)

Figure 40 *Applying the Advanced Lightning effect*

Advanced Lightning

Composite on Original

Figure 41 *Animating the Advanced Lightning effect*

Conductivity State

13 seconds

Working with Special Effects to Enhance Viral Videos - Adobe Premiere & Adobe After Effects CS5

Figure 42 *Adjusting the Alpha Obstacle property*

Alpha Obstacle

Full

8. On the Effect Controls panel, change the Direction values to **415.0** and **375.0**.

   The Direction values control specifies the x and y coordinates where the lightning strike will end. The actual end point may vary from the x, y based on the lightning type.

9. On the Effect Controls panel, change the Lightning type to **Breaking**.

   With the Breaking type, branches from the lightning are focused towards the Direction point as the distance between the Origin and Direction increases.

10. On the Effect Controls panel, change the Alpha Obstacle property to **4.50**.

    When the Alpha Obstacle value is greater than zero, the lightning attempts to wrap itself around the opaque areas in the layer by moving through the transparent areas.

11. On the Preview panel, change the Resolution to **Full**, as shown in Figure 42.

    If the Alpha Obstacle value is set to a value other than zero, it is important to preview in Full Resolution before exporting your project.

TIP On the Preview panel, click Full from the Resolution drop-down menu to preview in full resolution.

12. Click the **Play/Pause button** ▶ on the Preview panel to preview the clip.

13. Export your video to the FL format and name the file **Lightning Logo your name**.

14. Close the Lightning 1 your name.ae project file.

You animated the advanced lightning effect on a logo.

Animate Lips on an Animal
IN AFTER EFFECTS

What You'll Do

In this lesson, you will work with a special effect in After Effects that will give the appearance of an animal appearing to sing or talk.

Making an Animal Appear to Sing or Talk

A popular effect seen on commercials and the Internet is making babies or animals appear to speak. You have probably seen the E-trade baby or the dog in the Bush's Baked beans commercials. This effect can be accomplished in After Effects. In this lesson, we will make it appear that a dog is singing.

Using the Tracker Panel to Track Motion

Motion tracking is available within After Effects with the Tracker panel. The Tracker panel can be activated by selecting the Motion Tracking workspace, as shown in Figure 43, or by choosing Tracker from the Window menu.

Figure 43 *The Tracker panel*

Tracker panel

Motion tracking is used to track the movement of an object identified in footage. Tracking data is generated and then applied to another object in order to follow that same motion. For example, if you would like to add custom signage to a moving vehicle after the footage has been shot, you can design your sign in After Effects and then attach the tracking data to the sign so it moves with the vehicle.

The Tracker panel is where you specify settings, control tracking and apply tracking data. The first decision to be made is whether to choose Track motion or Stabilize motion as the method for tracking the motion of your footage.

Track motion and Stabilize motion are essentially the same processes. The main difference is that the Track motion option allows you to apply the tracking data to another layer, whereas the Stabilize motion applies tracking data to the source layer. By default, both processes activate a position, which creates only one track point on the Layer panel, as shown in Figure 44. Selecting either rotation or scale will activate another track point, which will generate tracking data for either the Rotation or Scale property.

A **track point** is the area that specifies what will be tracked. It contains a feature region, a search region, and an attach point. The **feature region** defines the area in the layer that will be tracked. The feature region should be sized to enclose the feature of the tracked region, including as little of the surrounding image as possible. The **search region** is a larger area around the feature region that defines the area where After Effects will look for the feature region.

Figure 44 *Moving Track Point 1 over the right eye*

Track Point 1

The size and location of the search region depends on the movement of the feature being tracked. The larger the search region, the longer the actual process of motion tracking will take. The search region needs to be large enough to accommodate the movement of the tracked feature from frame-to-frame, not the movement during the duration of the footage. If the movement is gradual, the search region needs to be only slightly larger than the feature region because the track point will adjust to the new location. If the area in the feature region

changes position and direction quickly, the search region needs to be large enough to include the largest position and direction change in any consecutive frames. The **attach point** is the designated place for the object you plan to attach to the motion. The attach point by default is at the center of the feature region and can be relocated anywhere on the Layer panel before tracking. For example, to animate a thought bubble above a person's head, you would place the attach point above the head and position the feature region on the head. If the attach point was left in the

default position, the thought bubble would be attached to that point and would hide the person's face.

During analysis the track points may move off of the area you have designated. The analysis can be paused so that adjustments can be made to the track points to improve the tracking data before it is applied. When adjusting the track points the Selection tool pointer icons change depending on what part of the track point you are moving. Refer to Figure 45 for more details.

Figure 45 *Track Point cursors*

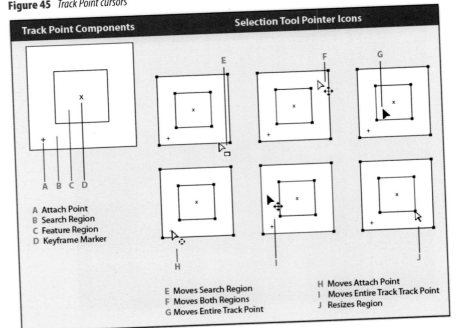

Working with Reverse Motion Tracking

Reverse motion tracking is a technique used to guarantee that any effects that rely on the motion tracking data stay in place. For example, if a drop shadow is applied to the thought bubble mentioned in the previous example, reverse motion tracking is necessary to keep the drop shadow effect on the bubble as it moves above the head.

Stabilize Motion generates tracking data for the anchor point, position, and rotation properties which are part of the Transform group. Often times, after stabilizing, motion-tracking data is applied, the tracking data causes the video that was tracked to drift out of the viewing area causing footage to be lost and black space to be seen, as shown in Figure 46. Reverse motion tracking also is used to correct this problem.

Two compositions are needed to work with reverse motion tracking. The first step is to create a pre-composition based on the layer that the Stabilizing motion-tracking data needs to be applied to. If the video is drifting out of the viewing area, it is necessary to resize the composition to accommodate the movement so that it has room to move without leaving the viewing area. Next, the workspace needs to be adjusted so that both compositions can be viewed at the same time, as shown in Figure 47, and so that Transform Expressions from the pre-composition can be connected to the main composition. The Transform Expressions are located under the Transform group on the Timeline panel for each property. **Expressions** use a scripting language to specify values of a property. A simple expression can be created to connect properties to one another. To add or remove expressions for a property, [Alt]-click (Win) or [option]-click (Mac) the stopwatch button. The Transform Expressions that will be

Figure 46 *Footage drifting out of viewing area after Stabilize motion applied*

Figure 47 *Viewing two compositions at the same time*

Lesson 3   Animate Lips on an Animal in After Effects

connected are: Anchor Point, Position, and Rotation. To stabilize motion, it will be necessary to connect the properties that are opposites. Anchor Point is the opposite of Position so those two expressions will be connected; Anchor Point to Position and Position to Anchor Point. This reverses the effect of the stabilization on the Anchor Point and Position expressions. Rotation does not have an opposite, so Rotation will point to Rotation and a mathematical expression *-1 will be added and cancel out any rotation that was added during the tracking process.

Creating a Garbage Matte

A **garbage matte** is a keying method used to remove portions of an image on a layer; the matte is then animated with the layer. If the image is a still image the garbage matte can be drawn close to the subject. This is done by drawing a garbage matte with the Pen tool. When drawing a matte on video it needs to be drawn loosely to accommodate the motion so the subject does not move outside the matted area.

It is possible to convert a video frame to a still image and create a garbage matte for that individual frame which will then last for the duration of the layer. In this case, you can be more exact when drawing your matte since the image will not be moving. This is done by using the Freeze Frame command. A Hold keyframe is created at the location of the CTI.

Applying the CC Split Effect

The CC Split effect is a distort effect which is often used to make a still image speak. The CC Split effect creates splits or holes in footage. Two crosshairs are provided,

Figure 48 *Adjusting crosshairs for CC Split effect*

Activate Points

Point A

Point B

Working with Special Effects to Enhance Viral Videos - Adobe Premiere & Adobe After Effects CS5

as shown in Figure 48, to place the location where the footage will create a split or hole in the footage. These crosshairs can be adjusted with keyframes to improve the effect. A garbage matte can be placed below a layer with the CC Split effect to fill the hole and then parented to that layer so the garbage matte follows the hole.

To attach an audio clip, the Split effect needs to be displayed on the Timeline panel and an expression added to the Split property. The next step is to connect the Split effect to

one of the sliders on the Audio Amplitude layer. The Pick Whip becomes available when expressions are activated and allows you to create simple expressions easily, by dragging from one parameter to another, as shown in Figure 49. A live link is created from the current parameter with values from the target parameter. For example, dragging the Pick Whip from the Anchor Point property to the Position property will create an expression that copies values from Anchor Point to Position.

(*Note*: If the Pick Whip is not available, [Alt]-click (Win) or [option]-click (Mac) the stopwatch button next to the parameter name in the Timeline.)

Which slider you connect to will depend on which audio channel has the audio track. If you have imported a music file, it is probably Both Channels; if you are recording your voice it may be on only one channel. Both channels are produced from audio that is stereo, one channel is produced if the audio track is mono.

Figure 49 *Attaching the CC Split effect to music*

Pick Whip   Audio Channel   Keyframe

Use the Track panel to track motion

1. Open the Talking Dog.ae file from the drive and folder where you store your Data Files, then save it as **Talking Dog your name**.

   A project file has already been started for you with two compositions and footage.

2. On the Timeline panel, click the **Tracking Head Movement composition**.

   The Tracking Head Movement composition is a pre-composition which includes the Dog Clip.avi footage. You need to track the movement of the dog's head. (*Note*: If the Tracking Head Movement composition is not on the Timeline panel, double-click it on the Project panel to open it on the Timeline panel.)

3. Click **Window** on the Application bar, point to **Workspace**, then click **Motion Tracking**.

   The current workspace is reset to Motion Tracking and the Tracker panel becomes available.

4. On the Timeline panel, click the **Dog Clip.avi layer**.

   You will be applying motion tracking to this layer.

5. On the Tracker panel, click the **Stabilize Motion button**.

   A track point appears on the Composition panel, however, you need to track two points and therefore need to activate the Rotation property.

   The first point will track the position and anchor point; the second point will track the rotation.

6. On the Tracker panel, click the **Rotation check box** to activate a second track point, as shown in Figure 50.

   (continued)

Figure 50 *Two track points are created*

Figure 51 *Moving Track Point 1 over the right eye*

Track Point 1

Search Region

Feature Region

Attach Point

Figure 52 *Moving the Track Point data with zoom feature*

Track Point 1 zoomed

Black cursor with four-arrow tail

Lesson 3   Animate Lips on an Animal in After Effects

7. On the Tracker panel click the **Options button.**

   The Motion Tracker Options dialog box opens, where the tracker can be customized to help improve the tracking analysis as it is being performed.

8. Make the following changes in the Motion Tracker Options dialog box: Channel: **Saturation,** on the drop-down menu, click **Stop Tracking,** and change the value for If Confidence is Below to **70%** and click **OK.**

   The Saturation option is selected because the dog's color does not have much contrast. The Stop Tracking if the Confidence is Below 70% was chosen so that you will be able to adjust the tracking when the analysis stops because the track points have moved too much from the target.

9. On the Composition panel, click and drag the **Feature Region square** on Track Point 1 over the dog's right eye, as shown in Figure 51.

   The cursor's appearance changes to a black cursor with a four-arrow tail, the area within squares will zoom when you click on the inner squares edge, and the entire track point should move together, as shown in Figure 52. (*Note*: If the arrow is white instead of black only the regions will move, the attach point will not.)

   (continued)

10. Drag **Track Point 2** over the dog's left eye.

    You are now ready to track the movement of the dog's head.

11. On the Tracker panel, click the **Analyze forward button** ▶.

    This will begin the tracking process on the footage. The analysis will stop if the tolerance falls below 70% and the track points will need to be re-adjusted so they are back on the dog's eyes.

12. When the tracking stops, move the track points so they are located on the dog's eyes, as shown in Figure 53.

13. If the track points move too far off of the dog's eyes, stop tracking manually and move the track points back to the dog's eyes.

    TIP Change the magnification of the Composition panel to make the tracking cursors easier to work with.

14. Click the **Analyze forward button** ▶ to resume the tracking process and continue to adjust track points if the track points move from the dog's eyes until the CTI reaches the end of the Timeline, then compare your Composition panel tracking data to Figure 54. Your results may vary.

    (continued)

Figure 53 *Tracking has stopped*

Track Point 1 needs to be readjusted

Figure 54 *Tracking data on last frame*

Tracking data

Magnification ratio popup

Working with Special Effects to Enhance Viral Videos - Adobe Premiere & Adobe After Effects CS5

Figure 55 *Tracking data on the Dog Clip.avi*

Tracking data

15. When Motion Tracking has reached the end of the video clip and has stopped, click **Apply**.

    The Motion Tracker Apply Options dialog box launches.

16. Click **OK**.

    The tracking data is placed on the Dog Clip.avi layer, as shown in Figure 55.

17. Save your project and leave it open for the next exercise.

You tracked the movement of the dog's head using the Tracker panel.

Apply reverse motion tracking

1. Open the Talking Dog your name.ae project file, with the Tracking Head Movement composition as the active composition, if necessary.

2. Click the **Play/Pause button** [>] on the Preview panel to preview the footage on the Composition panel.

   Notice the tracking data causes the entire layer to move, and at times causes empty space around the footage or the footage to move out of the viewing area, as shown in Figure 56.

3. Click **Composition** on the Application bar, then click **Composition Settings**.

   The Composition Settings dialog box opens.

4. Change the Width value to **1000,** verify that the Lock Aspect Ratio check box is checked, then click **OK**.

   This will give the video footage room to move with the tracking data applied to it.

5. On the Timeline panel, click the **Dog Clip.avi layer**, press [**A**] on your keyboard, press and hold [**Shift**], then press [**P**] and [**R**].

   The Anchor Point, Position, and Rotation properties become visible on the Timeline panel.

6. On the Timeline panel, click the **Tracking Head Movement composition tab**, then drag it above the Talking Dog composition, as shown in Figure 57.

   (continued)

Figure 56 *Tracking data applied to footage*

Empty space

Footage no longer in viewing area

Figure 57 *Customizing the workspace*

Drop Zone

Working with Special Effects to Enhance Viral Videos - Adobe Premiere & Adobe After Effects CS5

Figure 58 *Resizing the Timeline panels*

Resize cursor

7. On the Talking Dog Timeline panel, click the **Tracking Head Movement pre-composition**, press [**A**] on your keyboard, press and hold [**Shift**], then press [**P**] and [**R**].

   You will be using the Pick Whip to attach these properties from one composition to the other.

8. With the Tracking Head Movement pre-composition still selected, press and hold [**Alt**] (Win) or [**option**] (Mac), then click the **Time-Vary stop watch** for the Anchor Point, Position, and Rotation properties.

   This will add expressions for each of the properties.

9. Position your cursor above the Talking Dog Timeline panel tab, when the resize cursor appears, click and drag to resize the panel so you are able to see all of the properties, then do the same for the Tracking Head Movement Timeline, as shown in Figure 58.

TIP Resize the bottom Timeline panel first, it will size into the panel placed above it.

(continued)

Lesson 3   Animate Lips on an Animal in After Effects

10. On the Talking Dog Timeline panel, click the **Pick Whip** for the **Anchor Point property**, then drag to the Position property in the Tracking Head Movement Timeline panel, as shown in Figure 59.

The Anchor Point property is the opposite of the Position property so we need to connect these two properties to counteract their influence. You need to repeat this process with the Position property.

11. On the Talking Dog Timeline panel, click the **Pick Whip** for the **Position property** and drag to the Anchor Point property on the Tracking Head Movement Timeline panel.

12. On the Talking Dog Timeline panel, select the Pick Whip for the **Rotation property** and drag to the Rotation property on the Tracking Head Movement Timeline panel, then compare your Talking Dog Timeline panel to Figure 60.

Since there is not an opposite property for rotation, you will enter a mathematical formula multiplying the rotation by -1 to create the opposite.

13. On the Talking Dog Timeline panel, click at the end of the Rotation expression, then type *-1.

TIP Click anywhere to get out of the Rotation expression or just continue to the next step. Pressing [Enter] creates another line inside the expression.

14. Click **Workspace** on the Application bar, point to **Workspace**, then click **Standard**.

The workspace is set to Standard and returns the Tracking Head Movement Timeline panel to a stacked tab position.

You used the Pick Whip to attach expressions between two different compositions, and you added a mathematical formula to an expression.

Figure 59 *Using the Pick Whip*

Pick Whip

Figure 60 *Talking Dog properties after using Pick Whip*

Figure 61 *Drawing a garbage matte with the Pen tool*

Garbage matte

Time duration
0;00;05;08

Figure 62 *Adjusting the anchor point of the garbage matte*

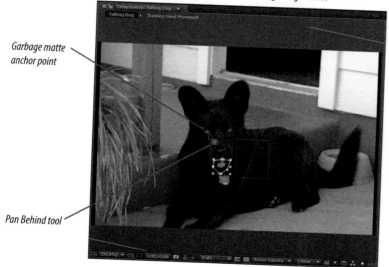

Garbage matte
anchor point

Pan Behind tool

Lesson 3 Animate Lips on an Animal in After Effects

Create a garbage matte

1. Open the Talking Dog your name.ae project file, with the Talking Dog composition as the active composition, if necessary.

   The dog's mouth opens just after 5 seconds; we will duplicate this to make our dog talk.

2. On the Timeline panel, click the **Open Mouth layer**, then drag the **CTI** to **0;00;05;08**.

   This is when the dog opens his mouth; we will be drawing a garbage matte around the open mouth.

3. Click the **Pen tool** on the Tools panel, verify that the RotoBezier check box is not checked on the Tools panel, then draw a selection around the open mouth, as shown in Figure 61.

4. On the Timeline panel, right-click the **Open Mouth layer**, point to **Time**, then click **Freeze Frame**.

   A snapshot of the garbage matte you just created is taken.

5. Click the **Pan Behind tool** on the Tools panel, then drag the **garbage matte anchor point** over the right pupil, as shown in Figure 62.

   This will attach the garbage matte anchor point to the Attach point we created during motion tracking over the dog's right eye.

(continued)

6. On the Timeline panel, on the Open Mouth layer, click the **Parent layer column drop-down menu**, then click 3. **Tracking Head Movement**, as shown in Figure 63.

   This will parent the Tracking Head Movement layer to the Open Mouth layer so that the matte we just created will follow the movement of the dog's head. You will make adjustments later to the garbage matte where it moves off track.

7. On the Timeline panel, drag the **CTI** to preview the footage, then drag the **CTI** to **00;00;00;00**.

   The open mouth should move with the dog's muzzle.

8. On the Timeline panel, drag the **Open Mouth layer** below the Tracking Head Movement layer, then compare your project to Figure 64.

   The Open Mouth layer should now be third in the stacking order.

9. On the Timeline panel, collapse the **Tracking Head Movement layer** and the **Open Mouth layer**.

   The layer properties are no longer in view.

10. Save your project and leave it open for the next exercise.

You drew a garbage matte around the dog's open mouth, created a freeze frame, parented a layer, and reordered the layers.

Figure 63 *Setting the Parent layer to the Tracking Head Movement layer*

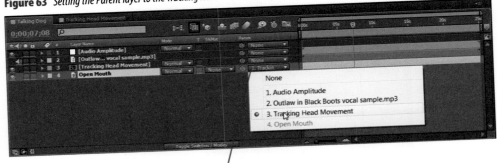

Parent Layer
drop-down menu

Figure 64 *Open Mouth layer moved to bottom of stacking order*

Open Mouth layer

Working with Special Effects to Enhance Viral Videos - Adobe Premiere & Adobe After Effects CS5

Figure 65 *Activating the crosshair points*

Point A crosshair

Point B crosshair

Figure 66 *Placing the Point A and Point B crosshairs*

Point A crosshair

Point B crosshair

Apply the CC Split effect

1. Open the Talking Dog your name.ae project file, with the Talking Dog composition as the active composition, if necessary.

   You now need to attach coordinates to the dog's mouth to create a hole in the video footage to make it appear he is talking.

2. On the Timeline panel, click the **Tracking Head Movement layer**, click **Effect** on the Application bar, point to **Distort**, then click **CC Split**.

   The CC Split effect is applied to the Tracking Head Movement layer and appears on the Effect Controls panel.

3. On the Effect Controls panel, click the **CC Split effect**.

   Crosshairs appear on the Composition panel, as shown in Figure 65. These crosshairs adjust the hole that is created in the dog's mouth.

4. Click the **crosshair** on the left side of the Composition panel, then drag it to the right side of the dog's mouth.

   This is Point A and creates the first reference point to make the mouth open.

5. Click the **crosshair** on the right side of the Composition panel, then drag it to the left side of the dog's mouth, as shown in Figure 66.

   This is Point B and creates the second reference point to make the mouth open.

6. On the Timeline panel, click and drag the **CTI** to preview the footage, then drag the **CTI** to **00;00;00;00**.

   Point A and Point B should move with the dog's muzzle.

7. Save your project and leave it open for the next exercise.

You applied tracking points to the dog's mouth.

THE VIDEO COLLECTION

Complete the CC Split effect

1. Open the Talking Dog your name.ae project file, with the Talking Dog composition as the active composition, if necessary.

   You now need to make the dog's mouth open coordinated to the music.

2. On the Timeline panel, click the **first layer** in the stacking order, click **Animation** on the Application bar, point to **Keyframe Assistant**, then click **Convert Audio to Keyframes**.

   A new layer is created at the top of the stacking order called Audio Amplitude creating keyframes on the audio channels.

3. On the Timeline panel, click the **Tracking Head Movement layer**.

4. Press and hold [**Alt**] (Win) or [**option**] (Mac), then click the **Time-Vary stopwatch button** in front of Split on the Effect Controls panel.

   This activates an expression for the Split property and makes it visible on the Timeline panel, as shown in Figure 67.

   You need to attach this expression to the Audio Amplitude layer to make the mouth open.

5. On the Timeline panel, expand the **Audio Amplitude Effects**, and **Both Channels layers**, as shown in Figure 68.

   This exposes the Slider property, which has the keyframes that the CC Split effect needs to reference in order to work. You may need to adjust the size of the panel.

6. On the Timeline panel, click the **Pick Whip** for the **Expression: Split property** and drag it to the **Slider property**, as shown in Figure 69.

   (continued)

Figure 67 *Adding an expression on Split*

Split Time-Vary stopwatch

Split Expression

Figure 68 *Expanding the Audio Amplitude layer to expose Slider under Both Channels*

Slider property

Figure 69 *Pointing the Pick Whip for the Expression: Split property to the Slider property*

Slider property   *Pick Whip*

Figure 70 *Adjusting points on the Timeline*

Point A

Point B

CC Split

Lesson 3   Animate Lips on an Animal in After Effects

7. On the Preview panel, click the **RAM Preview button** ▶ to preview the mouth opening, then drag the **CTI** to **00;00;00;00**.

   The audio may not play during the first RAM Preview, let it run through and repeat to hear the audio. The mouth needs some adjustments.

8. On the Timeline panel, click **CC Split**, then click the **Time-Vary stopwatch button** 🕑 in front of Point A.

9. On the Timeline panel, click **CC Split**, then click the **Time-Vary stopwatch button** 🕑 in front of Point B.

   Keyframes are now activated for both points. As you move the CTI and make adjustments to the locations of Point A and Point B on the Composition panel, a keyframe will be generated.

10. Drag the **CTI** to a location in the footage where the points are not on the mouth.

    The duration in the figure is 0;00;02;11, as shown in Figure 70, yours may vary.

11. On the Composition panel, click **Point A**, then drag to the right corner of the dog's mouth, click **Point B**, then drag to the left corner of the dog's mouth.

12. On the Timeline panel, drag the **CTI** to locate other areas where Point A and Point B need to be corrected and make corrections as needed.

    The music stops playing at approximately 20 seconds so the mouth should no longer be opening and closing. Therefore you will not need to make adjustments past this point.

13. Export your movie, including the audio, as an FLV resizing it as a Web Video.

You attached the CC Split effect to audio keyframes to make the mouth open and close in time to the music.

Apply the Time Remapping effect to a clip.

1. Open the Speed 4.prproj file from the drive and folder where you store your Data Files, then save it as **Speed 4 your name**.
2. Select the Bike Tricks sequence to activate the Timeline panel, then click the Play-Stop Toggle button on the Program Monitor to preview the clip.
3. Drag the CTI to 00;00;00;00.
4. On the Timeline panel, click the Clip Effect menu, point to Time Remapping, then click Speed.
5. [Ctrl]-click (Win) or ⌘-click (Mac) the rubber band at the location of the CTI (00;00;00;00).
6. Drag the CTI to 00;00;00;11 and on the Timeline panel, click the Add-Remove keyframe button.
7. Add additional speed keyframes at the following times: 00;00;01;28, 00;00;02;20, and 00;00;04;08.
8. Save your project and it leave open for the next step.

Adjust the speed of a clip.

1. Click the first rubber band segment, then drag in an upward direction until the tool tip reads 315.00%.
2. Drag the CTI to 00;00;00;00, then click the Play-Stop Toggle button on the Program Monitor to preview the clip.
3. Click the second rubber band segment and drag in a downward direction until the tool tip reads 25.00%.
4. Make the following adjustments along the rubber band segments: 3rd - 140.00%, 4th - 35.00%, and 5th - 300.00%.
5. Drag the CTI to 00;00;00;00, then click the Play-Stop Toggle button on the Program Monitor to preview the clip.

6. Export your video to the FLV|F4V format and name the file **Bike Tricks your name**.
7. Close the Speed 4 your name.prproj project file.

Play a clip backward then forward.

1. Open the Speed 5.prproj file from the drive and folder where you store your Data Files, then save it as **Speed 5 your name**.
2. On the Timeline panel, activate Time Remapping on the Clip Effect menu then resize the Video 1 track to get a better view of the rubber band control.
3. On the Timeline panel, drag the CTI to 00;00;02;18 then [Ctrl]-click (Win) or ⌘-click (Mac) the rubber band to create a speed keyframe.
4. Drag the CTI to 00;00;04;03 and on the Timeline panel, click the Add-Remove keyframe button.
5. [Ctrl]-click (Win) or ⌘-click (Mac) the second speed keyframe, then drag to the right until the first portion of the tool tip reads 00;00;05;18.
6. Drag the CTI to 00;00;00;00, then click the Play-Stop Toggle button on the Program Monitor to preview the clip.
7. Save your project and leave it open for the next step.

Add a speed transition.

1. On the Timeline panel, click and drag the right half of the speed keyframe that is in front of the left point brackets, until the first portion of the tool tip reads 00;00;04;20.
2. Drag the CTI to 00;00;06;05, and with the Timeline panel active, press the [=] key three times to zoom in.
3. Click the right handle of the blue curve control and drag right or left to adjust the speed ramp.

4. With the Timeline panel active, press the [-] key three times to zoom out.
5. Click the Razor tool on the Tools panel, and on the Timeline panel, drag the CTI to approximately 00;00;07;28 then point and click the location of the CTI to create a cut point.
6. On the Timeline panel, drag the CTI to approximately 00;00;08;20 then point and click the location of the CTI to create another cut point. (*Hint*: we are removing the portion of the clip where there is no action.)
7. Click the Selection tool on the Tools panel, then click the clip with the cut points that were just created.
8. Click Edit on the Application bar, then click Ripple Delete.
9. Drag the CTI to 00;00;00;00, then click the Play-Stop Toggle button on the Program Monitor to preview the clip.
10. Export your video to the FLV|F4V format and name the file **Skateboarding Tricks your name**.
11. Close the Speed 5 your name.prproj project file.

Adjust the speed of a clip with the Rate Stretch tool.

1. Open the Speed 6.prproj file from the drive and folder where you store your Data Files, then save it as **Speed 6 your name**.
2. Click the Play-Stop Toggle button on the Program Monitor to preview the clip.
3. Click the Rate Stretch tool on the Tools panel, then, on the Timeline panel, point to the right edge of the 18.avi clip.
4. Click and drag the right edge of the 18.avi clip to the right to fill the gap, then release the mouse button when you see the black line.
5. Click the Selection tool on the Tools panel.

6. Drag the CTI to 00;00;00;00, then click the Play-Stop Toggle button on the Program Monitor to preview the clip.

7. Save your project and leave it open for the next step.

Adjust the speed of a clip with the Clip Speed/Duration dialog box.

1. On the Timeline panel, right-click the 1.avi clip, then click Speed/Duration.

2. In the Clip Speed/Duration dialog box change the Speed value to 35%, click the Ripple Edit, Shifting Trailing Clips check box, then click OK.

3. On the Timeline panel, using the Selection tool, click the 1.avi clip.

4. Click Edit on the Application bar, then click Copy.

5. Place the CTI at the cut line after clip 1.avi.

6. Click Edit on the Application bar, then click Paste Insert.

7. On the Timeline panel, right-click the second instance of the 1.avi clip, then click Speed/Duration.

8. In the Clip Speed/Duration dialog box, click the Reverse Speed check box.

9. Drag the CTI to 00;00;00;00, then click the Play-Stop Toggle button on the Program Monitor to preview the clip.

10. Export your video to the FLV|F4V format and name the file **Biking your name**.

11. Close the Speed 6 your name.prproj project file.

Apply the CC Rain and Linear Color Key effects.

1. Open the Weather 2.ae file from the drive and folder where you store your Data Files, then save it as **Weather 2 your name**.

2. On the Timeline panel, click the us_15.mov layer, click Effect on the Application bar, point to Simulation, then click CC Rain.

3. Click the Play/Pause button on the Preview panel to preview the clip.

4. On the Timeline panel, click the us_15.mov layer, click Effect on the Application, point to Keying, then click Linear Color Key.

5. On the Effect Controls panel, click the Linear Color Key, then drag it above the CC Rain effect.

6. On the Effect Controls panel, under the Linear Color Key effect, select the Match colors drop-down menu, then click Using RGB.

7. Click the Key Color swatch, type **8CA5C1** in the # text box in the Key Color dialog box, then click OK.

8. On the Effect Controls panel, under the Linear Color Key effect, change the Matching Tolerance value to 39.0% and the Matching Softness value to 10.0%.

9. Click the Project panel, click the us_15 Mask composition, then drag it to the White House composition on the Timeline below the us_15.mov layer.

10. Click the Project panel, click the StormCloudsGathering2.mpeg footage, then drag it to the White House composition on the Timeline below the us_15 Mask composition layer.

11. Click the Play/Pause button on the Preview panel to preview the clip.

12. Save your project and leave it open for the next step.

Customize the CC Rain effect.

1. Verify that the Effect Controls panel is visible and that the CTI is at 00;00;00;00.

2. On the Timeline panel, click the us_15.mov layer, click the Effects expand arrow, then click the CC Rain expand arrow.

3. On the Effect Controls panel, in the CC Rain effect, click the Time-Vary stopwatch button in front of the Amount, Speed, Drop Size, and Source Depth properties, then change the Amount value to 0 and the Source Depth to 0.

4. Drag the CTI to 00;00;02;00, and on the Timeline panel, in the CC Rain effect, change the Amount value to 150.0.

5. Continue to adjust the CTI and the values as follows: 6 seconds: Amount: 200.0, Speed: 2.25, Drop Size: 3.0, and at 12 seconds: Amount: 350.0 and Source Depth: 100.0%.

6. Click the Play/Pause button on the Preview panel to preview the clip.

7. Save your project and leave it open for the next step.

Apply the CC Mr. Mercury effect.

1. Verify that the Effect Controls panel is visible and that the CTI is at 00;00;00;00.

2. On the Timeline panel, click the us_15.mov layer, click Effect on the Application bar, point to Simulation, then click CC Mr. Mercury.

3. On the Effect Controls panel, click the CC Mr. Mercury effect, then drag it above the CC Rain effect.

4. Click the Play/Pause button on the Preview panel to preview the clip.

5. On the Effect Controls panel, in the CC Mr. Mercury effect, click the Time-Vary stopwatch button in front of the Birth Rate property.

6. On the Effect Controls panel, make the following changes to the property values for the CC Mr. Mercury effect: Radius X: 45.0, Radius Y: 395.0, Velocity: 0.0, Birth Rate: 2.0, Gravity: 0.0, Influence Map: Constant Blobs, Blob Birth Size: 0.35, and Blob Death Size: 0.50.
7. Drag the CTI to 00;00;12;00 seconds, and on the Effect Controls panel, change the CC Mr. Mercury effect Birth Rate property value to 3.5.
8. Click the Play/Pause button on the Preview panel to preview the clip.
9. Export your video to the FLV format and name the file **White House Rain your name**.
10. Close the Weather 2 your name.ae project file.

Work with the Advanced Lightning effect on a logo.

1. Open the Lightning 2.ae file from the drive and folder where you store your Data Files, then save it as **Lightning 2 your name**.
2. On the Timeline panel, click the Halloween.ai layer, click Effect on the Application bar, point to Generate, then click Advanced Lightning.
3. On the Effect Controls panel, click the Composite on Original check box.
4. Click the Play/Pause button on the Preview panel to preview the clip.
5. On the Effect Controls panel, click the Time-Vary stopwatch button in front of the Conductivity State property.
6. Drag the CTI to 00;00;13;00, and on the Effect Controls panel, change the value of the Conductivity State to 2.5.

7. On the Effect Controls panel, change the Origin value to 100.0 and 45.0.
8. On the Effect Controls panel, change the Direction value to 560.0 and 480.0.
9. On the Effect Controls panel, change the Lightning type to Breaking.
10. On the Effect Controls panel, change the Alpha Obstacle value to 2.50.
11. On the Preview panel, change the Resolution to Full.
12. Click the Play/Pause button on the Preview panel to preview the clip.
13. Export your video to the FLV format and name the file **Halloween your name**.
14. Close the Lightning 2 your name.ae project file.

Use the Tracker panel to track motion.

1. Open the Singing Dog.ae file from the drive and folder where you store your Data Files, then save it as **Singing Dog your name**.
2. On the Timeline panel, click the Tracking Head Movement composition.
3. Click Window on the Application bar, point to Workspace, then click Motion Tracking.
4. On the Timeline panel, click the Dog Clip 2.avi layer.
5. On the Tracker panel, click the Stabilize Motion button.
6. On the Tracker panel, click the Rotation check box to activate a second tracking point.
7. On the Tracker panel, click the Options button.
8. Make the following changes in the Motion Tracker Options dialog box: Channel: Saturation, on the drop-down menu, select Stop Tracking, and change the value for If Confidence is Below to 70%, then click OK.

9. On the Composition panel, click and drag the Track Point 1 to an area over the dog's right eye.
10. Drag Track Point 2 over the dog's name tag. (*Note:* Resize the Search Regions to allow for the movement of the dog's head during the video.)
11. On the Tracker panel, click the Analyze forward button.
12. When the tracking stops, adjust the track points as needed.
13. Click the Analyze forward button to resume the tracking process and continue to adjust track points as necessary until the CTI reaches the end of the Timeline.
14. When motion tracking has completed click Apply.
15. Click OK.
16. Save your project and leave it open for the next step.

Apply reverse motion tracking.

1. Verify that the Tracking Head Movement composition is the active composition.
2. Click the Play/Pause button on the Preview panel to preview the footage on the Composition panel.
3. Click Composition on the Application bar, then click Composition Settings.
4. Change the Width value to 1500, verify that the Lock Aspect Ratio check box is checked, then click OK.
5. On the Timeline panel, click the Singing Dog 2. m2v layer, press [A] on your keyboard, press and hold [Shift], then press [P] and [R].
6. On the Timeline panel, click the Tracking Head Movement composition tab, then drag it to reposition the Timeline panel so that it is stacked above the Singing Dog composition.

7. On the Singing Dog Timeline panel, select the Tracking Head Movement pre-composition, press [A] on your keyboard press and hold [Shift], then press [P] and [R].

8. With the Tracking Head Movement pre-composition still selected, while holding the [Alt] (Win) or [option] (Mac) key, click the Time-Vary stopwatch button for the Anchor Point, Position, and Rotation properties.

9. Position your cursor above the Singing Dog Timeline panel tab, then when the resize cursor appears, resize the panel so you are able to see all of the properties, then resize the other Timeline.

10. On the Singing Dog Timeline panel, click the Pick Whip for the Anchor Point property and drag to the Position property on the Tracking Head Movement Timeline panel.

11. On the Singing Dog Timeline panel, click the Pick Whip for the Position property and drag to the Anchor Point property on the Tracking Head Movement Timeline panel.

12. On the Singing Dog Timeline panel, click the Pick Whip for the Rotation property and drag to Rotation property on the Tracking Head Movement Timeline panel.

13. On the Singing Dog Timeline panel, click at the end of the Rotation expression, then type *-1.

14. Click Workspace on the Application bar, point to Workspace, then click Standard.

Create a garbage matte.

1. Verify that the Singing Dog composition is the active composition.

2. On the Timeline panel click the Open Mouth layer, then drag the CTI to 0;00;00;10.

3. Click the Pen tool on the Tools panel, then draw a selection around the open mouth.

4. On the Timeline panel, right-click the Open Mouth layer, point to Time, then click Freeze Frame.

5. On the Timeline panel, click and drag the right edge of the Open Mouth layer to the right until it is the same length as the other layers.

6. Select the Pan Behind tool on the Tools panel, then move the garbage matte anchor point over the right pupil.

7. With the Selection tool, adjust the Open Mouth garbage matte to align with the mouth on the Tracking Head Movement pre-composition.

8. On the Timeline panel, on the Open Mouth layer, under the Parent layer column, select 3. Tracking Head Movement from the drop-down menu.

9. On the Timeline panel, drag the CTI to preview the footage, then return the CTI to 00;00;00;00.

10. On the Timeline panel, drag the Open Mouth layer below the Tracking Head Movement layer.

11. On the Timeline panel, click the arrow in front of the label on the Tracking Head Movement layer and the Open Mouth layer.

12. Save your project and leave it open for the next step.

Apply the CC Split effect.

1. Verify that the Singing Dog composition is the active composition.

2. On the Timeline panel, click the Tracking Head Movement layer, click Effect on the Application bar, point to Distort, then click CC Split.

3. On the Effect Controls panel, click the CC Split effect.

4. Click the crosshair on the left side of the Composition panel, then drag it to the right side of the dog's mouth.

5. Click the crosshair on the right side of the Composition panel and drag it to the left side of the dog's mouth.

6. On the Timeline panel, drag the CTI to preview the footage, then return the CTI to 00;00;00;00.

7. Save your project and leave it open for the next step.

Complete the CC Split effect.

1. On the Timeline panel, select the first layer in the stacking order, click Animation on the Application bar, point to Keyframe Assistant, then click Convert Audio to Keyframes.

2. On the Timeline panel, click the Tracking Head Movement layer.

3. On the Effect Controls panel, while holding the [Alt] (Win) or [option] (Mac), click the Time-Vary stopwatch button in front of Split.

4. On the Timeline panel, click the arrow in front of the Audio Amplitude layer, click the arrow in front of Effects, then click the arrow in front of Both Channels.

5. On the Timeline panel, select the Pick Whip for the Expression: Split property and point it to the Slider property.

6. On the Preview panel, click the RAM Preview button to preview the mouth opening, then return the CTI to 00;00;00;00.

7. On the Timeline panel, click CC Split, then click the Time-Vary stopwatch button in front of Point A.

8. On the Timeline panel, click CC Split, then click the Time-Vary stopwatch button in front of Point B.

9. Drag the CTI to a location in the footage where the points are not on the mouth.

10. On the Composition panel, click Point A, drag to the right corner of the dog's mouth, click Point B, then drag to the left corner of the dog's mouth.

11. On the Timeline panel ruler, drag the CTI to locate other areas where Point A and Point B need to be corrected and make corrections.

12. Export your movie as an FLV resizing it as a Web Video.

Figure 71 *Completed Skills Review, Part 1*

Your multimedia instructor would like to see you try some of the other weather effects that are available in After Effects. Work with the Weather 3.ae file to try your hand at some of the other effects, such as CC Drizzle and CC Snow. (*Note*: The sky in this footage does not need to be removed.)

1. Open the Weather 3.ae project file, then save it as **San Francisco Weather your name**.
2. Be creative and apply various weather effects to this video footage.
3. Use keyframes to make adjustments to customize the effects.
4. When you are happy with your work, export your file to the FLV file format.

Figure 72 *Completed Project Builder 1*

The local zoo would like you to use the antelope video clip and create a Flash video of the antelope speaking for their Web site. They would like you to record your own voice for the clip inviting people to come to the zoo and see the new antelope exhibit.

1. Open Antelope Talking.ae, then save it as **Antelope Talking your name**.
2. Using the Tracker panel, track the movement of the antelope's head on the Antelope Head composition.
3. Apply reverse tracking motion between the Antelope Talking composition and the Antelope Head composition.
4. Apply the CC Clip effect to the Antelope Talking composition.
5. Using Adobe Dynamic Link, create a new Premiere Pro sequence.
6. In Premiere Pro, record a short statement inviting people to the zoo to see the new antelope exhibit.
7. Export the file to the FLV|F4V file format named **Zoo Promo your name**.

Figure 73 *Completed Project Builder 2*

Your multimedia instructor would like you to use the skills you have acquired throughout the course of this book with Premiere Pro, After Effects, and Soundbooth. Using clips available in the Video Clips subfolder titled Sports, create a 90-second highlight video with background music. Use Premiere Pro to edit the footage, After Effects to add special effects, and Soundbooth to create background music.

1. Create a new Premiere Pro project and sequence and save it as **Highlight Video your name.**
2. Import the video clips into the Project panel.
3. Using the Source Monitor, preview the various clips and trim and place them on the sequence.
4. Add appropriate video transitions.
5. Use Time Remapping to emphasize various actions in the video footage.
6. Using Adobe Dynamic Link, create an After Effects composition.
7. Using After Effects, add special effects to the video you have edited in Premiere Pro.
8. Export your composition to the MPEG2 format.
9. Using Soundbooth, import the video; then, working with the Edit Score to Video workspace, create a soundtrack for your video.
10. Export your movie and soundtrack as an Audio Mixdown and save to the MPEG2 file format.

Figure 74 *Portfolio Project*

7

CHAPTER

CREATING AN ELECTRONIC PORTFOLIO USING ADOBE ENCORE CS5

Explore the Encore workspace

Create a project

Create timelines

Build a project

Adobe Encore CS5 is a video distribution-authoring tool that allows you to design, author, and build full-featured, menu-driven media projects that are on DVD, Blu-ray, or Web DVD. Encore is dynamically linked with Premiere Pro and After Effects, allowing you to work between applications without having to export or render. Alternatively, video and audio files can be used in their current format and Encore will transcode them to MPEG-2 video or Dolby Digital audio upon completion of the project.

Encore has a library of resources including menus, buttons, and backgrounds that

you can apply to a project. In addition, Resource Central provides an additional library of menus available for instant download. You can also use Photoshop to create and edit customized menus, buttons, and backgrounds. Photoshop supports the specialized naming convention for these items to import seamlessly.

In this chapter, we will explore the Encore workspace, import assets, and work with the library of available resources to create a custom DVD and a Web DVD.

Explore the ENCORE WORKSPACE

What You'll Do

In this lesson, you will start Encore and explore the workspace.

Exploring the Encore Workspace

Adobe Encore—like Premiere Pro, After Effects, and Soundbooth—includes a number of preformatted and customizable workspaces that optimize the arrangement of panels for particular tasks. Figure 1 shows the default workspace for Encore called Default.

You can change the workspace to another by selecting a preformatted workspace or by rearranging the panels to your individual preferences. Preformatted workspaces are available using the Workspace command on the Window menu or by making a selection from the drop-down menu on the Tools panel.

Panels are moved by clicking and dragging panel tabs. As you drag the panel, the area that you drag it to becomes highlighted; this is called the **drop zone**, and provides a visual reference to where the panel can be placed.

If you wish to save a customized workspace, you may do so by selecting New Workspace on the Workspace menu or from the drop-down menu on the Tools panel.

A basic workflow for creating a project in Encore follows eight steps.

1. Planning the project
2. Importing assets
3. Creating project elements
4. Creating menus
5. Indicating navigation
6. Transcoding audio and video for compatibility
7. Previewing the project
8. Building the project

Understanding Encore Preference Settings

The Preferences in Encore allow you to set a variety of defaults, as shown in Figure 2. The General section of the Preferences dialog box has the option to set the default television standard to either NTSC or PAL. **NTSC** is the standard used in North America and Japan, and **PAL** is the standard in Europe.

You can change the **Audio/Video Out settings**, allowing the project to be previewed on an external device, if connected by an IEEE 1394 Firewire. This option, if equipment is available, will allow the Menu Viewer to be viewed on the external device to verify the necessary elements remain in the viewing area. The Menu Viewer is a preview panel in Encore that is analogous to the Program Monitor in Premiere Pro.

Creating an Electronic Portfolio Using Adobe Encore CS5

Figure 1 *Encore Default workspace*

Project panel

Timeline panel tab

Monitor panel

Timeline Viewer

Properties panel

Default workspace

Library panel

Figure 2 *Preferences dialog box*

Preferences dialog box

Default Television Standard

Start Adobe Encore CS5 and explore the workspace

1. Click **Start** 🕹 on the Application bar, point to **All Programs**, then click **Adobe Encore CS5** (Win) or open the **Finder** from the dock, click **Applications** from the sidebar, select the **Adobe applications folder** then click **Adobe Encore CS5** (Mac).

   You may need to look in a subfolder for Adobe Encore CS5 if you have installed the Video Collection or Master Collection.

   TIP Pressing and holding [Shift][Ctrl] (Win) while starting Encore restores default preference settings. If you are working on a Mac you will need to drag the Preferences file to the trash and restart Encore.

2. Click **New Project** in the Adobe Encore CS5 window as shown in Figure 3.

   The New Project dialog box opens.

3. Click the **Browse button**, then navigate to the drive and folder where your Data Files are located.

   The Browse button allows you to choose a destination to save the project.

   The Browse For Folder dialog box opens, as shown in Figure 4.

   (continued)

Figure 3 *Adobe Encore CS5 window*

New Project

Figure 4 *Browse For Folder dialog box*

Figure 5 *New Project dialog box*

Name

Location

Authoring
Mode

Television
Standard

New Project

Basic   Advanced

Name and Location

Name: Sample Projects

Location: C:\Users\Debbie\Documents\TheVideoCollectionR...   ▼   Browse...

Project Settings

Authoring Mode: ○ Blu-ray   ● DVD

Television Standard: NTSC   ▼

Transcode Settings: Codec: MPEG-2; Dimensions: 720 x 480; Frame Rate: 29.97;
Fields:Lower Field First
Audio Transcoding Scheme: Dolby Digital
Maximum Audio/Video Bitrate: 8.0 Mbps

Default Transcode Settings...

ⓘ A project's authoring mode can be changed at any time in the Project Settings dialog.

OK   Cancel

4. Click **OK** to close the Browse For Folder window
   but keep the New Project dialog box open.

   As shown in Figure 5, the path where the project
   is saved appears in the Location field.

5. Type **Pollution your name** in the Name text box
   of the New Project dialog box.

6. Accept the default settings, then click **OK**.

   The Encore workspace is displayed.

7. Locate the Project panel, the Monitor panel, the
   Properties panel, and the Library panel.

(continued)

8. Click **Window** on the Application bar, point to **Workspace**, then click **Menu Design**.

The Menu Design workspace is used for designing menus, as shown in Figure 6. It includes the Menu panel, the Resource Central panel, and the Character panel.

9. Click **Window** on the Application bar, point to **Workspace**, then click **Default**.

The workspace is reset to the Default workspace.

10. Save your project and leave it open for the next exercise.

You started Adobe Encore CS5, created a new project named Pollution your name, and explored the workspace.

Figure 6 *Encore Menu Design workspace*

Menu Viewer

Layers panel

Menu Design

Styles panel

Character panel

Figure 7 *Preferences dialog box*

Audio/ Video Out

View the Encore preference settings

1. Open the Pollution your name.ncor file, if necessary.

2. Click **Edit** (Win) or **After Effects** (Mac) on the Application bar, point to **Preferences**, then click **General**.

   The Preferences dialog box opens.

3. Verify that the Television setting is set to NTSC.

   Encore can be set to preview on an external video source for verifying the appearance of the project.

4. Click **Audio/Video Out** on the left side of the Preferences dialog box, as shown in Figure 7.

   A video and audio external device can be selected in the dialog box if a device is available through an IEEE 1394 connection. The Menu Viewer will then preview on the external device.

5. Click the **Cancel button** to close the Preferences dialog box.

6. Save your project file, then leave it open for the next step.

Create
A PROJECT

What You'll Do

In this lesson, you will begin an Encore project.

Planning an Encore Project

It is important to plan your project before you begin the authoring process so that you understand what the project will contain and how you will present it. The scope of the project may be as minimal as organizing baby pictures and video, or as complicated as creating an interactive kiosk display. You should understand the following parameters by the end of the planning stage: **navigation scheme**, **playback environment**, and the **type and amount of content**.

The **navigation scheme** should be well organized so that the user has obvious and simple access to the content. The navigation scheme is the layout of the menus and buttons, which provide access to the various sections of the DVD.

The anticipated **playback environment**, or equipment where the final media project will be viewed, is important to know during the planning stage because the playback environment will affect what type of content can be included in the project and how it can

be accessed. For example, if the project will be only accessed on a computer, you can include content that would not be accessible from a television or Blu-ray player, such as data files. If you are going to export a project to the Flash file format, you can embed Web links.

It is essential to know the **type** and **amount of content** that will be included in your project so you know what type of media is needed: a single-layer DVD, a dual-layer (dual-sided DVD), or a Blu-ray disc. Small projects with mostly audio content will probably fit on a single-layer DVD. A project with a feature-length movie and supplemental materials could require a dual-layer DVD, or a Blu-ray disc.

It is a good idea to create a **storyboard** or flowchart on paper first before beginning your project. A storyboard is a visual representation that displays the structure of the project from start to end. It should start with the main menu with buttons to access the content. The content can be organized into chapters, like those that

Creating an Electronic Portfolio Using Adobe Encore CS5

are often seen on movie DVDs, requiring additional menus. For example, Figure 8 shows a storyboard for a DVD to chronicle a couple's new baby. In this example, there is a main menu with three buttons: Photos, Video, and Documents. Under each button, it shows what the couple plans to put on the next menu. A storyboard can show as much detail as you want to provide. Depending on the project, a storyboard can be simple or quite complex with nested submenus. As you become more proficient at designing storyboards and Encore projects, you can add additional details, such as video transitions between menus, slideshows, motion menus, and audio information.

Working with Projects

Encore files are called projects. Projects store links to the content, menus, and timelines in the project, and must conform to either the **NTSC** (National Television Standards Committee) or the **PAL** (Phase Alternating Line) television standard. These standards are specifications that any video must conform to in order to be viewed in a particular country or region. These requirements consist of specific frame rates and frame size conditions. The NTSC standard covers the regions of North America and Japan. The PAL standard covers Europe. The final output must conform to one of these standards.

When a project is created, Encore creates a project folder on the same directory where you have saved your project file. As assets are imported, menus are created and files are transcoded, Encore builds additional folders to hold the data. The folders are created in a hierarchy, as shown in Figure 9, and updated as changes are made to them. The Preferences file keeps track of any changes to the Encore interface. The Cache folder contains image files that will be used for thumbnails. The Sources folder organizes the data, such as video and audio assets, menus, and transcoded files.

Figure 8 *Sample Storyboard*

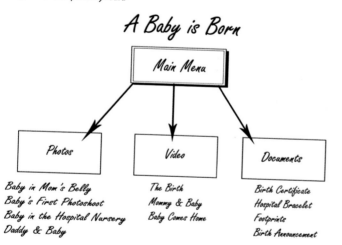

Figure 9 *Sample folder structure*

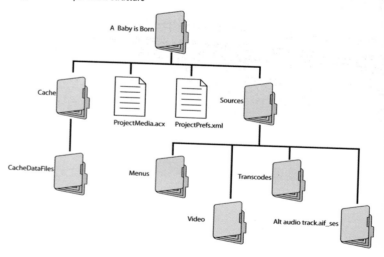

Organizing and Adding Assets

Assets include any type of multimedia, such as video clips, audio clips, and still images, used in the Encore project. Assets are organized in the Project panel, as shown in Figure 10. Assets that are specific to Encore only include menus, timelines, slideshows, playlists, and chapter playlists. Assets can be used multiple times. They can also be replaced, renamed, and updated.

A **menu** provides the viewer with access to the content in the project, as shown in Figure 11. Menus can be created and customized from the templates that are

Figure 10 *The Project panel*

Preview

Video clip

Menu

Timeline

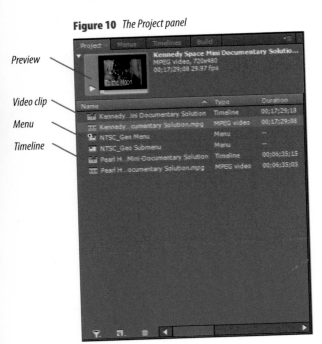

Figure 11 *Preview a menu in the Menu Viewer*

ENCORE CS5 SUPPORTED FILE FORMATS

Video

- AVI (Windows)
- DV-AVI (Mac OS)
- H.264
- MPEG-2 (including MPG, MPV, and M2V)
- Apple QuickTime® (MOV; including Reference Movies)—requires QuickTime installed on Windows systems
- WMV (Windows Media File)

Still Images

- Adobe Photoshop (PSD), RGB color space
- Bitmap (BMP)
- GIF
- JPEG
- PICT
- Portable Network Graphics (PNG)
- Targa (TGA)
- TIFF

Note: *PSD files must be 8-bit when imported as image assets; when imported as menus they can be 8-bit or 16-bit. TIFF files cannot be imported as menus.*

Audio

- AC3 (Dolby® Digital)
- Audio Interchange File Format (AIF, AIFF; not AIFF-C)
- Digital Theater Sound (DTS)
- mp3
- MPG or M2P (including MPEG-1, MPA, Layer II)
- QuickTime (MOV)
- WAV (32-bit floating-point files are transcoded; 96-kHz 16/24-bit files are not transcoded)
- WMA

Note: *DTS audio files will not play during Preview in Encore, even though they will play from the burned disc.*

included with Encore. They can also be downloaded from Resource Central, built from assets imported into the project, or designed in Photoshop and imported into Encore.

The Timeline Viewer, or **timeline**, is used to organize the assets that each button or menu item links to. These may include video clips, still images, and audio, as shown in Figure 12. The Timeline allows you to mark specific points in the project to create chapters or position subtitles.

Slideshows are a sequence of still images enhanced with special effects, such as pans and zooms, transitions and narrations, or music, and can be organized in the Slideshow viewer, as shown in Figure 13.

A **playlist** is a collection of timelines, slideshows, or chapter playlists set to play sequentially.

Figure 12 *The Timeline Viewer*

Timeline timecode
Video clip track
Source timecode
Audio clip track

Figure 13 *The Slideshow Viewer*

Slide Number
Preview

Slide Duration
Transition

Creating an Electronic Portfolio Using Adobe Encore CS5

A **chapter playlist** is similar to a playlist, but it provides a way to play a single timeline's chapters in non-sequential order.

Adding and Customizing Menus

The Library panel has a variety of categories, organizing the different assets available. Sets include all of the items from the same theme, themes have the same design elements, for example "Electric". Menus are one of the many sets available, as shown in Figure 14. The Toggle display buttons filter the various categories for simplified viewing. Menus can be created from either menus or backgrounds. Menus are created by choosing a menu or background in the Library panel and then clicking the New Menu button. After choosing a menu, you can customize it by using the Place button to add buttons, or the Text tool to highlight any of the text and then edit it, as shown in Figure 15.

Working with Backgrounds

Backgrounds can be added to a project as a menu by clicking the New Menu button on the Library panel. The background is then added to the Menu Viewer as a menu item. Using a background for a menu provides greater flexibility and allows the user to customize the layout of the menu. You can choose text items and buttons that

Figure 14 *The Library panel*

Library panel

Toggle displays

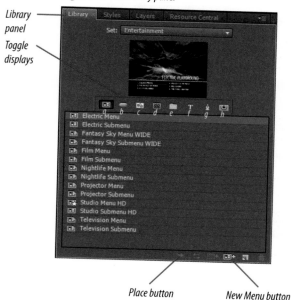

Place button

New Menu button

Toggle displays:

a. *Menus*

b. *Buttons*

c. *Images*

d. *Backgrounds*

e. *Layer Sets*

f. *Text Items*

g. *Shapes*

h. *Replacement Layers*

Figure 15 *Highlighted text in a menu for editing*

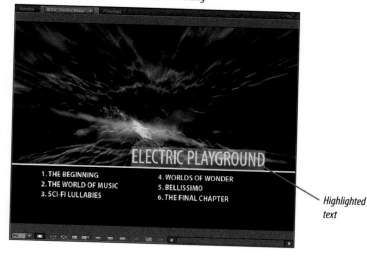

Highlighted text

complement the background, giving it a consistent look, as shown in Figure 16.

(*Note*: The Show Safe margins are available on the Menu Viewer to help aid in placement of assets and other visual elements.)

Working with the Flowchart Panel

The Flowchart panel assists with planning the project by showing the menu items and timelines graphically, in a tree structure. As you work with your project, the flowchart

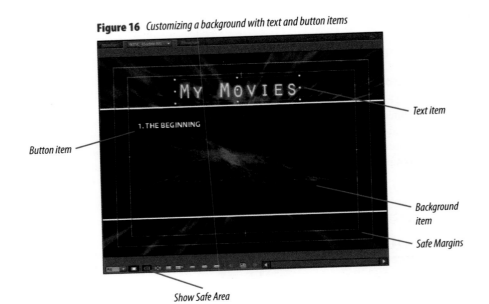

Figure 16 *Customizing a background with text and button items*

Text item

Button item

Background item

Safe Margins

Show Safe Area

Motion Menus

A Motion menu can also be created. This type of menu includes moving footage or audio. Video can be added to play in the background or in the thumbnail images of buttons. Music or a narration can also be added to play while the menu is displayed.

File Size and Quality

The available space, on the disc (DVD or Blu-ray) that you will be building your project to, limits the file size of the final project and as a result can influence the quality of the video. The video portion of the content occupies the most disc space. Depending on the data rate, 1 minute of standard-definition video for a DVD project can fill up to 73.5 MB, at a rate of 9.8 megabits per second (Mbps). The same length of high-definition video for a Blu-ray can occupy 270 MB, using a data rate of 36 Mbps.

continually updates showing the navigation layout of the project. The Flowchart panel can also be used to set project navigation.

The Flowchart panel is divided into two areas: the upper pane, and the lower pane. The upper pane displays the elements that are being used in the project and the lower pane displays the elements that are in the Project panel but have not been utilized. The arrows between the elements show how the buttons are connected to the timelines. A white line with an arrow indicates a normal link. A red line with an arrow indicated a broken link, as shown in Figure 17. Broken links occur when an item is removed from a project after a link has already been set.

Figure 17 *Working with the Flowchart panel*

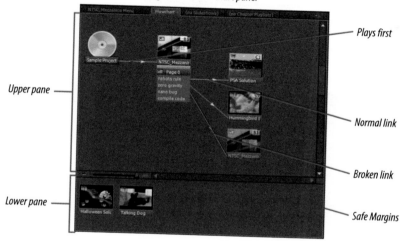

Plays first

Upper pane

Normal link

Broken link

Lower pane

Safe Margins

Figure 18 *Resource Central*

Refresh button

Categories

Download button

Using Resource Central

The Resource Central panel is also available in Encore. As in other applications, Resource Central provides access to tutorials, product related news, and product updates. In addition, a library of templates and assets can be downloaded into the project, as shown in Figure 18.

Organize and add assets

1. Open the Pollution your name.ncor file, if necessary.

2. Click **File** on the Application bar, point to **New**, then click **New Folder**.

   The New Folder Name dialog box opens, as shown in Figure 19.

3. Type **Air Pollution**, then click **OK**.

   A folder, named Air Pollution, is created on the Project panel.

4. On the Project panel, click the **Create a new item button** 🔳 then click **Folder**, as shown in Figure 20.

5. Type **Water Pollution** in the New Folder Name dialog box, then click **OK**.

   The Water Pollution folder is added to the Project panel.

6. Select the Air Pollution folder on the Project panel.

7. Click **File** on the Application bar, point to **Import As**, then click **Timeline**.

   The Import as Asset dialog box open.

   (continued)

Figure 19 *New Folder Name dialog box*

Enter name of folder here

Figure 20 *Creating a new folder*

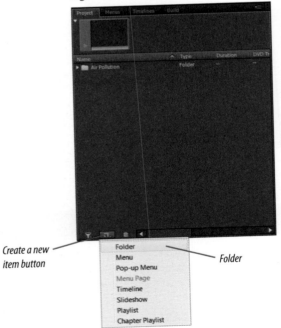

Create a new item button

Folder

Creating an Electronic Portfolio Using Adobe Encore CS5

Figure 21 *Importing assets*

Select files

Open

Figure 22 *Air Pollution Timeline assets*

Monitor
Viewer

Timeline
Viewer

8. Navigate to the drive and folder where your Data Files are stored, locate and open the **Environmental Issues folder**, click **EIS01**, press and hold [**Shift**], click **EIS10**, as shown in Figure 21, then click **Open**.

   The video footage is imported into the Project panel and placed inside the Air Pollution folder as a timeline and as individual clips. The Monitor Viewer and Timeline Viewer become active as shown in Figure 22.

9. On the Project panel, right-click the **Water Pollution folder,** point to **Import As**, then click **Asset**.

10. Select the files from EIS18 to EIS24, then click **Open**.

    The video footage is imported into the Water Pollution folder.

11. Save your project file and leave it open for the next step.

In the lesson, you created folders in the Project panel and imported video footage as individual timelines and associated assets or video clips into those folders.

Add and customize a menu

1. Open the Pollution your name.ncor file, if necessary.

2. Click **Window** on the Application bar, then click **Library**.

   The Library panel appears in the lower-right side of the Encore workspace.

   TIP The Library panel may already be open.

3. On the Library panel click the **Set drop-down menu**, then click **Corporate**, if necessary, as shown in Figure 23.

   The Library sets in the Corporate category are made available.

4. On the Library panel, click the **Toggle display of menus button** ▣ .

   This filters the Library panel to display menu templates for the Corporate category.

5. Select the Globe Menu, then click the **New Menu button** ▣▣ on the Library panel.

   The Globe Menu is added to the Project panel and appears in the Menu Viewer, as shown in Figure 24.

   (continued)

Figure 23 *The Library panel*

Library panel

Set drop-down menu

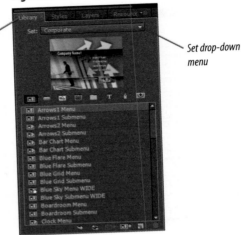

Figure 24 *Adding a menu template to a project*

Globe Menu

Menu Viewer

Globe Menu

Creating an Electronic Portfolio Using Adobe Encore CS5

Figure 25 *Customizing the Menu Template*

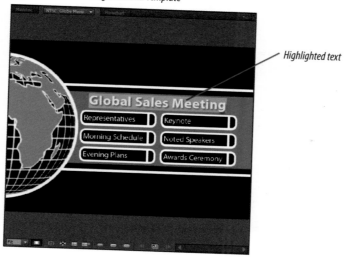

Highlighted text

Figure 26 *Modifying the submenu buttons*

Water Pollution

Air Pollution

6. Click the **Text tool** ▐ on the Tools panel, then click in front of the **letter "G"** in Global on the Menu Viewer.

   The text cursor is placed in front of the word Global so that the text can be edited.

7. Highlight the **Global Sales Meeting text**, then type **Pollution**, as shown in Figure 25.

   The title on the main menu is changed to Pollution.

8. Using the same method, change **Representative** to **Air Pollution** and **Keynote** to **Water Pollution**, as shown in Figure 26.

9. Click the **Selection tool** ▐ on the Tools panel, then click **Morning Schedule** in the Menu Viewer.

10. Click **Edit** on the Application bar, then click **Cut**.

    The Morning Schedule submenu buttons are removed from the main menu.

(continued)

11. Using the same method, remove **Noted Speakers**, **Evening Plans**, and **Awards Ceremony**.

The main menu now has two submenu buttons: Air Pollution and Water Pollution, as shown in Figure 27.

12. Click and drag the **Air Pollution button** towards the center of the green area to center the button vertically.

13. Click and drag the **Water Pollution button** towards the center of the green area to center the button vertically.

The submenu buttons are centered, as shown in Figure 28.

14. Save your project file and leave it open for the next step.

In this lesson, you added and customized a menu template.

Work with backgrounds

1. Open the Pollution your name.ncor file, if necessary.

You will create a custom submenu from a background image.

2. On the Library panel, click the **Toggle display of backgrounds button** .

The items in the Library panel are filtered to display just backgrounds; these backgrounds are complimentary to the menu templates viewed previously.

3. Click **Globe BG**, then click the **New Menu button** on the Library panel.

The Globe BG image is added to the Project panel as a blank menu and opens in the Menu Viewer, as shown in Figure 29.

(continued)

Figure 27 *Modified Main Menu*

Figure 28 *Adjusting the submenu buttons*

Figure 29 *Adding a background as a menu item*

Globe BG

Globe BG

Figure 30 *Adding a button to the submenu*

Rotators button

Figure 31 *Moving a button*

Figure 32 *Globe BG submenu with buttons*

4. On the Library panel, click the **Toggle display of buttons button** ▭.

The items in the Library panel are filtered to display only buttons.

5. Click **Rotators Button**, then click the **Place button** ▭ on the Library panel.

The Rotators Button is added to the Menu Viewer, as shown in Figure 30.

6. Click the **Move tool** ▭ on the Tools panel, then click and drag the **Company Overview** to the green rectangle, as shown in Figure 31.

7. Repeat this process to add 9 more Rotators Button buttons for a total of 10, and arrange the buttons as shown in Figure 32.

TIP Use the Selection tool and the Align command on the Object menu to help align the buttons.

8. Save your project file and leave it open for the next step.

You added buttons to the Globe BG submenu.

Work with the Flowchart panel

1. Open the Pollution your name.ncor file, if necessary.

2. Click the **Workspace drop-down menu**, then click **Navigation Design**.

   This resets the workspace making the Flowchart panel prominent, as shown in Figure 33.

3. On the Project panel, right-click the **NTSC_Globe Menu**, then click **Set as First Play**.

   This sets the NTSC_Globe Menu as the item that will play first and replaces the EIS01 Smokest in the Flowchart panel, as shown in Figure 34.

4. On the Project panel, right-click the **NTSC_Globe BG**, then click **Rename**.

   The Rename Menu dialog box opens.

   (continued)

Figure 33 *The Navigation Design workspace*

Flowchart panel

Navigation Design

Figure 34 *Setting NTSC_Globe Menu to play first*

NTSC_Globe Menu

Figure 35 *Rename Menu dialog box*

Enter a new
Menu name
text box

Figure 36 *Linking a button*

Air Pollution

Upper
pane

Lower
pane

Air Pollution
submenu

Air Pollution

Lesson 2   Create a Project

5. Type **Air Pollution submenu** in the Enter a new Menu name text box, as shown in Figure 35.

    This renames the title of the submenu making it easier to locate.

6. Click the **Selection tool** on the Tools panel, then click and drag **Air Pollution** from the NTSC_Globe Menu icon on the Flowchart panel to the **Air Pollution submenu** in the lower pane, as shown in Figure 36.

    The cursor changes to the Pick Whip, and the Air Pollution submenu is added to the upper pane with a link connecting the two items.

7. Using the same method select the first Company Over from the Air Pollution submenu and point to **EIS01** in the lower pane.

    The EIS01 timeline is added to the upper pane and links the first button on the Air Pollution submenu to the timeline.

(continued)

8. On the Properties panel, click the **Set Name from Link check box,** as shown in Figure 37.

   This changes the name of the button to EIS01 Smokestacks.

9. Repeat this process for each of the buttons from the Air Pollution submenu in the upper pane, point to the timelines in the lower pane in order from the left, then click the **Set Name from Link check box** for each button.

10. Compare your Footage panel to Figure 38.

    The timelines are removed from the lower pane once they are selected and moved to the upper pane.

    Save your project file and leave it open for the next step.

You renamed the buttons and linked them to the appropriate timeline.

Figure 37 *Renaming a button based on Timeline name*

Set Name from
Link check box

Button renamed

Figure 38 *All buttons on Air Pollution submenu linked*

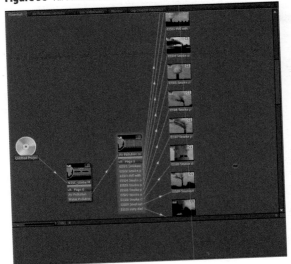

Creating an Electronic Portfolio Using Adobe Encore CS5

Figure 39 *Adding placeholder text to the submenu*

Placeholder text

Figure 40 *Using the Character panel*

Character panel

Font family

Font style

Edit a menu

1. Open the Pollution your name.ncor file, if necessary.

2. Reset the workspace to Menu Design.

   A title and a button to return to the main menu are needed on the Air Pollution submenu.

3. On the Library panel, click the **Toggle display of text items button** [T].

   This filters the items in the Library panel to display only text.

4. Click the **Scientific Title Text**, then click the **Place button** .

   Placeholder text is placed on the Monitor Preview.

5. Click the **Move tool** on the Tools panel, then click and drag the **placeholder text** above the button list, as shown in Figure 39.

6. Click the **Text tool** on the Tools panel, then change the placeholder text to **Air Pollution**.

7. Click the **Selection tool** on the Tools panel, click **Air Pollution**, then on the Character panel change the font family to **Nueva Std**, and the font style to **Bold Condensed**, as shown in Figure 40.

(continued)

8. Click the **Move tool** ⊕ on the Tools panel, then drag the **Air Pollution title** so it is centered over the button titles, as shown in Figure 41.

9. Click the **Scientific Title Text**, click the **Place button** ▣, then move the placeholder text to the bottom right of the Menu Viewer.

   You will rename this text placeholder and use it for a button that returns the viewer to the main menu.

10. Click the **Text tool** T on the Tools panel, change the placeholder text to **Return to Main Menu**, then change the font family to **Nueva Std**, and the font size to **36**.

11. On the Library panel, click the **Toggle display of buttons button** ▣ .

12. Click the **HiTech1 Previous Button**, click the **Place button** ▣, then move the button to the left of the Return to Main Menu text, as shown in Figure 42.

(continued)

Figure 41 *Moving the Air Pollution title*

Figure 42 *Creating a Return button with text*

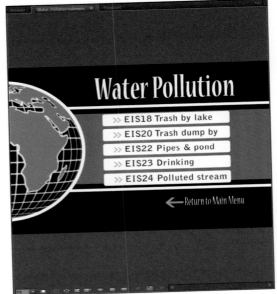

Creating an Electronic Portfolio Using Adobe Encore CS5

Figure 43 *Setting the Return button's action*

Link arrow

NTSC_Globe Menu

Default

13. Click the **Selection tool** 🔲 click the **HiTech1 Previous Button**, then on the Properties panel, click the **Link arrow**, point to **NTSC_Globe Menu**, and choose **Default** as shown in Figure 43.

This sets the button action to return to the main menu. Your figure may vary.

14. Save your project file and it leave open for the next step.

You edited the submenu to include a title and a button to return to the main menu.

Create TIMELINES

What You'll Do

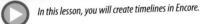
In this lesson, you will create timelines in Encore.

Previewing a Project

During the process of creating the project and setting links, it is a good idea to preview the project before you build your disc or Flash file. When you preview a project, you will see how it will appear at final output and be able to test the links in the Project Preview window with navigation controls such as Play, Pause, and Skip Forward, as shown in Figure 44.

Working with Timelines

As in Premiere Pro, timelines are used in Encore to arrange various assets or just hold one asset. Every linked asset needs to be placed on a timeline. The Timelines panel shows all the timelines in the current project. When a specific timeline is selected on the Timelines panel, its properties become active on the Properties panel, as shown in Figure 45.

Figure 44 *Project Preview window*

Highlighted button

Navigation controls

Creating an Electronic Portfolio Using Adobe Encore CS5

Timelines can be created at the same time assets are imported by selecting the Import As Timeline option from the File menu. The asset will be imported in its original format and a timeline will be created at the same time. Timelines may also be created after assets have been imported by creating a timeline using the Create a new

item button on the Project panel and then dragging the assets from the Project panel to the timeline.

The timeline needs an action set to control what happens when the clip ends. If an action is not set when the project is built, the video clip will remain on a black screen

when the clip is finished playing. This action is set in the Properties panel and is called an **end action**.

The end action is set by either using the Pick Whip or by using the drop-menu to select what the project should play when the video clip has ended, as shown in Figure 46.

Figure 45 *Working with Timelines*

Timelines panel

Properties panel

End Action

Figure 46 *End Action drop-down menu*

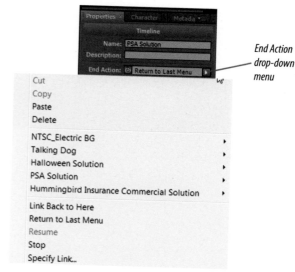

End Action drop-down menu

Creating Buttons with Timelines

Buttons can be created by dragging a timeline from the Project panel to the Menu Viewer. The button that is selected as the default in the set will be created automatically when the Timeline is dropped on the Menu Viewer, as shown in Figure 47. The default button can be set by right-clicking the button on the Library panel and then choosing Set as Default Button.

Creating a Playlist

A **playlist** is a group of timelines that are set to play sequentially. A playlist plays back all the elements that have been added to the playlist without stopping. The playlist is created by selecting the timelines on the Project panel while holding [Ctrl] (Win) or [⌘] (Mac). The playlist, when selected, can then be viewed on the Properties panel, as shown in Figure 48. The playlist is an excellent way to give the end user the opportunity to view multiple timelines at once.

Figure 47 *Creating a button from a timeline*

Selected Timeline

New button

Default button

Figure 48 *Creating a playlist*

Playlist

Timelines in playlist

Creating an Electronic Portfolio Using Adobe Encore CS5

Figure 49 *Project Preview window*

Figure 50 *Air Pollution submenu displayed in the Project Preview window*

Preview a project

1. Open the Pollution your name.ncor file, if necessary.
2. Reset the workspace to **Default**.

   The button names have been changed to reflect the name of the respective timeline to which they are linked.
3. Click **File** on the Application bar, then click **Preview**.

   The Project Preview window opens, as shown in Figure 49.
4. In the Project Preview window, click the **Air Pollution button**.

   The Air Pollution submenu is displayed, as shown in Figure 50.
5. Click the **EIS01 Smokestacks button**, then watch the video clip in its entirety.

   Notice the Project Preview goes to black when the video clip ends. The end action needs to be set so when the clip finishes, the Air Pollution submenu is again displayed.
6. Click the **Exit and return button** to return to the Encore workspace.
7. Save your project file and leave it open for the next step.

In this lesson, you previewed your project.

Set an end action for the timeline

1. Open the Pollution your name.ncor file, if necessary.
2. Click **Window** on the Application bar, then click **Timelines**.

   The Timelines panel appears in the upper-left section of the Encore workspace.

(continued)

3. On the Timelines panel, click the **EIS01 Smokestacks**, then on the Properties panel, click the **End Action arrow,** point to **Air Pollution submenu**, then click **Default**, as shown in Figure 51.

The video clip will now return to the Air Pollution submenu when it finishes playing, instead of staying on a black screen.

4. Repeat this process with the remaining timelines on the Timelines panel.

5. Save your project file and leave it open for the next step.

You set the end action for each of the timelines in the Timeline panel to return to the Air Pollution submenu.

Create buttons for a submenu with timelines

1. Open the Pollution your name.ncor file, if necessary.

2. Reset the Default workspace.

3. Click **File** on the Application bar, point to **Import As**, then click **Menu**.

The Import as Menu dialog box opens.

4. Locate the **Water Pollution submenu file** from your Data Files folder, then click **Open**.

The Water Pollution submenu has already been created for you; you need to set some links to add functionality.

5. Click the **Selection tool** , click the **light blue arrow** in the Menu Viewer, then on the Properties panel, click the **Link drop-down menu**, then click **NTSC_Globe Menu: Default**, as shown in Figure 52.

(continued)

Figure 51 *Setting the end action for a timeline*

End Action arrow

Air Pollution submenu

Default

Figure 52 *Setting the Link action for the light blue arrow*

Link

Light blue arrow

Creating an Electronic Portfolio Using Adobe Encore CS5

Figure 53 *Creating a button by dragging an asset from the Project panel*

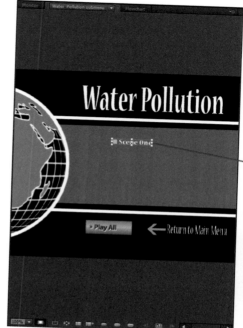

New button

Figure 54 *Button placement on the Water Pollution submenu*

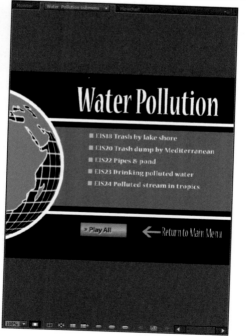

6. On the Library panel, click the **Toggle display of buttons button,** right-click the **Fire Button**, then click **Set as Default Button**.

7. On the Project panel, expand the contents of the **Water Pollution folder** to display the video footage assets.

8. Click and drag the **EIS18 Trash by lake shore.mov** video clip to the Water Pollution submenu in the Menu Viewer, as shown in Figure 53.

    A button is created in the Menu Viewer and a timeline is created on the Project panel.

9. Select the button, then on the Properties panel, click the **Set Name from Link check box** to reset the name of the button.

10. Click the **Move tool** on the Tools panel, then move the **EIS18 Trash by lake shore button** to the upper middle area of the green rectangle.

11. Repeat this process with the remaining video clips in the Water Pollution folder so that the buttons look like those shown in Figure 54.

TIP A red rectangle will alert you if you are overlapping buttons. To ensure buttons work correctly they cannot overlap.

(continued)

12. Click the **Menu Viewer drop-down menu**, then click **NTSC_Globe menu**.

   The NTSC_Globe menu will display in the Menu Viewer.

13. Click the **Water Pollution menu**, then on the Properties panel, set the Link to **Air Pollution submenu: Default**, as shown in Figure 55.

   This creates the link for the Air Pollution button to go to the Air Pollution submenu.

14. Preview the project to verify all of the buttons are working properly.

   All buttons should go to the appropriate place and all video clips should return to the appropriate submenu.

15. Make corrections if necessary.

16. Save your project file and leave it open for the next step.

You placed video assets on the Water Pollution submenu to create buttons, then you verified that all of the buttons and timelines in the project were working properly.

Create a playlist

1. Open the Pollution your name.ncor file, if necessary, then reset the Default workspace if necessary.

2. On the Project panel, expand the **Air Pollution folder**.

3. Select the **EIS01 Smokestacks timeline**, press and hold [**Ctrl**] (Win) or [⌘] (Mac), then select the remaining timelines in order.

4. Click the **New Item button** 🔲, then click **Playlist**.

   The New Playlist Name dialog box opens, as shown in Figure 56.

   (continued)

Figure 55 *Set the Water Pollution link on the main menu to go to the Water Pollution submenu*

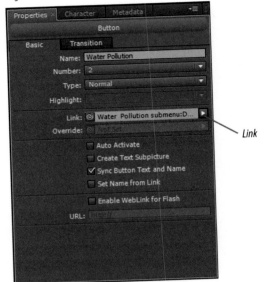

Link

Figure 56 *New Playlist Name dialog box*

New Playlist Name

Creating an Electronic Portfolio Using Adobe Encore CS5

Figure 57 *Setting the end action for a Playlist*

Air Pollution Playlist

End Action

Figure 58 *Moving the Air Pollution Playlist button*

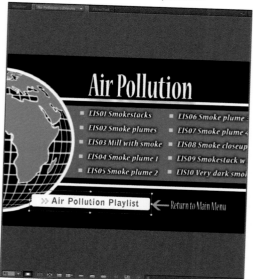

5. Type **Air Pollution Playlist** in the Enter a name for the new playlist text box, then click **OK**.

   The playlist is added to the Air Pollution folder on the Project panel.

6. Select the **Air Pollution Playlist**, then on the Properties panel, click the **End Action drop-down menu**, then click **Air Pollution submenu: Default**, as shown in Figure 57.

7. On the **Menu Viewer tab**, select the **Air Pollution submenu** from the drop-down menu, if necessary.

   The Air Pollution submenu needs to be active in the Menu Viewer panel.

8. Drag the **Air Pollution Playlist** from the Project panel to the Air Pollution submenu in the Menu Viewer, then click the **Set Name from Link check box**.

9. Click the **Move tool** ⬚, then move the **Air Pollution Playlist button** to the location shown in Figure 58.

   All of the Air Pollution video clips will play without stopping.

10. Save your project file and leave it open for the next step.

You created a playlist to play all of the Air Pollution video clips in order then return to the Air Pollution submenu.

Build
A PROJECT

What You'll Do

In this lesson, you will build your final project to the Flash format for the Internet and burn it to a DVD.

Checking the Project

Encore has a feature called Check Project, which is an important feature to use before actually building your project to its final output. The Check Project feature identifies problems with the project such as missing links or end actions not being set. This feature can be activated from the Build Project panel or from the File menu. You can choose which issues you want to check for by adding and removing check marks in the Check Project panel, as shown in Figure 59. Leaving all of the options checked will ensure that any possible problems will not be missed.

Figure 59 *The Check Project panel*

Check Project panel

Start button

Figure 60 shows some problems after running the Check Project feature. Selecting the name of the problem in the Check Project panel allows you to fix it on the Properties panel, as shown in Figure 61. Not all problems can be repaired on the Properties panel, for instance, an orphaned item like the Orphan Playlist problem shown in Figure 62, would need to be repaired on the Flowchart panel by moving it from the lower pane to the upper pane.

Figure 60   *Check Project results*

Identified problems

Orphan Playlist

Figure 61   *Fixing a problem on the Properties panel*

Selected problem

Problem on Properties panel

Figure 62   *Fixing a problem on the Flowchart panel*

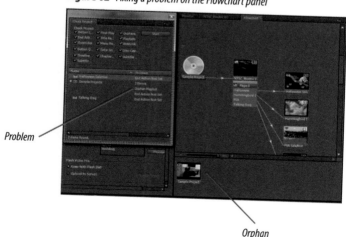

Problem

Orphan

Building the Project to the Flash Format

The Build panel offers the option to export an Encore project to a Flash format for interactive viewing on the Internet, as shown in Figure 63. The F4V and FLV formats are available, along with several presets to set the size and quality of the video. The F4V format is compatible with Flash Player 9 and higher, and is the new standard for published Flash files. The FLV standard is compatible with Flash Player 7 and higher.

In the Build panel, the name of the project is found in the Disc Info section of the panel and is named Untitled Project by default. It is not automatically the same as your Encore Project file. Templates are available to provide a background for the Flash project, as shown in Figure 64. If a template is not specified the default black background is used.

When a Flash project is built, Encore creates files and a folder in a separate folder named after the project in the Build panel. These files contain the necessary information for the project to play properly. Every Flash project produces an AuthorContent.xml, flshdvd.swf, and index.html file. In addition, there is a Sources folder created which contains the Flash videos, menu images, and icons needed for the project. (*Note*: The title of the Web page defaults to the name of the template; which can only be changed by editing the html code; it cannot be done in Encore.)

Figure 63 *Build panel*

Flash format

Build button

Name of Project Build

Flash file format

Preset

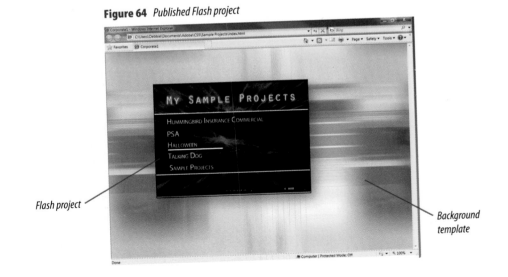

Figure 64 *Published Flash project*

Flash project

Background template

Creating an Electronic Portfolio Using Adobe Encore CS5

Building a DVD

The Build panel also offers the option to build a project to a DVD, as shown in Figure 65. You can burn the project directly to blank media that is in the appropriate drive. The DVD will auto play when inserted into the drive with DVD player software, as shown in Figure 66. You can also burn a DVD project to a folder that can be viewed on a computer with a DVD player.

The Disc Info area of the Build panel indicates if there is enough room on the selected media that has been designated for the project. As with the Flash build, you need to specify the name of the project. You can also copy-protect the disc so that it cannot be copied illegally.

Figure 65 *Build Project for a DVD*

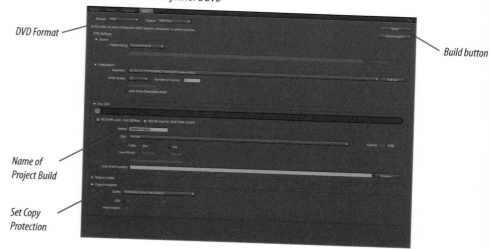

DVD Format

Build button

Name of Project Build

Set Copy Protection

Figure 66 *Published DVD project*

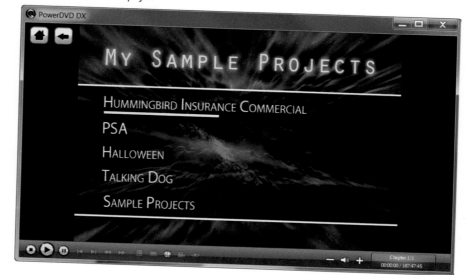

Build a project to the Flash format

1. Open the Pollution your name.ncor file, if necessary, then reset the Default workspace if necessary.

2. Click **Window** on the Application bar, then click **Build**.

   The Build panel becomes active in the upper-left area of the Encore workspace.

3. On the Build panel, click the **Format drop-down menu**, then click **Flash**.

   The Output drop-down menu automatically updates to Flash (.swf), and the Settings options update to Flash options, as shown in Figure 67.

4. On the Build panel, click the **Browse button**, navigate to the drive and folder where you save your work, then click **OK**.

   The Browse For Folder dialog box opens.

   (continued)

Figure 67 *The Build panel for Flash*

Format

Output

Browse

Settings

Working with Sequences in Encore

Adobe Dynamic Link is supported between Premiere Pro and Encore. A Premiere Pro sequence can be sent or imported into Encore, for output to DVD, Blue-ray, or SWF. The sequence can then be updated in Premiere Pro and it will be reflected in Encore without rendering, or while in Encore the sequence can be selected for editing by using the Edit Original command.

Creating an Electronic Portfolio Using Adobe Encore CS5

Figure 68 *Changing the Settings in the Build panel*

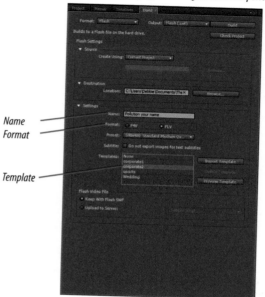

Name
Format

Template

Figure 69 *Checking the project for problems*

Problems

Start

5. In the Settings section complete the following: Name text box: **Pollution your name**, Format: **FLV**, and Templates: **corporate2**, then compare your screen to Figure 68.

6. Click the **Check Project button**.

   The Check Project dialog box opens.

7. Click **Start**.

   Problems are identified, as shown in Figure 69, and need to be repaired before building the project.

TIP If there are no errors, skip Steps 8 and 9.

8. In the Problems list select **EIS02**, then on the Properties panel, click the **End Action drop-down menu**, then click **Air Pollution submenu: Default**.

   The Timeline properties become active on the Properties panel when the problem is selected in the Check Project dialog box.

9. Repeat this process for each of the timelines in the Check Project dialog box.

(continued)

10. Click **Start**, then compare your results to Figure 70.

All the problems should be repaired. If you still have to make corrections, click Start again.

11. Close the Check Project dialog box.

12. On the Build panel, click the **Build button**, then click **OK** when the process is complete.

The Save Project dialog box is visible for a short time, then the Build Progress dialog box is displayed to show the progress of the build, as shown in Figure 71.

If you receive an error when attempting to build your project that a folder with that specific name is already taken, modify the name of your project in the Build panel.

(continued)

Figure 70 *Problems have been corrected*

Figure 71 *Build Progress dialog box*

Status of build

Creating an Electronic Portfolio Using Adobe Encore CS5

Figure 72 *Locating the Pollution your name folder*

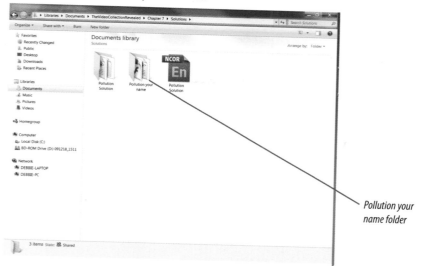

Pollution your
name folder

Figure 73 *Final project published for the Internet*

13. Minimize Encore, then navigate to and open the folder where you save your work, as shown in Figure 72.

A folder has been created with the files necessary for the Flash Web page to function properly.

14. Open the Pollution your name folder, then double-click **Index.html** to preview your project, as shown in Figure 73.

15. Save your project file and leave it open for the next step.

You built a project for the Flash format after verifying and correcting any problems.

Build a DVD

1. Open the Pollution your name.ncor file, if necessary.

2. On the Project panel, change the format to **DVD**.

   All the settings change accordingly to support the DVD output, as shown in Figure 74. (*Note*: You will need a blank DVD inserted in your DVD drive.)

   (continued)

Figure 74 *Build panel settings for a DVD build*

Format

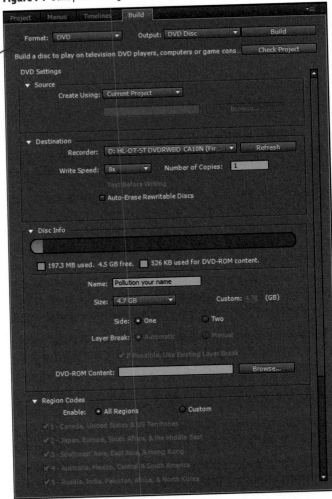

Figure 75 *Progress of build to a DVD*

Status of build

3. Click the **Build button**, then click **OK** when the process is complete.

   The Save Project dialog box is visible for a short time, then the Build Progress dialog box is displayed to show the progress of the build, as shown in Figure 75.

   (*Note*: The project has already been checked for errors before we built to the Flash format. If this was the only build, Check Project should have been completed prior to starting the build process.)

4. Minimize Encore and open the DVD, as shown in Figure 76.

   This disc will be ejected upon completion. Put it back into the drive; the DVD should launch automatically.

5. Save and close your project file.

You published your project to a DVD.

Figure 76 *Final project published to a DVD*

Start Adobe Encore CS5 and explore the workspace.

1. Click Start on the Application bar, point to All Programs, then click Adobe Encore CS5 (Win) or open the Finder from the dock, click Applications from the sidebar, select the Adobe applications folder then click Adobe Encore CS5 (Mac).
2. Click New Project in the Adobe Encore CS5 window.
3. Click the Browse button, then navigate to the drive and folder where your Chapter 7 Data Files are located.
4. Click OK to close the Browse for Folder window but keep the New Project dialog box open.
5. Type **Erosion Final your name** in the Name text box of the New Project dialog box.
6. Accept the default settings, then click OK.
7. Locate the Project panel, the Monitor panel, the Properties panel, and the Library panel.
8. Click Window on the Application bar, point to Workspace, then click Menu Design.
9. Click Window on the Application bar, point to Workspace, then click Default.

Organize and add assets.

1. Click File on the Application bar, point to New, then click New Folder.
2. Type **Deforestation**, then click OK.
3. On the Project panel, click the Create a new item button, then click Folder.
4. Type **Desertification** in the New Folder Name dialog box, then click OK.
5. Select the Deforestation folder on the Project panel.
6. Click File on the Application bar, point to Import As, then click Timeline.

7. Locate the Environmental Issues folder where your Data Files are stored, click EIS28 press and hold [Shift], select EIS37, then click Open.
8. On the Project panel, right-click the Desertification folder, point to Import As, then click Asset.
9. Select the files from EIS51 to EIS56, then click Open.

Add and customize a menu template.

1. Click Window on the Application bar, then click Library.
2. On the Library panel, click the Set drop-down menu, then click General, if necessary.
3. On the Library panel, click the Toggle display of menus button.
4. Locate the Sunset Menu, then click the New Menu button on the Library panel.
5. Click the Text tool on the Tools panel, then click in front of the letter "I" in Inspiration on the Menu Viewer.
6. Highlight Inspirational Thoughts, then type **Erosion**.
7. Using the same method, change the play movie text to **Deforestation** and the scene selections text to **Desertification**.
8. Click the Selection tool, then click special features in the Menu Viewer.
9. Click Edit on the Application bar, then click Cut.
10. Using the same method, remove languages.

Work with backgrounds.

1. On the Library panel, click the Toggle display of backgrounds button.
2. Locate and select Sunset BG, then click the New Menu button on the Library panel.

3. On the Library panel, click the Toggle display of buttons button.
4. Locate and select the Sunset Button, then click the Place button on the Library panel.
5. Repeat this process to add 9 more buttons for a total of 10, then arrange the buttons as you like.

Work with the Flowchart panel.

1. On the Project panel, right-click the NTSC_Sunset Menu, then click Set as First Play.
2. On the Project panel, right-click the NTSC_Sunset BG, then click Rename.
3. Type **Deforestation submenu** in the Enter a New Menu name text box.
4. Click the Workspace drop-down menu, then click Navigation Design.
5. Click the Selection tool, select Deforestation from the NTSC_Sunset Menu icon on the Flowchart panel, then drag to the Deforestation submenu in the lower pane.
6. Select the first introductions from the Deforestation submenu on the Flowchart panel, then point to EIS28 in the lower pane.
7. On the Properties panel, check the Set Name from Link check box.
8. Repeat this process for each of the buttons from the Deforestation submenu in the upper pane, point to the timelines in the lower pane in order from the left, then click the Set Name from Link check box for each button.

Edit a menu.

1. Reset the workspace to Menu Design.
2. On the Library panel, click the Toggle display of text items button.
3. Select 36 pt Gold Trajan Pro, then click the Place button.
4. Click the Move tool on the Tools panel, then click and drag the placeholder text above the button list.
5. Click the Text tool on the Tools panel, then change the placeholder text to **Deforestation**.
6. Click the Move tool, then move the Deforestation title so it is centered over the button titles.
7. Select 36 pt Gold Trajan Pro, click the Place button, then move the placeholder text to the bottom right of the Menu Viewer.
8. Click the Text tool on the Tools panel, then change the placeholder text to **Return to Main Menu**, and the font size to 10. (*Note*: Type Return to Main Menu on two lines, pressing [Enter] (Win) or [return] (Mac) after *to*.)
9. Right-click the Return to Main Menu text, then click Convert to Button.
10. Click the Selection tool, click the Return to Main Menu button, then on the Properties panel, click the Link arrow, point to NTSC_Sunset Menu, then click Default.

Preview a project.

1. Reset the workspace to Default.
2. Click File on the Application bar, then click Preview.
3. In the Project Preview window, click the Deforestation button.

4. Click the EIS28 Slash & burn plot Thailand button, then watch the video clip in its entirety.
5. Click the Exit and return button to return to the Encore workspace.

Set an end action for the timeline.

1. Click Window on the Application bar, then click Timelines.
2. On the Timelines panel, select the EIS37 Clear-cut hillside WA, then on the Properties panel, click the End Action drop-down menu, point to the Deforestation submenu, then click default.
3. Repeat this process with the remaining timelines on the Timelines panel.

Create buttons for a submenu with assets.

1. Reset the Default workspace.
2. Click File on the Application bar, point to Import, then click Menu.
3. Locate the Desertification submenu file from your Data Files folder, then click Open.
4. Click the Selection tool, select Return to Main Menu in the Menu Viewer, then on the Properties panel, click the Link drop-down menu, then click NTSC_Sunset Menu: Default.
5. On the Library panel, click the Toggle display of buttons, right-click the Sunset Button, then click Set as Default Button.
6. On the Project panel, expand the contents of the Desertification folder to display the video footage assets.

7. Click and drag the EIS51 Desertification Mai W Africa. mov video clip to the Desertification submenu in the Menu Viewer.
8. Click the Selection tool, select the button, then on the Properties panel, click the Set Name from Link check box to reset the name of the button.
9. Repeat this process with the remaining video clips in the Desertification folder.
10. Click the Menu Viewer drop-down menu, then click NTSC_Sunset menu.
11. Click the Desertification button, then on the Properties panel, click the Link drop-down menu, then click Desertification submenu: Default.
12. Preview the project to verify all of the buttons are working properly.
13. Make corrections if necessary.

Create a playlist.

1. Reset the Default workspace if necessary.
2. On the Project panel, expand the Desertification folder.
3. Select the EIS51 Desertification Mai W Africa timeline, press and hold [Ctrl] (Win) or ⌘ (Mac), then select the remaining timelines in order.
4. Click the New Item button, then click Playlist.
5. Type **Desertification Playlist** in the Enter a name for the new playlist text box, then click OK.
6. Select the Desertification Playlist, then on the Properties panel, click the End Action drop-down menu, then click Desertification submenu: Default.

Creating an Electronic Portfolio Using Adobe Encore CS5

7. Drag the Desertification Playlist from the Project panel to the Desertification submenu in the Menu Viewer, then click the Set Name from Link check box.

8. Click the Move tool, then move the Desertification Playlist button to the bottom of the list of buttons, as shown in Figure 77.

Build a project to the Flash format.

1. Reset the Default workspace if necessary.

2. Click Window on the Application bar, then click Build.

3. On the Build panel, click the Format drop-down menu, then click Flash.

4. On the Build panel, click the Browse button, navigate to the folder where you save your work, then click OK.

5. In the Settings section, complete the following: Name box: **Erosion your name**, Format: **FLV**, and Templates: **corporate2**.

6. Click the Check Project button.

7. Click Start.

8. In the Problems list, select EIS51 Desertification Mai W Africa, then on the Properties panel, click the End Action drop-down menu, then click Deforestation submenu: Default.

9. Repeat this process for each of the timelines in the Check Project dialog box.

10. Click Start.

11. Close the Check Project dialog box. (*Hint*: If there are no errors, continue to the next step.)

12. On the Build panel, click the Build button, then click OK when the process is complete.

13. Minimize Encore, navigate to and open the folder where you save your work.

14. Open the Erosion your name folder, then double-click Index.html to preview your project.

Build a DVD.

1. On the Project panel, change the format to DVD.

2. Click the Build button, then click OK when the process is complete.

3. Minimize Encore, then open the DVD.

4. Save and close your project file.

Figure 77 *Sample Skills Review*

A colleague has been working on a DVD that will be published for the Internet. Unfortunately, there has been a family emergency and he is not able to finish the project. You have been asked to complete the project so that the deadline is met for the client.

A playlist still needs to be created, which plays all the video clips sequentially without stopping and is linked to the Play Movie button on the Classic Menu SD main menu. The project then needs to be checked for problems and finally built to the Flash format.

1. Open the PB1.ncor project from the drive and folder where you save your Data Files.
2. Create a Playlist named **Issues** and use all of the clips in sequential order.
3. Create a link on the Play Movie button to the playlist.
4. In the Build panel, name the project **Environmental Issues**.
5. Check the project for problems and correct any problems that you need to. An example is shown in Figure 78.
6. Build the project to the Flash FLV file format.

Figure 78 *Example of the PB1 workspace*

Your multimedia instructor would like you to learn more about Adobe Encore. He would like you to open Encore and click the News tab on the Resource Central panel.

1. Open Encore and click the Resource Central panel.
2. Click the Get to know Encores CS5 on Adobe TV link, as shown in Figure 79.
3. Explore Adobe TV for an Encore video that interests you.
4. Write a brief summary to let your instructor know what you have learned.

Figure 79 *Resource Central panel*

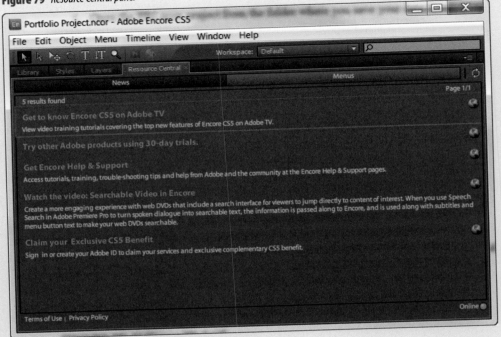

Creating an Electronic Portfolio Using Adobe Encore CS5

Design an electronic portfolio with the portfolio projects you have created through the course of this book. As you create the DVD, use your production logo to start the DVD and then go to the main menu. Include a playlist that plays all of your portfolio projects in order.

1. Create a new Encore project and name it **Your Name Portfolio**, using the default settings.
2. Import one final copy of each portfolio project you have created in either the MPEG-2 or FLV file format as a timeline.
3. Choose a template you would like to use for your project either from the Library panel or from Resource Central.
4. Modify the menu and submenus as you like. An example is shown in Figure 80.
5. Set the production logo to play first, then go to the main menu.
6. Create a playlist of your portfolio projects.
7. Link the buttons appropriately.
8. Check your project for problems, then fix the problems if there are any.
9. Build your project to the Flash format.
10. Preview your Flash project, then build your project to a DVD.

Figure 80 *Example Submenu for Portfolio Project*

ACE EXAM OBJECTIVES

Topic	Objective	Chapter(s)
1.0 Setting up projects and sequences	1.1 Given an option in the General tab and the Scratch Disk tab in the New Project dialog box, describe that option.	1 (p. 1-6)
	1.2 Given an option in the Sequence Presets tab, the General tab, and the Tracks tab in the New Sequence dialog box, describe that option.	1 (p. 1-7)
	1.3 Given an option in the Project Manager dialog box, explain the purpose of that option.	1 (p. 1-2)
	1.4 Configure preference options for a project. (Options include: General, Device control, Capture, media)	1 (p. 1-15)
2.0 Acquiring media assets	2.1 List and describe the features Premiere Pro provides for native HDV.	4 (p. 4-4 — 4-6)
	2.2 List and describe the features Premiere Pro provides for native tapeless assets such as DSLR cameras, RED, P2, AVCHD, XDCAM.	4 (p. 4-4 — 4-7)
	2.3 List and describe the features associated with the media browser.	1 (p. 1-11, 1-12)
	2.4 Given a video capture method, capture video by using that method. (Methods include: manual capture, setting in and out points, using Scene Detect)	4 (p. 4-4 — 4-7, 4-12)
	2.5 Given a device transport control, explain the purpose of or how to use that control.	1 (p. 1-6)
	2.6 Describe the workflow and steps required to perform a batch capture.	1 (p. 1-6)
	2.7 Capture video by using device control. (Device control capture options include: DV/ HDV, Serial)	1 (p. 1-6)
3.0 Editing footage in Premiere	3.1 Edit footage from a multiple-camera shoot.	1 (p. 1-6)
	3.2 Given an editing tool, edit footage by using that tool. (Tools include: ripple edit tool, rolling edit tool, slip tool, slide tool, trim tool)	1 (p. 1-6), 4 (p. 4-16 — 4-17)
	3.3 Discuss workflows related to 24p footage. (Workflow options include: interpreting, pulldown options)	4 (p. 4-9)
	3.4 Discuss workflow and implement nested sequences.	4 (p. 4-29 — 4-30)
	3.5 Discuss the functionality provided by time remapping. (Time remapping in the timeline)	6 (p. 6-4 — 6-5)
	3.6 Discuss functionality of the sync lock and lock track functions.	4 (p. 4-29)

ACE EXAM OBJECTIVES

Topic	Objective		Chapter(s)
4.0 Working with effects and transitions	4.1	Given a motion effect, adjust settings and apply that effect to a clip. (Motion effects include Position, Scale, and Rotation)	1 (p. 1-38 — 1-42)
	4.2	Given a keyframe interpolation method, describe the effect that method has on the motion of a clip. (Interpolation methods include: Bezier, Continuous Bezier, Ease In, Ease Out)	6 (p. 6-4)
	4.3	Describe the options available, and correct the color of a clip by applying the Fast Color Corrector effect. (Options include: White balance, Hue Balance and Angle, Input and Output levels)	4 (p. 4-23)
	4.4	Modify how a transition is applied by using options in the Effect Controls tab. (Options include: Alignment, Start, End)	1 (p. 1-30 — 1-31)
	4.5	Describe the process of adding transitions to more than one edit point at a time.	1 (p. 1-37)
5.0 Creating titles	5.1	List and describe the options available for working with text in titles. (Options include: aligning and distributing, paragraph and point text, text on a path, properties options)	1 (p. 1-53 — 1-54)
	5.2	Describe the process required to create a static title.	1 (p. 1-51 — 1-52)
	5.3	Describe the process required to create rolling or crawling titles.	1 (p. 1-51 — 1-52)
	5.4	Create a title from a template.	1 (p. 1-51)
6.0 Working with audio	6.1	Given a scenario, use the audio mixer. (Scenarios include: creating submix tracks and automation options)	5 (p. 5-10 — 5-11)
	6.2	Describe the differences associated with editing in timecode display versus audio units.	4 (p. 4-10)
	6.3	Discuss an effective use of the transcribe to text feature.	4 (p. 4-44)
	6.4	Given a clip, map the source channels of that clip. (Scenarios include: source channel mapping, treat mono as stereo, breakout stereo to mono)	4 (p. 4-10)
	6.5	List and describe how to work with 5.1 audio.	4 (p. 4-10)
7.0 Producing output from Premiere	7.1	Given an option in the Export Settings dialog box, explain the purpose of or when you would use that option. (Settings include: Flash, H.264, Blu-ray)	1 (p. 1-64 — 1-65)
	7.2	Given an option available in the Adobe Media Encoder, explain the purpose of or when you would use that option.	1 (p. 1-66 — 1-67)

Certification Grid

Topic	ACE EXAM OBJECTIVES		Chapter(s)
	Objective		
8.0 Authoring DVDs with Encore	8.1	Describe the options available in the Project panel including how to organize assets.	7 (p. 7-12)
	8.2	Given an option in the Disc panel, describe the purpose of that option. (Options include settings within the Project Settings, Check Project, and Build DVD dialog boxes)	7 (p. 7-4, 7-38 & 7-41)
	8.3	Given a scenario, create a motion menu. (Scenarios include adding a background video, adding video to buttons, setting the duration of menus, adding audio to a menu)	7 (p. 7-16)
	8.4	List and describe the audio, video, and still image file formats that can be used for source content in a DVD project.	4 (p. 4-17), 7 (p. 7-13)
	8.5	List and describe the options for exporting a sequence from Premiere to Encore and importing Premiere sequences from Encore.	7 (p. 7-42)

VIDEO COLLECTION DATA FILES				
Chapter	**Data File Supplied**	**Support Files**	**Linked Files**	**Student Creates File**	**Used In**
				Earth Day your name.prproj	Lesson 1
Chapter 1	None	None			Lesson 2
	Earth Day your name.prproj*	70s Soft Rock – 60.mp3			Lesson 3
		Scenic1.jpg			Lesson 4
		Scenic2.jpg			Lesson 5
		Scenic3.jpg			
		Scenic4.jpg			
		Scenic5.jpg			
		Scenic6.jpg			
		Scenic7.jpg			
		Scenic8.jpg			
		Scenic9.jpg			
		Scenic10.jpg			
		Scenic11.jpg			
		Scenic12.jpg			
		Scenic13.jpg			
		Scenic14.jpg			
		Scenic15.jpg			
		Scenic16.jpg			
		Scenic17.jpg			
		Scenic18.jpg			
		Scenic19.jpg			
		Scenic20.jpg			
		Scenic21.jpg			
		Scenic22.jpg			
		Scenic23.jpg			
		Scenic24.jpg			
		Scenic25.jpg			
		Scenic26.jpg			
		Scenic27.jpg			
		Scenic28.jpg			
		Scenic29.jpg			

*Created in previous Lesson or Skills Review in current chapter

Data Files List

Chapter	Data File Supplied	Support Files	Linked Files	Student Creates File	Used In
VIDEO COLLECTION DATA FILES					
Chapter 1, continued		Scenic30.jpg Scenic31.jpg Scenic32.jpg			
	Earth Day your name.prproj*	Earth Day Text.txt		Earth Day your name.mpeg Earth Day your name.flv	Lesson 6
	None	Subtle Storm - 60.mp3 Scenic16.jpg Scenic17.jpg Scenic18.jpg Scenic19.jpg Scenic20.jpg Scenic21.jpg Scenic22.jpg Scenic23.jpg Scenic24.jpg Scenic25.jpg Scenic26.jpg Scenic27.jpg Scenic28.jpg Scenic29.jpg Scenic30.jpg Scenic31.jpg Scenic32.jpg America Text.txt		America the Beautiful your name.proproj America the Beautiful your name.mpeg America the Beautiful your name.flv	Skills Review
	Italy.prproj		Subtle Storm.mp3 Italy1.jpg Italy2.jpg Italy3.jpg Italy4.jpg Italy5.jpg Italy6.jpg	Italy your name.prproj Italy your name.mpeg Italy your name.flv	Project Builder 1

*Created in previous Lesson or Skills Review in current chapter

Data Files List

VIDEO COLLECTION DATA FILES

Chapter	Data File Supplied	Support Files	Linked Files	Student Creates File	Used In
Chapter 1, continued			Italy7.jpg Italy8.jpg Italy9.jpg Italy10.jpg Italy11.jpg Italy12.jpg Italy13.jpg Italy14.jpg Italy15.jpg		
	SA Missions.prproj		Flat Calm.mp3 SA_Mission1.jpg SA_Mission2.jpg SA_Mission3.jpg SA_Mission4.jpg SA_Mission5.jpg SA_Mission6.jpg SA_Mission7.jpg SA_Mission8.jpg SA_Mission9.jpg SA_Mission10.jpg SA_Mission11.jpg SA_Mission12.jpg SA_Mission13.jpg SA_Mission14.jpg SA_Mission15.jpg SA_Mission16.jpg SA_Mission17.jpg SA_Mission18.jpg SA_Mission19.jpg SA_Mission20.jpg	SA Missions your name.prproj SA Missions your name.flv	Project Builder 2
	None	None		Space Program your name.prproj Space Program your name.mpeg	Portfolio Project

Chapter	Data File Supplied	Support Files	Linked Files	Student Creates File	Used In
Chapter 2	GridsPractice.aep	None	None	None	Lesson 1
	None	us_11.jpg		BUG your name.aep BUG Final your name.mpeg	Lesson 2
	Production Logo.aep	Channel 6 Logo.psd	EarthSpin_720x480.mpeg	Logo your name.aep Logo Final your name.flv	Lesson 3
	Title Sequence.aep		Nightscape.mp3 us_10.mov Title Sequence Text.psd	Title Sequence your name.aep Title Sequence Final your name.mpeg	Lesson 4
	None	us_10.jpg Nighttime Logo.psd	Nightscape.mp3 Skyline.jpg	Digital Graphic your name.aep Digital Graphic Final your name.mpeg Nighttime your name.aep Nighttime Final your name.flv	Skills Review
	Demo.aep	None	None	Animation Preset Demo your name.aep Animation Preset Demo Final your name.mpeg	Project Builder 1
	None	None	None	Elementary Title Sequence.aep Elementary Title Sequence Final your name.mpeg	Project Builder 2
	None	None	None	Title of your choice.aep Title of your choice.mpeg Title of your choice.flv	Portfolio Project

VIDEO COLLECTION DATA FILES

		VIDEO COLLECTION DATA FILES			
Chapter	**Data File Supplied**	**Support Files**	**Linked Files**	**Student Creates File**	**Used In**
Chapter 3	None	PopeyetheSailorMan.mp3	None	PopeyeRestored.mp3	Lesson 1
	None	Volcano.flv	None	Volcano your name.asnd Volcano Sound Effects your name.mp3	Lesson 2
	None	None	None	Savannah Spring Mix your name.asnd	Lesson 3
	None	GrandOldRag.mp3 airplane.m2v		GrandOldRagRestored.asnd Airplane your name.asnd Airplane Sound Effects your name.mpeg Lost Highway Mix Final your name.asnd Lost Highway Mix Final your name.wav	Skills Review
	None	rfkonmlkdeath45454.mp3		RFK Speech your name.mp3	Project Builder 1
	Elementary Title Sequence Final your name.mpeg**	None	None	Elementary Title Sequence with Music your name.asnd Elementary Title Sequence with Music your name.mpeg	Project Builder 2
	Charlie Chaplin.asnd	None	The_Kid_Auto_Race_In_Venice.mpeg	Chaplin Soundtrack your name.asnd Chaplin Soundtrack Final your name.mpeg	Portfolio Project

**Created in a previous chapter

Chapter					
	VIDEO COLLECTION DATA FILES				
	Data File Supplied	**Support Files**	**Linked Files**	**Student Creates File**	**Used In**
Chapter 4	None	AVCHD-Airshow Folder		Airshow your name.prproj	Lesson 1
	Pearl Harbor Reenactment. prproj		AirshowVideo1.m2v AirshowVideo2.m2v AirshowVideo3.m2v AirshowVideo4.m2v AirshowVideo5.m2v AirshowVideo6.m2v	Pearl Harbor Documentary your name.prproj	Lesson 2
	Pearl Harbor Documentary your name.prproj*	December7th.m2v	None		Lesson 3
	Pearl Harbor Documentary your name.prproj*	History PearlHarbor.mp3 FDR Speech.mp3	None	Pearl Harbor Documentary your name.MPEG	Lesson 4
	None Kennedy Space Documentary. prproj	AVCHD-Glassworks Folder apollo launch.m2v Kennedy Space.mp3 Kennedy Rice.mp3	space1.m2v space2.m2v space3.m2v space4.m2v space5.m2v space6.m2v	Glassworks your name.prproj Kennedy Space Documentary your name.prproj Kennedy Space Documentary your name.mpeg	Skills Review
	Chamber.prproj	None	Chamber1.m2v Chamber2.m2v Chamber3.m2v Chamber4.m2v	Chamber Commercial your name.prproj Chamber Commercial your name.mpeg Chamber Commercial your name.flv	Project Builder 1
	None	None	None	Great Speech Phrases your name.mp3	Project Builder 2
	None	Production Company Logo**	None	Documentary.prproj Documentary.mpeg	Portfolio Project

*Created in previous Lesson or Skills Review in current chapter
**Created in a previous chapter

Data Files List

		VIDEO COLLECTION DATA FILES			
Chapter	Data File Supplied	Support Files	Linked Files	Student Creates File	Used In
Chapter 5	PSA.aep PSA.prproj	PSA Script.txt	Ban044.mov Eri048.mov Eri50.mov Nic038.mov	PSA your name.aep PSA your name.prproj PSA your name.mpeg	Lesson 1
	Glassworks Commercial.prproj Glassworks 3D Text.aep	Blown Glass.avi	Frame.psd	Glassworks Commercial your name.prproj Glassworks Dynamic Link your name.aep Blown Glass.mocha Glassworks 3D Text your name.aep Glassworks Commercial your name.mpeg	Lesson 2
	Hummingbird Insurance.aep		scenic footage.prproj hummingbird.ai commercial.avi hummingbird.ai lighthousesunrise.avi malibusunset.avi mountain.avi nantucketsunset.avi redwoods.avi timelapseclouds.avi yellowstonewaterfall.avi	Hummingbird Insurance your name.aep Hummingbird Insurance your name.flv	Lesson 3
	Water Pollution.aep Water Pollution.prproj LuckenbachCommercial.prproj Luckenbach 3D Text.ae World Peace.ae	Water Pollution Script.txt	EIS19 Trash by culvert.mov EIS21 Trash on a tropical beach.mov EIS25 Brown water from mine.mov Luckenbach.avi Dove.avi londonbigben.avi sydneyaustralia.avi us_5.mov	Water Pollution your name.aep Water Pollution your name.prproj Water Pollution your name.mpeg Luckenbach Commercial your name.prproj Luckenbach Dynamic Link your name.ae Luckenback.mocha Luckenbach 3D Text your name.ae World Peace your name.ae World Peace Commercial your name.flv	Skills Review

Chapter	Data File Supplied	Support Files	Linked Files	Student Creates File	Used In
		VIDEO COLLECTION DATA FILES			
Chapter 5, continued	Cartoon Practice	None	ELS041.mov	Cartoon Practice your name.aep Cartoon Practice your name.flv	Project Builder 1
	Longhorn.ae		Longhorn.psd	Longhorn your name.ae Longhorn Commercial Spot your name.flv	Project Builder 2
	None	EIS62 Endangered Asian rhino.mov EIS63 Endangered African rhino.mov EIS64 Cheetah in grass.mov EIS65 Endangered antelope.mov EIS66 Male gorilla.mov EIS67 Young gorilla.mov EIS68 Mother Orang at Borneo refuge.mov EIS69 Orang with infant.mov EIS70 Panda in Beijing zoo.mov EIS71 Tiger SE Asia.mov EIS72 Manatee FL.mov EIS73 Andean condor.mov		Endangered species commercial.prproj Endangered species.mpeg Endangered species.flv	Portfolio Project

VIDEO COLLECTION DATA FILES					
Chapter	**Data File Supplied**	**Support Files**	**Linked Files**	**Student Creates File**	**Used In**
Chapter 6	Speed 1.prproj Speed 2.prproj Speed 3.prproj	None	42.avi 30.avi 7.avi 13.avi 22.avi	Speed 1 your name.prproj Skateboarding your name.flv Speed 2 your name.prproj Skateboarding Stunts your name.flv Speed 3 your name.prproj Bike Stunts your name.flv	Lesson 1
	Weather 1.aep Lightning 1.aep	None	Storm Clouds.m2v us_5.mov us_5 mask.psd Lightning Logo.ai	Weather 1 your name.aep Rain Effects your name.flv Lightning 1 your name.aep Lightning Logo your name.FLV	Lesson 2
	Talking Dog.aep	None	Dog Clip.avi Outlaw in Black Boots vocal sample.mp3	Talking Dog your name.aep Talking Dog your name.flv	Lesson 3
	Speed 4.prproj Speed 5.prproj Speed 6.prproj Weather 2.aep Lightning 2.aep Singing Dog.aep	None	42.avi 43.avi 1.avi 10.avi 18.avi StormCloudsGathering2.mpg us_15.mov us_15 mask.psd Boy Band vocals.mp3 Singing Dog 2.m2v Open Mouth 2.avi	Speed 4 your name.prproj Bike Tricks your name.flv Speed 5 your name.prproj Skateboarding Tricks your name.flv Speed 6 your name.prproj Biking your name.flv Weather 2 your name.aep White House Rain your name.flv Lightning 2 your name.aep Halloween your name.flv Singing Dog your name.aep Singing Dog your name.flv	Skills Review
	Weather 3.aep		us_7.mov	San Francisco Weather your name.flv	Project Builder 1
	Antelope Talking.ae		antelope.mov	Zoo Promo your name.flv	Project Builder 2
	none		Sports Folder	Highlight Video your name.prproj Highlight Video your name.mpeg	Portfolio Project

VIDEO COLLECTION DATA FILES					
Chapter	Data File Supplied	Support Files	Linked Files	Student Creates File	Used In
Chapter 7	None	EIS01 Smokestacks.mov EIS03 Mill with smoke.mov EIS04 Smoke plume 1.mov EIS05 Smoke plume 2.mov EIS06 Smoke plume 3.mov EIS07 Smoke plume 4.mov EIS08 Smoke closeup.mov EIS09 Smokestack w_trees.mov EIS10 Very dark smoke.mov EIS18 Trash by lake shore.mov EIS19 Trash by culvert.mov EIS20 Trash dump by Mediterranean.mov EIS21 Trash on a tropical beach.mov EIS22 Pipes & pond.mov EIS23 Drinking polluted water.mov EIS24 Polluted stream in tropics.mov Water Pollution submenu.psd		Pollution your name.ncor Pollution your name.flv	Lesson 1 Lesson 2 Lesson 3 Lesson 4
	None	EIS28 Slash & burn plot Thailand.mov EIS29 Burning cutover land Tropics.mov EIS30 Detail burning tree Tropics.mov EIS31 Smoke Amazon forest.mov EIS32 Deforested Amazon Brazil.mov EIS33 Slash & burn plot Venezuela.mov EIS34 Cutover hillside Guatemala.mov EIS35 Clear-cut operation OR.mov EIS36 Clear-cut hillside OR.mov EIS37 Clear-cut hillside WA.mov EIS51 Desertification Mali W Africa.mov EIS52 Overgrazed land Sahel Mali.mov EIS53 Desertification the Sahel Mali.mov		Erosion your name.ncor Erosion your name.flv	Skills Review

		VIDEO COLLECTION DATA FILES			
Chapter	**Data File Supplied**	**Support Files**	**Linked Files**	**Student Creates File**	**Used In**
Chapter 7, continued		EIS54 Disturbed desert floor CA.mov EIS55 Abandoned city Central Asia.mov EIS56 Hot rising sun.mov Desertification submenu.psd			
	PB1		EIS11 Smoke in distance.mov EIS12 Boat w_smoke.mov EIS13 85 Traffic jam with motocycles.mov EIS14 Snowmobiles in Yellowstone.mov EIS15 Smog over Guadalajara.mov EIS17 Air pollution & traffic Beijing.mov	Environmental Issues.ncor Environmental Issues.flv	Project Builder 1
	None	None	None	None	Project Builder 2
	None	Space Program your name.mpeg** (Chapter 1) Title of your choice.mpeg** (Chapter 2) Chaplin Soundtrack Final your name.mpeg** (Chapter 3) Documentary.mpeg** (Chapter 4) Endangered species.mpeg** (Chapter 5) Highlight Video your name.mpeg** (Chapter 6)	None	Your Name Portfolio Project.ncor Your Name Portfolio Project.flv	Portfolio Project

**Created in a previous chapter

A

action safe zone
The outer margin of the safe zone where content is guaranteed to be visible on all television displays.

Adobe Dynamic Link
Provides integration between After Effects, Premiere Pro, and Encore as long as they have been installed as part of the Creative Suite 5 Production Premium or the Creative Suite 5 Master Collection.

ambient (light)
In After Effects, a lighting effect which has no source but simply contributes to the overall brightness and casts no shadows.

amount of content
In an Encore project, the size of the project based on the type of content that has been used. This information is necessary when determining the media which will be needed to build the project.

amplitude
The change in pressure from crest to trough.

animation preset
A term in After Effects for a collection of animation settings that include keyframes and effects that can be applied to a layer.

anti-aliasing quality
A setting in the Premiere Pro Effect Controls panel which adjusts the smoothness of a transition's edges.

application window
The main window of an application comprising the various panels.

ASND
The Soundbooth file format which allows you to add effects, adjust fades, and store history snapshots.

assets
These can include video clips, digital images, and audio clips.

attach point
The designated place for the object you plan to attach to a motion in After Effects.

Audio/Video Out setting
A setting available in the Encore preferences which allows a project to be previewed on an external device that is connected by an IEEE 1394 Firewire.

AVCHD
Advanced video codec high definition is a format developed by Sony and Panasonic for recording and playback of high definition video, and is used in their tapeless video cameras.

B

Bezier spline
One of two splines available in Mocha; Bezier spline is the industry standard.

bins
Used to organize assets in the Project panel; work much the same way as folders in Windows Explorer or the Mac OS finder.

border color
A setting in the Effect Controls panel which allows the color of the transition border to be set.

border width
A setting in the Effect Controls panel which allows the adjustment of the optional border on a transition.

buffering
The delay before a video begins to play on the Internet.

bug
A term used in the United States and Canada for a digital on-screen graphic.

C

canvas
The work area in Mocha.

capturing
In Premiere Pro, the process which occurs when you connect a live video camera or an analog tape device, such as a camcorder or VCR that uses videotape, and you then record the video from the source to a hard disk.

CC Light Sweep effect
An effect available in After Effects which creates a light reflection along the layer.

CC Mr. Mercury effect
An effect available in After Effects which creates ever-changing blobs, which you can make appear like rain drops on a camera lens.

CC Rain effect
A self-animating effect available in After Effects that simulates rain.

chapter playlist
Similar to a playlist, but it provides a way to play a single timeline's chapters in non-sequential order.

clips
Another term for digital assets.

commercial
A short film broadcast for the public interest as a marketing device to raise awareness of a consumer product, service, or issue.

Composition panel
A panel in After Effects which represents layers spatially; it is where compositions are displayed at the location of the CTI on the Timeline panel.

compositions (comps)
In After Effects, the container that holds all the references for a movie; compositions can be dynamically linked to Premiere Pro or to Encore.

Conductivity State
The property in the Advanced Lightning effect which changes the path of lightning and can be used to animate the effect.

Constant Gain
A type of Crossfade which can sound abrupt because it changes the audio at a constant rate in and out as it transitions between clips.

Constant Power
A type of Crossfade; the default transition which creates a smooth, gradual transition between audio clips.

contrast
In After Effects, a setting found under the Color Emboss effect which determines the sharpness of the image.

crest
A waveform at its high point.

Crossfade
An audio transition used to fade in or fade out an audio clip.

current time display
Shows the timecode for the current frame.

current time indicator (CTI)
Indicates the current frame displayed in the Program monitor; *see* play head.

custom (transition settings)
A setting in the Effect, Controls panel specific to the transition.

custom workspace
A workspace that has been created by the user and saved with a unique name.

cut
The space between two clips. The vertical line between two clips marking a cut point. In Premiere Pro, the point where a clip has been split.

cut line
In Premiere Pro, the point where a clip has been split. It is marked by a vertical line between two clips and is also referred to as a cut or a cut line.

D

deform pin
A type of pin that you can place or move with the Puppet Pin tool.

digital assets
Video, audio, still images, Photoshop, and/or Illustrator files.

digital on-screen graphic
A logo overlaid on a portion of the television viewing area to identify the channel, much like a watermark.

digitizing
The process of converting analog video to digital form so that a computer can process and store it.

documentary
A broad category used to describe videos that are meant to "document" history.

DOG
A term used in the United Kingdom and New Zealand, an acronym for digital on-screen graphic (see digital on-screen graphic).

downstream
Another term for a composition that contains a nested composition.

Drag Video Only
An icon located on the Source Monitor in Premiere Pro which allows you to place a video clip without its audio track.

drop zone
The area that becomes highlighted as you drag a panel and provides a visual reference to where the panel can be placed.

duration
The span between the In point and the Out point of a video clip.

E

edge selectors
May be found on some transitions and will change the orientation or direction of the transition.

Edit in Soundbooth
A command in Premiere Pro used to edit an audio clip in Soundbooth.

Edit Source file
An option used in editing an audio clip in Soundbooth; makes changes to the actual source; any references made to the source file in Premiere will be updated when the file is saved in Soundbooth.

Editing (workspace)
The default workspace in Premiere Pro.

encoding
A procedure done during the export process so that other people will be able to view the movie.

end slider
The ending edge of a transition which may be adjusted.

Exponential Fade
A transition which fades out the first clip and fades up the second clip.

expressions
Expressions use a scripting language to specify values of property.

extract audio
When editing an audio clip in Soundbooth, a copy of the audio file is created from the source clip and appears on the Project panel and then opens in a new Soundbooth file.

Extract button
Located on the Program Monitor in Premiere Pro; removes a specified area of the sequence marked with In and Out points without leaving a gap in its place.

eyedropper
A tool used to select a color from an image or video clip.

F

fading
A basic effect used on images to fade in or out by applying the Opacity effect.

feature region
Defines the area in the layer that will be tracked in After Effects.

file-based
Another term for tapeless.

file-based media
The media to which a tapeless video camera records, for example a hard disk, a DVD, or flash memory.

Final Output (Linear Color Key Effect)
A view which displays a preview of the keyed area.

footage
The term used for assets in After Effects.

frequency
The number of cycles per second measured in Hertz.

frequency-space editing
Removing unwanted noise in the spectral display.

G

garbage matte
A keying method used in After Effects to remove portions of an image or layer; the matte can then be animated with the layer.

Go to Gap
A command in Premiere Pro used to jump between gaps and to find gaps that are very short and may be difficult to see.

Grid generator (Particle Playground effect)
Creates particles in a continuous stream from a set of grid intersections.

H

histogram
A chart that represents the changes of color in an image.

hold keyframe
In Soundbooth, the keyframe that is created by default and creates an abrupt change in value at each keyframe that is created; represented by a square.

I

icon view
In the Premiere Pro Project panel, shows thumbnails or smaller versions of the digital assets that have been imported.

In point
Marks the beginning of the layer in After Effects; in Premiere Pro it defines the first frame that is to be included in a sequence.

Insert edit
In Premiere Pro, a type of edit which shifts the contents of the selected track to the right when an asset is placed on a track.

K

Key Color (Linear Color Key effect)
A menu which has the Key Color swatch and the eyedropper available to select the color which will be keyed.

Key Color Swatch (Linear Color Key effect)
A palette of colors.

keyed
The term used to describe the removal of color from an image or video.

keyframe
Defined in the Effect Controls timeline, it is a "snapshot" of how you want a clip to look at a specified time.

L

layer duration bar
The bar that extends between the In point and the Out point.

Layer Exploder (Particle Playground effect)
A generator which creates new particles based on a layer.

layers
In After Effects, this is where footage may be added to a composition and is represented as a bar graph.

Lift button
Located on the Program Monitor in Premiere Pro; removes a specified area of the sequence marked with In and Out points leaving a gap in its place.

Linear Color Key effect
An effect available in After Effects which uses RGB, hue, or Chroma information to create a range of transparency across an image based on a specified color.

Linear keyframe
In Soundbooth, a keyframe that creates a gradual change in value from one keyframe to the next, and is represented by a diamond.

live streaming video
See streaming video.

M

master composition
In After Effects, the term used for a composition where a nested or pre-composition is placed.

Matching Softness (Linear Color Key effect)
A property which adjusts the softness of the edges between an image and the transparent area.

Matching Tolerance (Linear Color Key effect)
A property which determines how closely pixels must match the key color before they become transparent.

Matte Only (Linear Color Key effect)
A view which shows the alpha channel matte to view holes in the transparency.

metadata
Found in the Metadata panel, it may include the text transcript, the title, author, camera model, and day and time the video or image was taken.

mix down
In Soundbooth, it is the process of combining audio tracks for playback or for use in other devices.

mono
An audio file that was recorded with one sound source.

(continued)

motion path
The visual representation created when animating properties that change over space as well as time.

movie
A term in After Effects used for rendering or exporting an After Effects project.

MP3
The most widely used file format for portable media players and web-based audio; a highly compressed file that make downloads faster, but also results in poorer quality.

multitrack file
A Soundbooth document that allows you to mix audio files and scores together to create soundtracks for videos.

N

navigation scheme
The layout of the menus and buttons which provide access to the various sections of a DVD.

nest
A term used to place compositions in compositions or sequences within sequences.

nesting
To place one composition inside another.

New Workspace
A command on the Workspace menu that allows you to save a custom or customized workspace.

noise floor
The level of amplitude representing the near-constant background noise that has been identified and needs to be removed.

noise print
A sample of an audio clip created by selecting a small portion.

non-linear editing system
The ability to access any frame in a video in order to make changes to it.

NTSC
The National Television Standards Committee standard used in North America and Japan.

——————— O ———————

opacity
The level of transparency on a scale of 0% to 100%; if set to 0% the clip will be completely transparent; at 100% it will have no transparency.

Out point
Marks the end of a layer in After Effects; in Premiere Pro it defines the last frame that is to be included in a sequence.

overlay edit
In Premiere Pro, a type of edit in which you place a clip over an existing clip already on a track for the duration of the placed clip.

——————— P ———————

PAL
The Phase Alternating Line television standard used in Europe.

panels tab
The tabs found at the top of panels. You can move panels by dragging panel tabs.

parallel (light)
In After Effects, a lighting effect that approximates the light from a source like that of the sun.

parameter line
In Soundbooth, a line found in the Properties panel where keyframes may be added.

Particle Exploder (Particle Playground effect)
A generator which creates new particles based on a layer and then has the ability to explode a particle into more new particles.

Particle Playground effect
An effect available in After Effects used to animate an object by reproducing it randomly.

Paste insert
In Premiere Pro, behaves like an Insert edit.

Paste
In Premiere Pro, behaves like an Overlay edit.

phase
The position of a waveform in the cycle.

play head
Also known as the Current-time Indicator (CTI), a light blue triangle in the ruler with a vertical red line extending through the video and audio tracks.

playback environment
Equipment where the final Encore media project will be viewed.

playlist
In Encore, a collection of timelines, and/or slideshows set to play sequentially; may also include chapter playlists.

point (light)
In After Effects, a lighting effect that has no constraints. For example, a bare light bulb.

posterization
A process used to create a cartoon-like effect on a digital image or video.

pre-composition
The term used for a nested composition.

production logo
An opening or closing logo used by movie and television production companies at the beginning of a theatrical movie or at the end of a television program or movie to brand what they have produced.

program monitor
In Premiere Pro, the panel that displays the contents of the timeline, i.e., your project in progress.

progressive video
Looks like streaming video because it plays a movie without interruption; the movie player software determines how long it will take to download an entire movie for viewing and begins playing the movie when enough of the movie has been downloaded so it will playback uninterrupted.

project
In After Effects, it is a single file that stores compositions and references to footage used in the project.

project file
A term used for Premiere Pro, After Effects and Encore documents.

Project panel
The panel that organizes all the assets for your project, found in Premiere Pro, After Effects and Encore.

Property Mapper (Particle Playground effect)
Gives you the ability to control specific properties by using a layer map.

Public Service Announcement (PSA)
A type of commercial intended to modify public attitudes by raising awareness about specific issues.

R

Razor tool
In Premiere Pro, a tool used to split a clip at any point and creates a cut line.

rearrange edit
In Premiere Pro, an editing technique which allows you to click and drag a clip to a new location in the sequence. When the clip is released in place, the existing clips automatically shift to make room for the clip that is being placed.

reduce by
A setting in Soundbooth in the Noise dialog box used to adjust the noise floor.

reduction
A setting in Soundbooth in the Noise dialog box that sets the amplitude of the noise floor.

reference file
A file created to track assets which are referenced in the Premiere Pro Project panel.

Relief
In After Effects, a setting found under the Color Emboss effect which controls the maximum width of the highlighted edges.

Render and Replace
When editing an audio clip in Soundbooth, this option renders a new audio clip that is edited in Soundbooth and replaces it with the original clip on the Timeline panel; the original source clip remains untouched on the Projec panel.

render item
A term in After Effects for an item that has been added to the Render Queue panel.

rendered
See rendering.

rendering
The process of compiling a composition into its final output from all of its layers and settings; a rendered project will play more smoothly and much closer to real time.

Repel control (Particle Playground effect)
Specifies how nearby particles repel or attract each other, simulating a positive or negative magnetic charge to each of the particles.

reverse
A setting in the Effect Controls panel which allows you to play the transition backward.

ripple delete
Removes a clip from a sequence without leaving any gaps if the clip being removed is located between two other clips.

ripple edit
In Premiere Pro, a video editing technique that allows you to move the cut point either backward or forward in time (if the clip has frames available). The clip adjacent to the cut line adjusts accordingly, either shifting to the left or to the right by the amount of the ripple edit to compensate.

rolling edit
In Premiere Pro, a video editing technique that adjusts the In and Out points without affecting the rest of the Timeline.

rolls (title)
A title in which text moves vertically over the footage, also referred to as a Default Roll; if the text moves horizontally, it is referred to as a crawl, also referred to as a Default Crawl.

root composition
The term for the most downstream composition.

Rotobezier
An option used with the Pen tool in After Effects that makes paths easier to draw and makes the curves smoother.

S

safe zone
The viewing area designed to ensure that certain content is not missed when being played on television screens; broken down into two areas: title safe zone and action safe zone.

scores
Found in the Scores panel in Soundbooth; score templates are files that are downloaded from Resource Central to create soundtracks for video projects.

scrubbing
Clicking and dragging the CTI to preview the sequence.

search region
A larger area around the feature region that defines the area where After Effects will look for the feature region.

segment
The line or curve that connects the vertex.

sequence
Located on the Timeline panel, it is where most editing takes place.

show actual sources
An option in the Effect Controls panel which displays the starting and ending frames of clips to which the transition has been applied.

slideshows
A sequence of still images enhanced with special effects, such as pans and zooms, transitions and narrations, or music; can be organized in the Slideshow viewer, a panel available in Encore.

Source monitor
The panel that is used to preview assets from the project panel or the media browser before being placed in a sequence.

Source Only (Linear Color Key effect)
A view which shows the original footage without the key applied.

spatial
A term in After Effects for layer properties which have the ability to move, or add motion across composition space.

spectral display
Also known as the spectral frequency display, it appears below the waveform display on the Editor panel in Soundbooth.

speed
The playback rate compared to the rate at which the video was recorded.

speed ramp
The line between the Speed keyframe's two handles.

spline
A selection tool in Mocha used to track motion on a plane and can be used to determine position, scale, rotation, shear. and perspective.

spot (light)
In After Effects, a lighting effect that gives off light that is constrained by a cone, like a flashlight or spotlight.

Standard (workspace)
The default workspace in After Effects.

start slider
The beginning edge of a transition which may be adjusted.

stereo
An audio file that was recorded from two sound sources.

still (title)
A title that has fixed text; also referred to as Default Still.

storyboard
A visual representation that displays the structure of the project from start to end, used in the planning stage.

storyboarding
The way to plan your video by placing clips or digital assets in the order you plan to have them play.

streaming video
Video played much like a traditional live broadcast, and is affected by the bandwidth that is available; also referred to as live streaming video.

surface box
Used as a reference point in Mocha, it is resized and positioned as a stabilizing center.

synthetic layer
In After Effects, a layer that is created without using source footage.

——————— **T** ———————

tapeless
Digital video cameras that do not use video tape.

temporal
A term in After Effects for layer properties which change the layer over time.

thumbnails
A reduced size picture of the digital assets.

tick marks
In Premiere Pro, displayed along with numbers on the time ruler and are based on the timecode display.

time ruler
Measures the time in the sequence horizontally; also displays icons for markers and In and Out points.

timecode
Marks specific frames with unique addresses and is recorded onto videotape during the recording process.

Timeline panel
The panel where you place various assets and edit them.

Timeline Viewer
The term used for the timeline or Timeline panel in Encore.

Title Actions panel
A part of the Titler in Premiere Pro where you align, center, or distribute objects and text vertically and horizontally.

Title panel
A part of the Titler in Premiere Pro where you design and preview text and graphics; the central panel in the Titler window.

Title properties panel
A part of the Titler in Premiere Pro where you choose a font, change the font size, kerning, leading, or font characteristics such as bold or italics.

title safe zone
The inner margin of the safe zone that ensures text will be visible on all television displays.

title sequence
Shown at the beginning of a movie or television program to provide the title and credits to the actors.

Title Styles panel
A part of the Titler in Premiere Pro where you can apply preset styles to titles, and create and save your own titles.

Title tools panel
A part of the Titler in Premiere Pro where the tools are located to draw basic shapes, create text paths, and create vertical or horizontal text.

Titler
In Premiere Pro, a mini-application in a free-floating window used to create titles.

Tools panel
A panel which provides various tools such as the Selection tool and the Zoom tool; can be found in every application.

track point
The area that specifies what will be tracked in After Effects.

tracking data
Information that is created during the process of recording motion of a defined area of footage and creates keyframes for the Transform properties; can be generated from Mocha for After Effects or from the Track panel in After Effects.

tracks
Either video or audio, it is where the clips are assembled, edited, and enhanced with effects and transitions.

transition
Used to move from one clip to the next in a sequence; can add additional interest to video and can be as simple as phasing out one image and phasing in another.

trimming
In After Effects, changing the In and Out points on the Layer panel or the Timeline panel; in Premiere Pro, defining In and Out points for a video clip in the Source Monitor.

trough
A waveform at its lowest point.

type of content
Assets that are used in an Encore project, for example, video and audio clips, menus, buttons and data files.

—————— **U** ——————

upstream
Another term sometimes used for a nested composition.

—————— **V** ——————

vertex
The points on a path.

vertices
The plural for vertex.

video montage
A video created with digital images, words, transitions, and music.

Viewing area bar
The area which corresponds with the visible portion of the Timeline panel and allows you to quickly move to different parts of the sequence; located just above the Time ruler.

viral video
A video that gains popularity on the Internet through the process of sharing via Web sites and e-mail.

—————— **W** ——————

Wall Control (Particle Playground effect)
Creates an area restricting where particles can move.

waveform
The visual representation of sound.

wavelength
The distance measured between any two points; at the same degree on the phase in inches or centimeters.

work area bar
The area of the sequence you want to preview or export indicated by brackets just below the Time ruler.

workspace
The arrangement of the panels in an application window.

—————— **X** ——————

X spline
One of two splines available in Mocha; works well for tracking motion which involves perspective.

XMP metadata file
The file generated and shared between all video suite applications when a transcript is created.

—————— **Z** ——————

zoom slider
Increases or decreases the number of visible frames within the current viewing area.

Index